THE SPIRITUAL
LIFE CYCLE

THE SPIRITUAL LIFE CYCLE

Stages of Spiritual Growth From a Christian Perspective

Daryl Mitchell

For my wife Lylyn
and my parents
Elton and Betty Mitchell

CONTENTS

Stage	Learning Tasks	Crisis	Key	Symbol
Spiritual birth	1. God's authority 2. Responsibility to Him 3. Failure to live up to His standards 4. Jesus as Savior	Spiritual birth	Faith	Water/ Baptism
Spiritual childhood	1. Dependence on God 2. Rules to protect 3. Basic Doctrines 4. Allies and enemies in the spiritual dimension	Commitment/ dedication	Trust	Light/ Urim
Spiritual adolescence	1. Principles vs. rules 2. Cause and effect in the spiritual realm	Giant conflicts: Self-image Authority Conscience Forgiveness Meekness vs. Anger Moral Freedom Spiritual Purpose GenuineFriendships Financial Freedom	Strength	Integrity/ Thummim
Spiritual young adulthood	The way of God: death, burial, resurrection.	Willingness to wait vs. presumption	Patience	Treasure
Spiritual adulthood	Knowing God's way by experience	Meeting with God	Love	Children
Spiritual parenthood	Motivating and mentoring others	Death	Confidence	Heaven

PREFACE

AS a teenager I began to wonder why college aged church members would drop out. I was preparing to go to college myself and I was curious about the motivations of the age above me. Our church was good at teaching the doctrines of Christianity and the necessity of a lifetime commitment. Parents brought their children to church faithfully and families were active in the programs. But somehow religious training broke down for many when they went off to college. I would often hear that people trained up in the way of the Lord would eventually return, but in practice it didn't seem to happen much, and over the years I've seen very few people return who left the church as a young adult.

When I went to college myself I began to understand the problem better. I thought I was prepared to defend my faith, but I quickly learned I was not. I felt like a kindergartner going up against college graduates as far as spiritual matters were concerned. I did not have the knowledge or the character to deal with the skepticism and hostility of educated unbelievers.

God showed me that I was unprepared to live as a Christian adult, and that first of all I needed a stronger commitment to learning His ways. It was apparent that merely learning doctrinal positions and a few platitudes about putting faith into practice would be insufficient. A more life altering application of Christianity would be necessary to escape the fate of so many I knew who grew up to leave the church.

I never left the church, mainly because of my dogged commitment to find answers. I began to allow God to teach me and change my character, a long and difficult process.

As a young man I was a fiery idealist, ready to condemn church leaders and pastors trying to use the old ways that I knew didn't work. They didn't seem to understand what my problem was.

I saw some churches try new ways to nurture and educate the young, but after a while they mostly seemed to be the old ways tried harder: more Bible study, more prayer, more scripture memorization, more evangelism. They didn't work so well either. My measure of success was always different from the organizers of these youth programs. Theirs was how many young people it reached. Mine was how many young people were still in church at age 22.

Then, God showed me a different angle through secular knowledge. When I went to graduate school to get my Master of Social Work at age 27, I was introduced to several developmental theorists whom we studied extensively. I learned about the physical, psychological, emotional, and social development of people during the life cycle. But spiritual development wasn't talked about or studied much.

I began to wonder about spiritual development as the key to solving my riddle. Maybe young people drop out of church as young adults because their spiritual side is not young adult. They see it as a vestige of childhood that is no longer needed. Perhaps concentrating on spiritual development of the young would prepare people to live as Christians in the adult world.

In 1990, I began to study for and write the *Spiritual Life Cycle*. It is my attempt to show the pattern of spiritual growth for Christians. I started with the idea that since God has made people to grow in definite patterns in their other natures (physical, psychological, emotional, and social), there must be a definite pattern of spiritual growth as well.

I started a broad study of the scriptures to find the patterns of spiritual growth. I also studied everything I could find on development that seemed useful to the project. At the same time, I opened my life to God to allow Him to develop me in the path I saw in the scriptures.

It has taken several years for me to get the knowledge and experience to be able to write the *Spiritual Life Cycle*. The time has been well spent. If nothing else, my personal relationship with God has grown stronger. But I also hope that this work can be helpful to others. I believe that if churches put these principles into practice, they will be able to keep and nurture their people to spiritual maturity.

This is a beginning step toward a Christian understanding of spiritual development. I hope that as individuals and churches study and apply this book our knowledge will grow.

PART 1

Perspective

CHAPTER 1

The Fifth Dimension

"THE Fifth Dimension" was a popular singing group during the late 1960's. Judging from the time and its experimentation with drugs and mystical religions, it seems reasonable to assume the name meant a dimension beyond conscious reality. The first dimension is a straight line. The second dimension is a flat plane. The third dimension adds depth and height to the flat plane. Geometry ends with number three. The fourth dimension is time. Therefore, the fifth dimension must represent a condition beyond the physical.

I propose a definition of this fifth dimension. My "fifth dimension" is the spiritual dimension that rules over all and yet is beyond our physical senses.

The spiritual dimension affects our lives like water vapor. Water vapor is in the air at all times. Water from the ground, lakes, rivers and oceans evaporates and collects in the air. The measurement of water vapor in the air is called humidity. When the air becomes heavy enough with water vapor in a certain area and the temperature goes down, then the water collects on dust particles and falls as rain, sleet, snow, or hail. In the same way the spiritual dimension surrounds us at all times. When the vapor of the spiritual dimension gets heavy and condenses on the particles of experience, it collects on events and falls into our lives. We are only aware of spiritual rain when improbable events hit us on the head!

In truth, the spiritual dimension is the most powerful force in our lives. It has more influence on our plans, goals, decisions, and activities than any other factor. In this chapter I will show how the spiritual rain falls into our lives. First, I will describe the dimensions of a person: the spirit, the soul, and the body. The spiritual world interacts with each in a different way. Then I will describe the players of the spiritual dimension who try to influence natural events and how they do it. Finally, I will point out specific examples of spiritual intervention into the sensible world.

Pneuma, Psyche, Soma

"And the very God of peace sanctify you wholly; and I pray God your whole spirit and soul and body be preserved blameless unto the coming of our Lord Jesus Christ." 1 Thessalonians 5:23. Paul prays that the Thessalonians be sanctified (set apart for God) completely. He then lists the three sanctifiable natures of a person: the spirit, the soul, and the body; in Greek that's "pneuma, psyche, and soma." In this section I will define the elements of each nature and the boundaries among them: *"For the word of God is quick, and powerful, and sharper than any twoedged sword, piercing even to the dividing asunder of soul and spirit, and of the joints and marrow, and is a discerner of the thoughts and intents of the heart." Hebrews 4:12.*

Pneuma (Spiritual nature)

One way to define the spiritual nature is to say what it is not. Spirit is not made of intelligence: *"In that hour Jesus rejoiced in spirit, and said, I thank thee, O Father, Lord of heaven and earth, that thou hast hid these things from the wise and prudent, and hast revealed them unto babes: even so, Father; for so it seemed good in thy sight." Luke 10:21.* Jesus rejoiced that spiritual qualities aren't the exclusive domain of the wise and prudent of this world, but are often times revealed to babes in worldly wisdom. *"For the preaching of the cross is to them that perish foolishness; but unto us which are saved it is the power of God. For it is written, I will destroy the wisdom of the wise, and will bring to nothing the understanding of the prudent. Where is the wise? where is the scribe? where is the disputer of this world? hath not God made foolish the wisdom of this world?" 1 Corinthians 1:18-20.*

The spirit is not made of maturity. Jesus taught His disciples that spiritual insight is not based on physical and psychological maturity, but rather on childlike faith: *"At the same time came the disciples unto Jesus, saying, Who is the greatest in the kingdom of heaven? And Jesus called a little child unto him, and set him in the midst of them, And said, Verily I say unto you, Except ye be converted, and become as little children, ye shall not enter into the kingdom of heaven. Whosoever therefore shall humble himself as this little child, the same is greatest in the kingdom of heaven." Matthew 18:1-4.*

The spiritual nature is made up of five parts that can't be explained by intelligence or maturity: natural light, conscience, wisdom, sensitivity, and creativity.

1. Natural Light

"In the beginning was the Word, and the Word was with God, and the Word was God... That was the true Light, which lighteth every man that cometh into the world." John 1:1, 9. Natural light refers to that part of every one of us that recognizes the existence and authority of God. Every nation and people since time began has recognized the existence of deity. That's not by accident. God has put within each of His creations a little of His light that confesses His existence. *"Because that which may be known of God is manifest in them; for God hath shewed it unto them." Romans 1:19.*

2. Conscience

"For when the Gentiles, which have not the law, do by nature the things contained in the law, these, having not the law, are a law unto themselves: Which shew the work of the law written in their hearts, their conscience also bearing witness, and their thoughts the mean while accusing or else excusing one another;)" Romans 2:14, 15. The Bible teaches that even those who have not been trained in God's principles and teachings are without excuse before Him: *"Therefore thou art inexcusable, O man, whosoever thou art that judgest: for wherein thou judgest another, thou condemnest thyself; for thou that judgest doest the same things." Romans 2:1.* God has put within each person the ability to understand right and wrong. The rules and customs all people make for living are evidence that people judge behavior by standards beyond themselves. Morality is not relative in any society nor has it ever been. People's actions have always been judged by higher standards than individual preference. When people's actions don't conform to their understanding of the higher standard, they feel guilt. This recognition of a higher standard is further proof that people have an inborn recognition of God (the giver of the highest standard). Guilt feelings are indications that people know they don't live up to the "ideal" established by God.

Conscience is a function of the spirit and cannot be equated with intelligence or maturity. Conscience is exhibited by all people except those who have "seared their consciences" by continual immorality: *"Now the Spirit speaketh expressly, that in the latter times some shall depart from the faith, giving heed to seducing spirits, and doctrines of devils; Speaking lies in hypocrisy; having their conscience seared with a hot iron;" 1 Timothy 4:1, 2. "This I say therefore, and testify in the Lord, that ye henceforth walk not as other Gentiles walk, in the vanity of their mind, Having the understanding darkened, being alienated from the life of God through the ignorance that is in them, because of the blindness of their heart: Who being past feeling have given themselves over unto lasciviousness, to work all uncleanness with greediness." Ephesians 4:17-19.* "Being past feeling" is another phrase for "searing the conscience." *"When wisdom entereth into thine heart, and knowledge is pleasant unto thy soul; Discretion shall preserve thee, understanding shall keep thee: ... To deliver thee from the strange woman, even from the stranger which flattereth with her words; Which forsaketh the guide of her youth, and forgetteth the covenant of her God." Proverbs 2:10-11, 16-17.* The immoral woman forsakes "the guide of her youth" (her conscience).

3. Wisdom

"If any of you lack wisdom, let him ask of God, that giveth to all men liberally, and upbraideth not; and it shall be given him." James 1:5. James tells us that if we lack wisdom we should pray for it. Therefore, wisdom is not intelligence we are born with, neither is it something we can work for, nor is it something we receive when we are saved. James addresses people who were already saved. James boldly declares wisdom is spiritual and must be supernaturally given.

The "preacher" teaches explicitly that wisdom is not limited to the mature: *"Better is a poor and a wise child than an old and foolish king, who will no more be admonished." Ecclesiastes 4:13.*

"A scorner seeketh wisdom, and findeth it not: but knowledge is easy unto him that understandeth." Proverbs 14:6. This passage teaches that wisdom is easily comprehended, but only by those whose spirits are open to it and ready to receive (Proverbs 1:20-23; 8:1-9).

Jesus blessed Peter and his confession at Caesarea Philippi because *"flesh and blood hath not revealed it unto thee, but my father which is in heaven" Matthew 16: 17.*

James says that wisdom comes from above and not from within: *"Who is a wise man and endued with knowledge among you? let him shew out of a good conversation his works with meekness of wisdom. But if ye have bitter envying and strife in your hearts, glory not, and lie not against the truth. This wisdom descendeth not from above, but is earthly, sensual, devilish. For where envying and strife is, there is confusion and every evil work. But the wisdom that is from above is first pure, then peaceable, gentle, and easy to be intreated, full of mercy and good fruits, without partiality, and without hypocrisy. And the fruit of righteousness is sown in peace of them that make peace." James 3:13-18.*

The Bible definition of wisdom is given in *Proverbs 9:10: The fear ᴏ̨ ...
is the beginning of wisdom: and the knowledge of the holy is understanding.*
Wisdom begins when we are able to see from God's point of view.

4. Sensitivity

*"Beloved, believe not every spirit, but try the spirits whether they are of
God: because many false prophets are gone out into the world. Hereby know
ye the Spirit of God: Every spirit that confesseth that Jesus Christ is come in
the flesh is of God: And every spirit that confesseth not that Jesus Christ is
come in the flesh is not of God: and this is that spirit of antichrist, whereof ye
have heard that it should come; and even now already is it in the world. Ye
are of God, little children, and have overcome them: because greater is he
that is in you, than he that is in the world. They are of the world: therefore
speak they of the world, and the world heareth them. We are of God: he that
knoweth God heareth us; he that is not of God heareth not us. Hereby know
we the spirit of truth, and the spirit of error."* 1 John 4:1-6. John tells us to be
sensitive to the spirit of others. He teaches the spirit of the world denies the authority
of Christ over our lives but affirmation of Christ's work is testimony that God's
Spirit is in control.

The scriptures command us to be sensitive to the spirit of others. *"Brethren, if
a man be overtaken in a fault, ye which are spiritual, restore such an one in the
spirit of meekness; considering thyself, lest thou also be tempted."*
Galatians 6:1. Notice the words "ye which are spiritual." *"Flee also youthful
lusts: but follow righteousness, faith, charity, peace, with them that call on
the Lord out of a pure heart." 2 Timothy 2:22.* Young people are commanded to
seek companions with a "pure heart." This requires sensitivity. *"Make no
friendship with an angry man; and with a furious man thou shalt not go:
Lest thou learn his ways, and get a snare to thy soul." Proverbs 22:24,25.*
We are told here to discern the spirit of continual anger in a person and refuse to
be an amigo; on the other hand, we are supposed to search for wise people to be
friends: *"He that walketh with wise men shall be wise: but a companion of
fools shall be destroyed." Proverbs 13:20.*

The Bible teaches that sensitivity is a spiritual element: *"But as it is written,
Eye hath not seen, nor ear heard, neither have entered into the heart of man,
the things which God hath prepared for them that love him. 10 But God hath
revealed them unto us by his Spirit: for the Spirit searcheth all things, yea,
the deep things of God. 11 For what man knoweth the things of a man, save
the spirit of man which is in him? even so the things of God knoweth no*

man, but the Spirit of God. 12 Now we have received, not the spirit of the world, but the spirit which is of God; that we might know the things that are freely given to us of God. 13 Which things also we speak, not in the words which man's wisdom teacheth, but which the Holy Ghost teacheth; comparing spiritual things with spiritual. 14 But the natural man receiveth not the things of the Spirit of God: for they are foolishness unto him: neither can he know them, because they are spiritually discerned. 15 But he that is spiritual judgeth all things, yet he himself is judged of no man. 16 For who hath known the mind of the Lord, that he may instruct him? But we have the mind of Christ." 1 Corinthians 2:9-16. This passage contrasts the spirit of the world, which is natural to the people (Ecclesiastes 3:10-11), and the Spirit of God, which is received at the new birth. In verse 13 Paul says that the Holy Spirit wants us to compare and contrast the spirit of the world and the Spirit of God. Verse 15 explains that a spiritual person has the ability to discern both the spirit of the world and the Spirit of God in others.

5. Creativity

"And God blessed them, and God said unto them, Be fruitful, and multiply, and replenish the earth, and subdue it: and have dominion over the fish of the sea, and over the fowl of the air, and over every living thing that moveth upon the earth." Genesis 1:28. From the very beginning God commanded people to have dominion over all living things and over the physical earth itself. God's purpose for Adam and Eve was to use and develop the resources of the earth and to fill the earth to overflowing (replenish) with new people.

The special ability God gives to develop the potential of the earth is creativity. Creativity is the ability to take what is given and work out unique ways to solve problems. The results of creativity can be seen everywhere. We have highways and cars that allow us travel great distances in a short time. We have airplanes that transport us to the other side of the world in a few hours. We have household appliances, telephones, computers, fax machines, etc. All of these were created from natural resources. We also have art that inspires us to think spiritual thoughts.

We are most like God and reflect the spiritual nature He has put within us when we are creative. The very first words of God's revelation to people are, "In the beginning, God created."

Creativity is not limited by intelligence, maturity, or any other psychological ability. Little children, retarded people, and mentally ill people all demonstrate creativity.

Psyche (Psychological nature)

The word translated "soul" in I Thessalonians 5:23 is the same word we get "psychology" from. The psyche is the soul. Psychology is the study of the soul. Psychoanalysis is the taking apart and examination of the soul. Sigmund Freud coined the word "psychoanalysis" to emphasize the study of soulish matters.[1]

Likewise, the "soul" in the New Testament signifies the psychological nature. It is a mistake to use soul and spirit interchangeably as most Christians do. Rarely are they interchangeable in the scriptures. *"For what is a man profited, if he shall gain the whole world, and lose his own soul? or what shall a man give in exchange for his soul?" Matthew 16:26.* That's not talking about going to hell because of ambition; it's talking about the loss to the personality of not following Jesus. Hebrews 10:39 declares the just ones "are not of them that draw back unto perdition; but of them that believe to the saving of the soul." Salvation of the spirit does not require human effort, but salvation of the psychological nature (soul) requires living by faith in God.

"For the word of God is quick, and powerful, and sharper than any twoedged sword, piercing even to the dividing asunder of soul and spirit, and of the joints and marrow, and is a discerner of the thoughts and intents of the heart." Hebrews 4:12. This verse teaches there is a separation of the spirit and the soul. They are distinguished at the joints (the boundaries of each), and they are each delineated in the marrow (the elements that make them up). The word "heart" in the New Testament is usually interchangeable with soul.[2] It is in this verse. Thus we learn that thoughts (mind) and intents (will) are two elements of the soul.[3]

The other element of the soul is the emotions: *"Then saith he unto them, My soul is exceeding sorrowful, even unto death: tarry ye here, and watch with me." Matthew 26:38.*

Therefore, the soul (psychological nature) is made up of the mind, the will, and the emotions.

1. Mind - perception, reflection, reasoning

"Come unto me, all ye that labour and are heavy laden, and I will give you rest. Take my yoke upon you, and learn of me; for I am meek and lowly in heart: and ye shall find rest unto your souls. For my yoke is easy, and my burden is light." Matthew 11:28-30. If we learn of Him (a function of mind), we will find rest from anxiety in our psyches (souls). We are encouraged to do this

because He has a gentle heart. The "heart" here means personality and is interchangeable with soul.

"Be careful for nothing; but in every thing by prayer and supplication with thanksgiving let your requests be made known unto God. And the peace of God, which passeth all understanding, shall keep your hearts and minds through Christ Jesus. Finally, brethren, whatsoever things are true, whatsoever things are honest, whatsoever things are just, whatsoever things are pure, whatsoever things are lovely, whatsoever things are of good report; if there be any virtue, and if there be any praise, think on these things." *Philippians 4:6-8.* We are to be anxious about nothing. Instead, we are to pray and think on good things. By this our hearts (souls) and minds will have peace.

The King James Version translates "psyche" into mind three times: Acts 14:2; Philippians 1:27; Hebrews 12:3.[4]

2. Will - desires, purposes, wishes

"Servants, be obedient to them that are your masters according to the flesh, with fear and trembling, in singleness of your heart, as unto Christ; 6 Not with eyeservice, as menpleasers; but as the servants of Christ, doing the will of God from the heart;" *Ephesians 6:5,6.* Psyche is translated "heart" in verse 6.[5] Therefore, the will is a function of the soul.

"And the multitude of them that believed were of one heart and of one soul: neither said any of them that ought of the things which he possessed was his own; but they had all things common." *Acts 4:32.* The believers were in agreement about their desires, purposes, and wishes. They were of one "heart" and one "soul."

"Every man according as he purposeth in his heart, so let him give; not grudgingly, or of necessity: for God loveth a cheerful giver." *2 Corinthians 9:7.* Purposing is a function of the heart (soul).

"For the time past of our life may suffice us to have wrought the will of the Gentiles, when we walked in lasciviousness, lusts, excess of wine, revellings, banquetings, and abominable idolatries:" *1 Peter 4:3.* The "will of the Gentiles" refers to desires that are not tempered by the Spirit of God.

3. Emotions

"And Simeon blessed them, and said unto Mary his mother, Behold, this child is set for the fall and rising again of many in Israel; and for a sign which shall be spoken against; (Yea, a sword shall pierce through thy own

soul also,) that the thoughts of many hearts may be revealed." Luke 2:34,35. The "sword" as defined by Vine is "an instrument of anguish."[6] This anguish pierces through the emotional part of the soul.

"Men's hearts failing them for fear, and for looking after those things which are coming on the earth: for the powers of heaven shall be shaken." Luke 21:26. Fear is shown to be resident in the heart (soul).

"(For that righteous man dwelling among them, in seeing and hearing, vexed his righteous soul from day to day with their unlawful deeds;)" 2 Peter 2:8. The soul can be vexed or tormented emotionally.

"And they said one to another, Did not our heart burn within us, while he talked with us by the way, and while he opened to us the scriptures?" Luke 24:32. The heart (soul) can burn with emotion when touched by the Spirit of God.

"And I will say to my soul, Soul, thou hast much goods laid up for many years; take thine ease, eat, drink, and be merry." Luke 12:19. The soul can relax and be merry.

"Now is my soul troubled; and what shall I say? Father, save me from this hour: but for this cause came I unto this hour." John 12:27. The soul can be troubled.

"And one of the scribes came, and having heard them reasoning together, and perceiving that he had answered them well, asked him, Which is the first commandment of all? And Jesus answered him, The first of all the commandments is, Hear, O Israel; The Lord our God is one Lord: And thou shalt love the Lord thy God with all thy heart, and with all thy soul, and with all thy mind, and with all thy strength: this is the first commandment." Mark 12:28-30. In the light of this section, we now know that to love God with the heart, soul, mind, and strength means to love God with our personality: mind, will, emotions. The command implies that we are to go beyond the love our spirits have for God (our spirits are already in love with God), and allow the spiritual nature to remake and transform our souls.

Soma (Physical nature)

The soma is the physical nature. It transmits physical information to the psyche (soul) through the senses: sight, smell, hearing, taste, and touch. We use that information to make decisions.

The pneuma transmits spiritual information to the soul through the spiritual senses. The spirit also sees, smells, hears, tastes, and touches. The spirit is often in conflict with the physical nature because it has a different data set from the same events.

1. walk by faith, not by sight   2 Corinthians 5:7
2. an odor of a sweet smell   Philippians 4:18
3. hearing of faith   Galatians3:2
4. taste and see   Psalms 34:8
5. touch not the unclean thing   2 Corinthians 6:17

The Perpetual Conflict

The ideal is for all three natures to work together in harmony. This is Paul's wish in I Thessalonians 5:23. However, that doesn't often happen in our "messed up" world. In our world we usually have a conflict between the spiritual and the physical natures. The battleground is the soul (psychological nature).

Sigmund Freud studied the soul. His mission was to find a way to have harmony within. Freud well understood the combatants in the war. He called the spiritual nature the "above I," the psychological nature the "I," and the physical nature the "it."[7] These simple pronouns were translated into Latin for English speakers: id, ego, and superego (I don't know why). The "it" is the childish part that responds to physical sense data and primitive emotions. The "above I" is the judge of our actions that responds to spiritual sense data. The "it" and the "above I" fight for control of the "I." "I" take action. "I" do things or don't do things. "It" and "above I" try to influence me.

The New Testament described these same dynamics almost 2000 years before Sigmund Freud (and with much more authority): *"This I say then, Walk in the Spirit, and ye shall not fulfil the lust of the flesh. For the flesh lusteth against the Spirit, and the Spirit against the flesh: and these are contrary the one to the other: so that ye cannot do the things that ye would." Galatians 5:16,17.* If we have a regenerated spirit, and we follow the promptings of the "above I," we will be winning the battle against "it."

In the next section I will describe the details of this conflict and the players in the "fifth dimension" who try to influence the outcome.

Players on a Grand Scale

In the beginning Adam and Eve were without conflict in their spirits, souls, and bodies. Their triune natures harmonized.

Then the serpent walked onto the stage. He was more beautiful and clever than any of God's creations. He questioned the woman concerning God's directives about the tree of life. He found faulty reasoning in her understanding. She thought there was something evil or poison about the tree itself: *"But of the fruit of the tree which is in the midst of the garden, God hath said, Ye shall not eat of it, neither shall ye touch it, lest ye die." Genesis 3:3.*

The serpent beguiled her with his subtlety. He told her eating the fruit would not kill or poison her (true). He implied God had evil motives for keeping the tree away: "God does not want you to experience for yourself and decide what's good and evil": *"For God doth know that in the day ye eat thereof, then your eyes shall be opened, and ye shall be as gods, knowing good and evil." Genesis 3:5.*

The woman saw that the tree was good for food (lust of the flesh), that it was pleasant to the eyes (lust of the eyes), and that it was desired to make one wise (pride of life). She ate the fruit and persuaded Adam to eat also (Genesis 3:6).

The couple soon realized they had been duped and they were vulnerable to further deception: *"And the eyes of them both were opened, and they knew that they were naked; and they sewed fig leaves together, and made themselves aprons." Genesis 3:7.*

In the Forefront: Spirit vs. Flesh

The serpent successfully assaulted the soul through the physical nature. He triumphed by taking advantage of the woman's physical focus. He provoked her to ignore the spiritual consequences of disobeying God. Eating the fruit was not physically harmful, but it damaged Adam and Eve's relationship with God.

The natural world and its concerns hide the devil's ally in the war against our souls. This traitor is within the walls of the soul. The "flesh" is the Trojan horse of the personality. The flesh is energized by and responds to physical sense data. It's that part of the self that discounts God's intervention. Since Adam and Eve, the flesh has been part of every person's soul. Colossians 2:18-19 implies that paganism or polytheism is caused by a "fleshly mind": *"Let no man beguile you of your reward in a voluntary humility and worshipping of angels, intruding into those things which he hath not seen, vainly puffed up by his fleshly mind, And not holding the Head, from which all the body by joints and bands having nourishment ministered, and knit together, increaseth with the increase of God." Colossians 2:18,19.*

God offers reconciliation for this loss of harmony among the soul, spirit, and body, and the corruption caused by the flesh. Through Jesus Christ He seeks to destroy the creation of the devil in every one of us: *"He that committeth sin is of the devil; for the devil sinneth from the beginning. For this purpose the Son of God was manifested, that he might destroy the works of the devil." 1 John 3:8.* Through Jesus God dispels the darkness surrounding the spirit world and shows us the spiritual dimension: *"Then spake Jesus again unto them, saying, I am the light of the world: he that followeth me shall not walk in darkness, but shall have the light of life." John 8:12.*

God wants us to respond to our spiritual nature: natural light, conscience, wisdom, sensitivity, and creativity. Only by responding to spiritual sense data will we be able to subdue the flesh. We are reborn in our spirits when we trust in Christ as savior. We are transformed in our souls when we allow spiritual impulses to control us: *"There is therefore now no condemnation to them which are in Christ Jesus, who walk not after the flesh, but after the Spirit. For the law of the Spirit of life in Christ Jesus hath made me free from the law of sin and death. For what the law could not do, in that it was weak through the flesh, God sending his own Son in the likeness of sinful flesh, and for sin, condemned sin in the flesh: That the righteousness of the law might be fulfilled in us, who walk not after the flesh, but after the Spirit. For they that are after the flesh do mind the things of the flesh; but they that are after the Spirit the things of the Spirit. For to be carnally minded is death; but to be spiritually minded is life and peace." Romans 8:1-6. "If we live in the Spirit, let us also walk in the Spirit." Galatians 5: 25.*

Behind the Scenes: God vs. Satan

Satan animated the serpent. Satan wars against the soul through the physical senses and at the same time blinds us to spiritual reality (2 Corinthians 4:3-4). Satan wants us to believe the universe is a closed system that is never altered from without. Hewantstoremainhiddenandpersuadeusthatalleventshavenaturalcausesbecause he is a creature and not a creator (2 Peter 3:3-7; Ezekiel 28:13-17).

Satan's religion is pantheism: everything is divine and the divine is in everything. It leaves no gap for God to penetrate the boundary of a closed system. If everything is divine, then it's equally true to say everything is profane, since there is no difference between one divine thing and another. No person is more righteous than another. No culture is more desirable than another. All things in the universe must work together because the universe is all. C.S. Lewis said, "Pantheism is in fact the permanent natural bent of the human mind."[8]

Pantheism is very close to modern New Age. I had a New Age friend several years ago try to convince me she believed in the same God as me. I let her know for sure I didn't believe in the same god as her. The God I believe is not part of the physical universe, but He lives outside and interferes from time to time. This concept overloaded her circuits. Lewis also said, "each new relapse into this immemorial religion is hailed as the last word in novelty and emancipation."[9]

The spiritual world exists behind the scenes of the natural world. It can only be known through spiritual senses. In that world God and Satan fight first for the souls of people and ultimately the spirits of people. Satan's goal is to hide the spiritual world. God's goal is to reveal: *"But ye, brethren, are not in darkness, that that day should overtake you as a thief. Ye are all the children of light, and the children of the day: we are not of the night, nor of darkness. Therefore let us not sleep, as do others; but let us watch and be sober. For they that sleep sleep in the night; and they that be drunken are drunken in the night."* 1 *Thessalonians 5.4-7.*

The Bible gives us a few glimpses of this ongoing war. The temptation of Job is an example. The sons of God (angels) came to present themselves before God and Satan came also (Job 1:6). The Lord boasted to Satan of Job's faith and spiritual perception. Satan accused Job of serving God for reward and challenged God to take away His wealth. God allowed Satan to wreck Job's family, possessions, and health. Yet, Job remained faithful to God. He believed God controls reality and is able to restore losses. Job's story teaches that spiritual realities are not always reflected by physical appearances. Apparently, God cursed Job; but actually, God tested Job's faith and showed the world His power to save and restore.

In 1 Kings 22 the Kings of Judah and Israel prepared to go to battle with Syria (sounds like it could have happened last week, doesn't it?). They asked the prophets to predict the outcome. Four hundred false prophets said the battle would be easy. They looked at the fact that Ahab, the king of Israel, had already defeated Syria twice before without Jehoshaphat, the king of Judah. It seemed obvious their combined forces would win. But one prophet, whom Ahab did not want to hear from, Micaiah, reported the alliance's defeat: *"And he said, I saw all Israel scattered upon the hills, as sheep that have not a shepherd: and the LORD said, These have no master: let them return every man to his house in peace. And the king of Israel said unto Jehoshaphat, Did I not tell thee that he would prophesy no good concerning me, but evil? And he said, Hear thou therefore the word of the LORD: I saw the LORD sitting on his throne, and all the host of heaven standing by him on his right hand and on his left. And the LORD said, Who shall persuade Ahab, that he may go up and fall at Ramothgilead? And one said on this manner, and another said on that manner. And there came forth a spirit, and stood before the LORD, and said, I will persuade him. And the LORD said unto him, Wherewith? And he said, I will go forth, and I will be a lying spirit in the mouth of all his prophets. And he said, Thou shalt persuade him, and prevail also: go forth, and do so. Now therefore, behold, the LORD hath put a lying spirit in the mouth of all these thy prophets, and the LORD hath spoken evil concerning thee." 1 Kings 22:17-23.* God allowed a lying spirit, one of Satan's minions, to persuade Ahab. The lying spirit was eager because Satan's angels delight in destroying people with deception.

Then the false prophets mocked Micaiah and the king put him in prison. As a precaution before the battle, Ahab disguised himself as a common soldier. The Syrian king ordered his men to fight only with Ahab. And even though he was disguised, a lucky arrow killed Ahab.

The military victory that seemed obvious to worldly reasoning failed to occur. Spiritual intervention into the minds and attitudes of people prejudiced the outcome.

Daniel the Babylonian captive received a message from an angel. This is recorded in Daniel 10. He fasted and prayed for three weeks before the angel arrived. The angel told Daniel he would help, comfort, and teach him. The angel had been commissioned from the first day of Daniel's fast. But the angel was delayed by his fight with the "prince of Persia," one of Satan's angelic followers: *"Then said he unto me, Fear not, Daniel: for from the first day that thou didst set thine heart to understand, and to chasten thyself before thy God, thy words were heard, and I am come for thy words. But the prince of the kingdom of Persia withstood me one and twenty days: but, lo, Michael, one of the chief princes, came to help me; and I remained there with the kings of Persia." Daniel 10:12,13.* The angel delivered Daniel's message and returned to fight the spiritual prince of Persia.

Daniel was at the time an officer of the kingdom of Persia. The angel was not fighting with Cyrus the king. He was fighting with Satan's prince of Persia. Apparently, God's angels and Satan's angels have specific territories and peoples. Frank E. Peretti does a marvelous job of speculating on this theme in his books (*This Present Darkness, Piercing the Darkness*, etc.).

The scriptures say God's unseen forces are seeking to reward those who are faithful to Him: *"For the eyes of the LORD run to and fro throughout the whole earth, to shew himself strong in the behalf of them whose heart is perfect toward him. Herein thou hast done foolishly: therefore from henceforth thou shalt have wars." 2 Chron.16:9.*

The scriptures also warn us to prepare for battle with Satan's armies and rulers: *"Put on the whole armour of God, that ye may be able to stand against the wiles of the devil. For we wrestle not against flesh and blood, but against principalities, against powers, against the rulers of the darkness of this world, against spiritual wickedness in high places." Ephesians 6:11,12.*

Faust

Goethe's *Faust* depicts the dynamics of the spiritual conflict. Goethe paints both the inner battle between the spirit and the flesh and the behind the scenes war between God and Satan.

"The Prelude in the Theatre" involves a dialogue among the Poet, the Director, and the Comedian about their approach to the play. Each promotes his own style. The poet represents the spirit nature, the director the psychological nature, and the comedian the physical nature.

After the prelude the scene shifts to the "Prologue in Heaven." The angels of God praise Him: Raphael, Gabriel, and Michael. Mephistopheles (Satan) attends also. Just like with Job, the Lord praises Faust and Mephistopheles issues a challenge. If the Lord allows him, he will destroy Faust's soul. The Lord says "try" and tells the devil Faust's conscience and natural light will guide him in the right path: "a good man in his dark and secret longings is well aware which path to go."[10]

Faust is a man of erudition. He teaches the elite students of the land, yet he is dissatisfied with head knowledge. He wants to transcend book learning to know and develop his soul. Wagner the student only desires head knowledge. Faust says, "You're conscious only of a single drive; oh, do not seek to know the other passion! Two souls, alas, dwell in my breast, each seeks to rule without the other. The one with robust love's desires clings to the world with all its might; the other fiercely rises from the dust to reach sublime ancestral regions."[11]

Faust represents the soul straining to be in concert. He rejects mere mind and reason as insufficient to harmonize all parts of the person. Wagner represents the stunted soul who only understands the material.

Mephisto comes to Faust and offers every wish to command. When Faust asks his name, he says, "a portion of that power which always works for Evil and effects the Good."[12]Faust bets Mephisto that if he ever likes anything Mephisto gives enough to want more, then his soul is forfeit.

Mephisto represents Faust's flesh as well as Satan himself. In all their adventures, the Lord lives behind the scenes causing Faust to desire more than the mind, will, emotions, and flesh can offer.

The first woman Mephisto brings to Faust is Gretchen. She appeals to Faust's lust of the flesh. Faust's incontinence, however, destroys Gretchen and their relationship. After Gretchen, Faust is seemingly immune to merely fleshly impulses. He sees the dissipation of it all.

In Part 2, Faust desires to be with the spirit of Helen of Troy, who represents his striving for the spirit world (Colossians 2). Mephisto conjures her to comfort Faust.

Faust and Helen have a child named Euphorion. Euphorion dances and jumps upon the mountain peaks despite warnings from his mother and father, till he slips and falls to his death. Euphorion represents the ecstasy and danger of focusing on the spiritual without allowing it to change the soul. After this tragedy, Helen fades back into the spirit world also.

Faust learns that it is impossible to exclusively explore the spirit world while living in the body. We need input from both the physical senses and the spiritual senses. He learns that it's O.K. to have one's head in the clouds if one's feet are on the ground.

After Helen, Faust rejects Mephisto completely. He realizes that the flesh cannot add to the soul: "Shut out from life, you have no part in things that stir the human heart. Your bitter mind, where envy breeds, what can it know of human needs?"[13]

Then Faust embarks on a plan to reclaim land from the sea. He desires to overcome a small part of the force of nature. This shows Faust's maturity in that he realizes the development of his soul depends on pushing back the influence of the flesh (nature, the sea).

Although I don't think I fully understand or agree with Goethe's theology, I do believe he has given us powerful images of "the great conflict."

Precipitation From the Spirit World

Thunder, coolness of air, and the smell of condensation: these are all signals of an impending cloudburst. When the raindrops fall, you have your proof. In the same way the strivings of the spirit and flesh are signs of spiritual storms. Everyday events express the influence of good and evil, God and Satan. In this section, I will describe the emanations of the spiritual dimension in Health, Economy, Careers, Politics, and Love.

Health

Stephanie Simonton said a person's outlook and attitude has an effect on the propensity to contract cancer. She said depression and stress have a long-term effect on a person's immune system that makes them vulnerable to cancer.[14]

Depression and stress are partly psychological responses to events. Our response depends on which part of ourselves we listen to. If we listen to the flesh, then we are tempted to interpret almost any event as bad or potentially bad for us. People who are depressed badly interpret many events. If we listen to the Spirit, then we are led to interpret events as working together in the providence of God (Romans 8:28-29).

Therefore, if the spiritual conflict leads to either good or bad psychological responses, and bad psychological responses sometimes lead to diseases like depression and cancer, then sometimes diseases have a spiritual element as a precipitant, and their prevention depends on spiritual factors.

Dr. S.I. McMillan dealt with the spiritual roots of disease in his book *None of These Diseases*. The key verse of his thesis is *Exodus 15:26: "If thou wilt diligently hearken to the voice of the LORD thy God, and wilt do that which is right in his sight, and wilt give ear to his commandments, and keep all his statutes, I will put none of these diseases upon thee, which I have brought upon the Egyptians: for I am the LORD that healeth thee."* Following God's commands frees us from many diseases.

Dr. McMillan testified that chemical addiction, brought about by spiritual problems, destroys the physical. Emotional distress from attitudes of self-centeredness, envy, jealousy, resentment, hate, worry, oversensitivity, guilt-feelings, fear, sorrow, desire for approval, and frustration can cause or aggravate ulcers, colitis, high blood pressure, heart disease, kidney disease, headaches, arteriosclerosis, mental disturbances, goiter, diabetes, and arthritis.[15]These toxic emotional states sound like the "works of the flesh" from Galatians 5:19-21. Romans 1:28-32 also gives a similar list! *"And even as they did not like to retain God in their knowledge, God gave them over to a reprobate mind, to do those things which are not convenient; Being filled with all unrighteousness, fornication, wickedness, covetousness, maliciousness; full of envy, murder, debate, deceit, malignity; whisperers, Backbiters, haters of God, despiteful, proud, boasters, inventors of evil things, disobedient to parents, Without understanding, covenantbreakers, without natural affection, implacable, unmerciful: Who knowing the judgment of God, that they which commit such things are worthy of death, not only do the same, but have pleasure in them that do them." Romans 1:28-32.*

Dr. McMillan especially pointed out that brooding over resentments is harmful to health. He stated, "Man doesn't ever seem to learn that the high cost of getting even may be toxic goiter, strokes of apoplexy, and fatal heart attacks."[16] This makes me wonder at the meaning of *Matthew 18:34-35: "And his lord was wroth, and delivered him to the tormentors, till he should pay all that was due unto him. So likewise shall my heavenly Father do also unto you, if ye from your hearts forgive not every one his brother their trespasses."* The unforgiving servant was delivered to the tormentors and so will our Lord do to us if we do not practice forgiveness.

In contrast, *"A merry heart doeth good like a medicine: but a broken spirit drieth the bones." Proverbs 17:22.*

As I wrote this, I was sitting at my house in Sheridan, Arkansas, my hometown. About a year before, Sheridan was inundated by a storm of suicides and suicide attempts by teenagers. On April 31, 1990, Thomas Smith, 17, stood in front of his junior class at Sheridan High School to make an announcement. He then pulled out a gun and shot himself dead.[17] Within twenty-four hours, two other Sheridan teenagers took their own lives. This was followed by other attempts and preceded by a teen suicide in March 1990. Sheridan had a population of about 3,000 at the time.

There was some speculation that occult practices were involved. I don't think anyone ever proved that. Nevertheless, I do think it's appropriate to link suicide with the devil's influence. Even if the boys weren't involved in anything devilish, the devil was involved in their hopelessness and despairing. Suicide is a spiritual statement.

A dark spiritual cloud descended on Sheridan. I believe many people felt the drawing to do themselves in. I felt it also. The spiritual dimension was raining down hard on us during that time. It was an evil spiritual hurricane, leaving destruction in its passing.

"But the fruit of the Spirit is love, joy, peace, longsuffering, gentleness, goodness, faith, Meekness, temperance: against such there is no law. And they that are Christ's have crucified the flesh with the affections and lusts. If we live in the Spirit, let us also walk in the Spirit." Galatians 5:22-25.

Economy

The relationship between money and spiritual matters does not seem obvious. Yet, the Bible speaks often of finance. Jesus gave us the key principle that connects both worlds: *"He that is faithful in that which is least is faithful also in much: and he that is unjust in the least is unjust also in much. If therefore ye have not been faithful in the unrighteous mammon, who will commit to your trust the true riches?" Luke 16:10,11.* Money is for practice. If we learn how to use it properly, then God will give us greater riches: ministry, spouse, children, etc.

God told the children of Israel their disobedience would compel the need to borrow money: *"The stranger that is within thee shall get up above thee very high; and thou shalt come down very low. He shall lend to thee, and thou shalt not lend to him: he shall be the head, and thou shalt be the tail."* Deuteronomy *28:43,44.* This was listed as one of the curses of ignoring God's laws.

God allows our assets to increase or decrease in order to fulfill His purposes. In the days of Joseph the patriarch, God caused seven years of plenty to provide for the seven years of famine to follow: *"This is the thing which I have spoken unto Pharaoh: What God is about to do he sheweth unto Pharaoh. Behold, there come seven years of great plenty throughout all the land of Egypt: And there shall arise after them seven years of famine; and all the plenty shall be forgotten in the land of Egypt; and the famine shall consume the land; And the plenty shall not be known in the land by reason of that famine following; for it shall be very grievous. And for that the dream was doubled unto Pharaoh twice; it is because the thing is established by God, and God will shortly bring it to pass."* Genesis 41:28-32.

As a result of Joseph's interpretation of God's plans, Pharaoh made Joseph second ruler over Egypt. After the seven years of plenty, and the grievous famine began, Jacob and his family were forced to look to Egypt for food. This gave Joseph an opportunity to be reunited with his family: *"And Joseph said unto his brethren, Come near to me, I pray you. And they came near. And he said, I am Joseph your brother, whom ye sold into Egypt. Now therefore be not grieved, nor angry with yourselves, that ye sold me hither: for God did send me before you to preserve life. For these two years hath the famine been in the land: and yet there are five years, in the which there shall neither be earing nor harvest. And God sent me before you to preserve you a posterity in the earth, and to save your lives by a great deliverance. So now it was not you that sent me hither, but God: and he hath made me a father to Pharaoh, and lord of all his house, and a ruler throughout all the land of Egypt. Haste ye, and go up to my father, and say unto him, Thus saith thy son Joseph, God hath made me lord of all Egypt: come down unto me, tarry not: And thou shalt dwell in the land of Goshen, and thou shalt be near unto me, thou, and thy children, and thy children's children, and thy flocks, and thy herds, and all that thou hast: And there will I nourish thee; for yet there are five years of famine; lest thou, and thy household, and all that thou hast, come to poverty."* Genesis 45:4-11.

Warren T. Brooks taught that the Gross National Product depends upon spiritual values. In his essay, "Goodness and the GNP," he stated, "at its roots, economics is a metaphysical rather than a mathematical science, in which intangible spiritual values and attitudes are at least as important as physical assets and morale more fundamental than the money supply."[18]For example: people that are high on drugs aren't very productive; teenage mothers don't usually become a boon to our economy; insider-trading scandals don't promote investment in the stock market. Countries that sacrifice millions of potential workers to abortion can expect a labor shortage and a shrinking economy in the next generation. Countries that permit kickbacks, bribes, and cheating to go unchecked live with high levels of unemployment and poor services from the government. Brookes captured the essence when he said, "Without the civilizing force of universal moral standards, particularly honesty, trust, self-respect, integrity, and loyalty, the market place quickly degenerates."[19]

"Miser Dies; $33,000 Found in Cans, Bank." A seventy-two year old man in Spokane, Washington rented an $80 a month downtown apartment and shaved his head to save on haircuts. He was found dead in his shoddy studio: "his only obvious possessions were a small color television, a collection of hats, and a footlocker filled with papers and pictures." His money was turned over to the state since he had no known next of kin.[20]

I am reminded of Midas, king of Phrygia. He wished that everything he touched would turn to gold. His wish was granted. Midas changed all his possessions and all living things (flowers, trees) to gold until he found there was nothing living in his world anymore. There was only gold, which could not bring life, neither happiness, nor comfort. Midas couldn't even eat because his food and drink turned to gold. At least Midas was able to recant his error. The miser of Spokane apparently never did.

"There is that scattereth, and yet increaseth; and there is that withholdeth more than is meet, but it tendeth to poverty. The liberal soul shall be made fat: and he that watereth shall be watered also himself." Proverbs 11:24,25. "Charge them that are rich in this world, that they be not highminded, nor trust in uncertain riches, but in the living God, who giveth us richly all things to enjoy; That they do good, that they be rich in good works, ready to distribute, willing to communicate; Laying up in store for themselves a good foundation against the time to come, that they may lay hold on eternal life." 1 Timothy 6:17-19.

Careers

In 1986, a prominent Wall Street trader was fined $100,000,000 by the Securities Exchange Commission and was permanently banned from the securities business. He reportedly accepted advance tips on mergers and other large corporate decisions. He used the knowledge to make $millions$ in securities. The trader paid the fines out of his personal funds. The SEC said his trading companies had assets of $2 billion.[21]

In 1990, a southern Attorney General was found guilty of theft of state funds and fined $10,000. He reportedly had used a state credit card to treat family, girlfriends, and political contributors to meals and trips: "During the trial, five former girlfriends testified they accompanied the Attorney General at meals and on trips, including travel to Hawaii, New Orleans, and California... The women said they were unaware the expenses were paid by the state... Charges on the Visa card included a birthday party for his daughter, $80 shots of cognac and $500 worth of Don Perignon champagne at the Peabody hotel in Memphis."[22]

These men may have had cases of the "pride of life." The trader surely didn't need more money to make him happy. What was the need to cheat? The Attorney General was one of the most important politicians in the state. What was the need to abuse his trust? Surely getting to the top of the heap in careers doesn't always satisfy. Sometimes the spiritual dimension comes raining down: *"Pride goeth before destruction, and an haughty spirit before a fall. Better it is to be of an humble spirit with the lowly, than to divide the spoil with the proud." Proverbs 16:18,19.*

The decades of the 90's and 00's have given us many more examples of people high in public life who used their positions to satisfy their illicit longings, and there will continue to be an inexhaustible supply, because it is human nature to desire more, even when we should be satisfied.

Jesus addressed this problem with the man who wanted his inheritance. Jesus told the man that owning this world's goods and fame doesn't suffice. He taught there is more: *"And one of the company said unto him, Master, speak to my brother, that he divide the inheritance with me. And he said unto him, Man, who made me a judge or a divider over you? And he said unto them, Take heed, and beware of covetousness: for a man's life consisteth not in the abundance of the things which he possesseth. And he spake a parable unto them, saying, The ground of a certain rich man brought forth plentifully: And he thought within himself, saying, What shall I do, because I have no room where to bestow my fruits? And he said, This will I do: I will pull down my barns, and build greater; and there will I bestow all my fruits and my goods. And I will say to my soul, Soul, thou hast much goods laid up for many years; take thine ease, eat, drink, and be merry. But God said unto him, Thou fool, this night thy soul shall be required of thee: then whose shall those things be, which thou hast provided? So is he that layeth up treasure for himself, and is not rich toward God." Luke 12:13-21.*

The rich man built greater barns to show off his wealth. He thought this would finally quench his inner thirst. But God said, "thou fool, this night thy 'psyche' shall be required of thee." Apparently, material success is not enough. God requires more. He requires exploration of the spiritual dimension.

Joseph the Patriarch sought God's will for his life. Yet, his brothers sold him into slavery. Then, after proving himself to the captain of the guard, he was falsely accused by the captain's wife. Imprisonment. Joseph became the unofficial warden of the prison because of his diligence. It was only after God intervened in the politics and dreams of Egypt that Joseph was brought out of prison. He was elevated to be the second ruler of Egypt. Not a recommended career path, but God blessed him because of his love and his care to develop the spiritual side.

Politics

"Daniel answered and said, Blessed be the name of God for ever and ever: for wisdom and might are his: And he changeth the times and the seasons: he removeth kings, and setteth up kings: he giveth wisdom unto the wise, and knowledge to them that know understanding:" Daniel 2:20,21. "Surely men of low degree are vanity, and men of high degree are a lie: to be laid in the balance, they are altogether lighter than vanity. Trust not in oppression, and become not vain in robbery: if riches increase, set not your heart upon them. God hath spoken once; twice have I heard this; that power belongeth unto God." Psalms 62:9-11. "The king's heart is in the hand of the LORD, as the rivers of water: he turneth it whithersoever he will." Proverbs 21:1.

God interferes in politics. This is one of the plainest and most oft-repeated teachings of scripture. People want to write their own epic, but God finishes the final chapter: *"Man's goings are of the LORD; how can a man then understand his own way?" Proverbs 20:24. "A man's heart deviseth his way: but the LORD directeth his steps." Proverbs 16:9.*

The Assyrian empire under Shalmaneser destroyed Israel's northern kingdom in 721 B.C. Eight years later, the Assyrians under Sennacherib came back into the promised land to put down a revolt led by Hezekiah, king of Judah.

The Assyrians mocked the people and God. They said that the gods of other nations did not save them and neither would Jehovah save Israel. Jerusalem was the last stronghold. Hezekiah prayed to God and God gave this reply: *"And Isaiah said unto them, Thus shall ye say unto your master, Thus saith the LORD, Be not afraid of the words that thou hast heard, wherewith the servants of the king of Assyria have blasphemed me. Behold, I will send a blast upon him, and he shall hear a rumour, and return to his own land; and I will cause him to fall by the sword in his own land." Isaiah 37:6,7.* The Assyrians did hear a rumor that the Ethiopians were coming to attack, and they responded by threatening Judah more. Finally, God sent an angel at night and killed the majority of their army (Isaiah 37).

Later, Merodach-baladin, king of Babylon, who was also seeking to throw off the rule of the Assyrians, sent Hezekiah a present and envoys to congratulate him on his recovery from sickness. Hezekiah proudly showed the Babylonians all he had and I'm sure he told the story of how he had defeated the Assyrians: *"At that time Merodachbaladan, the son of Baladan, king of Babylon, sent letters and a present to Hezekiah: for he had heard that he had been sick, and was recovered. And Hezekiah was glad of them, and shewed them the house of his precious things, the silver, and the gold, and the spices, and the precious ointment, and all the house of his armour, and all that was found in his treasures: there was nothing in his house, nor in all his dominion, that Hezekiah shewed them not. Then came Isaiah the prophet unto king Hezekiah, and said unto him, What said these men? and from whence came they unto thee? And Hezekiah said, They are come from a far country unto me, even from Babylon. Then said he, What have they seen in thine house? And Hezekiah answered, All that is in mine house have they seen: there is nothing among my treasures that I have not shewed them. Then said Isaiah to Hezekiah, Hear the word of the LORD of hosts: Behold, the days come, that all that is in thine house, and that which thy fathers have laid up in store until this day, shall be carried to Babylon: nothing shall be left, saith the LORD. And of thy sons that shall issue from thee, which thou shalt beget, shall they take away; and they shall be eunuchs in the palace of the king of Babylon." Isaiah 39:1-7.*

The series of events that followed allowed Daniel to became an officer in the kingdom of Babylon. Daniel was a child of Judah's royal family. He was taken away by Nebuchadnezzar, king of Babylon, along with many other captives in 586 B.C. Daniel and his friends (Shadrach, Meshach, and Abednego) were to be trained as servants and wise men of the king.

God used Daniel and his friends to profoundly affect the rulers and king. When the king dreamed of the golden head, silver shoulders, brass belly, iron legs, and clay feet, Daniel (with the help of his friends) interpreted the dream and showed Nebuchadnezzar God's political program for "the times of the Gentiles" (Daniel

2). Because of his spiritual insight, Daniel became a high officer in Babylon: *"The king answered unto Daniel, and said, Of a truth it is, that your God is a God of gods, and a Lord of kings, and a revealer of secrets, seeing thou couldest reveal this secret. Then the king made Daniel a great man, and gave him many great gifts, and made him ruler over the whole province of Babylon, and chief of the governors over all the wise men of Babylon." (Daniel 2:47-48).*

Nebuchadnezzar later identified God's intervention in politics in a still more poignant way and testified: *"Nebuchadnezzar the king, unto all people, nations, and languages, that dwell in all the earth; Peace be multiplied unto you. I thought it good to shew the signs and wonders that the high God hath wrought toward me. How great are his signs! and how mighty are his wonders! his kingdom is an everlasting kingdom, and his dominion is from generation to generation… All this came upon the king Nebuchadnezzar. At the end of twelve months he walked in the palace of the kingdom of Babylon. The king spake, and said, Is not this great Babylon, that I have built for the house of the kingdom by the might of my power, and for the honour of my majesty? While the word was in the king's mouth, there fell a voice from heaven, saying, O king Nebuchadnezzar, to thee it is spoken; The kingdom is departed from thee. And they shall drive thee from men, and thy dwelling shall be with the beasts of the field: they shall make thee to eat grass as oxen, and seven times shall pass over thee, until thou know that the most High ruleth in the kingdom of men, and giveth it to whomsoever he will. The same hour was the thing fulfilled upon Nebuchadnezzar: and he was driven from men, and did eat grass as oxen, and his body was wet with the dew of heaven, till his hairs were grown like eagles' feathers, and his nails like birds' claws. And at the end of the days I Nebuchadnezzar lifted up mine eyes unto heaven, and mine understanding returned unto me, and I blessed the most High, and I praised and honoured him that liveth for ever, whose dominion is an everlasting dominion, and his kingdom is from generation to generation: And all the inhabitants of the earth are reputed as nothing: and he doeth according to his will in the army of heaven, and among the inhabitants of the earth: and none can stay his hand, or say unto him, What doest thou? At the same time my reason returned unto me; and for the glory of my kingdom, mine honour and brightness returned unto me; and my counsellors and my lords sought unto me; and I was established in my kingdom, and excellent majesty was added unto me. Now I Nebuchadnezzar praise and extol and honour the King of heaven, all whose works are truth, and his ways judgment: and those that walk in pride he is able to abase." Daniel 4:1-3, 28-37.*

All people esteemed Daniel's political skill and faithfulness. When the Persian engineers finally upended the Babylonians, Daniel inherited a high office in the new kingdom. The shift in government didn't alter his position. He became the Prime Minister under Darius: *"It pleased Darius to set over the kingdom an hundred and twenty princes, which should be over the whole kingdom; And over these three presidents; of whom Daniel was first: that the princes might give accounts unto them, and the king should have no damage." Daniel 6:1,2.*

And there's Esther. Esther was an orphan of the captivity. Her uncle Mordecai, an officer at Shushan the palace, adopted her. When Vashti the queen fell out of favor with Ahasuerus, the Persian king, and a search was made for another queen, Mordecai put Esther in the line-up.

The book of Esther tells the story of how Esther became the queen of Persia and saved her people from a pre-Hitler holocaust. The essence of the story is that God interferes in politics to accomplish His purposes. Esther went before the king at the risk of losing her life to set up a plea to save the Jews. God placed her in the position to thwart Satan's ever present plan to destroy the holy people: *"Again Esther spake unto Hatach, and gave him commandment unto Mordecai; All the king's servants, and the people of the king's provinces, do know, that whosoever, whether man or woman, shall come unto the king into the inner court, who is not called, there is one law of his to put him to death, except such to whom the king shall hold out the golden sceptre, that he may live: but I have not been called to come in unto the king these thirty days. And they told to Mordecai Esther's words. Then Mordecai commanded to answer Esther, Think not with thyself that thou shalt escape in the king's house, more than all the Jews. For if thou altogether holdest thy peace at this time, then shall there enlargement and deliverance arise to the Jews from another place; but thou and thy father's house shall be destroyed: and who knoweth whether thou art come to the kingdom for such a time as this? Then Esther bade them return Mordecai this answer, Go, gather together all the Jews that are present in Shushan, and fast ye for me, and neither eat nor drink three days, night or day: I also and my maidens will fast likewise; and so will I go in unto the king, which is not according to the law: and if I perish, I perish." Esther 4:10-16.* Esther bravely made her plea and saved her people.

Even today, God goes right on defending His people and interfering in politics. The new Israel has been at war four times since its inception in 1948. The first war, which started the day after Israel's independence, was against the Palestinians, Lebanon, Syria, Egypt, Jordan, Iraq, and Saudi Arabia. Israel occupied more area afterward.

In 1956, Israel defended itself again.

Then, in 1967, Israel defeated the Arab states in six days! They captured the Golan Heights from Syria, the West bank from Jordan, and the Gaza strip and the Sinai Peninsula from Egypt.

In 1973, Syria and Egypt tried to take the Promised Land but failed. This prompted Egypt to begin negotiations, which ended in the Camp David Peace Treaty (1979).

And then, in 1991, Israel won a remarkable victory without firing a shot. Iraq, under Saddam Hussein, vowed to destroy Israel. He actually fired ballistic missiles at them (SCUDS). Nevertheless, his air force never got off the ground, Patriots shot down his missiles, and the Allied army and air force slaughtered his troops. Iraq lost over 100,000 men while the Americans lost less than 200.

How a small country of a few million people could hold off the hordes of the Arab nation is baffling, except when you consider the protection of powers in the fifth dimension.

Love

Do spiritual powers intervene in matter of love? Glad you asked. Of course they do. Ever hear of a marriage made in heaven? A marriage made in hell? I intend to show that both exist. Both God and Satan work to influence the hearts of humans when they seek that special someone.

God placed Esther (Ishtar), the orphan, in a position to save the Jewish people from Satan's homicidal Haman. God saved His people through the device of the king's desire. After queen Vashti was deposed, the king's servants set out to look for her replacement from among the whole Persian Empire (Esther 2:2-4).

The girls were given one year to prepare themselves to meet the king. They had one shot to pierce his heart. And it came to pass, out of all the young women in the Persian Empire, Ahasuerus chose Esther. What a coincidence! (not really): *"And the king loved Esther above all the women, and she obtained grace and favour in his sight more than all the virgins; so that he set the royal crown upon her head, and made her queen instead of Vashti." Esther 2:17.*

Long before this, God was at work arranging marriages. How about Adam and Eve? *"And the LORD God caused a deep sleep to fall upon Adam, and he slept: and he took one of his ribs, and closed up the flesh instead thereof; And the rib, which the LORD God had taken from man, made he a woman, and brought her unto the man. And Adam said, This is now bone of my bones, and flesh of my flesh: she shall be called Woman, because she was taken out of Man. Therefore shall a man leave his father and his mother, and shall cleave unto his wife: and they shall be one flesh." Genesis 2:21-24.*

Isaac and Rebekah are another example. In Genesis 24, Moses tells the story of how Abraham charged his servant to find Isaac a wife from among his own people (Genesis 24:3-4). The servant traveled to Nahor and prayed for God's intervention. He prayed that God would reveal Isaac's wife by a sign. He prayed that the wife to be would not only offer him a drink from the well, but his camels also (Genesis 24:12-21). Rebekah was the first and only candidate and she completed the offer.

The servant then entered into negotiations with the family. Rebekah agreed to go and the story had a happy ending: *"Then Laban and Bethuel answered and said, The thing proceedeth from the LORD: we cannot speak unto thee bad or good. Behold, Rebekah is before thee, take her, and go, and let her be thy master's son's wife, as the LORD hath spoken… And they called Rebekah, and said unto her, Wilt thou go with this man? And she said, I will go… And Isaac went out to meditate in the field at the eventide: and he lifted up his eyes, and saw, and, behold, the camels were coming. And Rebekah lifted up her eyes, and when she saw Isaac, she lighted off the camel. For she had said unto the servant, What man is this that walketh in the field to meet us? And the servant had said, It is my master: therefore she took a vail, and covered herself. And the servant told Isaac all things that he had done. And Isaac brought her into his mother Sarah's tent, and took Rebekah, and she became his wife; and he loved her: and Isaac was comforted after his mother's death." Genesis 24:50-51, 58, 63-67.*

God goes to extremes to put people together. If it's too easy, it's not from God. Such was the case with David and Abigail: *"And there was a man in Maon, whose possessions were in Carmel; and the man was very great, and he had three thousand sheep, and a thousand goats: and he was shearing his sheep in Carmel. Now the name of the man was Nabal; and the name of his wife Abigail: and she was a woman of good understanding, and of a beautiful countenance: but the man was churlish and evil in his doings; and he was of the house of Caleb." 1 Samuel 25:2,3.*

David's men had protected Nabal's sheep near Mt. Carmel, and when the time came for the shearing David sent ten of his people to ask for a gift (1 Samuel 25:4-9). Nabal insulted David and threatened him by insinuating that he was nothing more than an escaped servant of Saul: *"And Nabal answered David's servants, and said, Who is David? and who is the son of Jesse? there be many servants now a days that break away every man from his master." 1 Samuel 25:10.*

David was stung by this reproach and organized a party to destroy Nabal, and he would have except that Abigail intervened on the behalf of her evil husband. She prepared a gift for David and his men and secretly delivered it to them personally. She also honoured David's place as the rightful king of Israel and counseled him to not kill in anger over the incident lest he engender hatred toward his rule (1 Samuel 25:12-31). *"And David said to Abigail, Blessed be the LORD God of Israel, which sent thee this day to meet me: And blessed be thy advice, and blessed be thou, which hast kept me this day from coming to shed blood, and from avenging myself with mine own hand." 1 Samuel 25:32,33.*

"And Abigail came to Nabal; and, behold, he held a feast in his house, like the feast of a king; and Nabal's heart was merry within him, for he was very drunken: wherefore she told him nothing, less or more, until the morning light. But it came to pass in the morning, when the wine was gone out of Nabal, and his wife had told him these things, that his heart died within him, and he became as a stone. And it came to pass about ten days after, that the LORD smote Nabal, that he died. And when David heard that Nabal was dead, he said, Blessed be the LORD, that hath pleaded the cause of my reproach from the hand of Nabal, and hath kept his servant from evil: for the LORD hath returned the wickedness of Nabal upon his own head. And David sent and communed with Abigail, to take her to him to wife. And when the servants of David were come to Abigail to Carmel, they spake unto her, saying, David sent us unto thee, to take thee to him to wife. And she arose, and bowed herself on her face to the earth, and said, Behold, let thine handmaid be a servant to wash the feet of the servants of my lord. And Abigail hasted, and arose, and rode upon an ass, with five damsels of hers that went after her; and she went after the messengers of David, and became his wife." 1 Samuel 25:36-42.

God used the wickedness of Nabal (Psalm 76:10) as a way to show David Abigail's wisdom and fine character. Then after God took Nabal's life, Abigail was free to become David's wife. Only God could know enough about the future and people's hearts to arrange a wedding for a widow before her spouse was dead.

And then, on the other hand, is Satan. His mission is to kill, to steal, and to destroy (John 10:10). He accomplished all in kingAhab's life through his Sidonian wife Jezebel: *"And Ahab the son of Omri did evil in the sight of the LORD above all that were before him. And it came to pass, as if it had been a light thing for him to walk in the sins of Jeroboam the son of Nebat, that he took to wife Jezebel the daughter of Ethbaal king of the Zidonians, and went and served Baal, and worshipped him. And he reared up an altar for Baal in the house of Baal, which he had built in Samaria. And Ahab made a grove; and Ahab did more to provoke the LORD God of Israel to anger than all the kings of Israel that were before him." 1 Kings 16:30-33.* It seems as though God took Ahab's marriage to Jezebel as the proverbial "straw that broke the camel's back."

Satan used Jezebel to kill, steal, and destroy. Ahab desired a vineyard next door to his place, but the owner wouldn't sell. So, he complained to his loving, caring wife. She promptly took care of her king and his problem. She helped him kill the vineyard owner: *"And Ahab came into his house heavy and displeased because of the word which Naboth the Jezreelite had spoken to him: for he had said, I will not give thee the inheritance of my fathers. And he laid him down upon his bed, and turned away his face, and would eat no bread. But Jezebel his wife came to him, and said unto him, Why is thy spirit so sad, that thou eatest no bread? And he said unto her, Because I spake unto Naboth the Jezreelite, and said unto him, Give me thy vineyard for money; or else, if it please thee, I will give thee another vineyard for it: and he answered, I will not give thee my vineyard. And Jezebel his wife said unto him, Dost thou now govern the kingdom of Israel? arise, and eat bread, and let thine heart be merry: I will give thee the vineyard of Naboth the Jezreelite." 1 Kings 21:4-7.*

Jezebel wrote letters in Ahab's name to the leaders of Naboth's city. She conspired with them to kill Naboth. They proclaimed a fast and put Naboth in the honored chair. Then they had two witnesses lie and say that Naboth had blasphemed God and the king. The people stoned him (1 Kings 21:8-14).

Then she helped Ahab steal: *"And it came to pass, when Jezebel heard that Naboth was stoned, and was dead, that Jezebel said to Ahab, Arise, take possession of the vineyard of Naboth the Jezreelite, which he refused to give thee for money: for Naboth is not alive, but dead. And it came to pass, when Ahab heard that Naboth was dead, that Ahab rose up to go down to the vineyard of Naboth the Jezreelite, to take possession of it." 1 Kings 21:15,16.*

God pronounced judgment on both Ahab and Jezebel and she was to be disgraced in the same way as her husband: *"And the word of the LORD came to Elijah the Tishbite, saying, Arise, go down to meet Ahab king of Israel, which is in Samaria: behold, he is in the vineyard of Naboth, whither he is gone down to possess it. And thou shalt speak unto him, saying, Thus saith the LORD, Hast thou killed, and also taken possession? And thou shalt speak unto him, saying, Thus saith the LORD, In the place where dogs licked the blood of Naboth shall dogs lick thy blood, even thine... And of Jezebel also spake the LORD, saying, The dogs shall eat Jezebel by the wall of Jezreel… But there was none like unto Ahab, which did sell himself to work wickedness in the sight of the LORD, whom Jezebel his wife stirred up." 1 Kings 21:17-19, 23, 25.*

Later, Ahab recruited the king of Judah to help him fight the Syrians. He disguised himself before the battle because he was afraid of another more recent prophecy of his demise. This did not help him, however, because the Lord was determined to judge him: *"And a certain man drew a bow at a venture, and smote the king of Israel between the joints of the harness: wherefore he said unto the driver of his chariot, Turn thine hand, and carry me out of the host; for I am wounded. And the battle increased that day: and the king was stayed up in his chariot against the Syrians, and died at even: and the blood ran out of the wound into the midst of the chariot. And there went a proclamation throughout the host about the going down of the sun, saying, Every man to his city, and every man to his own country. So the king died, and was brought to Samaria; and they buried the king in Samaria. And one washed the chariot in the pool of Samaria; and the dogs licked up his blood; and they washed his armour; according unto the word of the LORD which he spake." 1 Kings 22:34-38.*

Several years later Jezebel was thrown down from a tower window by her eunuchs during a *coup d'état.* The Lord did not forget His words concerning her: *"And when Jehu was come to Jezreel, Jezebel heard of it; and she painted her face, and tired her head, and looked out at a window. And as Jehu entered in at the gate, she said, Had Zimri peace, who slew his master? And he lifted up his face to the window, and said, Who is on my side? who? And there looked out to him two or three eunuchs. And he said, Throw her down. So they threw her down: and some of her blood was sprinkled on the wall, and on the horses: and he trode her under foot. And when he was come in, he did eat and drink, and said, Go, see now this cursed woman, and bury her: for she is a king's daughter. And they went to bury her: but they found no more of her than the skull, and the feet, and the palms of her hands. Wherefore they came again, and told him. And he said, This is the word of the LORD, which he spake by his servant Elijah the Tishbite, saying, In the portion of Jezreel shall dogs eat the flesh of Jezebel: And the carcase of Jezebel shall be as dung upon the face of the field in the portion of Jezreel; so that they shall not say, This is Jezebel." 2 Kings 9:30-37.*

Solomon, the wisest man who ever lived, was tormented because of the women he loved. Moses had given a stern warning to any future kings of Israel about women: *"Neither shall he multiply wives to himself, that his heart turn not away. Deuteronomy 17:17.*

Just as Satan had planted an evil woman in Ahab's life, surely he had an influence in Solomon's choices also. Solomon acquired many foreign wives in peace agreements with other countries. And to make his wives comfortable, he built places of worship for them and their gods: *"But king Solomon loved many strange women, together with the daughter of Pharaoh, women of the Moabites, Ammonites, Edomites, Zidonians, and Hittites; Of the nations concerning which the LORD said unto the children of Israel, Ye shall not go in to them, neither shall they come in unto you: for surely they will turn away your heart after their gods: Solomon clave unto these in love. And he had seven hundred wives, princesses, and three hundred concubines: and his wives turned away his heart. For it came to pass, when Solomon was old, that his wives turned away his heart after other gods... Then did Solomon build an high place for Chemosh, the abomination of Moab, in the hill that is before Jerusalem, and for Molech, the abomination of the children of Ammon. And likewise did he for all his strange wives, which burnt incense and sacrificed unto their gods." 1 Kings 11:1-4; 7,8.*

ISRAEL declined from that point forward. The backsliding started with Solomon's sins. God judged Solomon's wanderings by promising to divide the kingdom, which happened in the days of Solomon's son, Rehoboam: *"And the LORD was angry with Solomon, because his heart was turned from the LORD God of Israel, which had appeared unto him twice, And had commanded him concerning this thing, that he should not go after other gods: but he kept not that which the LORD commanded. Wherefore the LORD said unto Solomon, Forasmuch as this is done of thee, and thou hast not kept my covenant and my statutes, which I have commanded thee, I will surely rend the kingdom from thee, and will give it to thy servant. Notwithstanding in thy days I will not do it for David thy father's sake: but I will rend it out of the hand of thy son."*

1Kings11:9-12.

CHAPTER 2

Principles of Development

EVERY dimension of a person's life has its pattern of development. The physical nature develops in a prescribed plan from embryo to old age. The psychological nature is put together one building block at a time. Likewise, the spiritual nature has its sequence of growth.

The spiritual nature has seven stages: embryo to birth to childhood to adolescence to young adulthood to maturity to transcendence.

In this chapter I will explain the principles of physical and psychological development that are relevant to our study. I will then extrapolate them to the stages of spiritual growth. These principles are taken primarily from the work of Erik Erikson.

Epigenetic Principle

The epigenetic principle says, "Everything that grows has a ground plan, out of this ground plan the parts arise, each part having its time of special ascendancy, until all the parts have arisen to form a functioning whole."[1]

In the physical nature the ground plan is the DNA that orders all growth. DNA prescribes the pattern of the child. During growth, each part of the body has its time when it first appears and becomes functional. Eventually, all the parts of the unborn child develop to the point that the child can survive outside the womb. Outside, development continues, only less dramatically.

The psychological nature also develops in an ordered and sequential way. Language serves as an example. Noam Chomsky taught that people have an inborn language instinct that responds to the environment. This theory has gained more weight with time.[2] Children's inborn schemes of language find expression in the particular language of their culture. First, children learn names: mama, daddy. Then, verbs: mama play. At last, complete sentences: I want milk.

The spiritual nature as well develops according to the epigenetic principle. It makes sense that God would order spiritual development in the same style as the physical and psychological: *"Whom shall he teach knowledge? and whom shall he make to understand doctrine? them that are weaned from the milk, and drawn from the breasts. For precept must be upon precept, precept upon precept; line upon line, line upon line; here a little, and there a little:" Isaiah 28:9,10.*

Every one of a species grows the same way.

All people grow according to the same general pattern. They may grow at different speeds and with emphases at different times on specific parts, but the pattern remains unchallenged. This is true for both the physical and the psychological.

Therefore it is logical to believe spiritual growth has a specific pattern also. There is one path to spiritual maturity, and all must pass through the same stages to get there.

Exact Order of Mastery

Each stage of development has its tasks. New potentials are dependent on the mastery of previous challenges. You cannot run until you can walk. You cannot walk until you can pull up. You cannot pull up till you can crawl. A child making a pyramid with building blocks symbolically demonstrates what is happening to him or her. Just as each level of blocks depends on the strong base of the previous level, so the learning tasks of growth are dependent on previous learning.

The apostle Paul taught three phases of salvation: hearing, believing and calling: *"How then shall they call on him in whom they have not believed? and how shall they believe in him of whom they have not heard? and how shall they hear without a preacher? And how shall they preach, except they be sent? as it is written, How beautiful are the feet of them that preach the gospel of peace, and bring glad tidings of good things!" Romans 10:14,15.*

Each part has its time when conditions are best to develop.

Erik Erikson described this principle in his idea of life crises. The most famous life crisis is the identity crisis. Erikson said the identity crisis begins in adolescence because only then are the physical, psychological, and social conditions present to allow it.[3] The young person first grows to adult physical form. Then the young person begins to separate from parents psychologically and becomes aware of uniqueness. The adolescent is expected to begin making permanent decisions. A strong sense of identity prepares the adolescent to make solid decisions about marriage and career. The resolution of the identity crisis cannot be delayed because future development depends on it.[4]

In the same way, certain times of our lives are optimal for making specific spiritual decisions, and future growth depends on the quality of those decisions.

Engagement of Crises

Crises are the barriers that mark the stages of growth. The word "crisis" is from Greek and means "decision."[5] I've been told the Chinese symbol for "crisis" signifies both opportunity and danger. Developmental crises are opportunities if they are successfully navigated, but they are disasters if they become barriers to future potential.

Many crises are familiar to us all. Natural birth is a crisis we all must pass. Further growth is not possible in the womb, and the child enters the world to continue. Puberty produces adolescence from childhood. Economic self-sufficiency separates maturity from young adulthood. Reading divides the literate from the illiterate.

Likewise, there are spiritual crises: ordeals that we must go through if we want to go further.

Expectation of Growth

Continued development depends on constant diligence in those that grow. Children will come to their present crisis over and again until they gain the knowledge and skill to pass through. Even if they are frustrated at times and give up, children will persist with challenges. I observed this one Christmas day as I watched my two-year-old nephew. I had given him a plastic box with different shaped holes in it. The game was to put the plastic shapes into the holes they fit. He couldn't do it well at all in the beginning, but he stayed with it. He had a serious and determined look on his face that assured me he would one day put all the shapes into the right holes.

If children didn't display this need to grow and learn, we would think something was wrong with them. We would think they were developmentally delayed or depressed or sick or something else. The same applies to you and me when we give up on our spiritually shaped holes. There must be something unsound about us when we stop showing spiritual desire.

Evolving Schemes

While each step of growth depends on the success of the previous one, each step also gives new meaning to the previous ones.[6] As we learn more and reach higher levels, the past becomes clearer and more relevant to us. Entrance into a career job improves and draws on work skills learned as a youth. Marriage demands we pull up the interpersonal skills from our families into a new system. Effective childrearing depends on the ability to recast our past into teachable form.

In addition, the future gives new opportunities to improve the solutions to previous crises. The same crises appear again over the course of life, but maturity is shown in the ease and skill of resolving those recycled riddles. Very hard problems at one point of our lives may become very easy later. I used to have difficulty because of shyness in using the telephone or the library; now those activities are fun.

In like manner, higher levels of spiritual maturity cause us to respond with wisdom to spiritual crises. We learn to appreciate basic truths more. We learn that wisdom is not in understanding the heights of complexity, but in seeing the depths of the simple.

Effort to Reproduce and Teach Skills

When people reach maturity, they seek to reproduce that maturity in their children and in others. This happens physically, psychologically, socially, and spiritually. Erikson taught that the main virtues of adulthood are found in commitments to take care of persons and to take care for ideas.[7]

The implication for us spiritually is that true maturity is shown by willingness to reproduce the same growth in others. Spiritual grandchildren are the evidence of success: *"Thou therefore, my son, be strong in the grace that is in Christ Jesus. And the things that thou hast heard of me among many witnesses, the same commit thou to faithful men, who shall be able to teach others also." 2 Timothy 2:1,2.*

CHAPTER 3

The Spiritual Life Cycle

THE language of the New Testament implies that there is a spiritual life cycle: a pattern of growth and development of the spiritual nature. My task in this chapter is to outline the stages and in the remainder of the book to provide details.

Each stage of our natural life presents its opportunities and dangers. As children, we learn to trust our parents and other adults to provide for and teach us. As adolescents, we learn to make some of our own decisions and prepare for independence. As young adults, we make permanent decisions about relationships and lifestyles. As adults, we pursue our goals in love and work. Finally, as parents, we train and prepare the next generation.

The spiritual life cycle parallels the physical and psychological life cycles. The natural world provides symbols and metaphors for understanding the spiritual dimension. God teaches us about Himself and His work through the tasks and crises of development.

Scriptural Basis of the Spiritual Life Cycle

"Born again" is a physical metaphor for a spiritual reality. In John 3 Jesus tells Nicodemus that the spiritual nature has a birth just as the physical nature does. Jesus teaches that unless a person is born again spiritually he or she cannot enter the kingdom of God (the spiritual dimension under God's control): *"Jesus answered and said unto him, Verily, verily, I say unto thee, Except a man be born again, he cannot see the kingdom of God. Nicodemus saith unto him, How can a man be born when he is old? can he enter the second time into his mother's womb, and be born? Jesus answered, Verily, verily, I say unto thee, Except a man be born of water and of the Spirit, he cannot enter into the kingdom of God. That which is born of the flesh is flesh; and that which is born of the Spirit is spirit." John 3:3-6.*

Peter admonishes us to continue growing after spiritual birth: *"As newborn babes, desire the sincere milk of the word, that ye may grow thereby:" 1 Peter 2:2.*

Developmental crises are implied in the scripture. Paul tells the Corinthians that he feeds them with spiritual milk instead of meat because they haven't developed the will to put down the bottle: *"And I, brethren, could not speak unto you as unto spiritual, but as unto carnal, even as unto babes in Christ. I have fed you with milk, and not with meat: for hitherto ye were not able to bear it, neither yet now are ye able." 1 Corinthians 3:1,2.*

The writer of Hebrews explains that solid spiritual food belongs to those who have given up the bottle and have worked to appreciate the meat: *"For every one that useth milk is unskilful in the word of righteousness: for he is a babe. But strong meat belongeth to them that are of full age, even those who by reason of use have their senses exercised to discern both good and evil." Hebrews 5:13,14.* The next verse, Hebrews 6:1, in the Amplified Bible says this: *"Therefore let us go on and get past the elementary stage in the teaching and doctrine of Christ, the Messiah, advancing steadily toward the completeness and perfection that belongs to spiritual maturity."*

The apostle John notes that he is addressing persons in all stages of spiritual development with his first letter: *"I write unto you, little children, because your sins are forgiven you for his name's sake. I write unto you, fathers, because ye have known him that is from the beginning. I write unto you, young men, because ye have overcome the wicked one. I write unto you, little children, because ye have known the Father. I have written unto you, fathers, because ye have known him that is from the beginning. I have written unto you, young men, because ye are strong, and the word of God abideth in you, and ye have overcome the wicked one." 1 John 2:12-14.* The spiritual children know their sins are forgiven and that God has adopted them. The spiritual adolescents have grown strong enough to defeat their spiritual enemies with the teachings of God. The spiritual fathers understand God's design and have apprehended oneness with Him (Philippians 3:10-15).

Studying God in the Generations

God has given each earthly institution to teach us about Himself. The family teaches about God as we travel through the stages of the life cycle. As children we are under authority, just as Jesus was called the "son" on earth. Then as parents we are in authority, just as God was called the "father" in His relationship to Jesus during the earthly ministry. The terms Father and Son are not accidental. The earthly father and son display a relationship that is typical of the heavenly Father and Son. As children we are obedient and trusting of our parents: *"Children, obey your parents in the Lord: for this is right. Honour thy father and mother; (which is the first commandment with promise;) That it may be well with thee, and thou mayest live long on the earth." Ephesians 6:1-3.* Then, as parents, we diligently bring our children to physical, psychological, and spiritual maturity: *"And, ye fathers, provoke not your children to wrath: but bring them up in the nurture and admonition of the Lord." Ephesians 6:4.*

God and Jesus are not father and son the way we think of father and son. They used the terms to show their relationship in the redemption of people. Jesus put Himself under the authority of God and became human in order to save those that believe (Hebrews 5:8). Through experiencing the natural metaphor we appreciate more the spiritual reality of the heavenly Father and Son: *"Let this mind be in you, which was also in Christ Jesus: Who, being in the form of God, thought it not robbery to be equal with God: But made himself of no reputation, and took upon him the form of a servant, and was made in the likeness of men: And being found in fashion as a man, he humbled himself, and became obedient unto death, even the death of the cross. Wherefore God also hath highly exalted him, and given him a name which is above every name: That at the name of Jesus every knee should bow, of things in heaven, and things in earth, and things under the earth; And that every tongue should confess that Jesus Christ is Lord, to the glory of God the Father." Philippians 2:5-11.*

God created people to have relationship and purpose and these elements are present in all earthly institutions. The relevant relationships of the life cycle are children and parents. The child is under authority until he or she grows enough to be in authority over other children. The relevant purposes of the life cycle are to learn as a child, then to teach as a parent.

Stages of the Spiritual Life Cycle

Spiritual Birth

The first stage of spiritual development is the embryo. God plants the seed of truth in the womb of a person's experience. Then He nurtures it with His word and His Spirit. There are four learning tasks that lead to spiritual birth: the recognition of God's authority, responsibility to Him, failure to live up to His standards, and Christ as savior. Spiritual birth is the crisis of entry into God's kingdom (John 3:3). The key to the spiritual kingdom is faith. The symbol of spiritual birth is water. Baptism is a symbol of spiritual birth.

Spiritual Childhood

The spiritual newborn is a sponge for knowledge. He doesn't end his journey with birth, but immediately faces the learning tasks of childhood. There are four building blocks of spiritual childhood: learning dependence on God, rules to follow that will protect continued growth, basic doctrines of God, and one's allies and enemies in the spiritual dimension. The child enters spiritual adolescence by committing to God as Lord of all life. The amulet to secure safe passage is trust. The symbol of spiritual childhood is light.

Spiritual Adolescence

The spiritual adolescent is a warrior: *"I have written unto you, young men, because ye are strong, and the word of God abideth in you, and ye have overcome the wicked one." 1 John 2:14.* Spiritual warfare requires complete commitment to God. The ancient Hebrews under Moses symbolized the entry into adolescence by crossing over Jordan into the Promised Land. They could only claim their land by defeating their enemies. The learning tasks for the warfare of spiritual adolescence are to understand principles vs. simple rules and to understand cause and effect in the spiritual realm. These understandings are necessary to subjugate and subdue the basic conflicts that begin in physical adolescence but can only be resolved in spiritual adolescence. There are nine giants that must be conquered: poor self-image, rebellion, guilt, bitterness, anger, moral impurity, boredom and depression, using and abusing people, and financial bondage. These giants watch the gate into spiritual young adulthood. The power to subdue them is strength of character. The spiritual adolescent will either be dominated by these giants or will "put them to tribute." All nine must be held at bay or one or more will rise up to "vex and oppress." The symbol of spiritual adolescence is integrity.

Spiritual Young Adulthood

The spiritual young adult is a dreamer. To every person that commits to God and tackles the giants of spiritual adolescence, God gives a vision, a mission, a celestial city to dream of and move toward. The vision is an image of the special place the spiritual traveler has in God's drama. The mission is the work God has for the Christian pilgrim. The initiate must learn and understand the way of God to get to the Celestial City. The way of God is birth, death, burial, and resurrection. There first must be a birth of the vision, then death of the vision, then a time of waiting, and finally supernatural fulfillment. God touches the spiritual initiate with a personal version of Abraham's Isaac, Jacob's angel of Peniel, Moses' burning bush, or David's royal crown. Nevertheless, the spiritual young adult must not interfere with God's plan by using human means to accomplish the vision. The crisis is the willingness to wait vs. presumption. The energy to transport the spiritual young adult through the "valley of the shadow of death" comes from patience, experience, and hope. The symbol of spiritual young adulthood is treasure.

Spiritual Adulthood

The spiritual adult is a champion of faith. Spiritual maturity cannot be reached by self-will. It is bestowed on the one who waits on the Lord. The spiritual adult rests confidently in the purposes of God. The adult learns God's ways by experience and has a unique life message of how God has worked. The crisis is the meeting with God. The adult must recognize God's fulfillment of the vision and accept it to cross over into completeness. The mature person's hope turns into love through quiet expectation of the supernatural fulfillment of the vision (Romans 5:5). Love is the key to recognizing God. God is love, and when we see His pure love demonstrated in the fulfillment, we know it's His work: *"Hereby perceive we the love of God, because he laid down his life for us: and we ought to lay down our lives for the brethren." 1 John 3:16.* The symbol of spiritual adulthood is children. The adult wants others to know the love of God in a deep way also.

Spiritual Parenthood

The spiritual parent is a teacher. The spiritual adult recognizes God's fulfillment of the vision and accepts it. Then God gives the pilgrim a ministry based on experience. By this, the spiritual adult becomes a parent, in charge of bringing the next generation to spiritual maturity. The parent learns from his own experience and from God's example how to motivate and mentor others through the stages of spiritual growth. The crisis of spiritual parenthood is death. The spiritual parent must be willing to give up self for the growth of the children and demonstrate the true power of the resurrection: *"And Jesus answered them, saying, The hour is come, that the Son of man should be glorified. Verily, verily, I say unto you, Except a corn of wheat fall into the ground and die, it abideth alone: but if it die, it bringeth forth much fruit." John 12:23,24.* Confidence in God is the key to giving up self and transcending earthly concerns. We have confidence because we know firsthand the depths of God's love. The symbol of spiritual parenthood is heaven.

Conclusions and Exhortations

I pray that all spiritual pilgrims will adopt the attitude of the apostle Paul: *"That I may know him, and the power of his resurrection, and the fellowship of his sufferings, being made conformable unto his death; If by any means I might attain unto the resurrection of the dead." Philippians 3:10,11.* Reliance on God to complete the spiritual desires He has put within us is the key to spiritual maturity. We should never give up on the dreams He has given us: *"I press toward the mark for the prize of the high calling of God in Christ Jesus." Philippians 3:14.*

The spiritual journey does not end with spiritual birth, as many suppose; it only begins. Let's not teach people to be content with salvation only. There is so much more to Christianity in this life.

Those that are mature should be willing to bring others through the stages. We are not complete spiritually until we have seen our spiritual grandchildren.

CHAPTER 4

The Power of Myth

SPIRITUAL growth requires imagination. Imagination is the key to the spiritual world, and finding meaning for our lives.

Yet, in our time we only honor imagination in movies and the arts. We do not view it as a reliable motivator. We believe instead in something called reality, which is defined as those things that can be proven by sense data and statistics. We deride those who believe in their dreams as "wishful thinkers, those who live in a fantasy world, and those who have their heads in the clouds." Even we Christians are more pragmatic in our daily lives than willing to follow God's call into the unknown and unsure. We believe in our physical senses more than our spiritual senses. We rely on reality more than imagination. We walk more by sight than by faith.

We cannot discern spiritual truths through sense data, but the scientific method, which has influenced us all more than we think, has taught us that only sense data counts. We cannot know the spiritual dimension through scientific observation, and therein is the most serious flaw of relying exclusively on it as a means of knowing. Science cannot tell us how to live. The particulars of the natural world cannot give us meaning. The modern world and Christians have chosen Aristotle instead of Plato and have suffered the loss of the ideal as a result.

We usually only become aware of spiritual possibilities when natural explanations for events fail (John 3:8). We call unexpected disasters, "acts of God." We search the spiritual dimension for clues when people's behavior is either exceptionally evil or good (Luke 13:1-5).

We approach the spiritual dimension for motivation only when other inspirations prove insufficient. Even Carl Sagan, the famous scientist, was willing to use "the vision of the sacred" to help promote his desire to save the environment.[1]

In the closing decades of the twentieth century, many began to understand the failure of science to motivate us to higher causes than our own comfort and security. People have a thirst for meaning that will not be quenched by gadgets, styles, and conformity. We have seen a revival of fundamentalism in the religions of the world as people reject science as the savior of mankind.

While it may seem that the ascendance of fundamentalism is a victory for religion, focusing on the conflict between science and fundamentalism keeps people from growing spiritually. Fundamentalism teaches that the Scriptures are literally true. Science teaches that since the Scriptures cannot be literally true, they must be seen only as metaphorical, if they are useful at all. In the controversy, fundamentalism becomes a mere reaction against the scientific worldview.

Nevertheless, spiritual growth requires more than belief in the trueness of the Scriptures. It requires us to imagine that God will work in our lives the same way He did with the heroes of the Scriptures. It requires us to see the stories as metaphors for our lives. It requires us to search for the ideal will of God rather than settle for the particulars of our past.

So science undermines spiritual development by discounting the supernatural, and fundamentalism undermines spiritual development by discounting the metaphorical. Fundamentalism does not honor imagination as the power of spiritual growth. I'm not saying we should give up our fundamentalism. I'm saying we are spiritual paupers if we don't also look at the scriptures metaphorically.

The weakness of fundamentalism to inspire people for a lifetime is similar to the weakness of science to provide meaning. Meaning can only be achieved by believing that God has a plan for our lives. In other words, God has a story for us to live in. The examples in the Bible are stories of how God worked in the lives of others. They are metaphors for us. The recent popularity of the Bible study *Experiencing God*[2] shows that Christians are thirsty for individual meaning. The study uses the examples of Bible heroes as patterns of how God has worked with others, and goes further in promoting the expectation that God can work similarly in us.

There is a word whose definition connotes the trueness of a sacred story while at the same time describing it as a metaphor. We need to get acquainted with "myth."

What is Myth?

Webster's Collegiate Dictionary - Tenth Edition defines myth thus: "myth n [Gk mythos] (1830) 1 a: a usu. traditional story of ostensibly historical events that serves to unfold part of the world view of a people or explain a practice, belief, or natural phenomenon b: parable, allegory 2 a: a popular belief or tradition that has grown up around something or someone; esp: one embodying the ideals and institutions of a society or segment of society ... b: an unfounded or false notion 3: a person or thing having only an imaginary or unverifiable existence 4: the whole body of myths."[3]

It is apparent from the above definitions that the meaning of "myth" has changed over time. Webster's dictionary lists definitions from the ancient first to the most modern last. Ancient people regarded myth as "a story that unfolds or explains practices, beliefs, or natural phenomena" (definition 1a). But, modern people regard myth as "a person or thing having only an imaginary or unverifiable existence" (definition 3).

Definition 1 shows the ancient people's understanding that it takes imagination and symbols to understand the spiritual world. Definition 3 shows modern people's general disregard and contempt for anything that cannot be proven by sense data. Myth has "an unverifiable existence." Nevertheless, today it is the ancient view of myth that people are beginning to be interested in. This is due to our present revival of the spiritual side of man.

In the next few chapters I will try to restore the use of myth as a means of spiritual growth and to show that God is the best mythmaker in the ancient sense of the word. I will show that in Jesus myth became tangible and that God wants to make His myths real in our lives.

Joseph Campbell and C.S. Lewis have been my best teachers about myth. Although Campbell was not a Christian, he has been the most popular authority on myth in my lifetime and his views are insightful. The two men's basic views on myth are similar and can be summed up in four principles:

1. Myths teach divine truths that could not be comprehended by reason alone.
2. Myths are the doorways between the rational world and the spiritual world.
3. Myths are stories that put us in touch with the story of ourselves.
4. Myths appeal to the "natural light" of all of us. They are the "song of the universe—music we dance to even when we cannot name the tune."[4]

C.S. Lewis is the Christian authority on myth. The following quotes demonstrate the spiritual power that myth had for him:

"Myth in general is not merely misunderstood history (as Euhemerus thought) nor diabolical illusion (as some of the fathers thought) nor priestly lying (as the philosophers of the Enlightenment thought) but, at its best, a real and unfocused gleam of the divine truth falling on human imagination."[5]

"Every myth becomes the father of innumerable truths on the abstract level. Myth is the mountain whence all the different streams arise which become truths down here in the valley."[6]

"In the enjoyment of a great myth we come nearest to experiencing as concrete what can otherwise be understood only as an abstraction."[7]

"It is only while receiving the myth as a story that you experience the principle concretely."[8]

C. S. Lewis' attitude toward myth is summed up best when he quotes from *Pride and Prejudice*, ch xi, "'Would not conversation be much more rational than dancing?'said JaneAusten's Miss Bingly. 'Much more rational,' replied Mr. Bingly, 'but much less like a ball.'"[9]

The Power of Myth

God reveals Himself to us through His story or myth. The Bible is God's story of a "lovesick father"[10] who wins back the hearts of His rebellious children. Walter Wangerin Jr. put the Bible in novel form and called it the *Book of God*.[11] Perhaps stories are the best way we can understand God. Jesus used parables to teach the principles of the unseen kingdom.

People also reveal and understand themselves through their stories. Alcoholics Anonymous asks its members to tell and retell their life stories as a means of motivation and change. The members expect to change their stories and add new chapters as they grow spiritually and emotionally. A relatively new form of psychotherapy called Narrative Therapy encourages people to write their personal stories as a starting point to change perceptions. The therapist often focuses on the faulty life story itself as the problem instead of specific life circumstances. I once heard Shelby Foote say that we call schizophrenics mentally ill because their stories are incomprehensible to the rest of us. But they are still motivated by their personal myths. Carl Jung taught that the seriously mentally ill are people who are overwhelmed by the power of myth.[12]

The entertainment industry makes its billions from people's thirst for stories. In fact, the best selling books and movies are those that closest approach the mythological. Recent top movies carry on the tradition: *Harry Potter, Lord of the Rings, Star Wars*.

The power of myth is the power to change. God has made us mythmakers and myth responders for this very reason.

The Meaning of Myth

Joseph Campbell taught that mythology serves the practical function of helping people in the transitions from one life stage to another: "Mythology has a great deal to do with the stages of life, the initiation ceremonies as you move from childhood to adult responsibilities, from the unmarried state to the married state."[13] The myths provide guideposts for those who enter crisis stages along the way. The heroes of mythology are those who find unique solutions to common human problems.

Mythology uses symbols from the natural world to give authority to the messages. The symbols are usually interpreted as showing the stages of life. I believe the stages and the myths about them teach us about God's work in man. The natural world co-operates with the myth and is the source of it. All things that God created work together to show us the Creator. God is the invisible author of all that is: *"For the invisible things of him from the creation of the world are clearly seen, being understood by the things that are made, even His eternal power and Godhead; so that they are without excuse:" Romans 1:20.*

In Joseph Campbell's book, *The Transformations of Myth Through Time,* he talks about the significance of Navaho sand paintings. He describes one as showing the circuit of the sun symbolizing the stages of life: "The sun rises in the east. It is the place of birth, of emergence, of new life...The New Testament is a testament of Sunday, the rising of the new Eastern sun. In the height of the sky, the blue sky of noon is the midpoint, the thirty-fifth year of life. In the west the sun sinks, and the north is always an area of awe and mystery and danger, the danger of that which has not been accommodated in the forms of the social order."[14] The sun rising in the east symbolizes birth. The sun in the south symbolizes the strength of youth. The sun in the west represents maturity. And the setting sun represents death and the spiritual world: *"The heavens declare the glory of God; and the firmament sheweth his handywork. Day unto day uttereth speech, and night unto night sheweth knowledge. There is no speech nor language, where their voice is not heard. Their line is gone out through all the earth, and their words to the end of the world. In them hath he set a tabernacle for the sun, Which is as a bridegroom coming out of his chamber, and rejoiceth as a strong man to run a race. His going forth is from the end of the heaven, and his circuit unto the ends of it: and there is nothing hid from the heat thereof." Psalms 19:1-6.*

God used the same order of the four directions in telling Israel how to set up camp according to their tribes (Numbers 2).

Jesus Christ will enter Jerusalem in His second coming at the eastern gate, which is a symbol of a new birth.

The moon travels through a similar cycle to the sun and it also symbolizes the stages of life. The moon is born as a crescent of light and then passes through increasing strength to the fifteenth day (the midpoint of life) and slowly decreases in illumination until it becomes a crescent again (maturity). Finally, the moon enters the area of the unknown (new moon), which symbolizes death and rebirth.

The plant and animal worlds co-operate in showing us the cycles of life. Oak trees dress in new leaves in the spring. They grow to full strength and maturity in the summer. Then in the fall they lose their youthful color and vigor and fall to the ground where they cover and protect the seed of new trees. Finally, in winter, the trees sleep and are barren. They travel through cryptic territory awaiting the arrival of another spring.

All of these symbols explain to us the brevity of life and the tasks to be accomplished in it. The symbols teach us that we are to be attentive to our present but also to be preparing for the day we enter the unknown (the north, the new moon, winter): *"While the earth remaineth, seedtime and harvest, and cold and heat, and summer and winter, and day and night shall not cease."* Genesis 8:22. *"It is better to go to the house of mourning, than to go to the house of feasting: for that is the end of all men; and the living will lay it to his heart."* Ecclesiastes 7:2.

Pagan Myth vs. Christian Myth

Some will object to using the word "myth" in connection to God's word. Nevertheless, it is important to understand the Bible in the context of the ancient definition of myth because God's story fulfills the hopes and dreams of all mythmakers and students of myth. We search our entire lives for the perfect story. We spend lots of time and money listening, watching, and reading. God has the perfect story. God's story is unique in all the world of myth. In His story, myth comes to life, and is manifested in an actual person.

I learned about myth and its meaning primarily from the works of Joseph Campbell and C.S. Lewis. Although both Campbell and Lewis share the ancient view that myth forms the bridge between the natural world and supernatural world, they disagree as to what's out there in the supernatural world, and they disagree about the nature of the travelers on the bridge. Campbell believed that we can only go from here to the supernatural metaphorically, and that the gods do not come to us but are already in us. Lewis believed that God came to us across the bridge literally through Jesus and that we will one day literally go to Him.

C. S. Lewis believed that there are only two religions that could be taken seriously, Hinduism and Christianity: Hinduism because it is the purist and most mature expression of paganism or pantheism, which Lewis called "the permanent natural bent of the human mind,"[15] or Christianity because it is not only monotheistic but also fulfills the myths of the pagans.[16] Joseph Campbell and C. S. Lewis represent these two views of myth and religion to me.

The first major difference between Hinduism and Christianity is that Hinduism regards the universe as self-contained and the gods a part of it, but Christianity regards the universe as created by God and subject to His will and intervention.

Campbell: "Our way of thinking in the west sees God as the final source or cause of the energies and wonder of the universe. But in most oriental thinking, and in primal thinking, also, the gods are rather manifestations and purveyors of an energy that is finally impersonal. They are not its source."[17]

Lewis: "Speak about beauty, truth, and goodness, or about a God who is simply the indwelling principle of these three, speak about a great spiritual force pervading all things, a common mind of which we are all parts, a pool of generalized spirituality to which we can all flow, and you will command friendly interest. But the temperature drops as soon as you mention a God who has purposes and performs particular functions, who does one thing and not another, a concrete, choosing, commanding, prohibiting God with a determinate character."[18]

The second major difference between Hinduism and Christianity is that Hinduism regards the goal of myth as teaching us to attain godhood ourselves, while Christianity regards the goal of myth as pointing us to the one true God to worship.

Campbell: "In India there is a beautiful greeting, in which the palms are placed together, and you bow to the other person... the position of the palms together- this we use when we pray, do we not? That is a greeting which says that the god that is in you recognizes the god in the other. These people are aware of the divine presence in all things. When you enter an Indian home as a guest, you are greeted as a visiting deity."[19]

Lewis: "The heart of Christianity is a myth which is also a fact. The old Myth of the dying God, without ceasing to be myth, comes down from the heaven of legend and imagination to the earth of history. It happens at a particular date, in a particular place, followed by definable historical consequences. We pass from a Balder or an Osiris, dying nobody knows when or where, to a historical Person crucified (it is all in order) under Pontius Pilate. By becoming fact it does not cease to be myth: that is the miracle."[20]

"For we have not followed cunningly devised fables, when we made known unto you the power and coming of our Lord Jesus Christ, but were eyewitnesses of his majesty. For he received from God the Father honour and glory, when there came such a voice to him from the excellent glory, This is my beloved Son, in whom I am well pleased." 2 Peter 1:16,17.

Jesus and Myth

Jesus is the fulfillment of Pagan myth. It should not surprise Christians that the ancient myths are precursors of the historical story of Christ. The ancient myths show that God has put in us "natural light," and there is a part in our imaginations that relates to the story of God's work among people.

The Bible implies that Christ is the end of the world's search for God and that He is the culmination of the ancient myths: *"For we have not followed cunningly devised fables, when we made known unto you the power and coming of our Lord Jesus Christ, but were eyewitnesses of his majesty." 2 Peter 1:16.* Peter makes the distinction between Christianity and other myths. Jesus Christ was not the personification of natural forces or ideas but was an actual historical person. Peter knows this because he was an "eyewitness of his majesty": *"For he received from God the Father honour and glory, when there came such a voice to him from the excellent glory, This is my beloved Son, in whom I am well pleased. And this voice which came from heaven we heard, when we were with him in the holy mount." 2 Peter 1:17,18.* Peter states that God Himself actually spoke in an audible voice telling the world Jesus was His son. *"We have also a more sure word of prophecy; whereunto ye do well that ye take heed, as unto a light that shineth in a dark place, until the day dawn, and the day star arise in your hearts:" 2 Peter 1:19.* The word of prophecy about the Messiah is sure now. It has happened. The prophecy was like a light in a dark place, but the actual event is like the dawning of the day, dispelling the darkness.

When Paul addressed the Areopagus in Athens, he spoke to Greeks who were well aware of mythology. He explained to them that the "unknown God" (the god beyond their stories) was the creator of the world and had put within people the desire to seek and know Him. Paul told them that God had permitted people to think He could be worshipped with man-made things (idols and temples) because they were ignorant. But, now God commands everyone to understand His true nature and the true story of the universe. The proof is that He has appointed one who will judge the world. The sign of the appointed one is His resurrection from the dead: *"Then Paul stood in the midst of Mars' hill, and said, Ye men of*

Athens, I perceive that in all things ye are too superstitious. For as I passed by, and beheld your devotions, I found an altar with this inscription, TO THE UNKNOWN GOD… And the times of this ignorance God winked at; but now commandeth all men every where to repent: Because he hath appointed a day, in the which he will judge the world in righteousness by that man whom he hath ordained; whereof he hath given assurance unto all men, in that he hath raised him from the dead." Acts 17:22,23,30,31.

Not only did Jesus fulfill the pagan myths, He also completed the Jewish myths. The ceremonies and stories of the Jews are mythological in the sense that they point to truths beyond themselves. These truths were eventually embodied in an actual historical person. The book of Hebrews explains how Jesus Christ is the dawn of truth compared to a mere light shining in a dark place (the Old Testament). Jesus Christ is real but the laws were only a shadow of the true nature of God.

The book of Hebrews uses the images of shadow and substance to show the difference between the Law and Christ. The sacrifices were an "example and shadow of heavenly things" (Hebrews 8:5). The first tabernacle was a "figure for the time then present" (Hebrews 9:9). The patterns of the things in heaven were purified with animal sacrifices, but the heavenly things themselves required a greater sacrifice (Christ Himself): *"For Christ is not entered into the holy places made with hands, which are the figures of the true; but into heaven itself, now to appear in the presence of God for us:" Hebrews 9:24.* The true tabernacle is in heaven (Hebrews 9:8-11).

God taught the Jewish people through myths that were intended to inspire their imagination and cause them to look to Him in faith: *"Wherefore the law was our schoolmaster to bring us unto Christ, that we might be justified by faith." Galatians 3:24.*

An Example of Myth

C.S. Lewis retold the Greek and Roman myth of Cupid and Psyche in his novel *Till We Have Faces*. Lewis was fascinated by the myth and its application to Christian thought. It serves as a bridge between the best of pagan mythology and actual Christian events. Lewis made Psyche's world invisible to the nonbelievers and enlarged the myth's theme of sacrifice. Through it he hinted at Christ's work to join the worlds of reason and imagination (1 Corinthians 13:11-12).

The following is my abridgement of Cupid and Psyche from Apuleius: [21]

The Story of Cupid and Psyche

There was once a western king who had three daughters. The first two were more beautiful than all other women, but the third was more beautiful than all creatures of earth. And because of her extreme beauty, this third daughter became famous the world over, so that people said either Venus had been incarnated, or a new Venus had arisen.

Eventually the real Venus lost some of her worship, because people went on pilgrimages to see the king's daughter. Venus became jealous and vowed that the usurper would shortly repent. So Venus called on her son Cupid to revenge her of the king's daughter. She took Cupid to the western king's city and showed him Psyche (the girl's name). Venus asked him to make Psyche fall in love with the most crooked and vile creature living. But when he saw her, he secretly desired to have her himself, and made plans to save her from his mother.

Meanwhile, even with all her beauty and admiration, Psyche had no suitors. Her two older sisters were married to two kings without much difficulty, but Psyche's beauty was too intimidating for any mortal. She began to see her beauty as a curse.

Psyche's father believed that the gods and powers of heaven envied her and therefore withheld their favor. He went to the oracle of Apollo to get advice. Apollo answered that Psyche was destined to marry a terrible dragon serpent that terrified even the gods. He counseled the king to abandon her on a rock cliff to fate.

The king, who had been happy before his trip to the oracle, returned home sad and sorrowful, and told his wife the unhappy news. The entire kingdom mourned the fate of Psyche as she prepared for her black wedding day.

Her wedding procession was like a funeral. Her father and mother went forward weeping and crying. But Psyche said to them, "Why torment yourselves at your age? Why soil your faces with tears, and make me cry as well? Why beat your breasts for me? Now you see the evil reward of my excellent beauty. When the people praised me and called me Venus, it was bound to arouse her envy. Take me to my fate at the top of the rock. I want to be married and see my husband, the world destroyer."

So the procession reached its goal, and Psyche was abandoned on the high hill. The torches and lights were put out with the tears of the people, and the miserable parents gave their sorrowful hearts to darkness. There Psyche was left alone to weep and tremble on the top of the rock, but Zephyr, the wind, pitied her and carried her to a deep valley, where she was laid in a bed of sweet flowers. Psyche was comforted and soon refreshed with sleep.

She awoke and began to explore the place. It was filled with great and mighty trees, and a river ran as clear as crystal. She followed the river to a waterfall, and beside the waterfall stood a princely edifice, made not by man, but by the power of a god. It seemed in every point a heavenly Palace.

Psyche was so enchanted by the palace that she entered it and began to look at its treasures. And when with great pleasure she had viewed all those things, she heard a voice that said, "Why do you marvel at so great riches? Behold, all that you see is yours. Therefore, go into the bedroom; try out the bed, and the bath. We whose voices you hear will be your servants."

Then Psyche perceived divine providence at work, and she followed the advice of the voices. Psyche found the dining room and sat down. All sorts of divine meats and wines were brought in, not by anybody, but as it were by the wind, for she saw no person, but only heard voices on every side.

When all her pleasure of the evening was finished, she went to bed, and when she lay down, she began to be fearful, because she was alone. Then came her unknown benefactor, her new husband, the owner of the house. He slept with her and consummated the marriage, but before daybreak, before she could see him, he left. And so she stayed in the house a great while, and grew fonder of the place and her new situation.

During the time when Psyche was in the beautiful palace, her father and mother did nothing but weep and lament, and her two sisters did all they could to comfort them.

Then one night, Psyche's husband spoke to her. She could not see him, but could feel his eyes, his hands, and his ears. He said, "O my sweet wife, you are in imminent danger, and I want you to beware: for your sisters, thinking you are dead are greatly troubled, and are coming to look for you. If you hear their lamentations, do not answer or look up towards them, for if you do you will purchase to me great sorrow, and to yourself utter destruction." Psyche heard her husband and committed to follow his command.

After he left, Psyche lamented the whole day following, thinking that she was now past all hope of comfort. She felt imprisoned, and she was deprived of human conversation, commanded not to talk to her sisters, or to see them. She went bed that night having fasted the entire day.

Her husband came at night like before and embraced her sweetly and said. "Is this how you perform your promise, my sweet wife? You weep all day? And now you will not cease even though in my arms? Go ahead then, purchase your own destruction, and when you find it so, remember my words." Then she asked her husband more and more, assuring him that she would die, unless he would let her see her sisters. At this he relented, and said that she should give them gold and jewels as much as she wanted. But he told her, "Beware that you don't begin to desire to see my body (because he knew the sisters would counsel her to do so), lest by your curiosity you deprive yourself of so great and worthy estate."

Psyche was glad at this, and thanked him profusely. She said, "Sweet husband, I had rather die than to be separated from you, for whosoever you be, I love you as myself or Cupid himself: but I pray that you grant likewise, that Zephyr would bring my sisters down to the valley as he brought me."

The next day Psyche found her sisters calling for her on top of the rock, and she brought them down to the palace by the wind Zephyr. She showed them the storehouses of treasure. She caused them to hear the voices of the servants, and she fed them with the miraculous buffet. The sisters conceived great envy in their hearts, and one of them demanded news of her husband: his nature, name, and estate. But Psyche remembered her promise, and made up a story: he was a young man, of good stature, a flaxen beard, and loved to hunt in the hills and dales nearby. And fearing she would contradict herself

If she talked long about him, she filled their laps with gold, silver and jewels, and commanded Zephyr to carry them away.

On the way home her sisters began comparing their state to Psyche. They murmured that they had married foreign husbands, who had made them housekeepers, and they no longer were able to see their family and friends regularly. Whereas their younger sister lived in a house of treasure, as a goddess with invisible servants, and if her husband was as advertised, there could be no woman more happy than she. The sisters conspired to deprive Psyche of her happiness. They decided to withhold Psyche's good report from their father and mother, to return to their husbands, and to plan a scheme to put Psyche back in her place.

The two sisters hid their treasure, mussed their hair, and renewed their false and forged tears. When their father and mother beheld them weep and lament still, the sisters doubled their sorrow and grief, and full of Envy, they took their voyage home, preparing the slaughter and destruction of their sister.

In the mean time, the husband of Psyche warned her to beware her sisters' return, because he said they would do her harm. He said they would persuade her to look at his face, which if she did, she would see no more. He told her if she kept his secret she would have an immortal god as a child, if not she would have a mortal.

Then Psyche was glad that she would have a divine baby, and joyful in becoming a mother. She soon forgot the danger her husband warned her of.

Nevertheless her sisters, the pestilent and wicked furies, took shipping to bring their enterprise to pass. Cupid again warned her not to see her sisters, but Psyche begged to see them, reminding him that she had been faithful so far, and had endured the loss of human friendships. Her husband, compelled by the violence of her often embraces, wiped away her tears with his hair, and yielded to his wife.

Now her sisters arrived at the kingdom and immediately, barely letting their feet touch the ground, without visiting their parents, ran and jumped off the cliff into the arms of Zephyr. As soon as they were down the hill, they went to Psyche and unfolded their plot. They said, "O dear sister Psyche, you are no more a child, but a mother. How happy we will be to see the child grow up in such opulence. If he is like his parents, there is no doubt but a new Cupid shall be born." Psyche then treated her sisters to a fabulous meal and entertained them with the invisible instruments and their players.

Nevertheless, the wickedness of the sisters could not be stopped by her graciousness, but they were determined to work their treason. They began by asking again about her husband and his lineage. And she, having forgotten her former description, invented a new answer. Now she said that her husband was a middle-aged merchant, with a gray beard. Hoping to deflect them from further inquiries, she loaded them with more treasures and asked Zephyr to take them back to the hill.

On the way to their parent's house, the sisters compared the notes of the former visit and the present one. They discovered that Psyche's husband had suddenly grown from a young man with flaxen hair to a middle-aged one with a gray beard. They decided that Psyche's husband must really be a god and that she had never seen him. They also divined that her child was an immortal, a development their envy could not bear. They decided to color the matter to their parents.

The next day the sisters returned weeping deceitfully and told Psyche of the desperateness of her situation. They reminded her of Apollo's prophecy, that she would marry a terrible dragon serpent mightier than the gods. They bolstered their claim by reporting that people had seen the serpent hunting in that country. They warned her that he would not long pamper her with delicate meats, but would soon devour her and the child as soon as it was born. They further vouched for their own integrity by charging her to leave, and if she would not, they could not be thought guilty.

At this warning Psyche feared, and all her doubts about her husband lover seemed a reality, and her pleasant thoughts a delusion. She said, "O my dear sisters, I heartily thank you for your kindness toward me, and I am now persuaded of the truth, for I never saw my husband, nor do I know his country, I only hear his voice in the night. He loves not the light of day, and so I am suspicious of him, and wonder if he is a beast. Not only that, but he has told me not to see him, and has warned of unhappy consequences if I do. And now dear sisters, if you have a plan then tell me how I can escape."

Then the sisters opened the gates of their subtle minds, and egged her forward in her fearful thoughts. They counseled her to take a sharp razor and hide it under her pillow, and to prepare a lamp with oil, hid under the bed. They said, "When he comes as usual to the bed and sleeps soundly, then get up and quietly take the lamp for light, with the razor in your right hand, and with valiant force cut off the head of the poisonous serpent. Then we will get you married to a handsome man."

After they had inflamed their sister's heart, they began to fear for themselves and the unknown results of their plan. So they returned to the hill, ran toward the sea, and took shipping to their own lands.

When Psyche was left alone her mind was tossed like the waves of the sea, and although she had a strong desire to be loyal to her kind husband, yet she was in doubt because of the words of her sisters. Soon her husband came, kissed her, embraced her, and fell asleep.

Then Psyche, in order to ease her doubtful mind, took out the razor and the lamp to see him. She saw the meekest and sweetest beast of all beasts, Cupid himself, at whose sight the lamp increased its light for joy, and the razor turned its edge. Psyche was afraid then and intended to hide quickly the instruments of her treachery, but she was so enamored of his body that she stopped to look. She also examined his bow, quiver, and arrows, and when she touched the arrow, it pricked her hand. Her blood flowed, and by this she added love upon love. In her joy over the sight of him, she became careless with the lamp, and a drop of oil fell on his right shoulder.

Cupid woke up at the pain of the oil and perceived that his wife had broken her promise. He flew away without saying a word. But Psyche caught him as he was rising, and held him as he flew until she could not anymore, and fell to the ground. Cupid stopped and spoke to her. He said, "O simple Psyche, I disobeyed my mother, who wanted me to move you to marry a miserable man. Instead I loved you and wounded my own body with my proper weapons, to have you for a wife. And for that did I seem like a beast to you, that you would try to cut off my head with a razor?" Then he flew away for good.

Psyche tried to drown herself in the river, but the river threw her up on the bank, out of respect for Cupid. Pan was sitting by the riverside and he encouraged her to win back the heart of her husband by offering him service.

Psyche began to wander through the world in search of her beloved Cupid. By chance she entered the city of one of her sisters. When Psyche found her sister, she told the story of what happened that night. But Psyche wanted revenge on her sisters for their evil counsel and added to the story. She said, "Cupid vowed to get revenge by marrying my sister."

Psyche had hardly finished her tale, when the sister ran home, and lying to her husband about the death of her parents, took a ship and returned to the kingdom of her youth. She went to the hill and threw herself off, confident that Zephyr would take her down to her new home, But instead she fell among the rocks, and became a prey to birds and wild beasts, which she worthily deserved.

Then Psyche, seeing the success of her revenge, went and found the other sister, and repeated the same tale of deceit. The second sister met the same fate as the first.

Then the white bird Gull, which swims in the waves, went to Venus, and told her of Cupid's love, and his wounds, and his neglect of love in the world. Her told her that marriages were now filled with jealousy, fights, and arguments. Venus answered, "has my son fallen in love, which is contrary to his nature? Who is the usurper?" The Gull reported that he only knew the name, Psyche.

Venus then went to her bedroom, where she found her son wounded as it was told her. She accused him of betrayal, and told him that he had made a daughter out of her mortal foe. She determined to ask for help from Sobriety, whom she had often offended. Venus said she would ask Sobriety to take away his quiver, bow, and arrows, quench his fire, and subdue his body. She also vowed to cut off his hair and clip his wings.

Venus stormed out and straightway encountered Juno and Ceres. They chided her for her rage and asked her if she would now reprehend her own arts and delights when manifested in her son.

Venus was not appeased and took her voyage to the sea in all haste to look for Psyche.

Meanwhile, Psyche looked to and fro for her husband. She saw a temple on a hill and hiked up to it. When she reached the top, she saw grain lying in heaps, and hooks, scythes, sickles, and other instruments for reaping, but everything was out of order. When Psyche saw the disorder, she immediately went to work and put everything in its proper place. Then Ceres, the goddess of the harvest, came to her temple and saw Psych there. Psyche asked for protection from Venus but Ceres demurred because of a peace treaty with Venus.

Then Psyche driven away contrary to her hope, was double afflicted with sorrow. But, before she descended the hill, she saw afar off a temple standing in a forest. And Psyche, determined to ask the help of every god or goddess, purposed to go to it. The temple was that of Juno, the protector of pregnant women. Psyche asked for help from this goddess also. Juno declined to help Psyche for the same reason as Ceres, and because Venus was her daughter in law.

In her despair, Psyche decided to go to Venus herself in humility and ask for pardon. She also reasoned that her beloved might be in his mother's house.

In the meantime, Venus also wearied herself in chasing Psyche and went to find Mercury to help her. She charged Mercury to publish a reward to anyone who would deliver Psyche, and a punishment for those who would harbor her. The reward was seven sweet kisses from Venus, and with this every man was enflamed to seek out Psyche.

When Psyche arrived at the house of Venus, a servant called Custom came out and derided Psyche, and said; "now you will know that you have a mistress above you." She then took Psyche by the hair and brought her before Venus.

Venus laughed a mocking laugh and said, "O goddess, are you just now come to visit your sick husband, who is in danger of death by your doings. Rest assured that I will treat you like a daughter in law." Venus then called in her two servants called Sorrow and Sadness to torment Psyche.

When her torment was finished, Psyche was again brought before Venus. Venus denied that the unborn child was her grandchild and gave Psyche a task to prove her love. Venus took a great quantity of wheat, barley, poppy seed, peas, lentils, and beans and mingled them in a heap. Then she told Psyche to separate them into neat groups before nightfall.

Psyche sat down before the heap and did nothing; as such a task was impossible. Then a tiny ant took pity on her and called her sisters to help. The ants had mercy on Psyche and put the grain in order. When night came Venus returned drunk from a party and saw what had been done. She said to herself, "this is not your work, but rather of him that loves you." Venus then gave Psyche a morsel of bread and went to bed. In the meantime, Cupid was imprisoned in the most secure room of the house, so the two lovers were separated from one another.

The next day, Venus gave Psyche another task. She asked her to take wool from the man killing golden sheep. Psyche hastily went down by the river, not to get the wool, but to throw herself in. Then a green reed inspired by the gods said to her, "O Psyche, please do not pollute my water by your death, and beware that you go not near to the golden sheep, until the heat of the day is past. They are the most furious during the sunniest parts of the day, and they seek the destruction of mankind. Instead hide here safe by me, and when the sheep have finished drinking in the river, you may gather their wool from the thickets and bushes." Psyche followed the reed's advice, gathered the wool, and carried it home to Venus.

Venus was not satisfied by the works of Psyche and said that she would yet prove her courage and prudence by assigning her a more difficult task. She told Psyche to fetch a cup of water from the springs of the river Styx.

Psyche climbed the hill as she was instructed, but in her heart it was only to throw herself down. At the top of the hill Psyche saw what an impossible task she had been given. The spring cascaded down as a waterfall, as was guarded on each side by dragons that never slept. Psyche stood still as a stone. But the eagle, remembering his friend Cupid, came from the house of the skies and said to Psyche, "O simple naïve woman, don't think that you are able to dip of this dreadful water. The gods themselves are afraid of the sight." The eagle then took her bottle and filled it for her.

Venus would not be appeased, but became more menacing, and gave her an even more dangerous task. She said, "take this box to the underworld and bring back a little of the beauty of Proserpine, enough to last a day, and tell her that I have lost some of my own in caring for my sick son."

Then Psyche perceived that her luck had run out, because no one can return from the underworld. She went up to a high tower to throw herself off, thinking that was the quickest way to the underworld, but the tower spoke to her: "O poor miser, why are you going to kill yourself? Don't separate your spirit from your body by suicide, for then you can never return from the other side. Instead, go to Lacedemon, which is not far from here. Enquire there for the hill Tenarus, for in it is a bypath to the underworld, even the palace of Pluto. Do not go empty handed either. But take with you two barley cakes and some honey in your hands, and two coins in your mouth. And when you have passed a good way, you will see a lame donkey carrying wood, and a lame fellow driving him, who will ask you to give him the sticks that fall off, but do not assist him in any way. Go on and find the river of that world, where Chiron is the ferryman. Pay him one of the coins by dropping it to him out of your mouth. And it will come to pass that while you are in the ferry you will see and old man swimming in the water, desiring you to pull him into the boat. Do not regard his pleas. Then, when you reach the other side, you will see old women spinning, who will desire you to help them, but do not consent for any reason. These people who distract you all are traps of Venus, to make you drop your cakes. And don't think it's a light matter to drop your cakes, because without them you cannot return to the living.

"Then you will see at the gate a marvelous dog with three heads, barking continually at the souls of them which enter, but he can do no other harm. To him you must give a cake to ensure your safe entry. Proserpine afterward will be an excellent hostess and offer you treats, but ask only for brown bread, and give her your message. And when you receive some of her beauty for your offering, return past Cerberus, giving him the other cake, and Chiron, giving him the other coin. And above all, do not look into the box." Psyche proceeded to follow the tower's advice, and returned from the underworld with her cargo.

When Psyche returned from the underworld, she said within herself, "Am I not a fool, to have so great beauty in my possession, and not take a little for my face, to please my beloved?" So she opened the box and saw nothing therein. But a deep sleep invaded all her members so that she fell down on the ground, and lay as a corpse.

Cupid by this time was healed of his sickness and began to miss Psyche. So he secretly left his room, put his wings back on, and searched the countryside for his wife. He found her by and by and wiped the sleep from her face, and put it again into the box. He woke her with the tip of one of his arrows, saying: "O wretched Psyche, you almost perished again because of your curiosity. Go now, and complete your mission for my mother, and in the meantime, I will clear up everything." So Psyche took the box to Venus.

Cupid was more in love with Psyche every day, but he feared the displeasure of his mother. Therefore, he went to Jupiter to ask for help. Jupiter agreed to help him in return for his arrows directed toward the hearts of excellent maidens. Jupiter then held a council of the gods and asked them to forgive Cupid's trespasses and grant him marriage to Psyche, which would serve to tame his wild ways. Jupiter at that time commanded Venus to accept Psyche, and made Psyche into a goddess. So the marriage feast was sumptuously prepared. Psyche was then married to Cupid, and delivered a child called Pleasure.

The myth of Cupid and Psyche has often been called an allegory. It uses personifications of the abstract concepts of love (Cupid) and soul (Psyche) to enable us to understand their relationship. The myth answers the following questions: "How can the mind comprehend the divine? How can reason be reconciled to abstract powers that obviously influence us yet are not subject to the senses?" A Christian way to say this would be, "How can we as concrete creatures love a spiritual God?"

Cupid and Psyche answers these questions concisely and shows the steps of spiritual growth to reach a personal understanding of the divine powers. The author himself probably didn't understand fully the implications of the myth, and that is just right, because myth is truth that can't be distilled easily into principles, but is better comprehended through stories Perhaps that's why God Himself had to personify His love in the person and story of Jesus.

While it would be fascinating to speculate on the meanings in the story for women's psychology and development, I will limit my analysis to spiritual growth and the universal aspects for both genders.

Here is the meaning that the characters in the myth have for me:

Venus - represents the power of the divine. Psyche as reason must find a way to be reconciled to her in order to be complete and know the spiritual nature. Psyche as a girl was admired by all but not loved. There was something undefined about her that was missing. She did not have the unsayable and unknowable qualities that made suitors comfortable and at home with her. She did not make sacrifices to the power of love, to Venus.

Cupid - represents Psyche's treasure. Cupid was her symbol of completeness. If she could hold him, then she would have access to the divine world as well as the rational world.

Psyche - represents the initiate into spiritual matters. She possesses reason as her name implies, but she adds to herself spiritual secrets to reach the other side.

The sisters - represent the rational part of us that is faithless and refuses to believe in anything that cannot be proved by sense data.

Psyche was happy with Cupid until her sisters goaded her into looking at him. Psyche enjoyed her spirit lover but did not have knowledge of him as an equal. His substance was hid from her. The sisters caused her to doubt by demanding physical proof of his nature. Psyche took the wrong path by shining her light on the divine. She learned that the spirit world does not respond to scientific experiments.

Psyche injured Cupid with her lack of faith, but because of her loss she was motivated to learn the correct way about spiritual truths. The way was difficult because she could not depend on her reason alone; she had to rely instead on unseen forces to help her resolve her growth tasks. Psyche destroying her sisters represented her repentance of trusting more in the natural senses than the spiritual perspective.

Psyche began her life of repentance by trying to bring order to Ceres' temple. She tried to gain favor by working for the gods. But Ceres and Juno (protectors of women) quickly discouraged her. Psyche had to make peace with Venus personally, and rational work would not help.

She decided to go in humility and ask forgiveness from Venus. Venus did not forgive her but instead gave her a series of impossible tasks to perform in penance. Psyche did not understand the unreasonable power of love and could not be reconciled to Venus without a reverence for the mysterious motivations of God and men. She could only get that reverence by confrontation with impossible demands.

Each task was accomplished when Psyche received help from unexpected sources. Spiritual growth can't be done alone or in our own power. Grace has to manifest itself for the crises to be resolved. In Christian terms, God has to intervene for us.

1. Sorting the seeds - represents reviewing the experiences of the past and finding the truth about one's self. Specifically, sorting is examining past responses to the challenges of the divine intervention. Some would call this reviewing change points or decision provoking events. No human is able to do this honestly without grace. We can't overcome our tendency to justify ourselves or overlook our errors. The ants helped Psyche when she could not do it. They symbolized the diligent work and divine intervention required. Venus remarked, "this is not your work, but rather of him that loves you."

2. Retrieving the golden wool from the man-killing sheep - represents the work required to reform. We realize the gulf between God and ourselves. We see clearly the requirements of a relationship with God. We see the risk of pleasing God is the death of self-interest. Psyche could not get the wool without risking her own life.

    Once again she was given divine help. The reed told her the secret of gathering the wool: rely on the work of others. No one can reform herself. He told her to wait on the thorns to gather the wool for her.

    C.S. Lewis differs from Apuleius on this part. He added the concept of sacrifice. Lewis' main character in the tale is Orual, the sacrifice. Orual distracts the man killing sheep, allowing Psyche to pick the wool off the thorns without hindrance. Reformation cannot be accomplished by human effort; there must be sacrifice because there must be a death to self.

3. Fetching a cupful of water from the river of death (Styx) - represents the spiritual death to self that must come when we give up our efforts to reform. Psyche wanted to throw herself down and complete the loss of self physically. The eagle, a symbol of bravery and a friend of Cupid,

took pity on her and got the water for her. In Lewis'story, this symbolized Psyche's acceptance of the sacrifice.

4. Bringing Venus the beauty of Proserpine (Queen of the Underworld) - represents the reconciliation of the physical and spiritual natures by death to self. But the death cannot be literal. Psyche wanted to throw herself off of a tower to reach the underworld but was warned by a mysterious voice not to take the task so literally: "O poor miser, why are you going to kill yourself? Don't separate your spirit from your body by suicide, for then you can never return from the other side."

Apuleius solves this problem by providing Psyche with amulets. Lewis hints that the real solution is in the sacrifice. Psyche does not have to die to join the two worlds because Orual did this for her.

In her quest for the beauty of Proserpine, Psyche was to refuse to help those along the way who would hinder her, even if their causes were just and deserved her pity. These people represent those in the world that would hinder us from making a complete surrender to God.

Psyche was also forbidden to look inside the box. This represents the mystery of the spiritual realm and the futility of trying to understand it by sense data. The divine can't be comprehended by the mind alone.

Because of her accomplishment of the tasks, especially the last (death to self), Cupid returns. Psyche is reconciled to Venus and allowed to marry Cupid. Thus Psyche (the psychological nature), is transported to the divine sphere (spiritual nature) by realization that the spiritual world is not comprehended by sense and reason and must be entered by faith. She completes her metamorphosis into a spiritual creature, giving honor to the other meaning of her name, butterfly.[22]

Conclusion

The Cupid and Psyche myth illustrates how God chooses to instruct us through stories. These stories are of mythological figures, of historical people, and of our own lives. God uses stories to teach us because we must learn spiritual truths not only with our senses and reason but also with our imagination. We must learn through our psychological and spiritual natures. That is the power of myth.

CHAPTER 5

The Hero's Journey

THE stories in the Old Testament, especially the stories of the children of Israel, are designed to teach us spiritual truths and to guide us in our lives: *"Now all these things happened unto them for ensamples: and they are written for our admonition, upon whom the ends of the world are come." 1 Corinthians 10:11.*

In the remaining chapters, I will use examples of Old Testament characters and the nation of Israel to show that God has a definite pattern of dealing with people. He preserves the stories to teach us about Himself and to show us how to respond correctly to the spiritual crises and stages in our lives.

I will also use biographies, novels, and even fairy tales, because God has ordered the human mind to solve problems through the use of stories, and the understanding of our lives is limited by God's methodologies. People of all cultures and times have had the same tools to find their way to spiritual growth. Philip Yancey relates that in the old Soviet Union many people came to God through the works of Tolstoy and Dostoevsky even though the Bible was banned.[1] No one can escape the ways of God, and our artistic expressions contain the elements of God's design in making us to seek Him: *"That they should seek the Lord, if haply they might feel after him, and find him, though he be not far from every one of us: For in him we live, and move, and have our being; as certain also of your own poets have said, For we are also his offspring." Acts 17:27,28.*

Since God deals with us the same way as with others,[2] it is reasonable to believe that He will allow us to go through the same struggles as them: *"There hath no temptation taken you but such as is common to man: but God is faithful, who will not suffer you to be tempted above that ye are able; but will with the temptation also make a way to escape, that ye may be able to bear it." 1 Corinthians 10:13.* People have common temptations and common problems. There are also common solutions to those problems. God has given us examples in His word, in the world, in history, and in stories to guide us. Nevertheless, only His word can be fully relied on, and the scriptures must judge the truth of other knowledge.

In addition to the progression of the spiritual life cycle, I will also be alluding to the "hero's journey" in the remaining chapters. The hero's journey is the most prevalent mythological theme in the Bible and in other stories.[3] In *A Drunkard's Progress: AA and the Sobering Strength of Myth*, an anonymous author named Elpenor tells of the power of the hero's quest story to heal alcoholics as they identify with the overcomer.[4] William Kirk Kilpatrick advocated studying the hero's journey to gain models of virtue to imitate. He said that moral education should be based on lives of heroes rather than on situation ethics.[5]

Jesus Christ became the ultimate expression of the hero's adventure and is the model for all time: *"Wherefore seeing we also are compassed about with so great a cloud of witnesses, let us lay aside every weight, and the sin which doth so easily beset us, and let us run with patience the race that is set before us, Looking unto Jesus the author and finisher of our faith; who for the joy that was set before him endured the cross, despising the shame, and is set down at the right hand of the throne of God." Hebrews 12:1,2.* I believe God wants each of us to travel through a similar adventure in our lives, because it is the path of spiritual growth.

God uses the testimony of the life of the hero to turn others to faith. Hebrews 11-12:1-2 teaches us that God uses trials to demonstrate faith to the world. The hero must depend on God's power rather than self-effort. It is faith that pleases God: *"But without faith it is impossible to please him: for he that cometh to God must believe that he is, and that he is a rewarder of them that diligently seek him." Hebrews 11:6.* It is faith that causes others to believe in God: *"For I am not ashamed of the gospel of Christ: for it is the power of God unto salvation to every one that believeth; to the Jew first, and also to the Greek. For therein is the righteousness of God revealed from faith to faith: as it is written, The just shall live by faith." Romans 1:16,17.*

Joseph Campbell outlined the trail of the hero's journey in *The Hero With A Thousand Faces*. I will give a brief summary of the stages of the journey here as a guide. This typology is valid for Christians even though it is not directly mentioned in the Bible. It a common theme throughout the stories in the scriptures and can give us a much richer insight into them and into our own lives.

Outline of the Hero's Journey

Call To Adventure

The hero encounters events and relationships that do not respond to his knowledge, experience, and intervention. These new forces go beyond his repertoire of skills and challenge his spirit. He is led to consider spiritual solutions because of the ineffectiveness of mere reason and action. The hero at first is reluctant and may try to ignore signs of the call. Yet the problems grow and become more oppressive to his spirit. He sometimes answers the call to a spiritual quest out of curiosity or desire for gain, or sometimes is dragged into the journey by mysterious forces (the Holy Spirit).

Refusal of the Call

Many times a potential hero refuses the call and attempts to limit his world to reason and action. He restricts his life to mere physical and psychological experiences. The spiritual world is scary and is shunned. If he turns away, the hero's world becomes small, a prison, and "a wasteland of dry stones." "Walled in boredom," the potential hero becomes "a victim to be saved" instead of a liberator.[6]

Supernatural Helper

"For those who have not refused the call, the first encounter of the hero journey is with a protective figure who provides the adventurer with amulets against the dragon forces he is about to pass."[7] This supernatural helper in ancient mythology is clearly the Holy Spirit in Christian thought. The supernatural helper provides protection against evil forces and serves as a guide through the unknown spiritual world of the hero's journey. "What such a figure represents is the benign, protecting power of destiny."[8]

Crossing of the First Threshold

The first task of the hero, now with the supernatural helper, is to cross the threshold between the world of the senses and the spiritual world. At this threshold the hero encounters a guardian who does not allow anyone to pass except those who are worthy. The hero proves himself by defeating the guardian, by dying to self, or by extraordinary insight or wisdom. The key to defeating the threshold guardian is to abandon complete reliance on reason and sense data and instead to place faith in one's destiny and the supernatural power that called.

Belly of the Whale

The hero crosses the threshold into the world of the unknown, which cannot be seen or understood by reason alone. When Jesus Christ was asked by the Pharisees to give them a sign of His Messiahship, He told them the only sign would be that of Jonah. He then explained that just as Jonah went into the belly of the whale on a physical and spiritual journey, so would the Messiah prove His worthiness by descent into the world of death and the unknown. It is within the belly of the whale that the hero gains the supernatural power and wisdom to be a benefit to others (Matthew 12:38-40).

Road of Trials

Within the belly of the whale, the hero is presented with a series of tasks. These tasks test the hero's courage, moral power, and determination to survive and thrive in the spiritual dimension. Along the road of trials, the hero encounters supernatural forces that try to prevent (demon powers), and forces that try to help (angelic powers).

"The ordeal is a deepening of the problem of the first threshold and the question is still in balance: Can the ego put itself to death?"[9] In other words, how much faith is the hero willing to put in the power that called instead of relying on self? It is only through faith in the divine power and the hero's destiny that the tasks can be completed and the demon powers overcome.

Meeting with god

The hero learns that the wisdom of the world is insufficient to battle spiritual forces and gain supernatural power. This understanding is necessary to pass the ordeal. Once the tasks have been accomplished the hero is brought face to face with the power that called.

The hero stands before God to learn the answer to the mystery: How can man be overcome? How can I overcome myself? How can I transcend what I am to be what you are?[10]

God answers the mystery by sacrifice, the sacrifice of Himself. We cannot overcome by ourselves; it must be done for us. We cannot reach the other side by our own power; one must give us the power more powerful than ourselves.

The Bible declares the same principle: *"Behold, what manner of love the Father hath bestowed upon us, that we should be called the sons of God: therefore the world knoweth us not, because it knew him not. Beloved, now are we the sons of God, and it doth not yet appear what we shall be: but we know that, when he shall appear, we shall be like him; for we shall see him as he is. And every man that hath this hope in him purifieth himself, even as he is pure." 1 John 3:1-3.* Jesus provided the power for many heroes to transcend by His sacrifice. It is when we see Him *as He is* that *we shall be like him.* Jesus is the hero that made a way for other heroes to succeed: *"But we see Jesus, who was made a little lower than the angels for the suffering of death, crowned with glory and honour; that he by the grace of God should taste death for every man. For it became him, for whom are all things, and by whom are all things, in bringing many sons unto glory, to make the captain of their salvation perfect through sufferings." Hebrews 2:9,10.*

The hero learns from meeting with God that sacrifice and suffering are the sources of power.

Taking the Treasure

After meeting with God and receiving the sacrifice of God as a deep truth, the hero is given a treasure to take back to the physical world. This treasure is the knowledge and experience of sacrifice and suffering. The hero has learned that supernatural power comes through sacrifice and supernatural wisdom comes through suffering. He takes this treasure back into the physical world and uses it to solve real life problems.

Ambivalence of Returning

Now that the hero has gained supernatural wisdom and experience, what will he do? It would be much easier to live in the bliss of the image of God before your face without the distraction of the physical world; yet, the hero is not dead but alive. He is dead to self and able to comprehend God but yet is physically living in the world (Galatians 2:20). He could become a hermit and meditate on God, but that would hardly make him a hero because he must help others. Therefore, a true hero returns to share his treasure.

Wasn't even the apostle Paul himself caught up in this ambivalence? He describes the elements of meeting with God, the desire for the treasure, and the ambivalence of return in his writings.

1. Meeting With God

"I knew a man in Christ above fourteen years ago, (whether in the body, I cannot tell; or whether out of the body, I cannot tell: God knoweth;) such an one caught up to the third heaven. And I knew such a man, (whether in the body, or out of the body, I cannot tell: God knoweth;) How that he was caught up into paradise, and heard unspeakable words, which it is not lawful for a man to utter." 2 Corinthians 12:2-4. Paul describes how he was once completely lost in the spiritual reality of God.

2. Desire for Treasure

"That I may know him, and the power of his resurrection, and the fellowship of his sufferings, being made conformable unto his death; If by any means I might attain unto the resurrection of the dead. Not as though I had already attained, either were already perfect: but I follow after, if that I may apprehend that for which also I am apprehended of Christ Jesus." Philippians 3:10-12. Now that Paul has seen and understood the power of Christ's sacrifice and wisdom of his suffering, he wishes to use these mysteries himself to transcend the bounds of physical existence. His desire is to *"apprehend that for which I am apprehended of Christ."* He wants to experience the power and wisdom for himself.

3. Ambivalence of Return

"For to me to live is Christ, and to die is gain. But if I live in the flesh, this is the fruit of my labour: yet what I shall choose I wot not. For I am in a strait betwixt two, having a desire to depart, and to be with Christ; which is far better: Nevertheless to abide in the flesh is more needful for you. And having this confidence, I know that I shall abide and continue with you all for your furtherance and joy of faith; That your rejoicing may be more

abundant in Jesus Christ for me by my coming to you again." Philippians 1:21-26. Paul states at times he wishes to be completely lost in the spiritual realm and enjoy the presence of Christ; yet, he realizes the treasure he has received must be given to others.

Return

The hero goes back with treasure in hand. God who gave the treasure is now a full reality and he returns in that confidence.

The hero journeys under the auspices of God but at the same time must endure and fight off the dark powers. These dark powers do not want him to take treasures of supernatural power and wisdom to others in the physical world. The dark powers dominate the physical world by deceiving people into believing only in their senses and material things.

Therefore, the hero must pass through another road of trials and temptations in the return. Perhaps the greatest temptation of all is the feeling that others will not understand and will reject both the message and messenger.

Rescue From the Other Side

Somewhere during the return road of trials, the other side gives support. The natural world demands an explanation and an account of the journey and therefore pulls the hero to re-cross the threshold of adventure. At this time, he is close enough to the return threshold to be driven by a desire to complete the adventure. The adventure is not complete until the treasure has been taken back and new disciples are made.

Crossing the Return Threshold

The hero has been propelled by God and enticed by people to re-cross the threshold between the supernatural world and the natural world. The hero is ready to bestow his treasure. He has travelled to the fifth dimension and returns to a three dimensional world. Joseph Campbell explains: "the realm of the gods is a forgotten dimension of the world we know. And the exploration of that dimension, either willingly or unwillingly, is the whole sense of the deed of the hero."[11]

The hero must cross back into the natural world and learn how to relate spiritual realities to people who depend on sense data. He must show that the natural world is only a shadow of the spiritual and the world we take to be real is only a reflection of the rock solid world that is invisible: *"While we look not at the things which are seen, but at the things which are not seen: for the things which are seen are temporal; but the things which are not seen are eternal." 2 Corinthians 4:18.*

Master of the Two Worlds

The hero now has as opportunity to become a master of both worlds, since he has survived an initiation into the mysteries of the supernatural world. He has learned through the spiritual senses as well as the physical. The master of the two worlds sees a particular event not as merely naturally caused, but also as part of the workings of supernatural forces. All things work together. The spiritual world is not divorced from the physical world. It only seems so to those who are oblivious to the fifth dimension.

Freedom to Live

The hero has the freedom to live a life apart from evil motives. Evil motives come from a desire to protect the self. The hero doesn't have to protect the self because he died to self during the journey. He gave up total trust in the physical senses in order to experience the richness and power of the spiritual senses. Death-Burial-Resurrection: the path to power. No one can truly live until he has died. The hero learns from the sacrifice and suffering of God that these are necessary to truly live.

Jesus calls us to follow the same path that He has shown.

1. Death

"I am crucified with Christ: nevertheless I live; yet not I, but Christ liveth in me: and the life which I now live in the flesh I live by the faith of the Son of God, who loved me, and gave himself for me." Galatians 2:20.

2. Burial

"Therefore we are buried with him by baptism into death: that like as Christ was raised up from the dead by the glory of the Father, even so we also should walk in newness of life." (Romans 6:4).

3. Resurrection

"For if we have been planted together in the likeness of his death, we shall be also in the likeness of his resurrection:" Romans 6:5. "If ye then be risen with Christ, seek those things which are above, where Christ sitteth on the right hand of God." Colossians 3:1.

"Then said Jesus unto his disciples, If any man will come after me, let him deny himself, and take up his cross, and follow me. For whosoever will save his life shall lose it: and whosoever will lose his life for my sake shall find it. For what is a man profited, if he shall gain the whole world, and lose his own soul? or what shall a man give in exchange for his soul?" Matthew 16:24-26.

Those who refuse to take the spiritual journey lose the richness of life they could have had. The spiritual dimension remains unknown to them. Jesus warns, "what will it profit you, if you gain everything in the natural world, and yet impoverish the inner man? What physical thing will you give in exchange for your soul?"

An Example of the Hero's Journey

An excellent example of the hero's journey is Walt Disney's *The Little Mermaid*. Disney retold Hans Christian Anderson's story and in my mind made improvements. Disney's version is closer to the model of the hero's journey and more fully develops the key elements.

Call to Adventure: The heroine Ariel's call to adventure began with her inner voice. By "inner voice" I mean that she had a desire within to learn about and be a part of the human world. She collected objects from the world above the ocean and desired to learn about them. Ariel wanted to become human.

Ariel's desire for the world above is a symbol of the call to adventure. How would she go from the bounds of her physical world to the world of the unknown? This is the problem of the hero. In *The Little Mermaid* the girl under the sea desiring to live above the sea beautifully illustrates this principle.

Ariel's call strengthened when she saw the prince and later rescued him from the shipwreck. She saw her treasure and recognized her value in the other world. *Ariel stared, enchanted. She could not keep her eyes off the handsome prince… 'I've never seen a human this close before,' she whispered. 'He's very handsome, isn't he.'[12]*

In Anderson's story each of "her sister's gardens were filled with all sorts of things that they had collected from shipwrecks, but she had only a marble statue of a boy in hers. It had been cut out of stone that was almost transparently clear and had sunk to the bottom of the sea when the ship that had carried it was lost."[13] Later, when the little mermaid saw the prince, "she thought he looked like the statue in her garden."[14]

Therefore, in the original story, the symbol of her desire was given her before she realized the actuality (the prince) of her desire. This is an expression of how physical symbols foreshadow and point the way to spiritual realities.

Refusal of the Call: Ariel did not refuse the call, but instead was very eager to travel to the world above. In Disney's version her eagerness was motivated only by her love for prince Eric. Yet, in Anderson's version she says, "I would dare to do anything to win him and an immortal soul."[15] In the original story, the quest is shown to be a spiritual one.

Supernatural Helper: The Merking appointed Ariel's helper. Sebastian told the King that Ariel needed constant watching and guidance because of her otherworldly longings. Triton agreed and gave Sebastian the job.

Sebastian was reluctant at first to watch out for Ariel and he resisted her plan for the journey. Ambivalence is unusual for a supernatural helper, but that's the way it was in this case.

Sebastian was drawn into the expedition without his consent, but once in, he did his best to help Ariel complete her adventure. He coached her in how to win Eric's affection and later called together sea creatures to create a mood for Eric to kiss Ariel.

Crossing of the First Threshold: The little mermaid decided to cross the threshold after her father destroyed the statue of Eric and after she was tempted by Flotsam and Jetsam with the chance to become human and gain Eric's love. In this case, the heroine was directly enticed to cross by the minions of the dark power (Ursula). Nevertheless, the mission of the hero is universal regardless of the original agent, to gain the power and wisdom of the unknown world.

The guardians of the threshold were the polyps. These were described in Disney's version as "strange, writhing plants that grabbed at Ariel and tried to pull her down."[16] In Anderson's story, the polyps were "gigantic polyps that were half plant and half animal...Everything they could reach they grabbed, and never let go of it again."[17]

Anderson tells us that it was "with dread the little mermaid stood at the entrance to the forest; her heart was beating with fear, she almost turned back. But then she remembered her prince and the soul she wanted to gain and her courage returned."[18]

The little mermaid's fear at crossing indicated that the polyps were threshold guardians. Her only chance to gain her soul was by crossing, another evidence that this was the threshold. The mission of the hero's adventure is to develop the spiritual and psychological dimensions in one's self, and trials serve as the best motivators.

After the little mermaid regained her courage and determination she prepared to cross. "She braided her long hair and bound it around her head, so the polyps could not catch her by it. She held her arms folded tightly across her breast and then she flew through the water as fast as the swiftest fish."[19]

The little mermaid saw what the polyps had caught. She saw drowned human beings, she saw skeletons of land animals, "and then she saw a poor little mermaid who had been caught and strangled; and this sight to her was the most horrible."[20] The entrance to a dangerous world displays trophies of failure; only the worthy can cross.

Belly of the Whale: Ariel was now completely into the above world which was unknown and mysterious to her and which operated on different principles from the merworld. In the merworld, Ariel could not become human, but in the reverse "belly of the whale," becoming human was possible. This illustrates how the hero's adventure is the path to develop the spiritual dimension. Ariel was trying to move to a higher dimension of experience, and so are we.

Road of Trials: Ariel's desires were to win the love of the prince and to experience the wonders of the human world. In order to achieve these desires, she had to endure the road of trials.

The little mermaid met with Ursula, the sea witch, who gave her an opportunity to be human for three days. Ariel had to get the prince to kiss her with a kiss of true love. If she did not, she would turn back into a mermaid and become the sea witch's captive.

As payment for her potion, Ursula demanded that Ariel give up her voice. This symbolizes how the spiritual world operates on different principles than the natural world and cannot be understood solely by the senses. Ariel could not rely on her reason and senses alone to accomplish the task. She must also have faith in her own destiny and the power that called her to the journey.

Fully committed to her task, Ariel had to overcome the interference of demonic powers and take advantage of the help of angelic powers. Ursula and her eels represented the demonic powers that sought to prevent Ariel from succeeding. When Ursula saw the heroine had a chance of accomplishing her task she impersonated Ariel and used Ariel's voice to deceive Eric. Demonic powers use the natural senses to deceive.

Sebastian, the supernatural helper, led the angelic powers. Sebastian used all the power and wisdom he could to help Ariel, including conducting a symphony of "Kiss the Girl" with the sea creatures.

Scuttle the seagull is also important as a symbol of angelic powers. The "higher world" is his home and he helps with powers resident in that world (the birds).

The road of trials ended when the sun went down on the third day. Ariel's time was up. Even though Ariel came close to having the prince kiss her, it would take something more to succeed.

Meeting with god: The lesson of the road of trials is that the tasks cannot be accomplished by self-effort alone. Somehow we are insufficient within ourselves to gain supernatural power and wisdom. We are insufficient to gain "an immortal soul."

In Ariel's case, the meeting with god came only after her failure. What she could not do for herself had to be done for her. This is the meaning of the merking's sacrifice. He agreed to take Ariel's place as Ursula's captive. It was Triton's sacrifice that released the power to defeat Ursula. It was through his sacrifice that Eric was able to kill Ursula, and it was through his sacrifice that Ariel was able to reach her destiny.

Taking the Treasure: The little mermaid's true treasure was the knowledge that supernatural power and wisdom only come through sacrifice and suffering, not by self-effort. Nevertheless, her immediate treasure was the gift of a human (higher) life and marriage to the prince.

Return: In most hero stories, the return is an adventure in itself, but, in this story, Ariel did not return to the merworld. She lived the remainder of her days in the mysterious, enchanted world above the ocean.

To remain in eternal bliss is easy enough for the little mermaid. She lives happily ever after. But, for those of us who take the hero's journey, to return is part of the reason we go.

You might wonder how I can use fairy tales as examples of how people should live. I can do so because they are mythological. The tales explain truths that cannot be understood by the reason alone. The path is the same, whether the model is actual or imaginary.

Jesus and the Hero's Journey

Jesus Christ is the hero's model for all time and the historical reality of the ancient hero myths. The difference between Jesus and other heroes is that He took the journey in reverse. People are called to travel from the natural world to the spiritual world. Jesus travelled from the spiritual world to the natural world and back again. He did so to prove that He was the master of both dimensions: *"I came forth from the Father, and am come into the world: again, I leave the world, and go to the Father." John 16:28.*

Jesus passed the road of trials when He was tempted as a man and used spiritual means to overcome (Matthew 4:1-11).

His meeting with God was not a meeting, but a desertion: *"And about the ninth hour Jesus cried with a loud voice, saying, Eli, Eli, lama sabachthani? that is to say, My God, my God, why hast thou forsaken me?" Matthew 27:46* There was no one to sacrifice for Him. He was the sacrifice.

Jesus' treasure was the saints. He saved them through victory over sin, death, and hell. His return to heaven makes it possible for others to journey there: *"In my Father's house are many mansions: if it were not so, I would have told you. I go to prepare a place for you. And if I go and prepare a place for you, I will come again, and receive you unto myself; that where I am, there ye may be also. And whither I go ye know, and the way ye know. Thomas saith unto him, Lord, we know not whither thou goest; and how can we know the way? Jesus saith unto him, I am the way, the truth, and the life: no man cometh unto the Father, but by me." John 14:2-6.*

Our spiritual journey depends on His sacrifice. It's only trust in Him and death to self that qualifies us to go and be with Him: *"For it became him, for whom are all things, and by whom are all things, in bringing many sons unto glory, to make the captain of their salvation perfect through sufferings. For both he that sanctifieth and they who are sanctified are all of one: for which cause he is not ashamed to call them brethren, Saying, I will declare thy name unto my brethren, in the midst of the church will I sing praise unto thee. And again, I will put my trust in him. And again, Behold I and the children which God hath given me." Hebrews 2:10-13. (also see Philippians 2:5-11).*

CHAPTER 6

Birth of the Hero

THE legends and tales of the world have hardened the myth of the hero's birth and early life. Its pattern is archetypal: a story and personality so anchored in the human psyche that it manifests itself in every generation. Otto Rank studied this pattern and wrote *The Myth of the Birth of the Hero* in 1909:

> The hero is the child of most distinguished parents, usually the son of a king. His origin is preceded by difficulties, such as continence, or prolonged barrenness, or secret intercourse of the parents due to external prohibition or obstacles. During or before the pregnancy, there is a prophecy, in the form of a dream or oracle, cautioning against the birth, and usually threatening danger to the father or his representative. As a rule, he is surrendered to the water, in a box. He is then saved by animals, or by lowly people (shepherds), and is suckled by a female animal or by a humble woman. After he has grown up, he finds his distinguished parents, in a highly versatile fashion. He takes revenge on his father, on the one hand, and is acknowledged, on the other. Finally, he achieves rank and honors.[1]

Rank also gave examples of his pattern: Sargon, Moses, Karna, Oedipus, Paris, Telephus, Perseus, Gilgamesh, Cyrus, Tristan, Romulus, Hercules, Jesus, Siegfried, and Lehengrin.

Of course, Dr. Rank examined the myths from a psychological point of view. We know there is also a spiritual reality behind every true myth. Therefore, there is something spiritual to be learned here.

The True Historical Model of the Myth

1. The child - Jesus.
2. The distinguished parents - lineage of David.
3. The son of a King - son of God and son of man.
4. His origin preceded by difficulties - Joseph and Mary's struggles.
5. The prophecies - Genesis 3:15, Zacharias, Joseph's dream, Gabriel's announcement, Elizabeth, shepherds, Simeon, Anna.
6. His threatening danger to the father or representatives - Satan was the father of man by usurpation. Political and religious leaders were his representatives.
7. His surrender to the water, in a box, exposed - manger, flight to Egypt.
8. His rescue by animals, or lowly people - animals in manger, shepherds, poor parents.
9. He finds distinguished parents - triumphal entry into Jerusalem.
10. He takes revenge on father - destroys father of man, Satan.
11. He is acknowledged - day of Pentecost.
12. He achieves rank and honors - Philippians 2:5-11.

Child

Jesus was the child sought for millennia. Even the first child was honored with the notion that he might be the Messiah. Eve called her son Cain, and said, "I have gotten a man from the Lord" (Genesis 4:1). God had promised the serpent (and the personality animating the serpent) He would send a son to the woman who would crush his head, thus putting down the authority of the wicked one. I believe Eve thought Cain was the promised one. Nevertheless, we know she was severely disappointed.

Every Jewish woman hoped to have a son, and if she didn't, she felt disgraced (1 Samuel 1:1-8). Why? Because every one hoped her son would be the one to crush the serpent's head and restore the world to its proper order.

Paul said Jesus was this child: *"But when the fulness of the time was come, God sent forth his Son, made of a woman, made under the law, To redeem them that were under the law, that we might receive the adoption of sons. And because ye are sons, God hath sent forth the Spirit of his Son into your hearts, crying, Abba, Father." Galatians 4:4-6.* The writer of Hebrews also made the claim: *"Forasmuch then as the children are partakers of flesh and blood, he also himself likewise took part of the same; that through death he might destroy him that had the power of death, that is, the devil;" Hebrews 2:14.*

Most distinguished parents

Joseph and Mary both descended from the house of David the king. Matthew shows Joseph's genealogy from David, and Luke charts Mary's pedigree. When Caesar gave the order for the entire world to be taxed, and for everyone to return to his or her own city, Mary and Joseph went to Bethlehem, the city of David: *"And all went to be taxed, every one into his own city. And Joseph also went up from Galilee, out of the city of Nazareth, into Judaea, unto the city of David, which is called Bethlehem; (because he was of the house and lineage of David:) To be taxed with Mary his espoused wife, being great with child."* Luke 2:3-5.

Son of a King

Jesus was the son of God, the king of all creation: *"Now when the centurion, and they that were with him, watching Jesus, saw the earthquake, and those things that were done, they feared greatly, saying, Truly this was the Son of God."* Matthew 27:54.

His origin is preceded by difficulties

Joseph was alarmed by the announcement that his virgin Mary was pregnant. She must have been unfaithful. He decided to send her to a shelter for unwed mothers but God prevented him: *"Now the birth of Jesus Christ was on this wise: When as his mother Mary was espoused to Joseph, before they came together, she was found with child of the Holy Ghost. Then Joseph her husband, being a just man, and not willing to make her a publick example, was minded to put her away privily. But while he thought on these things, behold, the angel of the Lord appeared unto him in a dream, saying, Joseph, thou son of David, fear not to take unto thee Mary thy wife: for that which is conceived in her is of the Holy Ghost. And she shall bring forth a son, and thou shalt call his name JESUS: for he shall save his people from their sins."* Matthew 1:18-21.

Joseph and pregnant Mary were forced to travel on foot from Nazareth to Bethlehem, and when they got there, all the motel rooms were filled. Jesus was born outside and laid in a feeding trough for animals: *"And so it was, that, while they were there, the days were accomplished that she should be delivered. And she brought forth her firstborn son, and wrapped him in swaddling clothes, and laid him in a manger; because there was no room for them in the inn." Luke 2:6,7.*

Prophecy

The first prophecy of the coming Christ is Genesis 3:15. There are many others in the Old Testament, and the prophecies intensified before and during His incubation in the form of dreams and oracles:

1. Zacharias prophesied while Jesus was in the womb that God would visit His people with salvation through the house of David, and save them from their enemies (Luke 1:67-80).
2. Joseph dreamed and the angel showed him Jesus' true nature and calling - Jesus = Jehovah saves - "he shall save his people from their sins." (Matthew 1:18-25).
3. Gabriel told Mary she would bear the "son of the Highest," that He would rule on the throne of David, that He would reign forever, that His kingdom would continually increase, that God would be His father, and that He would be called the Son of God (Luke 1:26-35; Isaiah 9:6-7).
4. Elizabeth (Zachariah's wife and John's mother) prophesied that Mary's child would be her child's Lord (Luke 1:39-45).
5. The angels announced His birth to the shepherds: *"And the angel said unto them, Fear not: for, behold, I bring you good tidings of great joy, which shall be to all people. For unto you is born this day in the city of David a Saviour, which is Christ the Lord. And this shall be a sign unto you; Ye shall find the babe wrapped in swaddling clothes, lying in a manger. And suddenly there was with the angel a multitude of the heavenly host praising God, and saying, Glory to God in the highest, and on earth peace, good will toward men." Luke 2:10-14.*
6. Simeon said that Jesus would be "a light to lighten the Gentiles, and the glory of Israel." (Luke 2:21-33).
7. Anna, the prophetess "spake of him to all them that looked for redemption in Jerusalem." (Luke 2:36-38).

Threatening danger to the father or his representative

Jesus threatened the father of this world, the devil, and his representatives, the political and religious rulers: *"He that committeth sin is of the devil; for the devil sinneth from the beginning. For this purpose the Son of God was manifested, that he might destroy the works of the devil." 1 John 3:8.*

Satan claimed to be the father of this world: *"And the devil said unto him, All this power will I give thee, and the glory of them: for that is delivered unto me; and to whomsoever I will I give it." Luke 4:6.*

Paul said that Satan is a tyrant who tries to blind the eyes of the people to spiritual reality: *"But if our gospel be hid, it is hid to them that are lost: In whom the god of this world hath blinded the minds of them which believe not, lest the light of the glorious gospel of Christ, who is the image of God, should shine unto them." 2 Corinthians 4:3,4.*

Satan has political power and appointees: *"Put on the whole armour of God, that ye may be able to stand against the wiles of the devil. For we wrestle not against flesh and blood, but against principalities, against powers, against the rulers of the darkness of this world, against spiritual wickedness in high places." Ephesians 6:11,12.* One was Herod the king. When the wise men asked for "he that is born King of the Jews," Herod perceived the hazard of his position. He asked his chief priests and scribes to search their prophecy and find the place of the Messiah's birth. Then he sent the wise men to Bethlehem and insincerely instructed them to bring him word of the new king's whereabouts. Nevertheless, the magi were warned of God and did not return to Satan's servant. Seeing his scheme fail, Herod was enraged and sent soldiers to slay every male in Bethlehem less than two years old. Yet, Jesus and His parents had already escaped to Egypt (Matthew 2:1-18).

Jesus told the unbelieving Pharisees that Satan was their father and the generator of their scepticism: *"Jesus said unto them, If God were your Father, ye would love me: for I proceeded forth and came from God; neither came I of myself, but he sent me. Why do ye not understand my speech? even because ye cannot hear my word. Ye are of your father the devil, and the lusts of your father ye will do. He was a murderer from the beginning, and abode not in the truth, because there is no truth in him. When he speaketh a lie, he speaketh of his own: for he is a liar, and the father of it." John 8:42-44.*

When Jesus was brought before Pilate the procurator to be charged with a crime, it was for sedition against Caesar and for saying He was a king: *"And the whole multitude of them arose, and led him unto Pilate. And they began to accuse him, saying, We found this fellow perverting the nation, and forbidding to give tribute to Caesar, saying that he himself is Christ a King." Luke 23:1,2.*

He is surrendered to the water, in a box

Although Jesus was not actually surrendered to the water in a box, neither were many of Rank's heroes. The real motif is the exposure or abandonment of the hero.[2] How was Jesus exposed? He was born in a barn. Jesus' box was the manger.[3] He was then sent to Egypt (a Gentile nation) to flee the wrath of Herod (Matthew 2.13-15).

He is saved by animals, or lowly people

The Jesus birth is always associated with animals and shepherds, not with showers and cigars. The lowly people who saved Him were Mary and Joseph. Even though they descended from royalty, Joseph was only a carpenter. Jesus' townsfolk belittled Him over this: *"And when he was come into his own country, he taught them in their synagogue, insomuch that they were astonished, and said, Whence hath this man this wisdom, and these mighty works? Is not this the carpenter's son? is not his mother called Mary? and his brethren, James, and Joses, and Simon, and Judas? And his sisters, are they not all with us? Whence then hath this man all these things?" Matthew 13:54-56.*

He finds his distinguished parents

God had promised David that one of his line would sit on the throne of Israel forever: *"For unto us a child is born, unto us a son is given: and the government shall be upon his shoulder: and his name shall be called Wonderful, Counsellor, The mighty God, The everlasting Father, The Prince of Peace. Of the increase of his government and peace there shall be no end, upon the throne of David, and upon his kingdom, to order it, and to establish it with judgment and with justice from henceforth even for ever. The zeal of the LORD of hosts will perform this." Isaiah 9:6,7.* Therefore, Jesus found His distinguished parents by entering Jerusalem to take His throne: *"Tell ye the daughter of Sion, Behold, thy King cometh unto thee, meek, and sitting upon an ass, and a colt the foal of an ass. And the disciples went, and did as Jesus commanded them, And brought the ass, and the colt, and put on them their clothes, and they set him thereon. And a very great multitude spread their garments in the way; others cut down branches from the trees, and strawed them in the way. And the multitudes that went before, and that followed, cried, saying, Hosanna to the Son of David: Blessed is he that cometh in the name of the Lord; Hosanna in the highest." Matthew 21:5-9.*

Of course we know that God is Jesus' distinguished parent. The triumphal entry was presaged by three other prominent events. The first was Jesus' debate with the doctors in the temple at the age of twelve. He showed an understanding that God is His father: "wist ye not that I must be about my father's business?" (Luke 2:41-52). The second was Jesus' baptism. God said, "this is my beloved son, in whom I am well pleased" (Matthew 3:17). The third was Jesus' transfiguration at which God repeated His words from the baptism and added, "hear ye him" (Matthew 17:1-8).

He takes revenge on his father

This father is the god of this world: the father of lies. Satan and his representative Herod tried to destroy Jesus as a child. In truth, Satan tried to destroy Him all through history and prevent Him from coming (study Esther and Moses).

How did Jesus take revenge? He was killed at Golgotha. In the greatest twist of history, the very act of His self-sacrifice became revenge on Satan. Paul said: *"For I determined not to know any thing among you, save Jesus Christ, and him crucified...But we speak the wisdom of God in a mystery, even the hidden wisdom, which God ordained before the world unto our glory: Which none of the princes of this world knew: for had they known it, they would not have crucified the Lord of glory." 1 Corinthians 2:2,7,8.* The scripture implies that Satan and his representatives did not understand the consequences of killing the Messiah, their own ultimate destruction: *"Forasmuch then as the children are partakers of flesh and blood, he also himself likewise took part of the same; that through death he might destroy him that had the power of death, that is, the devil;" Hebrews 2:14.*

Through the death, burial, and resurrection of Jesus people are able to escape Satan's authority and enter God's kingdom: *"That if thou shalt confess with thy mouth the Lord Jesus, and shalt believe in thine heart that God hath raised him from the dead, thou shalt be saved. For with the heart man believeth unto righteousness; and with the mouth confession is made unto salvation." Romans 10:9,10.* Listen to Paul's testimony of Christ's commission to him: *"To open their eyes, and to turn them from darkness to light, and from the power of Satan unto God, that they may receive forgiveness of sins, and inheritance among them which are sanctified by faith that is in me." Acts 26:18.*

He is acknowledged

Many acknowledged Jesus as the Son of God. On the day of Pentecost, three thousand accepted Jesus as the Messiah and Savior in Jerusalem. On another occasion, five thousand more believed on Jesus. So many people acknowledged Jesus that the religious leaders feared for their positions: *"Saying, Did not we straitly command you that ye should not teach in this name? and, behold, ye have filled Jerusalem with your doctrine, and intend to bring this man's blood upon us." Acts 5:28.*

Finally, he achieves rank and honors

Rank and honors came from the highest source, God Himself: *"Let this mind be in you, which was also in Christ Jesus: Who, being in the form of God, thought it not robbery to be equal with God: But made himself of no reputation, and took upon him the form of a servant, and was made in the likeness of men: And being found in fashion as a man, he humbled himself, and became obedient unto death, even the death of the cross. Wherefore God also hath highly exalted him, and given him a name which is above every name: That at the name of Jesus every knee should bow, of things in heaven, and things in earth, and things under the earth; And that every tongue should confess that Jesus Christ is Lord, to the glory of God the Father." Philippians 2:5-11.*

Raglan's system

Jesus is also the archetypal hero of Raglan's system, especially the first thirteen parts (that part of his system that corresponds to Rank's).[4]

1. Mother is a royal virgin - Mary was a virgin of royal descent.
2. Father is a king - Joseph was also of royal descent. God, His real father, is king of the universe.

3. Father related to mother - Joseph and Mary were both of the lineage of David.

4. Unusual conception - Jesus was conceived of the Holy Spirit, one of the trinity (Luke 1:35).

5. Hero reputed to be the son of a god - The prophecies of Jesus gave Him the reputation of the Son of God.

6. Attempt (usually by father) to kill the hero - The father of lies and his representatives attempted to destroy Jesus.

7. Hero spirited away - Joseph and Mary hid Jesus in Egypt at God's command.

8. Reared by foster parents in a far country - In a sense, Joseph and Mary were foster parents. They raised Him in Egypt and Galilee, away from His throne in Jerusalem (Matthew 2:13-23).

9. No details of childhood - The only detail we have of Jesus before age thirty was His debates with the doctors at age twelve, which foreshadowed His mission (Luke 2:46-49).

10. Goes to future kingdom - Jesus entered triumphally into Jerusalem during the week of Passover.

11. Is victor over king, giant dragon, or wild beast - Jesus was victorious over Satan, who was the king (Luke 4:6), the giant dragon (Revelation 12:7-10), and the animator of the wild beast (Revelation 13:1-2).

12. Marries a princess, often the daughter of predecessor - Jesus marries His bride, the church, which He redeemed from Satan (Romans 7:4; Acts 20:28; Ephesians 5:25-27; Revelation 19:6-10).

13. Becomes king - *"And I saw heaven opened, and behold a white horse; and he that sat upon him was called Faithful and True, and in righteousness he doth judge and make war. His eyes were as a flame of fire, and on his head were many crowns; and he had a name written, that no man knew, but he himself. And he was clothed with a vesture dipped in blood: and his name is called The Word of God. And the armies which were in heaven followed him upon white horses, clothed in fine linen, white and clean. And out of his mouth goeth a sharp sword, that with it he should smite the nations: and he shall rule them with a rod of iron: and he treadeth the winepress of the fierceness and wrath of Almighty God. And he hath on his vesture and on his thigh a name written, KING OF KINGS, AND LORD OF LORDS." Revelation 19:11-16.*

The Spiritual Struggle: God vs. Satan.

Satan tempted Adam and Eve in the Garden of Eden apparently to take revenge against God. God had cast him out of the celestial sphere and Satan subtly sabotaged God's creation (Luke 10:18; Revelation 12:12; Isaiah 14:12- 17; Genesis 3:1).

Satan was successful in his deception of Eve and Adam, and he gained the mastery of the world through their error (2 Corinthians 4:3-4; Luke 4:6). But God sent a baby, the seed of a woman, to crush his head. That child was Jesus (Genesis 3:15).

This supernatural drama is played out on a physical level because the prizes are the hearts and minds of people. Satan comes to blind people to spiritual realities and to keep them in darkness. Jesus comes to take back the spirits of people who were dead under Satan's rule: *"Forasmuch then as the children are partakers of flesh and blood, he also himself likewise took part of the same; that through death he might destroy him that had the power of death, that is, the devil; And deliver them who through fear of death were all their lifetime subject to bondage." Hebrews 2:14,15. "To open their eyes, and to turn them from darkness to light, and from the power of Satan unto God, that they may receive forgiveness of sins, and inheritance among them which are sanctified by faith that is in me." Acts 26:18.* Even the angels are an audience to this (1 Peter 1:10-12).

The Psychological Struggle: Spirit vs. Flesh.

Adam and Eve responded to Satan's temptation through the physical senses. In doing so, they corrupted the input from their spiritual senses by bringing the physical sense data to a higher level of importance. Satan acquired an ally within people: the "flesh." The flesh responds to physical sense data and is subject to spiritual deception. This is the "old man" of Paul's letters.

The old man sits as a king on the throne of the psyche. He is Satan's representative in our mind, will, and emotions. But Jesus came to energize and give birth to the "new man." He came to give us a spiritual birth and to take back the psyche by a regenerated spirit: *"There was a man of the Pharisees, named Nicodemus, a ruler of the Jews: The same came to Jesus by night, and said unto him, Rabbi, we know that thou art a teacher come from God: for no man can do these miracles that thou doest, except God be with him. Jesus answered and said unto him, Verily, verily, I say unto thee, Except a man be born again, he cannot see the kingdom of God. Nicodemus saith unto him, How can a man be born when he is old? can he enter the second time into his mother's womb, and be born? Jesus answered, Verily, verily, I say unto thee, Except a man be born of water and of the Spirit, he cannot enter into the kingdom of God. That which is born of the flesh is flesh; and that which is born of the Spirit is spirit." John 3:1-6.*

The old man has had time to develop and grow strong in us. He is the strong man in his house: *"Or else how can one enter into a strong man's house, and spoil his goods, except he first bind the strong man? and then he will spoil his house." Matthew 12:29.* We have had him since birth (Ephesians 2:2-3). But Jesus brought to life the new man: the spiritual nature to fight the strong man: *"And you hath he quickened, who were dead in trespasses and sins;" Ephesians 2:1. "That ye put off concerning the former conversation the old man, which is corrupt according to the deceitful lusts; And be renewed in the spirit of your mind; And that ye put on the new man, which after God is created in righteousness and true holiness." Ephesians 4:22-24.*

The new man is a babe at the beginning. He begins to grow just as the old man has done for years. We are exhorted to feed this babe so he can be strong: *"As newborn babes, desire the sincere milk of the word, that ye may grow thereby:" 1 Peter 2:2.* At first, the old man is much stronger and can easily defeat the babe. If the babe is not fed, protected, and developed, he will be crushed. Galatians 5:16-17 tells us to "walk in the spirit." In other words, respond to the renewed spiritual senses. This is how the new man develops muscle.

The introduction of the new man into the psyche is an important part of how Jesus came to "destroy the works of the devil" (1 John 3:8). Romans 6:6-11 teaches us to reckon our old man to be dead in order to gain a psychological advantage over him.

Conclusion

Jesus, the eternal hero, slayed the dragon on a physical level by His earthly life, on a spiritual level by regaining the lost kingdom, and on a psychological level by creating the new man to defeat the old man.

And, there is also a personal level: *"Be ye therefore followers of God, as dear children; And walk in love, as Christ also hath loved us, and hath given himself for us an offering and a sacrifice to God for a sweetsmelling savour." Ephesians 5:1,2.* The Greek for follower is "mimetes,"[5] which comes from "mimos," a mime. Therefore we are to copy the actions of God. Specifically, to love others as Christ loves us. And how does He love us? By giving himself as an offering and sacrifice. The hero gives his life for others: *"This is my commandment, That ye love one another, as I have loved you. Greater love hath no man than this, that a man lay down his life for his friends." John 15:12,13. "And he said to them all, If any man will come after me, let him deny himself, and take up his cross daily, and follow me." Luke 9:23.*

I believe every person has a spiritual destiny. If this were not so, we would not be told to imitate Jesus. Every person who dedicates his or her life to God receives a vision of God's glorious blessing. Each one has a treasure to bring back from the hero's journey and share. If the hero fails, everyone suffers.

Satan hates all children. He knows each one has the potential to tear down his work. He hated the first child because of prophecy (Genesis 3: 15), and he's hated every one since. He is the father-king who is threatened by the birth of potential heroes. Abortion in our day is evidence of Satan's hatred of children: snuff them out before they get here, or better yet, convince people that children are a burden instead of a blessing so they won't have them. But, God teaches children are a blessing: *"Lo, children are an heritage of the LORD: and the fruit of the womb is his reward. As arrows are in the hand of a mighty man; so are children of the youth. Happy is the man that hath his quiver full of them: they shall not be ashamed, but they shall speak with the enemies in the gate." Psalms 127:3-5.*

Satan's other devices to destroy potential heroes include broken homes, sexual abuse, physical abuse, neglect, etc. In the teenage years he conquers young people with guilt over sexual sins and immorality: *"None that go unto her return again, neither take they hold of the paths of life." Proverbs 2:19.* Teenagers are thus immunized against spiritual development.

If Satan hates physical children, he hates spiritual children even more. He blinds the eyes of people to keep them from entering the spiritual dimension through Jesus Christ: *"But if our gospel be hid, it is hid to them that are lost: In whom the god of this world hath blinded the minds of them which believe not, lest the light of the glorious gospel of Christ, who is the image of God, should shine unto them." 2 Corinthians 4:3,4.* He walks about, seeking whom he may devour (1 Peter 5:8). He tries to stop spiritual development every step of the way.

Satan wants to protect his ally, the old man, in every one of us. He resists the birth and growth of the new man.

In the remaining chapters, I will outline spiritual development from birth to maturity. I pray you will take the challenge to learn, grow and respond to crises. Because so few take this journey, our churches are weak, our families are weak, and our own hearts are weak. Most do not grow to maturity because so few lead. I pray you will be a mime of Christ: *"Strengthen ye the weak hands, and confirm the feeble knees. Say to them that are of a fearful heart, Be strong, fear not: behold, your God will come with vengeance, even God with a recompence; he will come and save you. Then the eyes of the blind shall be opened, and the ears of the deaf shall be unstopped. Then shall the lame man leap as an hart, and the tongue of the dumb sing: for in the wilderness shall waters break out, and streams in the desert. And the parched ground shall become a pool, and the thirsty land springs of water: in the habitation of dragons, where each lay, shall be grass with reeds and rushes. And an highway shall be there, and a way, and it shall be called The way of holiness; the unclean shall not pass over it; but it shall be for those: the wayfaring men, though fools, shall not err therein." Isaiah 35:3-8.*

PART 2

Stages of Spiritual Growth

CHAPTER 7

Spiritual Birth

FROM May to October in the holy land there is no rain and clouds rarely form.[1] Instead, heavy dew descends on the earth every night and provides refreshment to all life.[2]The dew protects those who would perish without moisture. The dew is like God's shielding of the children who don't yet understand His ways or how to enter the spiritual dimension. The lonely cloud represents God's pledge that the first drops of rain from the spiritual world are on the way.

The First Drops

Piaget's theories of intelligence lead us to believe that very young children's evaluations of spiritual matters are modest. Common experience confirms this. To explain why, I will first define the terms animism and finalism, which partly make up the worldview of the young child. Then I will show how children begin at around age seven to ask the questions that can lead to a stronger spiritual understanding.

Animism is an immature worldview, common to children under or around seven years of age, that attributes living qualities to all things and events. The young child doesn't distinguish inanimate from animate, instinctual from purposeful, unconscious from conscious. Why did that leaf fall? Did it want to? Does that big rock like for you to sit on it? Is that car thirsty? Is that why we had to stop for gas? Animism is why stories like *Alice In Wonderland* are so appealing.

Animism implies motivation. Everything thing that moves seems to have power within, like an energizer. The thing seems to have its own intentions. The young child does not realize forces from without sometimes cause change without the consent of the changee.

Finalism is the child's doctrine of cause. To a child cause is inevitably attributed to result. The result is the reason for the event. Why does the water in the rivers run into the sea? To fill it up. But why then, don't the rivers run dry? Why do trees have leaves? To keep them warm. Won't they get cold without them? The child doesn't understand that rain refills the rivers, because he is only looking at the river's final intentions. The first time he sees a tree's leaves fall, he doesn't believe they will come back, because they must have had a good reason to leave the tree, or the tree didn't want them anymore.

Children don't understand chance the same as adults. They don't know chance events can cause rivers and leaves to change against their will. Rivers change course because of storms, erosion, and manmade obstacles. The tree with leaves naturally has them unless it is diseased, or infested with gypsy moths, it is winter, a fire has charred it, etc. The young child believes inanimate objects have life and moving objects act on their own.[3]

To a child, "life is a perfectly normal phenomenon, without any elements of surprise (*or chance*) in it, up till the moment when the child takes cognizance of the difference between life and death. From this moment, the idea of death sets the child's curiosity in action, precisely because, if every cause is coupled with a motive, then death calls for a special explanation."[4] Why did he leave? Why did he want to die? It is beyond the young child's view of the world that anything would not choose life. Death begins a search for causes from the outside. Contemplating death is the door of spiritual life. Piaget states it is those questions that "refer to death that will cause the child to leave behind him the stage of pure finalism, and to acquire the notion of...chance."[5]

This marks the beginning of Piaget's stage of concrete operational thought. Around age seven, children learn to see cause and effect and leave animistic thinking. They come to understand the relationships among variables impacting an event. They start to think logically. Nevertheless, their logic is still limited to only what they can see, hear, touch, taste, and smell. They are not yet able to compare ideas.

I grew up in a Christian home. I had many questions about conversion at six or seven. Yet, it was not until I *saw* a dramatic depiction of the death, burial, and resurrection of Christ that I finally understood the implications of His sacrifice. A group of teenagers from our church re-enacted Christ's passion in a play on a Sunday night. Along with me there were also several other children that professed faith in Christ that night. I was eight years old.

Animism is the doctrine of New Agers. Pantheism demands it.[6] Everything is divine and the divine is in everything. This is a pre-seven-year-old philosophy. Perhaps New Agers are people who got stuck at the door of the spiritual dimension.

When they began to understand that death is an interruption of the will, they feared the power that interrupted it. They were shot by Satan's arrows at the wicket gate.[7] Then they adopted the safe and appealing philosophy of Pantheism: the universe is all there is and it survives on its own.

These people are like the lover that loves his feelings about his lady more than the lady. They would rather look at a picture of the beloved than the beloved. They wait by the mailbox for letters from far away with pictures and descriptions, but they do not ever intend to go to that far country. This is the essence of idolatry, to love the symbols, myths, and images of God more than God Himself. And why do they love pictures more? Because pictures don't require anything. They are only to be looked at and admired. *"And we know that the Son of God is come, and hath given us an understanding, that we may know him that is true, and we are in him that is true, even in his Son Jesus Christ. This is the true God, and eternal life. Little children, keep yourselves from idols. Amen." 1 John 5:20,21.*

Instead of entering the spiritual realm on God's terms, New Agers learn to flirt with demonic powers while staying (they think) on this side. They become spiritually promiscuous. I think that's the meaning of the terms "fornication"[8]and "whoredom"[9]applied to spiritual matters in the scriptures. Babylon, the seat of false religion, is called the *"MOTHER OF HARLOTS AND ABOMINATIONS OF THE EARTH." Revelation 17:5.*

It's not surprising to those who study the Bible; the notion that looking at death begins the quest for meaning: *"It is better to go to the house of mourning, than to go to the house of feasting: for that is the end of all men; and the living will lay it to his heart." Ecclesiastes 7:2.*

Even the ancient Babylonians understood that death inspired the search for everlasting life. Gilgamesh went to find Utnapishtim (the Babylonian Noah) after the death of his friend Enkidu. He went because of his fear: "How can I rest, how can I be at peace? Despair is in my heart. What my brother is now, that shall I be when I am dead. Because I am afraid of death I will go as best I can to find Utnapishtim whom they call the Faraway, for he has entered the assembly of the gods... and to him alone of men they gave everlasting life."[10]Gilgamesh hoped to lay hold of eternal life.

Robert Coles presented children's conceptions of death in his book, *The Spiritual Life of Children.* He gave examples of children considering death and how that consideration led to spiritual speculations. Showing a fourth grade art history class *The Doctor* by Sir Luke Fildes (1844-1927) sparked a serious conversation: "In it, a physician sits by the bed (a makeshift arrangement of chairs, actually) of an ailing child; the doctor's left hand is held to his beard-covered chin. On a table nearby, a cup and a spoon are to be seen, and a bottle of medicine. The child (most likely a girl because of her longish hair) is sleeping, her left arm outstretched, her right arm on top of her chest, a blanket covering her. In the background, the dim outline of a man, presumably the child's father, can be discerned. The children are unusually hushed once they see the slide of that sickbed scene, and they refrain from immediate comment. I have learned to ask nothing, to say nothing. Eventually the questions always come - inquiries that, of course, make their own statements."[11] He went on to say that the children speculate on whether the girl is dying, whether the doctor will be able to heal her, and whether God will hear prayers on her behalf and perhaps heal her.

Coles said, "For children, even those quite healthy and never before seriously sick, death has a powerful and continuing meaning. They hear what their elders hear in sermons and stories, in songs, in spiritual warnings. They also experience death personally when grandparents and other people depart."[12]

In his book, Dr. Coles related a very personal encounter with death by an eleven-year-old boy named Tony. Tony was a polio victim before the Salk vaccine was available and had to be put on an "iron lung" respirator. Dr. Coles recorded some of Tony's remarks: "The priest says pray, but I don't feel like praying. My uncle (a high school athletic coach) says I should 'keep smiling' and I'll get through it all. I try to - I get low, and then I talk myself out of it. But a lot of the time I'm thinking to myself - if you go, Tony, then where will you go to? I ask and ask. I know I'll never get the answer until I go, and I don't want to go, not until I'm as old as my grandpa! But I might, so I should be wondering, I guess."[13]Dr. Coles commented on Tony's spiritual introspection by saying, "His spirituality was, I think, evoked by the distinct possibility of death."[14]

Maybe it's because meditation on death is integral to the beginning of the hero's journey that so many are afraid to embark. Nevertheless, the Bible teaches the way to understand life is through understanding death: *"I am crucified with Christ: nevertheless I live; yet not I, but Christ liveth in me: and the life which I now live in the flesh I live by the faith of the Son of God, who loved me, and gave himself for me." Galatians 2:20. "And he said to them all, If any man will come after me, let him deny himself, and take up his cross daily, and follow me. For whosoever will save his life shall lose it: but whosoever will lose his life for my sake, the same shall save it. For what is a man advantaged, if he gain the whole world, and lose himself, or be cast away?" Luke 9:23-25.*

Learning Tasks

Children soon learn that life can be interrupted and cut short by divine intervention. This can lead them to recognize the authority of God and responsibility toward Him. Indeed, these are the first two learning tasks of spiritual birth. When people become aware of God's authority and responsibility to Him they take the first steps toward spiritual growth. They are then compelled to the conviction that they don't live up to His standards, because, after all, people can't even live up to human standards, and God must be more perfect than us. The search for a Savior begins with these understandings.

The Four Learning Tasks of Spiritual Birth

1. Recognizing God's Authority
2. Recognizing our Responsibility to Him
3. Recognizing our Failure to Live up to His Standards
4. Recognizing our Need for a Savior

Although a child the age of seven or so is cognitively capable of completing these tasks, very few can articulate the experience. Thankfully, we have men from history and stories whose lives have charted the process of conversion. Even as adults, they still went through the same spiritual awakening as children.

In this section I will show the progress of spiritual education in the lives of Charles Colson, C.S. Lewis, John Bunyan, and Robinson Crusoe.

Charles Colson

Perhaps the most scrutinized conversion of our time is the case of Charles Colson. He was a lawyer and the Special Counsel to the president under Richard Nixon. He was Nixon's right hand man. Because of his reputation for ruthlessness and his nickname, the "Nixon hatchet-man," Colson was a suspect from the beginning of the Watergate scandal. He was ultimately convicted of obstruction of justice in the Daniel Ellsberg incident. Even though it is questionable whether Colson committed a crime, he confessed to a "crime of conscience."[15]

In the midst of the Watergate hearings, Colson accepted Christ as his Savior. It was a media feast. On December 17, 1973, the story of Charles Colson's conversion appeared in the *Los Angeles Times* and the *New York Times*. Eric Sevaried of CBS devoted his entire commentary to it. Colson was later interviewed on *60 Minutes* by Mike Wallace, and by Barbara Walters for the *Today Show*.

In his book, *Born Again,* Colson explained how he came to accept Christ. His curiosity was sparked when he noticed the change in his friend, Tom Phillips, president of the Raytheon Company, after Phillip's conversion to Christianity. Colson went to meet with Mr. Phillips, and after their conversation, Phillips gave him a copy of *Mere Christianity* by C.S. Lewis. Colson went through all four learning tasks in that meeting.

In these quotes from *Born Again*, I will point out the beginning of each new phase. Some of it quotes from *Mere Christianity* and some is from Colson's own thoughts:[16]

1. God's Authority: "In God you come up against something which is in every respect immeasurably superior to yourself. Unless you know God as that - and, therefore, know yourself as nothing in comparison - you do not know God at all. As long as you are proud you cannot know God. A proud man is always looking down on things and people: and of course, as long as you are looking down, you cannot see something that is above you."[17]
2. Responsibility to Him: "Suddenly I felt naked and unclean, my bravado defenses gone. I was exposed; unprotected, for Lewis's words were describing me. As he continued, one passage in particular seemed to sum up what had happened to all of us at the White House: 'for Pride is spiritual cancer: it eats up the very possibility of love, or contentment, or even common sense.'"[18]
3. Failure to live up to His standards: "Just as a man about to die is supposed to see flash before him, sequence by sequence, the high points of life, so, as Tom's voice read on that August evening, key events in my life paraded before me as if projected in a screen. Things I hadn't thought about in years - my graduation speech at prep school - being 'good enough' for the marines - my first marriage, into the 'right' family - sitting on the Jaycees dais while civic leader after civic leader praised me as the outstanding young man of Boston - then to the White House - the clawing and straining for status and position - 'Mr. Colson, the President is calling - Mr. Colson, the President wants to see you right away.'

   "For some reason I thought of an incident after the 1972 election when a reporter, an old Nixon nemesis, came by my office and contritely asked what he could do to get in the good graces of the White House. I suggested that he try 'slashing his wrists.' I meant it as a joke, of course, but also to make him squirm. It was the arrogance of the victor over an enemy brought to submission.

"Now, sitting there on the dimly lit porch, my self-centered past was washing over me in waves. It was painful. Agony. Desperately I tried to defend myself. What about my sacrifices for government services, the giving up of a big income, putting my stocks into a blind trust? The truth, I saw in an instant, was that I wanted the position in the White House more than I'd wanted money. There was no sacrifice. And the more I had talked about my own sacrifices, the more I was really trying to build myself up in the eyes of others. I would eagerly have given up everything I'd ever earned to prove myself at the mountaintop of government. It was pride - Lewis's 'great sin' - that had propelled me through life."

In those brief moments while Tom read, I saw myself as I never had before. And the picture was ugly.[19]

4. Need for a savior: "'How about it, Chuck?' Tom's question jarred me out of my trance. I knew precisely what he meant. Was I ready to make the leap of faith as he had in New York, to 'accept' Christ?"

Charles Colson still had not become a Christian, but he had reached the crisis point of spiritual birth.

C. S. Lewis

Lewis' lonely cloud was joy. His experience of joy and search for enduring joy drew him toward the door of the spiritual dimension. In his book, *Surprised By Joy,* he told of simple early encounters that launched his life long quest: the smell and sight of a flowering currant bush on a summer day, the idea of Autumn drawn from the pages of a book, and the feeling of the vastness of the northern sky which came through poetic work.[20]

Of these experiences Lewis said, "It was something quite different from ordinary life and even from ordinary pleasure; something, as they would say, 'in another dimension.' ... For those who are still disposed to proceed I will only underline the quality common to the three experiences; it is that of an unsatisfied desire which is itself satisfaction. I call it Joy, which is here a technical term and must be sharply distinguished from Happiness and Pleasure. Joy (in my sense) has indeed one characteristic, and one only, in common with them, the fact that anyone who has experienced it will want it again.... I doubt whether anyone who has tasted it would ever, if both were in his power, exchange it for all the pleasures in the world."[21]These moments "are not the thing in itself; they are only the scent of a flower we have not found, the echo of a tune we have not heard, news from a country we have never yet visited."[22]

In all his experiences and philosophical studies Lewis continually sought lasting joy, but it would never stay. It would slip away artfully like a butterfly being chased with a net. C.S. Lewis relates, "to 'get it again' became my constant endeavor; while reading every poem, hearing every piece of music, going for every walk, I stood anxious sentinel at my own mind to watch whether the blessed moment was beginning and to endeavor to retain it if it did."[23]

Nevertheless, during his quest, Mr. Lewis rejected Christianity. He did not want to turn over his will to a higher power: "But, of course, what mattered most of all was my deep-seated hatred of authority, my monstrous individualism, my lawlessness. No word in my vocabulary expressed deeper hatred than the word *Interference*. But Christianity placed at the center what then seemed to me a transcendental Interferer."[24] Lewis tried to get away from God's authority by vain philosophies, but everywhere he turned God had laid traps for him.[25]

C.S. Lewis eventually gave in to God's insistence. He was intellectually and emotionally forced to accept God's authority by reason and conscience: "In the Trinity Term of 1929 I gave in, and admitted that God was God, and knelt and prayed: perhaps, that night, the most dejected and reluctant convert in all England."[26] Learning task No. 1 had been accomplished.

In Lewis's logical mind, to accept the authority of God was also to understand responsibility to Him. Learning task No. 2: "God was to be obeyed simply because he was God... He had taught me how a thing can be revered not for what it can do but for what it is in itself. That is why, though it was a terror, it was no surprise to learn that God is to be obeyed because of what he is in Himself. If you ask why we should obey God, in the last resort the answer is, 'I am.'"[27]

C.S. Lewis also recognized his failure to live up to God's standards: Learning task No. 3. In *Mere Christianity*, Book III, "The Great Sin," Lewis talked about pride being "the complete anti-God state of mind." We already know it was his pride that caused him to fear the Great Interferer. And, through hearing this section of *Mere Christianity*, Charles Colson was convicted of his need for a savior.

Learning task No. 4: recognizing the need for a savior. Mr. Lewis examined all the religions of the world, and found that only one "full-grown." He discovered that Jesus of Nazareth was the fulfillment of the world's savior myths and an actual historical person. His learning and logic drove him to conclude that Jesus Christ is the Son of God.

John Bunyan

John Bunyan finished the masterpiece allegory of spiritual growth, *The Pilgrims Progress,* in 1678. He also authored his own spiritual autobiography *Grace Abounding: To the Chief of Sinners,* which outlines his progress from a mischievous youth to a champion for Christ.

Bunyan recognized God's authority from the beginning. Even in the midst of his debauched and dissolute life he respected piety: "I was in the height of vanity, yet upon hearing one swear that was reckoned for a religious man, it had so great an impact upon my spirit that it made my heart ache."[28] He reflected the culture of his day, which had a healthy fear of God.

Bunyan married a Christian woman and went to church to keep her happy. He enjoyed the trappings and the rituals. Yet godliness remained a mystery to him. He recalls the first time he recognized his responsibility to God: "But one day, among all the sermons our parson made, his subject was the treatment of the Sabbath day and of the evil of breaking that, either with labor, sports, or otherwise... Wherefore I fell in my conscience under this sermon, thinking and believing that he made that sermon on purpose to show me my evil-doing."

Nevertheless, John Bunyan erred the same as many, he felt in his mind he was too lost to be saved: "I had been a great and grievous sinner, and it was now too late for me to look toward heaven, for Christ would not forgive me nor pardon my transgressions... I resolved in my mind to go on in sin, because I reasoned, if the case be thus, my state is surely miserable - miserable if I leave my sins and miserable if I follow them. I can but be damned; and if it must be so, I might as well be damned for many sins as be damned for few."

A month later he emotionally recognized his failure to live up to God's standards at the reproof of an ungodly wretch of a woman. He was cursing so heartily it hurt even her ears. After that he tried reforming himself.

His attitude at the time was this: "Yes, to relate it in my own way, I thought no man in England could please God better than I. But, poor wretch that I was, I was all this while ignorant of Jesus Christ, going about to establish my own righteousness, in which I would have perished had not God in mercy showed me more of my state by nature."

Mr. Bunyan went several years before he was convinced of his need for the Savior and that Jesus would really save him. "I remember that one day, as I was traveling into the country and musing on the wickedness and blasphemy of my heart, and considering the enmity that was in me to God, that scripture came into my mind *'And, having made peace through the blood of his cross' Colossians*

1:20. By this I was made to see, both again and again, that God and my soul were friends by His blood. Yes, I saw that the justice of God and my sinful soul could embrace and kiss each other, through His blood. This was a good day to me; I hope I shall never forget it."

Robinson Crusoe

Robinson Crusoe as a teenager rejected a career in law, and set his heart to be a sailor. He went to sea against the commands of his father and the entreaties of his mother. His father prophesied misery to the young man. At last, after several mishaps and false starts, he was hopelessly shipwrecked alone on an island in the Caribbean.

On the "Island of Despair" God rebuked Robinson Crusoe. He had been shipwrecked for about ten months when the jungle fever possessed him. It was then, in his dreams and deliriums, that God revealed His authority: "I thought that I was sitting on the ground, on the outside of my wall, where I sat when the storm blew after the earthquake, and that I saw a man descend from a great black cloud, in a bright flame of fire, and light upon the ground. He was all over as bright as a flame, so that I could but just bear to look towards him; his countenance was most inexpressibly dreadful, impossible for words to describe; when he stepped upon the ground with his feet, I thought the earth trembled, just as it had done before in the earthquake, and all the air looked, to my apprehension, as if it had been filled with flashes of fire."[29]

"He was no sooner landed upon the earth but he moved forwards toward me, with a long spear or weapon in his hand, to kill me; and when he came he spoke to me, or I heard a voice so terrible, that it is impossible to express the terror of it; all that I can say I understood was this: 'Seeing all these things have not brought thee to repentance, now thou shalt die.' At which words, I thought he lifted up the spear that was in his hand to kill me."

It was only after this dream that Robinson Crusoe recognized his responsibility to God: "I began to reproach myself with my past life, in which I had so evidently, by uncommon wickedness, provoked the justice of God to lay me under uncommon strokes, and to deal with me in so vindictive a manner."

Crusoe began to consider the works of God's hands: "we are all made by some secret Power who formed the earth and the sea, the air and the sky; and who is that?… If God has made all these things, He guides and governs them all, and all things that concern them; for the Power that could make all things must certainly have power to guide and direct them."

Robinson was now ready for his third lesson: recognizing his failure to live up to God's standards. He thought, *Why has God done this to me? What have I done to be thus used?* He said, "my conscience presently checked me in that inquiry, as if I had blasphemed, and me thought it spoke to me like a voice: WRETCH! dost thou ask what thou hast done? Look back upon a dreadful misspent life and ask thyself what thou hast not done; ask, why is it that thou wert not long ago destroyed? Why wert thou not drowned in Yarmouth Roads? Killed in the fight when the ship was taken by the Sallee man-of-war? Devoured by the wild beasts on the coast of Africa? Or drowned here, when all the crew perished but thyself? Dost thou ask, what have I done?"

After about a week, Robinson recovered from his sickness and began to search the scriptures for answers. He quickly recognized his need for a savior, or perhaps he already had and was searching for Him: "In the morning I took the Bible, and beginning at the New Testament, I began seriously to read it, and imposed upon myself to read a while every morning and every night, not tying myself to the number of chapters, but as long as my thoughts should engage me. It was not long after I set seriously to this work but I found my heart more deeply and sincerely affected with the wickedness of my past life. The impression of my dream revived, and the words, 'All these things have not brought thee to repentance,' ran seriously in my thoughts. I was earnestly begging of God to give me repentance, when it happened providentially the very day that reading the Scripture, I came to these words, 'He is exalted a Prince and a Savior, to give repentance, and to give remission.'"

Crisis

"There was a man of the Pharisees, named Nicodemus, a ruler of the Jews: The same came to Jesus by night, and said unto him, Rabbi, we know that thou art a teacher come from God: for no man can do these miracles that thou doest, except God be with him." John 3:1,2.

Nicodemus knew the prophecy that Moses had given, "*The LORD thy God will raise up unto thee a Prophet from the midst of thee, of thy brethren, like unto me; unto him ye shall hearken;*" *Deuteronomy 18:15.* The working of miracles was the connection between Moses and the Prophet: *"Then those men, when they had seen the miracle that Jesus did, said, This is of a truth that prophet that should come into the world." John 6:14. (Acts 3:18-23).*

Nicodemus was in essence asking, are you the Messiah? the Savior? the Prophet? The Jews of the day weren't really sure what the Messiah would be like.

They were looking for the Christ's earthly kingdom, which will come only at the end of time, at Jesus' second coming (John 1:19-25). Nicodemus' questions indicate his progress toward spiritual birth. As a Jewish scholar he recognized God's authority and his responsibility toward Him. He also recognized his need for a savior since he was inquiring about Jesus' identity.

Jesus responded by convincing Nicodemus of the crisis of spiritual birth: *"Jesus answered and said unto him, Verily, verily, I say unto thee, Except a man be born again, he cannot see the kingdom of God." John 3:3.*

"Nicodemus saith unto him, How can a man be born when he is old? can he enter the second time into his mother's womb, and be born?" John 3:4. Nicodemus at first ignored the implication of a spiritual birth. He tried to keep the conversation on a physical level.

"Jesus answered, Verily, verily, I say unto thee, Except a man be born of water and of the Spirit, he cannot enter into the kingdom of God. That which is born of the flesh is flesh; and that which is born of the Spirit is spirit. Marvel not that I said unto thee, Ye must be born again." John 3:5-7. Our first birth was not defective. That's not why we must be born again. We need to be born the second time, the spiritual birth. The physical nature has a birth, and the spiritual nature, much later, has a birth.

This is the crisis. The growing spiritual embryo cannot progress anymore till it's born. If it is not born, it will die. The big difference between physical birth and spiritual birth is that spiritual birth is a choice. We can't imagine a baby that does not want to be born, but we can imagine a person refusing to enter the spiritual world.

Spiritual birth is beyond the understanding of the natural man (the un-spiritually-born): *"But the natural man receiveth not the things of the Spirit of God: for they are foolishness unto him: neither can he know them, because they are spiritually discerned."1Corinthians2:14.* Spiritual birth can only be discerned through spiritual means, through metaphors: *"The wind bloweth where it listeth, and thou hearest the sound thereof, but canst not tell whence it cometh, and whither it goeth: so is every one that is born of the Spirit. Nicodemus answered and said unto him, How can these things be? Jesus answered and said unto him, Art thou a master of Israel, and knowest not these things? Verily, verily, I say unto thee, We speak that we do know, and testify that we have seen; and ye receive not our witness. If I have told you earthly things, and ye believe not, how shall ye believe, if I tell you of heavenly things?" John 3:8-12.*

Jesus then showed Nicodemus why He is the only true Savior: *"And no man hath ascended up to heaven, but he that came down from heaven, even the Son of man which is in heaven. And as Moses lifted up the serpent in the wilderness, even so must the Son of man be lifted up: That whosoever believeth in him should not perish, but have eternal life. For God so loved the world, that he gave his only begotten Son, that whosoever believeth in him should not perish, but have everlasting life." John 3:13-16.* No person has ever reached God through self-effort: New Age, Pantheism, Self-Actualization. God must come down from outside the universe to reach people. Jesus identified Himself as the Savior by showing the wilderness serpent as a metaphor for Himself. Jesus prophesied His own sacrifice and its saving power.

Although these scriptures do not record Nicodemus' acceptance of Jesus, I believe he was later saved. When the chief priests and Pharisees sent officers to capture Jesus, Nicodemus defended Him. The Pharisees made two mistakes. They assumed no ruler had believed in Jesus, and they did not understand their law as a schoolmaster to lead them to Christ: *"Then came the officers to the chief priests and Pharisees; and they said unto them, Why have ye not brought him? The officers answered, Never man spake like this man. Then answered them the Pharisees, Are ye also deceived? Have any of the rulers or of the Pharisees believed on him? But this people who knoweth not the law are cursed. Nicodemus saith unto them, (he that came to Jesus by night, being one of them,) Doth our law judge any man, before it hear him, and know what he doeth?" John 7:45-51.*

After Jesus' death, Joseph of Arimathea, a member of the ruling council of the Jews, and a secret disciple, prepared and buried the body. Nicodemus assisted him in this, indicating that he was a disciple also. It's marvelous that while Jesus' twelve ran away for fear, two of the rulers, who risked their jobs and their lives, came forward to help with His burial (John 19:38-42).

Robinson Crusoe passed through his crisis of spiritual birth quickly. As soon as he read the scripture that Jesus had been exalted to be a "Prince and a Savior, to give repentance and to give remission," he accepted God's gift: "I threw down the book, and with my heart as well as my hands lifted up to Heaven, in a kind of ecstasy of joy, I cried out aloud, 'Jesus, Thou Son of David, Jesus, Thou exalted Prince and Savior, give me repentance!'"

John Bunyan also went immediately from his recognition of Christ to salvation. Hebrews 2:14-15 became his confirmation: *"Forasmuch then as the children are partakers of flesh and blood, he also himself likewise took part of the same; that through death he might destroy him that had the power of death, that is, the devil; And deliver them who through fear of death were all their lifetime subject to bondage." Hebrews 2:14,15.* He said, "I thought that the glory of these words was then so weighty on me, that I was once or twice ready to faint as I sat, yet not with grief and trouble, but with solid joy and peace."

For C.S. Lewis, the intellectual understanding that Jesus was indeed the Son of God brought him to the crisis. The logic of the work of God backed him into a corner. He called himself "the most dejected and reluctant convert in all of England." He saw God's invasion into his mind and soul as unavoidable.

To such a man, failure to accept truth when it is revealed is unthinkable; to live a lie is impossible. In *The Pilgrim's Regress*, which is an allegorical autobiography, Lewis' hero John is coerced by Reason and Death to descend a steep cliff down to Mother Kirk (Christianity) or else be thrown down. When John reaches the bottom of the chasm he says to Mother Kirk, "I have come to give myself up."[30]

Charles Colson had been led to the crisis point but his own human reasoning guarded the threshold. The meeting with Tom Phillips had touched his emotions but he lacked an intellectual understanding of "accepting Christ." He and his wife rented a cottage on the sea in Maine and there Colson studied *Mere Christianity*. He hoped it might explain his emotional experience, but instead he quickly found a persuasive, intellectual, and logical argument for Christianity and "accepting Christ."

Colson explained the process of spiritual birth. He described the learning tasks and the crisis: "Each of the steps I'd labored through was an essential building block to get to this point, but once I had, the others seemed almost irrelevant... I knew the time had come for me: I could not sidestep the central question Lewis (or God) had placed squarely before me. Was I to accept without reservations Jesus Christ as Lord of my life? It was like a gate before me. There was no way to walk around it. I would step through, or I would remain outside. A 'maybe' or 'I need more time' was kidding myself."[31]

At last, Colson walked through the gate: "And so, early that Friday morning, while I sat alone staring at the sea I love, words I had not been certain I could understand or say fell naturally from my lips: 'Lord Jesus, I believe You. I accept You. Please come into my life. I commit it to You.'"

Key - Faith

The "key" in scripture is used as a symbol or metaphor for special knowledge or divinely appointed power.[32] It is an appropriate symbol for the ability to pass through crises. The spiritual traveler must master the learning tasks and then open the door.

The *Road of Life* is a symbol game I play with many of my friends and acquaintances. In this game I give a series of universal symbols and ask the life traveler to react to them. One of the symbols is the "key." The key symbolizes knowledge and authority. In the game the traveler has the option to pick up a key to indicate his or her stance toward knowledge. Often the key is used to unlock gates or house doors.

Each stage of the spiritual life cycle has its key, and it takes a full set to be spiritually mature. The key to the entrance is faith: *"Now faith is the substance of things hoped for, the evidence of things not seen." Hebrews 11:1.* Faith is an infrared lens. It allows us to see the spiritual dimension that is otherwise obscure: *"(For we walk by faith, not by sight:)" 2 Corinthians 5:7.* The learning tasks convince us that He is. Faith in Jesus is the belief that He rewards those who turn the key to His treasure house: *"But without faith it is impossible to please him: for he that cometh to God must believe that he is, and that he is a rewarder of them that diligently seek him." Hebrews 11:6.*

Just as a keyhole is made so that only one type of key will work, so faith is the only type of key that will open the door to the spiritual world. There may be many copies of this key in people's hearts, but it always has the same grooves.[33]

We cannot learn magic words and do magic tricks to enter. We must use the only type of key given. All the gyrations and ceremonies of those who are disposed to perform will not budge God's door: *"Now to him that worketh is the reward not reckoned of grace, but of debt. But to him that worketh not, but believeth on him that justifieth the ungodly, his faith is counted for righteousness." Romans 4:4,5. (Romans 5:1-2; Ephesians 2:8-9).*

The Jews thought their law was the hoop they would jump through into God's kingdom. They didn't understand that their law was the mythology but Jesus Christ was the fact: *"Wherefore the law was our schoolmaster to bring us unto Christ, that we might be justified by faith." Galatians 3:24. "What shall we say then? That the Gentiles, which followed not after righteousness, have attained to righteousness, even the righteousness which is of faith. But Israel, which followed after the law of righteousness, hath not attained to the law of righteousness. Wherefore? Because they sought it not by faith, but as it were by the works of the law. For they stumbled at that stumblingstone; As it is written, Behold, I lay in Sion a stumblingstone and rock of offence: and whosoever believeth on him shall not be ashamed." Romans 9:30-33.*

Symbol - Water

Carl G. Jung, in his book *Man and His Symbols,* describes what a symbol is and does: "a word or an image is symbolic when it implies something more than its obvious and immediate meaning… As the mind explores the symbol, it is led to ideas that lie beyond the grasp of reason… Because there are innumerable things beyond the range of human understanding, we constantly use symbolic terms to represent concepts that we cannot define or fully comprehend. This is one reason why all religions employ symbolic language or images."[34] Jesus Himself taught that spiritual concepts could only be comprehended through symbols (John 3:8-12).

The symbol for spiritual birth is water. Water represents life and birth. The Word makes the connection between water and the new birth: *"Jesus answered, Verily, verily, I say unto thee, Except a man be born of water and of the Spirit, he cannot enter into the kingdom of God." John 3:5. "In the last day, that great day of the feast, Jesus stood and cried, saying, If any man thirst, let him come unto me, and drink. He that believeth on me, as the scripture hath said, out of his belly shall flow rivers of living water." John 7:37,38. (Isaiah 12:1-3).*

Several passages in the Old and New Testaments show the symbolism of water for life and spiritual birth. Water from the rocks showed God's life giving spiritual supply to the children of Israel: *"Behold, I will stand before thee there upon the rock in Horeb; and thou shalt smite the rock, and there shall come water out of it, that the people may drink. And Moses did so in the sight of the elders of Israel." Exodus 17:6. "And Moses lifted up his hand, and with his rod he smote the rock twice: and the water came out abundantly, and the congregation drank, and their beasts also." Numbers 20:11. "And did all drink the same spiritual drink: for they drank of that spiritual Rock that followed them: and that Rock was Christ." 1 Corinthians 10:4. (Isaiah 44:3-4; Ezekiel 16:3-9; John 4:7-14; Revelation 21:6; 22:1,17).*

Baptism is a water symbol. It is an outward symbol of passing the crisis of spiritual birth. It represents the work done in salvation. The believer becomes one with Christ on the cross and symbolically goes through the death, burial, and resurrection with Him. Baptism, like all good symbols, pictures to the mind this fathomless and mystical work. Baptism does not save, but it presents the work of salvation: *"Know ye not, that so many of us as were baptized into Jesus Christ were baptized into his death? Therefore we are buried with him by baptism into death: that like as Christ was raised up from the dead by the glory of the Father, even so we also should walk in newness of life. For if we have been planted together in the likeness of his death, we shall be also in the likeness of his resurrection: Knowing this, that our old man is crucified with him, that the body of sin might be destroyed, that henceforth we should not serve sin." Romans 6:3-6. "I am crucified with Christ: nevertheless I live; yet not I, but Christ liveth in me: and the life which I now live in the flesh I live by the faith of the Son of God, who loved me, and gave himself for me." Galatians 2:20.*

The Bible says directly that baptism is a figure of salvation: *"when once the longsuffering of God waited in the days of Noah, while the ark was a preparing, wherein few, that is, eight souls were saved by water. The like figure whereunto even baptism doth also now save us (not the putting away of the filth of the flesh, but the answer of a good conscience toward God,) by the resurrection of Jesus Christ:" 1 Peter 3:20,21.* The flood killed others, but it was a symbol of Noah's salvation. Noah and his family were destined to be rescued by God, and He chose water as the agent. In the same way, water is the metaphor for us. It does not wash the sins from our flesh, but it does show we have a good conscience toward God because of spiritual birth.

History of Israel

The history of Israel is an accurate road map of spiritual development: *"Now all these things happened unto them for ensamples: and they are written for our admonition, upon whom the ends of the world are come." 1 Corinthians 10:11.* From the time God appeared to Moses in the burning bush, He began to show us the way. God called Israel His child, and we can learn from the experience.

God also provided the patriarchs as examples of the way. The first was Abraham and his promise from God was the bridge between the patriarchs and the nation: *"And he said unto Abram, Know of a surety that thy seed shall be a stranger in a land that is not theirs, and shall serve them; and they shall afflict them four hundred years; And also that nation, whom they shall serve, will I judge: and afterward shall they come out with great substance. And thou shalt go to thy fathers in peace; thou shalt be buried in a good old age. But in the fourth generation they shall come hither again: for the iniquity of the Amorites is not yet full." Genesis 15:13-16.*

When God appeared to Moses, it was in response to this promise. Moses was keeping his father-in-law's flock of sheep at the mountain of God, a task he had done for decades. He suddenly saw a bush on fire, but that did not burn up. God called to him out of the bush and declared that He was the God of the patriarchs: Abraham, Isaac, and Jacob. God commissioned Moses to go back to Egypt and bring the children of Israel to the Promised Land.

"And Moses said unto God, Behold, when I come unto the children of Israel, and shall say unto them, The God of your fathers hath sent me unto you; and they shall say to me, What is his name? what shall I say unto them?

And God said unto Moses, I AM THAT I AM: and he said, Thus shalt thou say unto the children of Israel, I AM hath sent me unto you. And God said moreover unto Moses, Thus shalt thou say unto the children of Israel, The LORD God of your fathers, the God of Abraham, the God of Isaac, and the God of Jacob, hath sent me unto you: this is my name for ever, and this is my memorial unto all generations. Go, and gather the elders of Israel together, and say unto them, The LORD God of your fathers, the God of Abraham, of Isaac, and of Jacob, appeared unto me, saying, I have surely visited you, and seen that which is done to you in Egypt: And I have said, I will bring you up out of the affliction of Egypt unto the land of the Canaanites, and the Hittites, and the Amorites, and the Perizzites, and the Hivites, and the Jebusites, unto a land flowing with milk and honey. And they shall hearken to thy voice: and thou shalt come, thou and the elders of Israel, unto the king of Egypt, and ye shall say unto him, The LORD God of the Hebrews hath met with us: and now let us go, we beseech thee, three days' journey into the wilderness, that we may sacrifice to the LORD our God." Exodus 3:13-18.

God's name reminded the Israelites and proved to them His authority. His mention of Abraham, Isaac, and Jacob reminded them of their relationship and responsibility toward Him. The mention of a sacrifice in the wilderness reminded them of their failure to live up to His standards. Finally, Moses represented the savior they were looking for and expecting.[35]

We know the story. Moses and Aaron went before Pharaoh and pleaded for him to let the people go. When he hardened his heart, God judged Egypt with ten plagues. The last plague, Passover, pictured the crisis of spiritual birth because it required faith to escape and to begin a new life with the emerging nation: *"Then Moses called for all the elders of Israel, and said unto them, Draw out and take you a lamb according to your families, and kill the passover. And ye shall take a bunch of hyssop, and dip it in the blood that is in the bason, and strike the lintel and the two side posts with the blood that is in the bason; and none of you shall go out at the door of his house until the morning. For the LORD will pass through to smite the Egyptians; and when he seeth the blood upon the lintel, and on the two side posts, the LORD will pass over the door, and will not suffer the destroyer to come in unto your houses to smite you." Exodus 12:21-23.* *"And it came to pass, that at midnight the LORD smote all the firstborn in the land of Egypt, from the firstborn of Pharaoh that sat on his throne unto the firstborn of the captive that was in the dungeon; and all the firstborn of cattle. And Pharaoh rose up in the night, he, and all his servants, and all the Egyptians; and there was a great cry in Egypt; for there was not a house where there was not one dead. And he called for Moses and Aaron by night, and said, Rise up, and get you forth from among my people, both ye and the children of Israel; and go, serve the LORD, as ye have said." Exodus 12:29-31.*

In the remaining chapters I will continue the epic of the children of Israel and show how their journey symbolizes our own on the road to spiritual maturity.

CHAPTER 8

Spiritual Childhood

THE early rains descend on the Promised Land in October and November. No ploughing is done until the early rains because the ground is hard and resistant (Psalms 65:9-10). The farmers wait patiently and expectantly. Jeremiah explains what happens when the early rain is delayed: *"Because the ground is chapt, for there was no rain in the earth, the plowmen were ashamed, they covered their heads." Jeremiah 14:4.*

The early rains loosen the soil and prepare it for planting.[1] Hosea uses the early rain as a metaphor for God's instruction: *"Sow to yourselves in righteousness, reap in mercy; break up your fallow ground: for it is time to seek the LORD, till he come and rain righteousness upon you." Hosea 10:12.* Spiritual birth loosens the soil of our souls for God's ploughing. Just as the farmer is prompted by the early rain to open the ground for physical refreshment from the first heaven, so are we prompted by God's grace to open our minds, wills, and emotions for spiritual refreshment from the third heaven.[2] *"For as the rain cometh down, and the snow from heaven, and returneth not thither, but watereth the earth, and maketh it bring forth and bud, that it may give seed to the sower, and bread to the eater: So shall my word be that goeth forth out of my mouth: it shall not return unto me void, but it shall accomplish that which I please, and it shall prosper in the thing whereto I sent it." Isaiah 55:10,11.*

Early Rains

Piaget's cognitive stage of concrete operations begins around age seven and extends to age eleven or twelve. The child at this stage understands cause and effect relationships and can think logically about sights, sounds, touches, tastes, and smells.[3]

At this age children begin to play games with rules that require cooperation:[4] whether it's the highly structured and many-player games of boys that focus on justice and fairness (football, baseball), or the friendship games of girls that focus on kindness and deference (jump rope, hopscotch).[5]The ability to see another's point of view enables them to play with community.[6]

It's no coincidence that people of all cultures begin systematic training of children at age seven or eight.[7]Only when they have their concrete operations and the ability to cooperate with groups do children learn the rules and technologies (including literacy) of their cultures.[8]

The new cognitive and social skills of school age children also enable them to advance spiritually. This is the optimal age for children to begin their spiritual journey, because the following skills are necessary for a person to be trained in spiritual matters: cooperation, justice, deference, empathy, and understanding. These are essential ingredients for growth in God's spiritual institutions: Israel, churches. God never endorsed a purely individual path to spiritual maturity. He promotes development in relation to a group.

Too many times when young children of seven or eight profess faith in Christ they are ignored or not taken seriously. Yet, this is the best time to teach them the basics of the Christian life. We should never underestimate or belittle the work of God in a young life. Children of this age are able to respond to the Spirit of God in them and are capable of more spiritual insight than we expect. I saw a girl of eight walk the aisle once and state that God was calling her to work in foreign missions. The pastor took her at her word. So did I. *"And Jesus called a little child unto him, and set him in the midst of them, And said, Verily I say unto you, Except ye be converted, and become as little children, ye shall not enter into the kingdom of heaven. Whosoever therefore shall humble himself as this little child, the same is greatest in the kingdom of heaven. And whoso shall receive one such little child in my name receiveth me. But whoso shall offend one of these little ones which believe in me, it were better for him that a millstone were hanged about his neck, and that he were drowned in the depth of the sea." Matthew 18:2-6.*

Learning Tasks

Children of seven or eight years have the cognitive and social equipment to learn the tasks of spiritual childhood. An early start can give the opportunity for further advancement. This is one advantage of accepting Christ at a young age. New Christian adults must begin at the same level spiritually even though they are more advanced cognitively. Nevertheless, adults often more quickly pass through the stages.

The Four Learning Tasks of Spiritual Childhood

1. Learning dependence on God - In the same way a child depends on its parents for nourishment and protection, so a spiritual child must learn to depend on God and petition Him in prayer.
2. Learning the technologies to ensure continued growth - Just as a child needs food, water, and nurturing to grow physically, and guidance and education to grow psychologically, so the spiritual child needs wise counsel and the Word of God to grow spiritually. The spiritual neophyte needs daily obedience to God's word to be healthy: *"But he answered and said, It is written, Man shall not live by bread alone, but by every word that proceedeth out of the mouth of God." Matthew 4:4.*
3. Learning the basic rules of the spiritual dimension - Children learn rules of survival: don't stand in the road; don't touch the hot stove. Spiritual children must learn the rules also. We call them doctrines. Doctrinal ignorance leaves spiritual children vulnerable to deception and injury.
4. Learning one's allies and enemies in the spiritual dimension - School age children know that not everyone is their friend or helper. In the same way, spiritual children need to know who are deadly enemies in the spiritual realm.

In the next two sections I will illustrate the learning tasks of spiritual childhood using the history of Israel. Then I will further develop the theme in specific tasks of individual Christian development.

History of Israel

1. Call To Adventure

"When Israel was a child then I loved him, and called my son out of Egypt." Hosea 11:1.

God's "call to adventure" came to the children of Israel through Moses and the burning bush. They accepted the call after they heard God's words and saw the supernatural signs: *"And Moses and Aaron went and gathered together all the elders of the children of Israel: And Aaron spake all the words which the LORD had spoken unto Moses, and did the signs in the sight of the people. And the people believed: and when they heard that the LORD had visited the children of Israel, and that he had looked upon their affliction, then they bowed their heads and worshipped." Exodus 4:29-31.*

2.   Refusal of the Call

Yet, the children doubted when Pharaoh had them make bricks without straw. They questioned Moses and his motives. *"And the officers of the children of Israel did see that they were in evil case, after it was said, Ye shall not minish ought from your bricks of your daily task. And they met Moses and Aaron, who stood in the way, as they came forth from Pharaoh: And they said unto them, The LORD look upon you, and judge; because ye have made our savour to be abhorred in the eyes of Pharaoh, and in the eyes of his servants, to put a sword in their hand to slay us." Exodus 5:19-21.*

God quickly tried to reassure them: *"I have also heard the groaning of the children of Israel, whom the Egyptians keep in bondage; and I have remembered my covenant. Wherefore say unto the children of Israel, I am the LORD, and I will bring you out from under the burdens of the Egyptians, and I will rid you out of their bondage, and I will redeem you with a stretched out arm, and with great judgments: And I will take you to me for a people, and I will be to you a God: and ye shall know that I am the LORD your God, which bringeth you out from under the burdens of the Egyptians. And I will bring you in unto the land, concerning the which I did swear to give it to Abraham, to Isaac, and to Jacob; and I will give it you for an heritage: I am the LORD. And Moses spake so unto the children of Israel: but they hearkened not unto Moses for anguish of spirit, and for cruel bondage." Exodus 6:5-9.*

God then confirmed His will to the people by sending ten plagues on Pharaoh and the Egyptians for resisting. The last was the death of the firstborn of Egypt at the Passover.

Israel finally demonstrated their faith in God through sacrificing the Passover lamb. Slaying the lamb and applying its blood symbolized acceptance of God's provision: *"For even Christ our passover is sacrificed for us:" 1 Corinthians 5:7.* God spared every house with the lamb's blood on the door and lintels. And through their faith in God the aptly called children of Israel entered spiritual childhood.

3.   Supernatural Helper

As the children prepared to leave Egypt, they met their supernatural helper: *"And the LORD went before them by day in a pillar of a cloud, to lead them the way; and by night in a pillar of fire, to give them light; to go by day and night: He took not away the pillar of the cloud by day, nor the pillar of fire by night, from before the people." Exodus 13:21,22.* The cloud represented the work of the Holy Spirit in its leadership of God's people.

The cloud, however, did not lead them in the shortest and easiest way: *"And it came to pass, when Pharaoh had let the people go, that God led them not through the way of the land of the Philistines, although that was near; for God said, Lest peradventure the people repent when they see war, and they return to Egypt: But God led the people about, through the way of the wilderness of the Red sea: and the children of Israel went up harnessed out of the land of Egypt." Exodus 13:17,18.* God knew the children were not prepared for the battles ahead. They first had to accomplish the learning tasks of spiritual childhood. Therefore, the supernatural helper led them into the wilderness to be trained.

We often mistakenly assume those who have been "born again" will be able to handle the pressures of the spiritual world without much preparation. We count on their enthusiasm to propel them. God doesn't assume. He knows there is a long path between birth and fruitfulness (Matthew 13:23; John 15:1-8; 2 Peter 1:5-8).

Generals do not like to send untrained and inexperienced soldiers into battle, and for good reason. Likewise, we should not expect spiritual newborns to fight our battles. For example, asking Christian children to transform their secular schools. Babes can't do it. I've often heard those opposed to private Christian schools or home schools exclaim, "but they must know how to live in the world!" Yes! but not without training. Full-scale spiritual warfare will crush the unprepared.

4.   Crossing of the First Threshold

The cloud pillar led them directly to a great barrier, the Red Sea, the first threshold. The Red Sea symbolized the wall between the physical world and the spiritual world.

The children were trapped with the Egyptians behind and the sea ahead. The Egyptians thought they had their chance for revenge: *"And it was told the king of Egypt that the people fled: and the heart of Pharaoh and of his servants was turned against the people, and they said, Why have we done this, that we have let Israel go from serving us? And he made ready his chariot, and took his people with him: And he took six hundred chosen chariots, and all the chariots of Egypt, and captains over every one of them. And the LORD hardened the heart of Pharaoh king of Egypt, and he pursued after the children of Israel" Exodus 14:5-8.*

The pursuing Egyptians represented how the world tries to stop pilgrims from fully entering the spiritual realm. They attempted to stop the children by force. There are other methods. Christian in *Pilgrim's Progress* experienced the following: emotional abuse from his family; threats and pleads from his neighbors; an attempt by Obstinate and Pliable to bring him back forcefully; and the evil temptations of the Slough of Despond and Worldly Wiseman.[9]

The children of Israel could not turn back. Their destiny was to cross on dry land. The threshold guardians, the Egyptians, were defeated with supernatural help. Reason and sense data could not provide a solution to this dilemma. Rational methods often fall short in spiritual warfare. They leave out the chance factor of spiritual intervention: *"And when Pharaoh drew nigh, the children of Israel lifted up their eyes, and, behold, the Egyptians marched after them; and they were sore afraid: and the children of Israel cried out unto the LORD." Exodus 14:10. "And Moses said unto the people, Fear ye not, stand still, and see the salvation of the LORD, which he will shew to you to day: for the Egyptians whom ye have seen to day, ye shall see them again no more for ever. The LORD shall fight for you, and ye shall hold your peace." Exodus 14:13,14. "And the angel of God, which went before the camp of Israel, removed and went behind them; and the pillar of the cloud went from before their face, and stood behind them: And it came between the camp of the Egyptians and the camp of Israel; and it was a cloud and darkness to them, but it gave light by night to these: so that the one came not near the other all the night. And Moses stretched out his hand over the sea; and the LORD caused the sea to go back by a strong east wind all that night, and made the sea dry land, and the waters were divided. And the children of Israel went into the midst of the sea upon the dry ground: and the waters were a wall unto them on their right hand, and on their left. And the Egyptians pursued, and went in after them to the midst of the sea, even all Pharaoh's horses, his chariots, and his horsemen. And it came to pass, that in the morning watch the LORD looked unto the host of the Egyptians through the pillar of fire and of the cloud, and troubled the host of the Egyptians, And took off their chariot wheels, that they drave them heavily: so that the Egyptians said, Let us flee from the face of Israel; for the LORD fighteth for them against the Egyptians. And the LORD said unto Moses, Stretch out thine hand over the sea, that the waters may come again upon the Egyptians, upon their chariots, and upon their horsemen. And Moses stretched forth his hand over the sea, and the sea returned to his strength when the morning appeared; and the Egyptians fled against it; and the LORD overthrew the Egyptians in the midst of the sea. And the waters returned, and covered the chariots, and the horsemen, and all the host of Pharaoh that came into the sea after them; there remained not so much as one of them. But the children of Israel walked upon dry land in the midst of the sea; and the waters were a wall unto them on their right hand, and on their left." Exodus 14:19-29.*

Crossing the Red Sea represents baptism to the Christian: *"Moreover, brethren, I would not that ye should be ignorant, how that all our fathers were under the cloud, and all passed through the sea; And were all baptized unto Moses in the cloud and in the sea;" 1 Corinthians 10:1,2.* They were covered with a wall of water on both sides and the water in the cloud above them. Just as the children of Israel actually entered the place of no return on the other side of the sea, so the Christian symbolically enters the place of no return when he or she emerges from the water. The world may ignore the inner work of salvation, but it will not ignore the outer symbol of that salvation. A Christian's baptism is a mark that forever brands him as a repudiator of the world. The prince of the world makes war against those with the mark.

5.   Belly of the Whale

Once the children crossed over, they were completely in the world of the unknown. They could no longer depend on their experience to guide them. Moses was the only one who had been in the wilderness before (Exodus 2:15), and the pillar of the cloud became their true guide.

When a Christian is born again and baptized, the old rules no longer apply. He must trust in the guidance of the Holy Spirit to navigate the spiritual dimension.

The wilderness is the belly of the whale, a dark void of acid and dead men's bones. The place where the hero will be tested to discover worthiness of spiritual power and wisdom: many are called, but few are chosen.

Jesus of Nazareth modeled this crossing into the wilderness after baptism: *"And Jesus, when he was baptized, went up straightway out of the water: and, lo, the heavens were opened unto him, and he saw the Spirit of God descending like a dove, and lighting upon him: And lo a voice from heaven, saying, This is my beloved Son, in whom I am well pleased. Then was Jesus led up of the Spirit into the wilderness to be tempted of the devil." Matthew 3:16-17; 4:1.*

The wilderness journey is not unique to the lives of Israel and Jesus. It is a necessary developmental event of the spiritual life.

6.   The Road of Trials

The children of Israel began their road of trials. It extended all the way from the Red Sea to the time of Jesus' death on the cross. The road of trials does not end until the hero experiences the sacrifice of God.

Tasks of the Children

The tasks of spiritual childhood prepare us for sustained growth. The narrative of Exodus outlines the learning tasks of spiritual childhood.

1.   Learning Dependence on God

After the crossing, the first trial teaches trust and dependence on God. Erickson's first developmental stage is trust vs. mistrust.[10]And so it is spiritually. The children must learn that God will provide their basic needs and trust Him to do so in a world they don't understand.

"So Moses brought Israel from the Red sea, and they went out into the wilderness of Shur; and they went three days in the wilderness, and found no water. And when they came to Marah, they could not drink of the waters of Marah, for they were bitter: therefore the name of it was called Marah. And the people murmured against Moses, saying, What shall we drink? And he cried unto the LORD; and the LORD shewed him a tree, which when he had cast into the waters, the waters were made sweet: there he made for them a statute and an ordinance, and there he proved them, And said, If thou wilt diligently hearken to the voice of the LORD thy God, and wilt do that which is right in his sight, and wilt give ear to his commandments, and keep all his statutes, I will put none of these diseases upon thee, which I have brought upon the Egyptians: for I am the LORD that healeth thee. And they came to Elim, where were twelve wells of water, and threescore and ten palm trees: and they encamped there by the waters." Exodus 15:22-27.

When the people said to Moses, "What shall we drink?" he immediately went to the Lord in prayer. Then the Lord provided a tree that made the waters sweet. The tree is a symbol of psychic growth.[11] One definition of "psychic" is "apparently sensitive to forces beyond the physical world."[12]Therefore, the tree represented growth in the spiritual dimension.[13]Isaiah 65:22 states, "as the days of a tree are the days of my people." God wants us to see the journey of Israel as a spiritual journey.

The tree changed the bitter water to sweet. The bitter waters represented the loss of the old way of life: comfort, safety, and pleasure of the known. The tree as the sugar of the spiritual world gave promise of new ways.

God then declared the chance and the symbolism of the bitter water and the tree: "there he made for them a statute and an ordinance... I will put none of these diseases upon you, which I have brought upon the Egyptians." The bitter waters of Egyptian bondage, although they were known and comfortable, did not allow the people to develop their full potential. Neither did the Egyptian religion allow its own people to grow spiritually. The bitter water turned to sweet showed the power of God to change corruption into health: *"Bless the LORD, O my soul, and forget not all his benefits: Who forgiveth all thine iniquities; who healeth all thy diseases;" Psalms 103:2,3.*

After Marah, the cloud led them to twelve wells of water. God could have brought them straight to Elim, but the lesson would have been lost. Bitter experience at times is a great teacher.

"And they took their journey from Elim, and all the congregation of the children of Israel came unto the wilderness of Sin, which is between Elim and Sinai, on the fifteenth day of the second month after their departing out of the land of Egypt. And the whole congregation of the children of Israel murmured against Moses and Aaron in the wilderness: And the children of Israel said unto them, Would to God we had died by the hand of the LORD in the land of Egypt, when we sat by the flesh pots, and when we did eat bread to the full; for ye have brought us forth into this wilderness, to kill this whole assembly with hunger." Exodus 16:1-3.

Another issue of trust and dependence: "What shall we eat?" (Matthew 6:31-33). God provided them bread from heaven every day after, as long as they were in spiritual childhood: *"I have heard the murmurings of the children of Israel: speak unto them, saying, At even ye shall eat flesh, and in the morning ye shall be filled with bread; and ye shall know that I am the LORD your God. And it came to pass, that at even the quails came up, and covered the camp: and in the morning the dew lay round about the host. And when the dew that lay was gone up, behold, upon the face of the wilderness there lay a small round thing, as small as the hoar frost on the ground. And when the children of Israel saw it, they said one to another, It is manna: for they wist not what it was. And Moses said unto them, This is the bread which the LORD hath given you to eat ... And they gathered it every morning, every man according to his eating: and when the sun waxed hot, it melted… And the children of Israel did eat manna forty years, until they came to a land inhabited; they did eat manna, until they came unto the borders of the land of Canaan." Exodus 16:12-15, 21, 35.*

Children must be fed until they are old enough to feed themselves. In the same way, spiritual children need direction and leadership in discovering the basic truths of their new life.

The people traveled farther to Rephidim where there was no water. For the third time, God proved His trustworthiness. He gave them water out of the rock: *"And the LORD said unto Moses, Go on before the people, and take with thee of the elders of Israel; and thy rod, wherewith thou smotest the river, take in thine hand, and go. Behold, I will stand before thee there upon the rock in Horeb; and thou shalt smite the rock, and there shall come water out of it, that the people may drink. And Moses did so in the sight of the elders of Israel. And he called the name of the place Massah, and Meribah, because of the chiding of the children of Israel, and because they tempted the LORD, saying, Is the LORD among us, or not?" Exodus 17:5-7.*

The water from the rock represented the solidness of God's commitment. He can break open the hardest problems and obstacles to provide for us. The impossible situations are the tests of His love.

Notice that in all three incidents, the children of Israel were like crying infants. "I'm thirsty! I'm hungry!" The people had to be ministered to before they could minister to others. In our day, we expect the newborns to provide the enthusiasm and work in God's kingdom. But it's a long way from birth to giving birth.

All three events pictured the work of Jesus Christ. The sweet tree represented Christ's work on the cross. His blood saturated the tree with holiness. The cross was cast into our lives to give us promise of a new life and healing of old wounds: *"Who his own self bare our sins in his own body on the tree, that we, being dead to sins, should live unto righteousness: by whose stripes ye were healed." 1 Peter 2:24.*

Jesus declared the manna a symbol that He would give followers His flesh to eat (John 6:31-35, 51). Jesus taught that belief and dependence on Him would nourish us spiritually as much as manna did the children physically: *"Give us this day our daily bread." Matthew 6:11.*

The rock was another symbol of Christ. When Simon Peter made his great confession, "Thou art the Christ, the son of the Living God," Jesus responded by comparing Peter (the little rock) to Himself (the big rock): *"And I say also unto thee, That thou art Peter, and upon this rock I will build my church; and the gates of hell shall not prevail against it." Matthew 16:18.* Jesus is "Petra" (a mass of rock); Peter is "petros" (a detached stone or boulder).[14]Petra and petros are more metaphors of parent and child: daddy rock and baby rock.

1 Corinthians 10:3-4 sums up the work of Christ in the children's lives: *"And did all eat the same spiritual meat; And did all drink the same spiritual drink: for they drank of that spiritual Rock that followed them: and that Rock was Christ."*

The children of Israel learned dependence on God for protection from their enemies: *"Then came Amalek, and fought with Israel in Rephidim. And Moses said unto Joshua, Choose us out men, and go out, fight with Amalek: to morrow I will stand on the top of the hill with the rod of God in mine hand. So Joshua did as Moses had said to him, and fought with Amalek: and Moses, Aaron, and Hur went up to the top of the hill. And it came to pass, when Moses held up his hand, that Israel prevailed: and when he let down his hand, Amalek prevailed. But Moses' hands were heavy; and they took a stone, and put it under him, and he sat thereon; and Aaron and Hur stayed up his hands, the one on the one side, and the other on the other side; and his hands were steady until the going down of the sun. And Joshua discomfited Amalek and his people with the edge of the sword.... And Moses built an altar, and called the name of it Jehovahnissi:" Exodus 17:8-13, 15.*

Aaron and Hur held up Moses' hands symbolizing their constant prayer to God throughout the battle. They depended on God for the victory. God was their strength. Moses acknowledged God as their protector with the altar. "Jehovah-nissi" means "God is my banner." The banner or flag represents the strength and power of the people. The loss of a banner is a source of great discouragement. Armies will die to keep their banner flying. In the battle of Rephidim, God the banner showed the people they could trust Him to always be strong and victorious on their behalf.

2. Learning the Technologies to Ensure Continued Growth

Spiritual childhood is the time to learn two key technologies: hearing and obeying wise counsel (Proverbs 11:14; 19:20), and hearing and obeying God's word (John 6:63).

After the battle with Amalek, God sent Jethro, Moses' father-in-law, to counsel him. Jethro came to Moses at Horeb (the site of the burning bush), to bring Moses' wife and two sons. Moses had left them behind when he went into Egypt.

Jethro discovered Moses sitting to judge the more than two million people from morning till night! Jethro feared the human Moses would burn out and see the scattering of Israel: *"And Moses' father in law said unto him, The thing that thou doest is not good. Thou wilt surely wear away, both thou, and this people that is with thee: for this thing is too heavy for thee; thou art not able to perform it thyself alone." Exodus 18:17,18.*

He counseled Moses to divide the responsibility of judgment among rulers of thousands, rulers of hundreds, rulers of fifties, and rulers of tens, then hear only the hard cases personally. Jethro told Moses this would prevent a breakdown and ensure peace: *"If thou shalt do this thing, and God command thee so, then thou shalt be able to endure, and all this people shall also go to their place in peace." Exodus 18:23.*

Moses obeyed Jethro's counsel and divided the people under different levels of leadership: *"So Moses hearkened to the voice of his father in law, and did all that he had said. And Moses chose able men out of all Israel, and made them heads over the people, rulers of thousands, rulers of hundreds, rulers of fifties, and rulers of tens. And they judged the people at all seasons: the hard causes they brought unto Moses, but every small matter they judged themselves." Exodus 18:24-26.*

In the same way children cannot learn the technologies of their culture without teaching and guidance, so spiritual children cannot learn the Way without God-sent counsel. Without godly guidance they are like sheep with no shepherd (Matthew 9:36).

At Horeb (mountain of God, Sinai), God declared the other essential technology of spiritual childhood: obedience to His word. God spoke to them in an audible voice so they would know His word was tangible and had authority. Children need concrete experiences to learn. They learn by sense data: sight, sound, touch, taste, and smell. Their ability to learn by abstract reasoning is undeveloped.

The voice of God frightened the people, but He did it as an immunization against sin: *"And when the voice of the trumpet sounded long, and waxed louder and louder, Moses spake, and God answered him by a voice." Exodus 19:19. "And all the people saw the thunderings, and the lightnings, and the noise of the trumpet, and the mountain smoking: and when the people saw it, they removed, and stood afar off. And they said unto Moses, Speak thou with us, and we will hear: but let not God speak with us, lest we die. And Moses said unto the people, Fear not: for God is come to prove you, and that his fear may be before your faces, that ye sin not. And the people stood afar off, and Moses drew near unto the thick darkness where God was. And the LORD said unto Moses, Thus thou shalt say unto the children of Israel, Ye have seen that I have talked with you from heaven." Exodus 20:18-22.*

God let them know that if they obeyed His voice, He would bless them: *"Ye have seen what I did unto the Egyptians, and how I bare you on eagles' wings, and brought you unto myself. Now therefore, if ye will obey my voice indeed, and keep my covenant, then ye shall be a peculiar treasure unto me above all people: for all the earth is mine: And ye shall be unto me a kingdom of priests, and an holy nation… And all the people answered together, and said, All that the LORD hath spoken we will do" Exodus 19:4-6, 8.*

3. Learning the Basic Rules of the Spiritual Dimension

God spoke the Ten Commandments from heaven that day. He gave order and protection to their society. The Ten Commandments were designed to save them and us from ignorance and harm.

Commandment 1: *"Thou shalt have no other gods before me." Exodus 20:3.* Do not make anyone else or anything else an object of worship. Worship is "an extreme devotion or intense love or admiration of any kind."[15] Another definition is from the Sermon on the Mount: *"For where your treasure is, there will your heart be also." Matthew 6:21.* When we invest our time, money, and energy into something we are close to worship. CharlesAllen named five objects of modern worship: wealth, fame, pleasure, power, and knowledge.[16] These false five have been around since Moses. Let us be careful so we don't fall for the distractions around us: *"For my people have committed two evils; they have forsaken me the fountain of living waters, and hewed them out cisterns, broken cisterns, that can hold no water." Jeremiah 2:13.*

Commandment 2: *"Thou shalt not make unto thee any graven image, or any likeness of any thing that is in heaven above, or that is in the earth beneath, or that is in the water under the earth: Thou shalt not bow down thyself to them, nor serve them: for I the LORD thy God am a jealous God, visiting the iniquity of the fathers upon the children unto the third and fourth generation of them that hate me; And shewing mercy unto thousands of them that love me, and keep my commandments." Exodus 20:4-6.*

Charles Allen expressed well the nature of the image problem: "primitive man found it hard to realize a God he could not see, so he made aids to assist his imagination, to bring reality into his worship."[17] We have noted that children have difficulty with what they cannot see. Spiritual children are naturally tempted to make idols. Yet God said, "I am not like corruptible man, birds, four-footed beasts, or creeping things" (Romans 1:23). A mere image of God constricts Him to a time and a place and leads to a lack of proper fear for Him (Romans 1:26-32). *"I am the LORD: that is my name: and my glory will I not give to another, neither my praise to graven images." Isaiah 42:8.*

Spiritual children restrict God's work in their lives when they limit Him to the physical buildings of worship. It's a common belief that God can only be worshipped properly in His "house." The church building itself becomes an image of God. In the same way, the use of statues, relics, prayer wheels, etc. as aids to worship can lead to a sort of permanent immaturity.

The word "image" in Exodus 20:4 means "a shadow, a phantom."[18] Otto Rank said of the shadow: "folklorists are in agreement in emphasizing that the shadow is equivalent with the human soul."[19] Primitive people believe you can injure someone's soul if you step on their shadow. They also believe the devil can steal your soul by stealing your shadow.[20] Rank attests: "savages believe that the soul is embodied in the image reproduced by glass, water, portrait, or by a shadow."[21] If the preceding is true, then making an image of God is to steal His shadow, and the image of God captures Him in time and place. God will not submit to time and place, except in the person of Jesus Christ: *"But will God indeed dwell on the earth? behold, the heaven and heaven of heavens cannot contain thee; how much less this house that I have builded?" 1 Kings 8:27.*

The second commandment educated the people away from Egyptian ideas. The Egyptians also believed the soul or essence could be captured: "In Egypt too, the shadow was the oldest form of the soul… there were alternative terms for soul: double (ka), image, shadow, and name."[22]

And finally, God did not want the people to make a graven image because of Jesus Christ. Jesus was to be His graven image. Jesus embodied the essence of God in time and place on earth: *"Who being the brightness of his glory, and the express image of his person" Hebrews 1:3.* This is the only verse that uses the Greek word "charakter" for image. It means "a tool for engraving" and "a stamp or impress."[23] The word for tool is substituted for the thing made, metonymy of cause. The graving tool makes an exact copy of the image in the substance. In other words, God's engraved image is Jesus Christ.

Commandment 3: *"Thou shalt not take the name of the LORD thy God in vain; for the LORD will not hold him guiltless that taketh his name in vain." Exodus 20:7. The International Children's Bible* says: "You must not use the name of the Lord your God thoughtlessly."[24] We misuse God's name when we use it as a banner for a private cause. As a personal banner, God's name loses its glory. It becomes vain. We are representatives of God's name, and have responsibility to Him for the causes to which we give our loyalties. We are cautioned to not make our causes God's causes. God will give us clear direction about His priorities and mission. We do not have a right to substitute our program for His.

Jesus denounced the Pharisees for this very sin: *"Howbeit in vain do they worship me, teaching for doctrines the commandments of men." Mark 7:7.*

The first three commandments are to put God first, to get the right picture of God, and to think about God in the right way. We are to think of ourselves in God's service, not vice-versa.

Commandment 4: *"Remember the sabbath day, to keep it holy. Six days shalt thou labour, and do all thy work: But the seventh day is the sabbath of the LORD thy God: in it thou shalt not do any work, thou, nor thy son, nor thy daughter, thy manservant, nor thy maidservant, nor thy cattle, nor thy stranger that is within thy gates: For in six days the LORD made heaven and earth, the sea, and all that in them is, and rested the seventh day: wherefore the LORD blessed the sabbath day, and hallowed it." Exodus 20:8-11.* Remember the day of rest and communion with God. Keep it dedicated and consecrated to Him. Unger says, "The rest of God is the goal which the whole creation is destined to reach."[25] The day of rest is a constant reminder that one day we will rest with God from all our work, labor, and suffering.

This rest includes resting from the work we do for God. "Work" in this passage means "to dispatch as a messenger or deputy of God." The word is used in the context of work done for God.[26] We are not to busy ourselves in physical activity on our consecrated days. We are to devote ourselves to our relationship to God. The sabbath is a day of relationship, not purpose. We need time to talk and visit with God. We are to honor Him, not doing our own ways, nor finding our own pleasure, nor speaking our own words (Isaiah 58:13).

The observance of the consecrated day is a symbol of the relationship between God and His people: *"Wherefore the children of Israel shall keep the sabbath, to observe the sabbath throughout their generations, for a perpetual covenant. It is a sign between me and the children of Israel for ever: for in six days the LORD made heaven and earth, and on the seventh day he rested, and was refreshed." Exodus 31:16,17.*

God intends the day of rest to be for the entire body. As a result of relaxing the body, His people become more attuned to the spiritual dimension. Through contemplating the ways of God, His people find the right ways of relating to others: *"Is not this the fast that I have chosen? to loose the bands of wickedness, to undo the heavy burdens, and to let the oppressed go free, and that ye break every yoke? ... Then shalt thou call, and the LORD shall answer; thou shalt cry, and he shall say, Here I am. If thou take away from the midst of thee the yoke, the putting forth of the finger, and speaking vanity; And if thou draw out thy soul to the hungry, and satisfy the afflicted soul; then shall thy light rise in obscurity, and thy darkness be as the noonday:" Isaiah 58:6, 9-10.*

Although Christians are not required to keep Saturday as a sacred day, the principle is still valid. We can individually and collectively consecrate Sunday instead as a day we will seek God and build our relationship to Him. Our society makes this easy by sanctioning Sunday as a day of rest. God will bless those who honor the spirit of this commandment in their lives. The promise of Isaiah still applies: *"And the LORD shall guide thee continually, and satisfy thy soul in drought, and make fat thy bones: and thou shalt be like a watered garden, and like a spring of water, whose waters fail not. And they that shall be of thee shall build the old waste places: thou shalt raise up the foundations of many generations; and thou shalt be called, The repairer of the breach, The restorer of paths to dwell in." Isaiah 58:11,12.*

Commandment 5: *"Honour thy father and thy mother: that thy days may be long upon the land which the LORD thy God giveth thee." Exodus 20:12.* It has been said that the first four commandments concern our relationship to God and the last six our relationship to people. But it looks like number five concerns our relationship to God and people. Our fathers and mothers are the middle management between God and us. God rules their hearts to counsel and guide us in ways that are good for us (Proverbs 21:1).

"My son, keep thy father's commandment, and forsake not the law of thy mother: Bind them continually upon thine heart, and tie them about thy neck. When thou goest, it shall lead thee; when thou sleepest, it shall keep thee; and when thou awakest, it shall talk with thee." Proverbs 6:20-22. Our parents' direction will lead us, keep us safe, and instruct us. This guidance is a lifetime commitment: *"Hearken unto thy father that begat thee, and despise not thy mother when she is old." Proverbs 23:22.* Those who despise their parents' instruction are in danger: *"The eye that mocketh at his father, and despiseth to obey his mother, the ravens of the valley shall pick it out, and the young eagles shall eat it." Proverbs 30:17.*

Our parents are precursors of spiritual parentage. When we learn to relate properly to them we will be ready for spiritual guidance. We are to learn from the natural world and apply that knowledge to the spiritual world: *"For though ye have ten thousand instructors in Christ, yet have ye not many fathers: for in Christ Jesus I have begotten you through the gospel." 1 Corinthians 4:15. "Obey them that have the rule over you, and submit yourselves: for they watch for your souls, as they that must give account, that they may do it with joy, and not with grief: for that is unprofitable for you." Hebrews 13:17.*

Commandment 6: *"Thou shalt not kill." Exodus 20:13.* "Kill" here means "to dash in pieces, to murder." The issue is the sanctity and sacredness of life. Charles Swindoll called this and sexual purity (Commandment 7) "the inescapable issues of our time."[27](This chapter was first written in 1991 and 1992). Homicide and suicide are a continual and growing problem in the United States.[28] Abortions are performed at the rate of 1.6 million per year. Infanticide and euthanasia are accepted by some people. Washington State had Initiative 119 on the ballot in November 1991. It would have allowed doctors to administer "aid in dying" to patients with less than six months to live.[29] A book called *Final Exit* (which tells you how to kill yourself) has been on the bestseller list.[30] The respect for life is so low that articles about parents killing their own children are common: "Texas boy, found starved and chained in family trailer, dies at 13."[31] "Father confesses he fed son to dog."[32]

"Whoso sheddeth man's blood, by man shall his blood be shed: for in the image of God made he man." Genesis 9:6. The word "image" in this verse means "shadow, phantom," the same definition as in Commandment 2. God honors His image so that to injure it is an offense against Him. People are the shades of God. God wants us to honor His shadows. We are to respect all human life as sacred: *"I will praise thee; for I am fearfully and wonderfully made: marvellous are thy works; and that my soul knoweth right well." Psalms 139:14.*

Many people reject the God of the Bible and seek to make Him in their own image. They believe God is a dull shadow of themselves, a larger than life human. Yet, without a transcendent God, people's individual lives become expendable. Only the community retains meaning. Thus we no longer weep over the loss of millions of individuals. In such a milieu, people truly become faceless phantoms, not fearfully and wonderfully made.

There is also the sanctity of God's will and life plan for individuals (Psalm 139:14; Philippians 1:6). We cannot presume to know the details of God's will for others. But often we allow hate to destroy our relationships with people whose life plans seem to conflict with our own goals. We wish they were not in our way, that they were removed. Instead, we need to observe and reverence God's work in other's lives as well as our own. Jesus addressed this very issue in the Sermon on the Mount: *"Ye have heard that it was said by them of old time, Thou shalt not kill; and whosoever shall kill shall be in danger of the judgment: But I say unto you, That whosoever is angry with his brother without a cause shall be in danger of the judgment: and whosoever shall say to his brother, Raca, shall be in danger of the council: but whosoever shall say, Thou fool, shall be in danger of hell fire." Matthew 5:21,22.*

Commandment 7: *"Thou shalt not commit adultery." Exodus 20:14.* What is adultery? To adulterate something means to "make inferior, impure, or not genuine by adding a harmful, less valuable, or prohibited substance."[33]God intended for

144

people to have one sexual partner in a lifetime. To add another sexual experience to the one is to add something harmful. God has made us so that we develop an emotional bond to the one with whom we have sex. The bond becomes adulterated when we introduce a second person into our experience. Even if we marry a later partner, the "ghosts" of earlier ones may haunt us.[34] For this reason, adultery includes any sexual experience outside the marriage, including those before marriage.

In the New Testament, the seventh commandment is repeated: *"For this is the will of God, even your sanctification, that ye should abstain from fornication:" 1 Thessalonians 4:3.* The word "fornication" comes from the Greek "porneia." This word includes "homosexuality, incestuous relationships, unnatural acts with beasts, premarital sexual relationships, and extramarital sex."[35] Fornication is a more inclusive word than adultery and it represents the idea better. Any form of sex outside the marriage bond interferes with our set-apart-ness, sanctification. Jesus even included lust in the definition of adultery: *"But I say unto you, That whosoever looketh on a woman to lust after her hath committed adultery with her already in his heart." Matthew 5:28.* It is easy to see how the Greek "porneia" travels to our language as "pornography." Pornography is a root of many sexual sins and a destroyer of sexual bonding.

Why is it spiritually important for the Children of Israel and us to know and keep Commandment 7? First, because the earthly relationship of marriage symbolizes the heavenly relationship we have with God: *"What? know ye not that he which is joined to an harlot is one body? for two, saith he, shall be one flesh. But he that is joined unto the Lord is one spirit." 1 Corinthians 6:16,17.* God wants the earthly picture to be right so we will know what to look for in Him. He wants us to grow in our relationship to Him by relating in the right ways to our partner. He wants us to be faithful to our partner, whether we are already married or haven't yet found that partner.

Secondly, we damage other people's spirits by adultery. In the restating of the commandment in 1 Thessalonians 4, Paul tells the consequence of violation: *"That no man go beyond and defraud his brother in any matter: because that the Lord is the avenger of all such, as we also have forewarned you and testified." 1 Thessalonians 4:6.* The word "defraud" means "to overreach with covetousness."[36] To defraud by adultery means, "to take for yourself the bond that is reserved exclusively for two others." It is overreaching, thievery. God says He will avenge those who have lost the spirit of marriage to defrauders.

Thirdly, failure harms our own selves: *"Flee fornication. Every sin that a man doeth is without the body; but he that committeth fornication sinneth against his own body." 1 Corinthians 6:18.* Paul said coming together sexually is to be one body. Therefore, to violate that bond is to harm your own body, the oneness between you and your spouse: *"That every one of you should know how to possess his vessel in sanctification and honour; Not in the lust of concupiscence, even as the Gentiles which know not God: ...For God hath not called us unto uncleanness, but unto holiness." 1 Thessalonians 4:4-5,7.* A look at Greek definitions led me to write it this way: "That every one of you should understand how to acquire your spouse (The one who contributes to your usefulness, Gen. 2:18 "help fitting") in purity and with value; not suffering from the disease of passion, which leads to longing for the forbidden, even as the Gentiles who don't understand God. For God has not called us to impurity (adultery), but to purity."[37] God wants us to have a one-man, one-woman relationship that symbolizes our faithfulness to Him and His faithfulness to us.

Finally, sex outside its place stunts our spiritual growth. It decreases our spiritual power: *"None that go unto her return again, neither take they hold of the paths of life." Proverbs 2:19.* A haunting verse that explains the consequences of following the strange woman. The way is lost; the paths of development are altered. Potential for spiritual power is sacrificed.

Commandment 8: *"Thou shalt not steal." Exodus 20:15.* Steal means more than to take what doesn't belong to you. It also means "to deceive and get by stealth."[38] You could be stealing even if the other person gives it to you, if they were giving under wrong assumptions.

Stealing destroys others for profit, whether for money, pleasure, or power. Roget's Thesaurus includes such synonyms for stealing as "robbery, abduction, kidnapping, rape, poaching, extortion, blackmail, graft, piracy, burglary, housebreaking, embezzlement, fraud, swindle, pick pocketing, and shoplifting." Those are just the nouns, and not all of them.

Instead of stealing, God wants us to give to others out of our abundance. He in turn will increase blessings for all: *"Give, and it shall be given unto you; good measure, pressed down, and shaken together, and running over, shall men give into your bosom. For with the same measure that ye mete withal it shall be measured to you again." Luke 6:38. "He that hath pity upon the poor lendeth unto the LORD; and that which he hath given will he pay him again." Proverbs 19:17.*

According to Charles Allen, the story of the Good Samaritan illustrates three different philosophies of possession (Luke 10:25-37): "The philosophy of the thieves was: What belongs to my neighbor belongs to me and I will take it... The philosophy of the priest and the Levite was: What belongs to me is mine and I will keep it... the Good Samaritan saw his brother's needs and his philosophy was: What belongs to me belongs to others, and I will share it."[39] Everything belongs to God and we are only His stewards in that which He gives us.

In a spiritual sense, we steal when we promise spiritual growth to people but instead only use them for our own purposes (2 Peter 2:3). We steal their time, devotion, and spiritual energy, and can leave them bitter and unwilling to try. Many spiritual children become discouraged when factions in churches use them for purposes other than the advancement of the kingdom.

Jesus contrasted Himself to false teachers, the stealers of spiritual energy, in John 10:8-10. Their mission is to steal, to sacrifice others for their own benefit,[40] and to utterly ruin other people's well-being.[41] Jesus wants to give us more in abundance and to enhance our lives. Spiritual leaders who follow Jesus will do the same.

Commandment 9: *"Thou shalt not bear false witness against thy neighbour." Exodus 20:16.* In other words, "Do not respond wrongfully for the record in order to beat down your companion."[42] False words are a source of great discouragement (beating down). False words against a companion are doubly discouraging. The word for "neighbour" in this verse includes "companion, brother, friend, husband, or lover." We most often wrong those with whom we spend the most time. And those are usually our cherished ones.

False witnessing becomes even more serious when we realize we are accountable to God for every word we say about others. It all goes in God's record book: *"But I say unto you, That every idle word that men shall speak, they shall give account thereof in the day of judgment." Matthew 12:36.*

Lies about others are usually an attempt to discredit them after we have been offended. But, it is always unwise to begin a reputation war: *"Dearly beloved, avenge not yourselves, but rather give place unto wrath: for it is written, Vengeance is mine; I will repay, saith the Lord." Romans 12:19. (Proverbs 24:17-18).*

False words are another form of stealing. They steal reputation. Even if the charges are proven false, the damage is done. In a sense, commandments 6-9 are all about stealing: killing is stealing another's life; adultery is stealing another's "oneness"; stealing is taking another's wealth; and bearing false witness is stealing another's reputation.

Commandment 10: *"Thou shalt not covet thy neighbour's house, thou shalt not covet thy neighbour's wife, nor his manservant, nor his maidservant, nor his ox, nor his ass, nor any thing that is thy neighbour's." Exodus 20:17.* The prohibition doesn't stop with actual stealing; even wanting the things God has given others is forbidden. The word "covet" means "to delight in and desire a precious thing."[43] Delight and desire are not evil in themselves, but evil follows delighting in and desiring other's relationships and possessions.

God's answer to covetousness is contentment: *"Let your conversation be without covetousness; and be content with such things as ye have: for he hath said, I will never leave thee, nor forsake thee." Hebrews 13:5.* God Himself is our shield, and our exceeding great reward (Gen.15: 1). He owns it all, and He will give us all good things: *"For the LORD God is a sun and shield: the LORD will give grace and glory: no good thing will he withhold from them that walk uprightly." Psalms 84:11.*

God gave ten basic rules of spiritual childhood that day from the black mountain. He then applied and elaborated them with His judgments (Exodus 22:1-23:19), and with His ordinances, which were the regulations concerning worship (Hebrews 9:1).

4. Learning One's Allies and Enemies in the Spiritual Dimension

After giving the commandments and judgments, God instructed the children about their allies and enemies: *"20 Behold, I send an Angel before thee, to keep thee in the way, and to bring thee into the place which I have prepared. 21 Beware of him, and obey his voice, provoke him not; for he will not pardon your transgressions: for my name is in him. 22 But if thou shalt indeed obey his voice, and do all that I speak; then I will be an enemy unto thine enemies, and an adversary unto thine adversaries. 23 For mine Angel shall go before thee, and bring thee in unto the Amorites, and the Hittites, and the Perizzites, and the Canaanites, the Hivites, and the Jebusites: and I will cut them off. 24 Thou shalt not bow down to their gods, nor serve them, nor do after their works: but thou shalt utterly overthrow them, and quite break down their images. 25 And ye shall serve the LORD your God, and he shall bless thy bread, and thy water; and I will take sickness away from the midst of thee. 26 There shall nothing cast their young, nor be barren, in thy land: the number of thy days I will fulfil. 27 I will send my fear before thee, and will destroy all the people to whom thou shalt come, and I will make all thine enemies turn their backs unto thee. 28 And I will send hornets before thee, which shall drive out the Hivite, the Canaanite, and the Hittite, from before thee. 29 I will not drive them out from before thee in one year; lest the land become desolate, and the beast of the field multiply against thee. 30 By little and little I will drive them out from before thee, until thou be increased, and inherit the land. 31 And I will set thy bounds from the Red sea even unto the sea of the Philistines, and from the desert unto the river: for I will deliver the inhabitants of the land into your hand; and thou shalt drive them out before thee. 32 Thou shalt make no covenant with them, nor with their gods. 33 They shall not dwell in thy land, lest they make thee sin against me: for if thou serve their gods, it will surely be a snare unto thee." Exodus 23:20-33.*

A. Allies

1. Angel - This Angel is the one in the cloud (Ex.14: 19). He is the supernatural helper that "keeps us in the way," and "brings us to the place God has prepared for us." The Angel represents the work of the Holy Spirit to the Christian. The Holy Spirit heads us in the right way and seeks to bring us to spiritual maturity.

2. God and His word - In verse 25 God promises the children blessings if they will serve Him. He will bless their provisions: bread and water, which symbolize spiritual meat and drink (1 Corinthians 10:3-4). And He will take away their sicknesses of body and soul (Psalm 103:2-3).

3. Ancestors - v.31 There was a sense of history about their mission. God had promised Abraham the land of Palestine and they were going to take it (Gen.15: 12-21; 17:8; Ex. 6:8). It is as if the patriarchs are watching and cheering them. We also have spiritual ancestors that cheer us as we build on their work. The feelings expressed in Hebrews 12:1 apply to the children: *"Wherefore seeing we also are compassed about with so great a cloud of witnesses, let us lay aside every weight, and the sin which doth so easily beset us, and let us run with patience the race that is set before us," Hebrews 12:1.*

B. Enemies

1. Nations of Canaan - v.23 This passage lists six nations but Deuteronomy 7:1 adds the Girgashites. The Amalekites were also enemies (Ex. 17:13-16). The Bibles implies these nations were to be driven out because of their immorality and wickedness: *"But in the fourth generation they shall come hither again: for the iniquity of the Amorites is not yet full." Genesis 15:16. "And the land is defiled: therefore I do visit the iniquity thereof upon it, and the land itself vomiteth out her inhabitants." Leviticus 18:25.* These nations had rejected God and followed their own hearts. They had sunk to the low state of those who refuse to follow God's ways. God could not allow

them to live with the children because of their corrupting influence (Romans 1:18-32).

God does not tell us today to destroy our enemies, instead He tells us to make them into friends through the gospel (Romans 8:37). But God still warns young Christians to separate themselves from the principles of the world, in order to build a distinct worldview (Colossians 2:8): *"Wherefore come out from among them, and be ye separate, saith the Lord, and touch not the unclean thing; and I will receive you, And will be a Father unto you, and ye shall be my sons and daughters, saith the Lord Almighty." 2 Corinthians 6:17,18.*

2. Compromise - v. 24,32,33 Not only were the enemies themselves dangerous, but their ideas were also. God did not want His children to be influenced by the Canaanites. He especially forbade them to marry: *"Neither shalt thou make marriages with them; thy daughter thou shalt not give unto his son, nor his daughter shalt thou take unto thy son. For they will turn away thy son from following me, that they may serve other gods: so will the anger of the LORD be kindled against you, and destroy thee suddenly." Deuteronomy 7:3,4. (2 Corinthians 6:14).*

Children must be protected from bad ideas. God's example is clear. Children have to be taught absolute truths (basic rules) without interference from false teachers. There must be a time of separation from the world so children can learn the truth without being preyed upon.

Children must learn the best about their own culture first. The time of debate with other thoughts and ways of life is for adolescence; it is only when children reach adolescence that they are able to adequately compare different points of view about such things. Only then will they be able to "reason correctly about propositions they do not yet believe."[44] Only when they are able to judge their own culture will they be able to judge others. And yes, judgment of thoughts and ways is necessary if we expect spiritual growth. Spiritual growth from a Christian perspective does not mean that we accept all viewpoints as truth.

The saying, "children must be exposed to other cultures," has no validity for those who have not passed the stage of concrete operations; that is, to those who are under 12 or so, because they do not have the capacity to evaluate those cultures or religions by standards of truth. They instead tend to accept whatever is taught them as truth, or to learn that differences don't matter.

The push for multicultural education has a noble aim, to increase tolerance for others. Yet, tolerance implies that you start from a set of values and beliefs you hold dear. When children are taught foreign cultures and religions before they can judge their own, they do not learn tolerance, instead they learn to trivialize values, beliefs, and culture.

Christian Elementary School

The New Testament also defines the basic elements of spiritual childhood: *"12 For when for the time ye ought to be teachers, ye have need that one teach you again which be the first principles of the oracles of God; and are become such as have need of milk, and not of strong meat 13 For every one that useth milk is unskilful in the word of righteousness: for he is a babe. 14 But strong meat belongeth to them that are of full age, even those who by reason of use have their senses exercised to discern both good and evil. 6:1 Therefore leaving the principles of the doctrine of Christ, let us go on unto perfection; not laying again the foundation of repentance from dead works, and of faith toward God, 2 Of the doctrine of baptisms, and of laying on of hands, and of resurrection of the dead, and of eternal judgment." Hebrews 5:12-6:2.*

This passage lists six teachings that make up the foundation of the Christian life. They are the Christian rules and culture that must be learned by every spiritual child. They form the base from which the child grows up to maturity, perfection. They are the "first principles of the oracles of God" and the "milk" of the Christian life. They should not be re-laid when once put down.

Gromacki groups these six teachings under three categories:

1. Salvation
2. Initial church experience
3. Future things.[45]

This list represents the first three types of learning in which spiritual children need to be grounded. The fourth type of learning is the push toward maturity.

1. Salvation

   A. Repentance from dead works - The realization that we need a savior, that we cannot save ourselves or be good enough in the eyes of God, and that we cannot perform any ritual that will win us favor with God.

B. Faith toward God - Our faith in God's son Jesus Christ saves us. He was the sacrifice for our sins. It is only through our trust in His work that we can be justified before God: *"Now to him that worketh is the reward not reckoned of grace, but of debt. But to him that worketh not, but believeth on him that justifieth the ungodly, his faith is counted for righteousness."* Romans 4:4,5.

2. Initial church experience

   A. Baptisms - The use of the plural is confusing since we only have one type of baptism today (Ephesians 4:5). Perhaps the plural is used because the early Jewish Christians had learned of different types of baptism: ceremonial washings, proselyte baptism, John's baptism, the baptism of Jesus and His disciples. Nevertheless today we have only one type of baptism: church baptism (see Chapter 7 - Symbol), Matthew 28:18-20.

   B. Laying on of hands - The Bible speaks of laying on of hands in several contexts: the priests symbolically put their hands on the offerings; Jacob laid his hands on Joseph's children when he blessed them (Genesis 48:14); The children of Israel consecrated the Levites for service by the laying on of hands (Numbers 8:10-11); Moses transferred leadership to Joshua by placing his hands on him (Numbers 27:18-20); Jesus laid His hands on the children when He blessed them (Matthew 19:13-15); Jesus also laid His hands on people when He healed them (Luke 4:40). In the early church, the laying on of hands involved the acknowledgment of special gifts and the appointment of service to God (Acts 6:3-6; 1 Tim. 4:14; 5:22; 2 Tim. 1:6). Today also, the laying on of hands is given to express recognition of fellowship (Acts 8:14-17), and to ordain pastors and deacons.

       Gromacki says the laying on of hands "symbolizes recognition, identification, and approval."[46] These purposes of the act can be seen from the previous discussion. For spiritual children, the giving of the hand of fellowship is the most significant. It symbolizes their recognition by the church, their identification with the church, and their approval by the church. Thus their stand for Christ in salvation and baptism is acknowledged.

   C. Also under initial church experience we could include the Lord's Supper. (1 Corinthians 11:23-26).

3. Future things

    A. Resurrection of the dead - The resurrection is the means of our salvation (Romans 10:9). It is also the hope of a new body and life with God (1 Corinthians 15:19, 50-53). The resurrection is the final victory over the flesh, the world, and Satan: *"But thanks be to God, which giveth us the victory through our Lord Jesus Christ. Therefore, my beloved brethren, be ye stedfast, unmoveable, always abounding in the work of the Lord, forasmuch as ye know that your labour is not in vain in the Lord." 1 Corinthians 15:57,58.*

    B. Eternal Judgment - This is the doctrine of ultimate accountability of all toward God (Philippians 2:10-11): *"And as it is appointed unto men once to die, but after this the judgment:" Hebrews 9:27.* The Bible specifically says the unsaved will be judged by their works and will be separated from God eternally (Revelation 20:11-15). The Bible also teaches those who place their faith in Christ are free from the sentence of hell (Romans 5:1; 8:1). Believers in Christ will live with Him in glory (Revelation 21:1-4).

        Young Christians are usually interested in the study of future things. The word that ties resurrection and judgment together is victory. It's the reassurance of victory that spiritual children are after. The doctrines of resurrection and judgment both teach that in the end those who side with God will be winners.

    C. The study of end-time events and Revelation could be included here.

4. On to Perfection

Beyond the basic elements is the goal of maturity. The spiritual child should eventually leave elementary school and go on toward the completion of his education.

The idea of Hebrews 6:1 is that spiritual children grow like plants or trees. The trunk or base grows first, then the branches that eventually bear fruit. The writer tells the children that the trunk is in place, the roots have gone down, and it's time to let the branches grow. He encourages them to stretch their arms and hands like the branches of a tree seeking the sun, trying to grab hold of God's power: *"Therefore let us go on and get past the elementary stage in the teachings and doctrines of Christ, the Messiah, advancing steadily toward the completeness and perfection that belongs to spiritual maturity. (Hebrews 6:1a, Amplified)."*

Parents give with the hope of producing excellence in their children. But, what a sad thing it would be for a parent to never see the outcome of their provision and training, to never have the joy of relating to their children as adults. The reward for parents is to see their children grow up happy and eventually provide for and train the next generation: *"Children's children are the crown of old men; and the glory of children are their fathers." Proverbs 17:6.*

God also wants His children to grow. He wants to rejoice in our excellence.

Childhood is fun. It is relatively free of responsibilities. Children take and receive and give little. Nevertheless, many of us would like to be spiritual Peter Pans, to live in the Never-Never Land of childhood and never grow up. But to have a spiritual family and a "crown" requires us to leave Never-Never Land and take on adult responsibilities. We can only help our own children grow to the point we have. Let's leave our Peter Pan ways and grasp for the goal of maturity.

Lets go back up in the passage of Hebrews 5:11-6:2 to see the mechanism of this growth. I will use a technique of Bro. Tom McElmurry. He once said that if you got a letter from Aunt Rita and read the last paragraph, and didn't understand the letter, then it would be appropriate to read backward and find the source of her shocking close.

"But strong meat belongeth to them that are of full age, even those who by reason of use have their senses exercised to discern both good and evil." Hebrews 5:14. The word "strong" comes from the Greek "stereos."[47] "Stereos" means "solid, firm, three dimensional." The word "stereo" makes us think of stereophonic sound as opposed to monophonic sound. Stereophonic sound is produced by "using two or more channels to carry and reproduce the sound from the directions in which they were picked up"[48] Monophonic sound uses only one channel.[49] The author of Hebrews uses "stereo" in the same sense of richness. He uses the developmental terms of "milk" and "strong meat" to show the advancement from perceiving spiritual things one dimensionally (mono) to perceiving them multidimensionally (stereo).

"Stereo" as a developmental advancement can be observed in young children. Young children before age seven usually "link two events in all ways because they are similar in one way."[50] They make errors in judgment because they attend to only one dimension. At the age of concrete operations, 7-11, children's judgment becomes better because they can think in "stereo": the senses pick up data (sights, sounds, etc.) from different dimensions which are finally perceived together in all their richness. Spiritually, a similar advance in development allows one to effectively evaluate the richness of the spiritual world.

"Stereo" belongs to those of full age. "Full age" means "complete growth, complete mental or moral character."[51] With the advent of "stereo," the child has the ability to advance to adult levels of thinking. The foundation gets a framework. The equipment gets delivered and the carpenters, masons, and electricians of the mind go to work.

"Stereo" enters through the doorway of use. The young child acts on the environment and learns bit-by-bit, piece-by-piece with monodimensional tools until one day he makes a breakthrough. "By reason of use" actually means "the channel of an act; through practice or habit."[52] Isaiah described this process: *"Whom shall he teach knowledge? and whom shall he make to understand doctrine? them that are weaned from the milk, and drawn from the breasts. For precept must be upon precept, precept upon precept; line upon line, line upon line; here a little, and there a little:" Isaiah 28:9,10.*

Hebrews 5:14 teaches us that young children reach the threshold of stereo by "exercising their senses." The senses are the organs of perception used for judgment.[53] Vine says the spiritual senses are "capacities for spiritual apprehension."[54] These were described in detail in Chapter 1. The word "exercise" in this verse was used by the Greeks to describe young athletes' special training for Olympic type games. The word is "gumnazo" and it means "to practice naked."[55] Greek athletes practiced in the raw.[56] From "gumnazo" comes the word "gumnasion" (gymnasium),[57] the reserved place where athletes trained. Therefore, exercising the senses in the verse means to train spiritual senses like an athlete would for a contest. The training is to be done in a systematic and disciplined way.

Young children naturally train themselves in this manner. Piaget taught that children learn first by touching and handling. Then they learn next to estimate the results of their actions beforehand. They use their experience to predict. The ability, however, to be accurate in their assessments of outcomes is not possible until the age of seven or so.[58] Children need repeated experiments in order to accurately predict. Piaget's explanation of the results of these sense experiments resembles our concept of "stereo." He said children before the age of seven think in static, two-dimensional images. Nevertheless, because of experience and action on the environment by age seven, they learn to imagine in three dimensions and anticipate movements and formations.[59]

Through the analogy of exercise, the writer of Hebrews encourages us to train our spiritual senses so we can reach spiritual "stereo": *"Train yourself toward godliness (piety) - Keeping yourself spiritually fit, for physical training is of some value - useful for a little; but godliness [spiritual training] is useful and of value in everything and in every way, for it holds promise for the present life and also for the life which is to come." (1 Timothy 4:7-8, Amplified Bible).*

The advantage of reaching the three-dimensional level spiritually is the ability to "discern both good and evil." "Discern" means "to separate thoroughly, to carefully consider the facts in coming to a decision."[60] Good and evil are contrasted in the original language as "valuable vs. worthless."[61] These terms from the original are exactly what we would expect from a developmental perspective. Young spiritual experimenters train their senses through practice until they are able to keep the valuable and throw away the useless. They learn to predict the beneficial in the spiritual world and avoid the harmful.

Only through "stereo" will the child be able to grasp for the goal of maturity. "Stereo" belongs to those who are ready to advance, those who have trained their spiritual senses to separate the valuable from the worthless.

But what do we say for those who don't reach this level, for those who lag behind in their spiritual growth. They remain on the bottle. They live in a monophonic, two-dimensional world: *"For every one that useth milk is unskilful in the word of righteousness: for he is a babe." Hebrews 5:13.* The spiritual traveler who sees the world through two-dimensional eyes has not yet experimented enough with the computations that give rise to effective actions; he or she is still a spiritual infant (without language).

The Greek words in Hebrews 5:13 continue to connote developmental ideas. "Unskilful" literally means "no experiment."[62] "Word" (Logos) implies "reasoning and computation."[63] "Righteousness" means "right actions".[64] And "babe" literally means "without the power of speech."[65]

The writer leads us to think of a baby less than two years old. "Babe" is used in Romans 2:20 to describe those possessing only natural knowledge. "Babe" is used in 1 Corinthians 3:1-2 where Paul says he cannot speak to their spiritual nature, but only to their physical nature, because they are without spiritual language (babes).

The writer of Hebrews laments this condition: *"For when for the time ye ought to be teachers, ye have need that one teach you again which be the first principles of the oracles of God; and are become such as have need of milk, and not of strong meat." Hebrews 5:12.* He sighs because the Hebrew Christians have grown physically and psychologically, but they remain stuck in spiritual infancy. They have not grown enough to face the crisis of spiritual childhood. They now require retraining because they have forgotten: *"But he that lacketh these things is blind, and cannot see afar off, and hath forgotten that he was purged from his old sins." 2 Peter 1:9.*

Here is Hebrews 5:12 more bluntly: At your age in life, you should be teachers of others, but now you need those who are mature and complete to teach you once more the ABC's from the alphabet, not Word, of God; you have become those that need milk (two-dimensions), and not solid food (stereo). You have reverted back to the stage where you cannot feed yourself or chew your food.[66]

How did the Hebrew Christians get into this quagmire, this Slough of Despond?[67] They did not look for the proper steps. They failed to exercise their spiritual senses, and they became dull, lazy, sluggish, and unresponsive.[68] The writer of Hebrews said they could not advance in their understanding of Christ because of this lethargy: *"Of whom we have many things to say, and hard to be uttered, seeing ye are dull of hearing." Hebrews 5:11.* In other words, he had many things to teach them about Jesus, but they were difficult to relate in spiritual words, because the people had not developed their spiritual senses, their hearing in particular.[69]

Crisis

Somehow, the Hebrew Christians came to a place in their Christian life where they balked at going farther. They were unwilling to confront their crisis. They did not want to leave Never-Never Land. Therefore, they lost the sights and sounds of the spiritual dimension they had begun to know. The Bible teaches that neglect of going forward leads to the loss of insights already gained. In contrast, going forward leads to greater understanding: *"If any man have ears to hear, let him hear. And he said unto them, Take heed what ye hear: with what measure ye mete, it shall be measured to you: and unto you that hear shall more be given. For he that hath, to him shall be given: and he that hath not, from him shall be taken even that which he hath." Mark 4:23-25.*

The children of Israel also faced the crisis of going on to perfection. We left them at Mount Sinai where they received the Ten Commandments, the judgments, and the ordinances. The children learned the tasks of spiritual childhood and were ready to approach the barrier between them and spiritual adolescence.

The cloud moved from Sinai in the second year from their escape (Numbers 10:11-13). The book of Numbers describes how they were organized to march under the direction of the cloud (Numbers 9:15-23). They were to go forward when the cloud went forward, and to stop when the cloud stopped. This demonstrated their following of the Lord's leadership.

The text turns to military matters after the encounter with God at Sinai. The people were divided into armies according to their tribes (Numbers 10:28, 33-36). Discipline and warfare are the work of spiritual adolescence.

God also sent them a counselor, Jethro (Numbers 10:29-32). He became their eyes: "and thou mayest be to us instead of eyes." Jethro as the spiritual mentor had trained his senses to discern good and evil and was able to lead the less mature.

The Israelites soon arrived at their crisis point: Kadesh-barnea in the wilderness of Paran. At Kadesh God commanded Moses to send twelve spies (one for each tribe) into the Promised Land on a reconnaissance mission (Numbers 13:1-25). Moses exhorted the men to "be of good courage." Courage is a necessary character trait in the spiritual land they were to explore: adolescence.

Probing into the next developmental level is natural. Children often admire teenagers and try to be near them. I believe we also probe in our spiritual growth.

The twelve spies came back after forty days with a majority and a minority report (Numbers 13:26-33). The majority report (v.32) was a slander against the land. They saw the sons of Anak, the giants. They saw themselves as grasshoppers in the reflection of the giants (v.33). Even though the majority testified of the richness of Canaan (surely it flows with milk and honey), they assumed the sons of Anak were invincible. The ten looked at the obstacles from only a physical point of view.

The giants represented the crises of spiritual adolescence, which must be defeated by warfare. They must be wrestled to the ground if one is to live peaceably and at rest. The majority were not prepared to fight. In contrast, a latter group of Israelites were prepared: *"Blessed be the LORD my strength, which teacheth my hands to war, and my fingers to fight:" Psalms 144:1.* David the king and his men finally destroyed the last of the giants hundreds of years later (2 Samuel 21:18-22).

The minority report, given by Caleb, was filled with faith, trust, and courage: "Let us go up at once, and possess it; for we are well able to overcome it." What was the difference? Caleb and Joshua saw the giants from a spiritual perspective. They knew it was God's will to move forward. He would supply the weapons and strategies to win (Numbers 14:6-10).

The children of Israel believed the majority report and stopped their growth that day. They cried to Moses and Aaron and lamented their impending deaths at the hands of the natives. They did not believe that they could conquer the giants of Canaan, which in a spiritual sense are those crises that arise from renouncing the values of the world and moving into the unknown world of the spirit. They even elected a captain to take them back to Egypt, which in symbolic terms equals a repudiation of the spiritual life (Numbers 14:1-4).

"And the LORD spake unto Moses and unto Aaron, saying, How long shall I bear with this evil congregation, which murmur against me? I have heard the murmurings of the children of Israel, which they murmur against me. Say unto them, As truly as I live, saith the LORD, as ye have spoken in mine ears, so will I do to you: Your carcases shall fall in this wilderness; and

all that were numbered of you, according to your whole number, from twenty years old and upward, which have murmured against me, Doubtless ye shall not come into the land, concerning which I sware to make you dwell therein, save Caleb the son of Jephunneh, and Joshua the son of Nun. But your little ones, which ye said should be a prey, them will I bring in, and they shall know the land which ye have despised. But as for you, your carcases, they shall fall in this wilderness. And your children shall wander in the wilderness forty years, and bear your whoredoms, until your carcases be wasted in the wilderness. After the number of the days in which ye searched the land, even forty days, each day for a year, shall ye bear your iniquities, even forty years, and ye shall know my breach of promise. I the LORD have said, I will surely do it unto all this evil congregation, that are gathered together against me: in this wilderness they shall be consumed, and there they shall die. And the men, which Moses sent to search the land, who returned, and made all the congregation to murmur against him, by bringing up a slander upon the land, Even those men that did bring up the evil report upon the land, died by the plague before the LORD. But Joshua the son of Nun, and Caleb the son of Jephunneh, which were of the men that went to search the land, lived still." Numbers 14:26-38.

The Lord responded to their unbelief with judgment: They would die in the wilderness; they would die as spiritual children. All over the age of 20 would never see the Promised Land.

Everyone over 20 who turned away from the crisis made a final decision. From this example, it seems that 20 is on the higher end of the Bell Curve for the ability to enter spiritual adolescence. God would not have cut off those too immature to decide. Erikson taught that a firm identity requires 20 years to develop: "twenty years is about the span of human development needed for the individual to acquire a sense of identity firm enough and informed enough to act."[70] So we have a biblical example and the corollary of social development to show that 20 is a reasonable benchmark (see Chapter 9 Spiritual Adolescence).

Only two people of the over two million had the spiritual vision to enter the land. They had the character qualities of trust and commitment, which are requirements of spiritual warfare. Joshua and Caleb were willing to fight for the privilege of entering the next level.

Commitment is the crisis of spiritual childhood. Romans 12:1-2 is an excellent explanation of spiritual commitment: *"I beseech you therefore, brethren, by the mercies of God, that ye present your bodies a living sacrifice, holy, acceptable unto God, which is your reasonable service. And be not conformed to this world: but be ye transformed by the renewing of your mind, that ye may prove what is that good, and acceptable, and perfect, will of God." Romans 12:1,2.*

The word "beseech" is translated in other places "exhort." The original word means "to call near/alongside for the purpose of asking or begging to action, encouraging to go forward, and to comfort."[71] Paul, the writer of Romans, was able to "beseech" the brethren to higher levels of growth because he had more maturity. Joshua and Caleb also were able to exhort because in their hearts they had already crossed over into spiritual adolescence.

"By the mercies of God" - Remembering that God watches over us and will save us from harm motivates us to commit to Him: *"He made known his ways unto Moses, his acts unto the children of Israel…Like as a father pitieth his children, so the LORD pitieth them that fear him. For he knoweth our frame; he remembereth that we are dust." Psalms 103:7, 13-14.* Joshua and Caleb remembered God's ways and trusted Him to protect them from the giants of the land.

"Present your bodies a living sacrifice" - To "present" is "to act on commitment." It means "to offer all we are to God for acceptance."

To "sacrifice" means "to dedicate something to God." The children of Israel were familiar with sacrificing animals. But, Paul exhorts spiritual children to offer "living sacrifices" rather than dead ones. In the context of the phrase our bodies are the dedicated sacrifice. We are not to kill our bodies in dedication to God, but we are to offer them as if we were already dead to our own wants and wills. A soldier dedicates himself to fight and perhaps sacrifice on a daily basis: *"And the things that thou hast heard of me among many witnesses, the same commit thou to faithful men, who shall be able to teach others also. Thou therefore endure hardness, as a good soldier of Jesus Christ." 2 Timothy 2:2,3. "I am crucified with Christ: nevertheless I live; yet not I, but Christ liveth in me: and the life which I now live in the flesh I live by the faith of the Son of God, who loved me, and gave himself for me." Galatians 2:20.*

"Holy, acceptable to God" - The word "holy" signified to the Greeks "dedicated to the Gods."[72] The word "holy" carries the ideas of physical purity and moral blamelessness. The term "holy" signifies the quality of the sacrifice. God would not accept a blemished sacrifice from the Israelites (Leviticus 1:2-3).

The term "without blemish" means "entire, complete."[73] God wants His living sacrifices, those ready to enter spiritual adolescence, to offer themselves totally, with no part uncommitted.

"Which is your reasonable service" - Vine's dictionary implies the word "reasonable" here is used to contrast the sacrifice of a rational being (human) to the sacrifice of an irrational being (animal).[74]God taught the Israelites to sacrifice animals to Him, but they were only shadows of the real, living sacrifices God wanted.

"And be not conformed to this world: but be ye transformed" - This phrase is an allusion to Ovid's *Metamorphoses*. Ovid was a poet laureate of Rome in the early 1st century.[75] But, he offended Caesar Augustus and was banished in 8A.D. to Romania.[76] The reasons for his banishment were Augustus' objections to his poem *"Ars Amatoria,"* the Art of Love, and a mistake/error, not a crime, committed in 8 A.D. Ovid never told what the mistake was. He only implied that he saw something he was not supposed to see. Apparently, Ovid's biggest offence was his encouragement of loose morals through his poetry in a day when Augustus was trying to make adultery a capital crime. Ovid's books were removed from the public libraries and he died in exile in 17A.D. Ovid's friends tried to persuade the emperor to have him return, but his works circulated only privately under Augustus.

Such a scandal of a famous Roman artist must have been well known in Rome in A.D. 57, the date of Paul's letter. By the year 57, the people of Rome must have been as familiar with *Metamorphoses,* Ovid's masterpiece, as Americans today are familiar with *Huckleberry Finn*. Paul, as a Roman citizen from a cosmopolitan city, Tarsus, must have known about Ovid and his book. I believe this because of Paul's use of the word "metamorphoo," which has been translated in Romans 12:2 as "transformed."

The first line of *Metamorphoses* tells its theme; "My intention is to tell of bodies changed to different forms; the gods, who made the changes, will help me."[77] The poem gives explanations of the nature and character of the physical world by showing how people were changed by the gods into trees, flowers, and animals. The individuals were changed into things that symbolized their character: Lycaon put Jove to the test by killing a hostage and preparing the body for Jove to eat. Jove punished him by changing him into a wolf. This is why the wolf "delights in slaughter."[78] Apollo pursued Daphne for love. She refused him. Her hardness toward love was her downfall. She was changed into something hard and lifeless, a laurel tree, which Apollo loved.[79] Cygnus mourned for the fallen Phaethon and became a mournful swan.[80] Ocyrhoe prophesied about Coronis' son. For this she was sentenced to neigh and whinny, to make the sounds of prophecy.[81] Echo talked and chattered to create diversions for Jove in his trysts. She was condemned by Juno to say the last thing she heard and nothing further. Ovid said, "She could not start a conversation, nor fail to answer other people talking." After Narcissus rejected her, Echo pined away until only her voice remained.[82]Narcissus rejected Echo but lost his heart to his own reflection in a pool. He became a thing that can never move but only look pretty, a flower.[83] The mulberry tree once had white mulberries but now they are red in honor of the blood of Pyramus and Thisbe, who were lovers like Romeo and Juliet.[84] Clytie loved the sun god but because of her jealousy and for telling of his affair with Leucothoe (for which Leucothoe was killed by her father), the sun god rejected her. Still Clytie turned toward the sunlight. She pined away and became a sunflower.[85] The nine daughters of Pierus loved the sound of their own voices and challenged the Muses to a duel of singing. They lost and were changed to magpies, which chatter and imitate any kind of sound.[86] These examples are from only the first five books of *Metamorphoses* (there are fifteen).

Ovid's heroes were "conformed to this world." They became living sacrifices to the Roman gods and were like things in the world.[87] Vine's dictionary says the word translated "conformed," "suschematizo," could not be used of inward transformation. It could only be used of that which is worldly: transitory, changeable, and unstable.[88] Vine also said "schema" of "suschematizo" stresses outward change while "morphe" of "metamorphoo" stresses an inward change. He said that Luke in his account of the transfiguration avoided using "metamorphoo" because it would have "suggested to Gentile readers the metamorphoses of heathen gods."[89] The Jewish gospel writers used "metamorphoo," but Luke was the only Gentile writer of the NT.

Since the Romans were used to seeing metamorphosis as a change initiated by a god based on character, and Paul contrasted the word "conformed," which refers only to outward change, to "transformed," then "metamorphoo" implied inward change by God based on character. Paul counseled the Romans to present themselves to the true God for a different kind of metamorphosis. Paul did not want them to be transformed like Ovid's subjects, only in the physical world, but also in the heart. He wanted them to go beyond the inward change of initial salvation. He beseeched them to have a total transformation of heart.

Paul taught that God required presentation and holiness for His metamorphosis.

"By the renewing of your mind" - Paul's metamorphosis is a renovation of the mind; it's to be made new again and brought back to an uncorrupted condition.[90] The "mind" in this context refers to "thoughts, feelings, and will":[91] the elements of the psychological nature (see Chapter 1). While the crisis of spiritual birth was a renovation of the "pneuma," the crisis of spiritual childhood is a renovation of the psyche. This transformation is accomplished not by self-will, but by the presentation to God in commitment. By God's grace, the Spirit within works His way outward; *"But we all, with open face beholding as in a glass the glory of the Lord, are changed into the same image from glory to glory, even as by the Spirit of the Lord." 2 Corinthians 3:18.* Changed = "metamorphoo."

Metamorphosis is a process.[92] It is change in stages. In biology, metamorphosis means "a change in form, structure, or function as a result of development."[93]

Caterpillar, chrysalis, butterfly: these are all the same insect at different stages. We call the process of its change, metamorphosis. It's fascinating that Paul under the inspiration of the Holy Spirit used such a versatile word. The inward change God produces in us also follows a definite pattern.

"That ye may prove what is that good, and acceptable, and perfect, will of God." The process of metamorphosis gives the spiritual traveler what the babe of Hebrews 5:13 lacks, experience. The spirit man grows by experience, the same way as the physical man, by reaching out and learning with his senses. We prove God's will by testing with our spiritual senses.[94]

The word "perfect" in this verse is different from the "perfection" in Hebrews 6:1. The verse in Hebrews tells us to be carried on to full growth (perfection). Here we are to "test the already complete (perfect) will of God for us."[95] God's will is already perfect. We become perfect, or mature, as we follow His will.

The only way to experience His complete will for us is to take the challenge of each stage. The challenge of spiritual childhood is "to present our bodies a living sacrifice," to commit to God.

The children of Israel failed to present themselves to God in commitment. Therefore, when they presumed to fight without that inward metamorphosis, they were turned back: *"And they rose up early in the morning, and gat them up into the top of the mountain, saying, Lo, we be here, and will go up unto the place which the LORD hath promised: for we have sinned. And Moses said, Wherefore now do ye transgress the commandment of the LORD? but it shall not prosper. Go not up, for the LORD is not among you; that ye be not smitten before your enemies. For the Amalekites and the Canaanites are there before you, and ye shall fall by the sword: because ye are turned away from the LORD, therefore the LORD will not be with you. But they presumed to go up unto the hill top: nevertheless the ark of the covenant of the LORD, and Moses, departed not out of the camp. Then the Amalekites came down, and the Canaanites which dwelt in that hill, and smote them, and discomfited them, even unto Hormah." Numbers 14:40-45.*

"The Lord is not among you" - The word "among" in the Hebrew could be literally translated as "inward parts or thoughts": "the Lord is not in your inward parts."[96] Moses implied they would not be able to defeat their enemies because of their lack of inward dedication and transformation.

"Ye are turned away" - You have retreated from the crisis between you and a closer relationship with God.[97]

"But they presumed to go up" - They went to battle without the weapons of spiritual adolescence; they went as children. The Amalekites and Canaanites "discomfited" them; they were "crushed, destroyed, and utterly routed" without God's protection and blessing.[98]

This example teaches us that there is a definite order of spiritual tasks and challenges. We must follow the plan to win: *"And if a man also strive for masteries, yet is he not crowned, except he strive lawfully." 2 Timothy 2:5.*

Why were the children of Israel given such a harsh sentence: death in the wilderness? Why were they not given a second chance from a merciful God? The answer is found back in Hebrews 6.

The Hebrew Christians were also blocked in their growth because they did not develop their spiritual senses. The writer exhorted them to go on to spiritual maturity and used the failure of Israel at Kadesh-barnea as an example of those who "refuse Him that speaketh." I will explain later how I know the following passage refers to Kadesh.

"1 Therefore leaving the principles of the doctrine of Christ, let us go on unto perfection…3 And this will we do, if God permit. 4 For it is impossible for those who were once enlightened, and have tasted of the heavenly gift, and were made partakers of the Holy Ghost, 5 And have tasted the good word of God, and the powers of the world to come, 6 If they shall fall away, to renew them again unto repentance; seeing they crucify to themselves the Son of God afresh, and put him to an open shame. 7 For the earth which drinketh in the rain that cometh oft upon it, and bringeth forth herbs meet for them by whom it is dressed, receiveth blessing from God: 8 But that which beareth thorns and briers is rejected, and is nigh unto cursing; whose end is to be burned. 9 But, beloved, we are persuaded better things of you, and things that accompany salvation, though we thus speak." Hebrews 6:1, 3-9.

"If indeed God permits"[99] - The writer implies that God has stopped some in their journey. He goes on to explain that there have been some who after they experienced the incipience of their spiritual senses turned away from the spiritual world.

"Those who were once enlightened" - In v.4-5 the writer continues the developmental perspective of the previous verses by using sense words four times: enlightened ("photizo" - made to see[100]), tasted (twice), and partakers.

"Iftheyshallfallaway"-"Tofallinone'swayorpath,tostumble,tohaltprogress."[101]   The phrase suggests a halt to growth, not a loss of the spiritual nature.

"It is impossible…to renew them again to repentance" - Definition 2 of my blue dictionary for renew is "to give new spiritual strength to."[102] It's like in a video game where you must pick up a sword, hammer, or gun to gain strength and keep going against adversity. In the spirit world, if you do not meet your crisis and gain from its resolution, you lose your spiritual strength and become vulnerable: *"And he said unto them, Take heed what ye hear: with what measure ye mete, it shall be measured to you: and unto you that hear shall more be given. For he that hath, to him shall be given: and he that hath not, from him shall be taken even that which he hath." Mark 4:24,25.* Repentance means, "change of mind, altered perception."[103] Repentance is the prerequisite of metamorphosis. Without repentance there could be no commitment to God. Repentance prepares us for the renewing of our minds and for our metamorphosis. Those who turn away from the moment of crisis sometimes lose the power to change their minds. The children of Israel later desired to change their minds about going into the land, but "the Lord was not among them."

"Seeing they crucify to themselves the Son of God afresh, and put Him to an open shame" -Those who fall away show their unbelief in God's power to transform. They show their unbelief in God even though He has already proved Himself to them in salvation. They in effect say, "Did He rise again? Did God really save me?" They fall back to a lower level of faith. A Christian who refuses to grow crucifies Christ afresh because he puts himself back in the camp of unbelief. In contrast, Paul expressed his hope in God's transforming power: *"That I may know him, and the power of his resurrection Philippians 3:10.*

The children of Israel ran away from the crisis at Kadesh and put God to a public shame before the heathen even though He had already showed His power to them: *"11 And the LORD said unto Moses, How long will this people provoke me? and how long will it be ere they believe me, for all the signs which I have shewed among them? 12 I will smite them with the pestilence, and disinherit them, and will make of thee a greater nation and mightier than they. 13 And Moses said unto the LORD, Then the Egyptians shall hear it, (for thou broughtest up this people in thy might from among them;) 14 And they will tell it to the inhabitants of this land: for they have heard that thou LORD art among this people, that thou LORD art seen face to face, and that thy cloud standeth over them, and that thou goest before them, by day time in a pillar of a cloud, and in a pillar of fire by night. 15 Now if thou shalt kill all this people as one man, then the nations which have heard the fame of thee will speak, saying, 16 Because the LORD was not able to bring this people into the land which he sware unto them, therefore he hath slain them in the wilderness." (Numbers 14:11-16).*

God threatened to disinherit them because of their rebellion. Yet, Moses appealed for them on the basis of God's reputation (v.15 -16). God spared them but did not allow them to move forward on their journey. He led them instead to wander in the wilderness. This was the only merciful thing He could do. They were not ready to fight for the right to be in the Promised Land. Only Caleb (and Joshua) "had another spirit and followed God fully." God promised that their "seed would possess it." (Numbers 14:17-25).

"For the earth which drinketh in rain" - Rain is used as a symbol in Hebrews 6:7-8 of spiritual nurturance to the soil of people's hearts. It is another metaphor of spiritual growth. The writer says those who bear fitting herbs are blessed of God, but those who receive God's rain and yet bear thorns and briars are nigh unto cursing. God expects a return on His investment (Isaiah 55:10-11).The parable of the sower (Matthew 13:18-23) is about this very principle. Some people are soil by the wayside; they do not understand. Some are stony soil; they have no place for roots and soon wither. Some soil already has the seeds of thorns in it, and the good herbs are choked. Finally, some are good soil; they exercise their spiritual senses and hear with spiritual ears; they bear fitting herbs.

The children of Israel received God's rain: His spiritual milk. Yet, God did not receive a return for His work. They turned away at the crucial moment. Therefore, they "found no place of repentance, though they sought it carefully with tears": *"And Moses told these sayings unto all the children of Israel: and the people mourned greatly." Numbers 14:39.*

"We are persuaded better things of you" - The writer of Hebrews implies in 6:9 that even though the children of Israel failed at Kadesh-barnea, his audience (the Hebrews of the 1st century) would not. He has confidence they will meet the crisis of spiritual childhood. He is "persuaded better things of them, things that *echo*[104] salvation." Remember Echo? She says the last thing she hears. Echo responds to the words of salvation without doubt. She is the good soil that hears.

Key - Trust

How do I know the writer of Hebrews in Chapter 6 is using the incident at Kadesh-barnea as an example? Because that's what he was talking about in Chapters 3 and 4. It fits the context.

In Chapter 3 he teaches that the key to entering spiritual adolescence is trust. He uses the children of Israel as a negative example: *"Wherefore (as the Holy Ghost saith, To day if ye will hear his voice, 8 Harden not your hearts, as in the provocation, in the day of temptation in the wilderness: 9 When your fathers tempted me, proved me, and saw my works forty years. 10 Wherefore I was grieved with that generation, and said, They do alway err in their heart; and they have not known my ways. 11 So I sware in my wrath, They shall not enter into my rest.) 12 Take heed, brethren, lest there be in any of you an evil heart of unbelief, in departing from the living God. 13 But exhort one another daily, while it is called To day; lest any of you be hardened through the deceitfulness of sin. 14 For we are made partakers of Christ, if we hold the beginning of our confidence stedfast unto the end; 15 While it is said, To day if ye will hear his voice, harden not your hearts, as in the provocation. 16 For some, when they had heard, did provoke: howbeit not all that came out of Egypt by Moses. 17 But with whom was he grieved forty years? was it not with them that had sinned, whose carcases fell in the wilderness? 18 And to whom sware he that they should not enter into his rest, but to them that believed not? 19 So we see that they could not enter in because of unbelief." Hebrews 3;7-19*

The writer begins by telling us the Holy Spirit is leading him to quote Psalm 95. He says, "Hear God's voice. Exercise your spiritual senses. Take note of where you are on your journey."

He then warns us not to be like the children of Israel: "harden not your hearts." God had indignation against them because they went astray in their hearts and did not follow the road to spiritual maturity.[105] The writer says in v.12 and 13, "Take heed, look, watch out. Do not have a heart that fails to trust in God, that causes you to desert from God's army. Instead, exhort one another to stay on the path."[106]

Why should we be so diligent? Because we have an opportunity to become partakers of Christ's spiritual nature (v.14). This goal is the hope of our confidence. Our confidence in God's blessing is the foundation of growth.[107] We must hang onto the confidence we started with all the way to the end of our labor, till the building is complete.

Then, the writer repeats the exhortation in v.15-18 to hear God's voice and follow Him. He emphasizes that only those who failed to trust God were not allowed to take the next step (v.19).

Chapter 4 talks about the "rest of God." This is a stage beyond Kadesh-barnea and spiritual adolescence. It is a vision of what can be, designed to encourage spiritual travelers. The metaphors of the journey and the race continue.

Rest is beyond Kadesh because some stopped short at Kadesh and did not enter rest: *"Let us therefore fear, lest, a promise being left us of entering into his rest, any of you should seem to come short of it." Hebrews 4:1.* Rest is beyond adolescence because even Joshua did not provide it for the children of Israel, even though he helped them defeat their enemies, which is the crisis of spiritual adolescence: *"For if Jesus had given them rest, then would he not afterward have spoken of another day. There remaineth therefore a rest to the people of God." Hebrews 4:8,9.* The literal meaning of remaineth is "reserved."[108] God has reserved a rest to His people who continue to follow Him in growth.

The writer encourages us to labor, to use speed,[109] to enter rest (4:11). In fact, the whole book of Hebrews is an exhortation to "run the race set before us." The first few verses of Chapter 2 provide its theme: *Therefore we ought to give the more earnest heed to the things which we have heard, lest at any time we should let them slip. For if the word spoken by angels was stedfast, and every transgression and disobedience received a just recompence of reward; How shall we escape, if we neglect so great salvation; which at the first began to be spoken by the Lord, and was confirmed unto us by them that heard him;" Hebrews 2:1-3.* In other words, "Don't let God's words slip. Don't be careless and let them glide by."[110] TheAmplified Bible says: "lest in any way we drift past [them] and slip away." The images remind me of a relay race, where winning depends on proper timing. As in a relay race, we can't misjudge the timing in receiving the baton of God's word. Otherwise it will fall to the ground and we will be guilty of running the race carelessly.[111]

Wandering In The Wilderness

I must not neglect to explain the fate of those left to wander in the wilderness. John Bunyan's Formalist and Hypocrisy are apt personifications of the attitudes they develop. When Christian, Formalist, and Hypocrisy came to the hill Difficulty, their Kadesh-barnea, Christian went straight up, while Formalist and Hypocrisy tried to go around. Christian said:

> The hill, though high, I covet to ascend;
> The difficulty will not me offend;
> For I perceive the way to life lies here:
> Come, pluck up, heart, let's neither faint nor fear.
> better, though difficult, the right way to go,
> Than wrong, though easy, where the end is woe.[112]

Formalist and Hypocrisy "saw the hill was steep and high, and that there were two other ways to go... Now the name of one of those ways was Danger, and the name of the other Destruction. So the one took the way which is called Danger, which did lead him into a great wood; and the other took directly up the way to Destruction, which led him into a wide field, full of dark mountains, where he stumbled and fell, and rose no more."[113]

Formalist and Hypocrisy believed they could follow God by their own rules. They did not realize easy-looking ways lead to Danger and Destruction. Christian told them, "I walk by the rule of my Master: you walk by the rude working of your fancies."[114]

On his way up the hill, Christian also met Timorous and Mistrust running back down. They turned away from their journey because "the farther we go, the more danger we meet with."[115] They were also afraid of the "lions in the way." But Christian decided to go forward: "To go back is death: to go forward is fear of death, and life everlasting beyond it: I will yet go forward."[116] Timorous and Mistrust exemplified the children of Israel at Kadesh. Christian acted like Joshua and Caleb.

1 Corinthians 10:5-11 summarizes the problems of the children of Israel and those like Formalist and Hypocrisy who are sentenced to wander in the wilderness. Paul warns the Corinthians to go forward in their spiritual growth or suffer the fate of the wilderness.

"But with many of them God was not well pleased: for they were overthrown in the wilderness." 1 Corinthians 10:5. Joshua and Caleb and the children under 20 were the only exempt ones. The rest refused to commit themselves to God and use the key of trust.

"Now these things were our examples, to the intent we should not lust after evil things, as they also lusted." 1 Corinthians 10:6. The theme of the people's spiritual lives after Kadesh was boredom. Since they did not go forward in their growth, they atrophied in those spiritual senses they had begun to develop. They became "dull of hearing." As a consequence of their lack of spiritual discernment, and the resulting boredom with spiritual things, they began to long again for the pleasures of the world, of Egypt. They even elected a captain to help them return (Numbers 14:4). But that was impossible because of two reasons: they had already crossed the threshold of baptism at the Red Sea and Egypt would not let them back in.

"Neither be ye idolaters, as were some of them; as it is written, The people sat down to eat and drink, and rose up to play." 1 Corinthians 10:7. One of the outgrowths of spiritual boredom is idolatry: worshiping the works of your own hands (Isaiah 2:8). The children in the wilderness were far away from God in their hearts. Yet they felt a continual need to make a show of piety. An example is the golden calf. In the story of the golden calf, Moses took a long time in coming down from Mt. Sinai, and the people began to feel far away from God. They tried to contrive closeness to God by forming an image of Him. As a result, Aaron made the molten calf: *"And all the people brake off the golden earrings which were in their ears, and brought them unto Aaron. And he received them at their hand, and fashioned it with a graving tool, after he had made*

it a molten calf: and they said, These be thy gods, O Israel, which brought thee up out of the land of Egypt. And when Aaron saw it, he built an altar before it; and Aaron made proclamation, and said, To morrow is a feast to the LORD." Exodus 32:3-5.

Spiritual wanderers today show their boredom by becoming overly attached to certain songbooks, rituals, pastors, or buildings: the style of worship more than the substance.

"Neither let us commit fornication, as some of them committed, and fell in one day three and twenty thousand." 1 Corinthians 10:8. Boredom leads to lust. The lust of the flesh is one of the big three of an idle, carnal mind. It's one of the giants of the land. Those who refuse to fight give up control to the giants. Their spiritual man remains weak and underdeveloped in the giant's dungeon. Their natural man becomes muscular and well fed as an ally of giant lust (1 Corinthians 2:11-15).

The children of Israel saw themselves as grasshoppers compared to the giants of Canaan. They were afraid to fight. As a consequence, they did not develop spiritual strength and were easily led into idolatry and fornication: *"And Israel abode in Shittim, and the people began to commit whoredom with the daughters of Moab. And they called the people unto the sacrifices of their gods: and the people did eat, and bowed down to their gods. And Israel joined himself unto Baalpeor: and the anger of the LORD was kindled against Israel... And those that died in the plague were twenty and four thousand." Numbers 25:1-3, 9.*

"Neither let us tempt Christ, as some of them also tempted, and were destroyed of serpents." 1 Corinthians 10:9. Spiritual sluggishness makes you forget lessons of the past. You can forget that "you were once purged from your old sins." (2 Peter 1:9). You can forget that God has always provided for you. The people were discouraged by "the way." Their harvest of blessings had been curtailed.[117] They were stunted in their growth. They began to question God's provision. They forgot their first lesson of spiritual childhood: learning dependence on God: *"And they journeyed from mount Hor by the way of the Red sea, to compass the land of Edom: and the soul of the people was much discouraged because of the way. And the people spake against God, and against Moses, Wherefore have ye brought us up out of Egypt to die in the wilderness? for there is no bread, neither is there any water; and our soul loatheth this light bread. And the LORD sent fiery serpents among the people, and they bit the people; and much people of Israel died." Numbers 21:4-6.*

"And our soul loatheth this light bread" - More evidence of their boredom. They were tired of the manna. They had probably tried every form of manna possible: manna cakes, manna pies, fried manna, manna fries, manna sandwiches, etc. They said: *"We remember the fish, which we did eat in Egypt freely; the cucumbers, and the melons, and the leeks, and the onions, and the garlick: But now our soul is dried away: there is nothing at all, beside this manna, before our eyes." Numbers 11:5,6.*

Nevertheless, the symbolic purpose of the manna was to show God's provision for children unable to feed themselves. It was spiritual baby food in the fifth dimension. If they had gone into the land and entered spiritual adolescence, they would have enjoyed more variety. When their children entered the land under Joshua, the manna ceased: *"And the manna ceased on the morrow after they had eaten of the old corn of the land, neither had the children of Israel manna any more; but they did eat of the fruit of the land of Canaan that year." Joshua 5:12.*

But the children in the wilderness were unable to eat solid food. They were fed with milk (manna). They were like the Corinthians: *"And I, brethren, could not speak unto you as unto spiritual, but as unto carnal, even as unto babes in Christ. I have fed you with milk, and not with meat: for hitherto ye were not able to bear it, neither yet now are ye able." 1 Corinthians 3:1,2.*

Christians who do not commit to God also get stuck in spiritual childhood. They too can only handle baby food. If their teachers try to give them more, they resist. They have turned back from the crisis point already, and stubbornness has become their cardinal characteristic. They are a "stiffnecked" group. They get bored with the same old same old. Yet, that is the fate to which they have assigned themselves.

"Neither murmur ye, as some of them also murmured, and were destroyed of the destroyer." 1 Corinthians 10:10. The chief occupation of bored saints is murmuring. The New Testament definition for "murmur" is "to grumble,"[118] but the Old Testament word means "to lodge, stay, stop, abide," and "to be obstinate and complain."[119] The Old Testament word contains the concepts of both spiritual boredom and grumbling. The Old Testament "murmur" gives me the image of houseguests that are cordial in the presence of the hosts, but later get together and complain about the accommodations.

The Old Testament word for "murmuring" fits the spirit of those who failed at Kadesh. The people were spiritually idle; they had stopped to stay in the wilderness, and thus they began to complain. They had plenty of time to find troubles.

There are several instances of the children murmuring, so much so that it could be seen as their fatal flaw. They were condemned to die in the wilderness because of it: *"And the LORD spake unto Moses and unto Aaron, saying, How long shall I bear with this evil congregation, which murmur against me? I have heard the murmurings of the children of Israel, which they murmur against me. Say unto them, As truly as I live, saith the LORD, as ye have spoken in mine ears, so will I do to you: Your carcases shall fall in this wilderness; and all that were numbered of you, according to your whole number, from twenty years old and upward, which have murmured against me, Doubtless ye shall not come into the land, concerning which I sware to make you dwell therein, save Caleb the son of Jephunneh, and Joshua the son of Nun." Numbers 14:26-30.*

Destruction was the consequence of murmuring. And even though some of the children were destroyed quickly and miraculously (Numbers 16), most of them died slowly. The secret agent Destroyer usually worked undercover. His *modus operandi* lay in stealth. His minions were like spiritual AIDS viruses. They got in undetected and slowly multiplied. They were not noticed at first. Yet, every time their victims suffered stress, the invaders became stronger. Finally, their victims were overcome after a long siege. Vines dictionary defines "destroy" this way: "the idea is not extinction, but ruin, loss, not of being, but of well-being."[120]

The Greek verb for "destroy" is "apollumi," and the agent for "apollumi" is Apollyon.[121] Remember him? He's the king of the demonic locusts unleashed on the earth in Revelation 9:1-11. The locusts did not kill the people, but only tormented them and made them wish to die. Their stings hurt like the stings of scorpions. Misery and loss of well-being is the work of Apollyon, the destroyer.

The fatal flaw of murmuring opens the way for Apollyon. The Greek word for "destroyer" means "a ruiner, a venomous serpent."[122] The people's attitudes made them vulnerable to the destroyer's poison. Their murmuring allowed the poison into their spiritual lives first, and then metastasize into their psyches and bodies. Finally, it cost them their lives. They wandered in the wilderness for forty years, bored, until they were consumed (Numbers 14:29; 32:13).

Today, murmurers are frequently found in bored churches that have balked at committing themselves to God. And they too suffer from the slow poison of their own attitudes.

"Now all these things happened unto them for ensamples: and they are written for our admonition, upon whom the ends of the world are come." 1 Corinthians 10:11. The children of Israel are examples to us of the consequences of rebellion. "We ought to give more earnest heed" to this admonition since we live at the end of the ages. The children of Israel lived at the beginning of the journey, but we live at the time of their destination.[123] We have the advantage of knowing where they got off the track, but we also have the pressure of knowing that "the time is short." (1 Corinthians 7:29).

Symbol - Light

The symbol for spiritual childhood is light.

The natural world is described as a place of darkness while the spiritual world is portrayed as a place of light: *"But ye are a chosen generation, a royal priesthood, an holy nation, a peculiar people; that ye should shew forth the praises of him who hath called you out of darkness into his marvellous light:"* 1 Peter 2:9.

Natural people are shown to be children of darkness while spiritual people are depicted as children of light: *"Ye are all the children of light, and the children of the day; we are not of the night, nor of darkness."* 1 Thessalonians 5:5.

Natural deeds are represented as works of darkness while spiritual deeds are characterized as works of light: *"For ye were sometimes darkness, but now are ye light in the Lord: walk as children of light:"* Ephesians 5:8. Darkness is natural to us before spiritual birth. Light becomes our environment afterward. The god of the natural world keeps us lost by keeping us in the dark. When we enter the spiritual world through the new birth, we see the light: *"But if our gospel be hid, it is hid to them that are lost: In whom the god of this world hath blinded the minds of them which believe not, lest the light of the glorious gospel of Christ, who is the image of God, should shine unto them."* 2 Corinthians 4:3,4.

God judged the Egyptians by darkness, but gave light to the children of Israel (Exodus 10:21-23). God led the children out of Egypt by His light: *"And the LORD went before them by day in a pillar of a cloud, to lead them the way; and by night in a pillar of fire, to give them light; to go by day and night:"* Exodus 13:21. The cloud separated the children from the Egyptians by being light to one and darkness to the other: *"And it came between the camp of the Egyptians and the camp of Israel; and it was a cloud and darkness to them, but it gave light by night to these: so that the one came not near the other all the night."* Exodus 14:20.

Light is necessary for the developmental tasks of spiritual childhood. Some of the skills needed for the tasks are co-operation and fellowship, which cannot happen in the dark. John reminded his spiritual children of the importance of light for growth and relationships: *"This then is the message which we have heard of him, and declare unto you, that God is light, and in him is no darkness at all. If we say that we have fellowship with him, and walk in darkness, we lie, and do not the truth: But if we walk in the light, as he is in the light, we have fellowship one with another, and the blood of Jesus Christ his Son cleanseth us from all sin." 1 John 1:5-7.*

In the next chapter, we will learn what it takes to take down the giants and continue the journey toward the "rest" of God.

CHAPTER 9

Spiritual Adolescence

HEAVY rains fall on Israel during December, January, and February. Violent thunderstorms crash down with lightning and hail.[1] The prophet Joel listed this rain in his three stages of rain: the early rain, the violent rain, and the latter rain (Joel 2:23).[2] The violent rain is a good metaphor for spiritual adolescence.

During the early rains (spiritual childhood), the heart and mind are softened and broken up and the seeds of truth are planted. But to grow to maturity, the seeds need lots of rain. The heavy rains provide the water but are accompanied by turbulence. During spiritual adolescence, God waters the Word that has been planted in the heart. Yet along with the opportunity for growth comes the danger of stormy emotions and confusion.

Just like the heavy rains are the main effect on the seed's growth, spiritual adolescence makes or breaks the hero. If few people reach spiritual adolescence, even fewer graduate from it; they often are victims of the *sweeping rain that leaves no food* (Proverbs 28:3).

Violent Rain

Children from 7 to 11 or 12 years can evaluate spiritual matters and think logically about what can be seen, heard, touched, tasted, or smelled. They learn cooperation, rules, and technologies. They grow in their ability to conduct experiments. Then, at the age of 11 or 12, they break through to a new level. Children begin to think in terms of concepts, possibilities, and hypotheses of things beyond the senses.[3] They conduct experiments by imagination rather than by merely physical senses. This new ability of the mind provides for more advanced spiritual growth because experiments in the spiritual realm must be done without the aid of sense data.

Preteens and teenagers can begin to understand and follow principles behind rules. They are no longer limited to the parameters of their own society or its rules. They often seem to be idealistic because they are for the first time envisioning perfect systems of living. They can think about ideas and societies that have existed, do exist, or can exist.[4]

Young people use their powers of imagination to experiment in their minds with different roles, partners, and lifestyles. They may be intellectuals one month and singers the next. They may go with middle class partners one month and working class partners the next. They may be New Agers one month and Christians the next.

Then, from about ages 17-23, young people begin to choose from all alternatives their adult identity. They decide on the type of job they want, the type of mate they want, and the type of lifestyle they want. Young people choose the best parts of people, ideals, and systems they admire to make their own.

Nevertheless, once this identity is fully formed, there will not be much chance of changing it peacefully. Once a person reaches about 25, and has invested time, energy, and feelings into the chosen career, mate, and lifestyle, it becomes difficult to reconsider. Usually, only an extreme crisis, such as job loss, divorce, death of a loved one, life threatening illness or trauma, etc. can provoke a re-evaluation.[5]

Therefore, the ages of 11-25 are extremely important spiritually. There will never again be such an opportunity for spiritual development. The ability to think hypothetically gained in preadolescence provides the basis to reflect on spiritual matters. Permanent commitments to Christ are not likely before 11 or 12. At the same time, lifetime commitments to Christ are not likely after age 25. By age 25, a person's spiritual choices are usually eternal. Very few people accept Christ as Savior past 25.

This truth implies that churches should provide the very best teachers and role models for young people, instead of mere babysitters and game leaders. Young people are the target of Satan. He wants to derail them from Christianity to ride the tracks of vanity. Satan wants them concerned about everything else but God because he fears the potential they have to harm him and his work.

Learning Tasks

The ability to think beyond rules and regulations begins at age 11 or 12. Young people begin to learn principles that can be applied to many situations.

Even so, many people never use that ability in spiritual matters. They don't because they fail to dedicate their lives to God and cross into spiritual adolescence. These people choose to remain spiritual children and to live by a clear and confining set of rules. They don't want to do the hard work of thinking for themselves, so they limit their experience of God's power. In order to grow up in the spiritual realm, it's necessary to learn the reasons behind the rules and how to apply principles in all situations.

The ability to experiment in the mind enables us to learn cause and effect in the spiritual dimension. We can examine probable responses from God and others toward us by learning from examples in scripture: *"Now all these things happened unto them for ensamples; and they are written for our admonition, upon whom the ends of the world are come."* 1 *Corinthians 10:11.* God wants us to learn from other's spiritual experiences. The Old Testament is filled with case studies from which spiritual adolescents can learn: *"Be not deceived; God is not mocked: for whatsoever a man soweth, that shall he also reap. For he that soweth to his flesh shall of the flesh reap corruption; but he that soweth to the Spirit shall of the Spirit reap life everlasting."* *Galatians 6:7,8.*

The Two Learning Tasks of Spiritual Adolescence

1. Understanding Principles vs. Rules
2. Understanding Cause and Effect in the Spiritual Realm

History of Israel

The children of Israel did not use the key of trust at Kadesh-barnea and did not enter the Promised Land. As a result, they died in the wilderness. They died in a suspended state of spiritual mediocrity: *"And the space in which we came from Kadeshbarnea, until we were come over the brook Zered, was thirty and eight years; until all the generation of the men of war were wasted out from among the host, as the LORD sware unto them. For indeed the hand of the LORD was against them, to destroy them from among the host, until they were consumed."* *Deuteronomy 2:14,15.*

After the rebels had passed on, Moses addressed a younger crowd to prepare them to pass over. He reviewed their progress as a nation in Deuteronomy and challenged them to continue their growth. He repeated the Ten Commandments in Deuteronomy 5, then added new directions in Chapter 6:1-9.

Understanding Principles vs. Rules

Spiritual adolescence, possessing the land of promise, required new ways of relating to God and one another:

1. Love the Lord thy God: *"And thou shalt love the LORD thy God with all thine heart, and with all thy soul, and with all thy might."* Deuteronomy 6:5.
2. Meditate on God's word: *"And these words, which I command thee this day, shall be in thine heart:"* Deuteronomy 6:6.
3. Teach God's word: *"And thou shalt teach them diligently unto thy children, and shalt talk of them when thou sittest in thine house, and when thou walkest by the way, and when thou liest down, and when thou risest up. And thou shalt bind them for a sign upon thine hand, and they shall be as frontlets between thine eyes. And thou shalt write them upon the posts of thy house, and on thy gates."* Deuteronomy 6:7-9.

The new commandments show us God's expectations of the people to grow under the Law of Moses. They were not to be content with the letter of the Law; they were to form a relationship with the heart of God through it.

When we love people, we seek out their secret wishes and dreams. We try to understand the motivations behind what they do. We seek to please them with our actions. What other reason would there be for God to command the children to love Him with all their "hearts, minds, and souls?" He knew that the people would grow only if they knew the lawgiver better than the Law.

When we memorize and meditate on the words of a play we will perform, we do so to understand the meaning, motivation, and character of the writer. This enables us to perform the play according to the author's intent. God knew that meditation of His Word would expose His character and reveal His principles of the abundant life.

When we prepare to teach others, we study very hard all the supporting materials to provide a solid base to defend our position. We think about possible questions and points of confusion. We look for ways to illustrate the lessons. God knew that preparation to teach would lead people to seek His wisdom: *"If any of you lack wisdom, let him ask of God, that giveth to all men liberally, and upbraideth not; and it shall be given him."* James 1:5.

The new commands led the children of Israel to look beyond the letter of the Law and into the principles behind it. They were an open invitation to ask "why?" That is a favorite word of adolescents. They need to ask "why?" Asking questions and finding answers is the only way for them to build a worldview strong enough to think for themselves.

Jesus Christ rebuked the Pharisees for their failure to do this. Instead of asking "why?" and searching for the heart of God, the Pharisees multiplied laws to keep from breaking God's original laws. They did not look for the reasons and meaning behind the laws. To stay holy, the Pharisees created the "seyag" and the "gezerot."[6]

The "seyag" were fence rules that protected them from breaking God's laws. They put a fence between the worshiper and the offense. They are the source of some of the silliness we see in the New Testament.The Pharisees took the functional and ceremonial washings of Moses' Law and extended them to their personal lives (Leviticus 15; Numbers 31:21-24). They condemned Jesus' disciples for not following their fence rules: *"Then came together unto him the Pharisees, and certain of the scribes, which came from Jerusalem. And when they saw some of his disciples eat bread with defiled, that is to say, with unwashen, hands, they found fault. For the Pharisees, and all the Jews, except they wash their hands oft, eat not, holding the tradition of the elders. And when they come from the market, except they wash, they eat not. And many other things there be, which they have received to hold, as the washing of cups, and pots, brasen vessels, and of tables. Then the Pharisees and scribes asked him, Why walk not thy disciples according to the tradition of the elders, but eat bread with unwashen hands?" Mark 7:1-5.*

But Jesus told them they were laying aside the command of God to follow the tradition of men: *"He answered and said unto them, Well hath Esaias prophesied of you hypocrites, as it is written, This people honoureth me with their lips, but their heart is far from me. Howbeit in vain do they worship me, teaching for doctrines the commandments of men. For laying aside the commandment of God, ye hold the tradition of men, as the washing of pots and cups: and many other such like things ye do. And he said unto them, Full well ye reject the commandment of God, that ye may keep your own tradition." Mark 7:6-9.*

The Pharisees took the command to observe the Sabbath and extended it to exclude anything done on the Sabbath (Luke 13:10-14). Jesus pointed out their hypocrisy, which is inevitable when you merely observe outward rules in order to gain people's favor: *"The Lord then answered him, and said, Thou hypocrite, doth not each one of you on the sabbath loose his ox or his ass from the stall, and lead him away to watering? And ought not this woman, being a daughter of Abraham, whom Satan hath bound, lo, these eighteen years, be loosed from this bond on the sabbath day? And when he had said these things, all his adversaries were ashamed: and all the people rejoiced for all the glorious things that were done by him." Luke 13:15-17.*

The "gezerot" were new rules invented to cover new developments. The Pharisees treated the Law of Moses like some treat the Constitution of the United States. They reason that the founding fathers, or God, couldn't see new things coming so we have to make new rules for modern times, even when they violate the principles of the original laws.[7]

Jesus contrasted love to blind obedience and rules as guiding motives. Loving God and others leads us to live by principles rather than rules, because we want our love to show in every circumstance, even those not covered by rules. With these considerations, we can better understand Jesus' answer to the lawyer's question: "which is the greatest commandment in the law?" (Matthew 22:37-40): *"For, brethren, ye have been called unto liberty; only use not liberty for an occasion to the flesh, but by love serve one another. For all the law is fulfilled in one word, even in this; Thou shalt love thy neighbour as thyself." Galatians 5:13,14. "Stand fast therefore in the liberty wherewith Christ hath made us free, and be not entangled again with the yoke of bondage." Galatians 5:1.*

James, who addressed his letter to the "twelve tribes which are scattered abroad," evoking the analogy between Israel and the church, exhorted his readers to go beyond the Law to the law of liberty. The law of liberty is a higher standard than the Law of Moses. Living by principles is a higher standard than living by rules. Principles can be applied to every new situation. Rules fall short because they are specific and fixed: *"For whosoever shall keep the whole law, and yet offend in one point, he is guilty of all. For he that said, Do not commit adultery, said also, Do not kill. Now if thou commit no adultery, yet if thou kill, thou art become a transgressor of the law. So speak ye, and so do, as they that shall be judged by the law of liberty." James 2:10-12.*

Paul explained to the Corinthians that while he had been made free by Christ from the Law and other's expectations, yet he lived by the law of Christ, a higher law which is not a law but a principle, which is to serve others out of love: *"For though I be free from all men, yet have I made myself servant unto all, that I might gain the more. And unto the Jews I became as a Jew, that I might gain the Jews; to them that are under the law, as under the law, that I might gain them that are under the law; To them that are without law, as without law, (being not without law to God, but under the law to Christ,) that I might gain them that are without law. To the weak became I as weak, that I might gain the weak: I am made all things to all men, that I might by all means save some." 1 Corinthians 9:19-22.*

James and Paul built on the teachings of Jesus, who condemned the Jews for not looking beyond the Law. Jesus told them specifically how they should have applied Deuteronomy 6:1-9: *"Think not that I am come to destroy the law, or the prophets: I am not come to destroy, but to fulfil. For verily I say unto you, Till heaven and earth pass, one jot or one tittle shall in no wise pass from the law, till all be fulfilled. Whosoever therefore shall break one of these least commandments, and shall teach men so, he shall be called the least in the kingdom of heaven: but whosoever shall do and teach them, the same shall be called great in the kingdom of heaven. For I say unto you, That except your righteousness shall exceed the righteousness of the scribes and Pharisees, ye shall in no case enter into the kingdom of heaven." Matthew 5:17-20.* Jesus told the people their righteousness must exceed the righteousness of the Pharisees. The people must have thought, "How can we do that?" Then Jesus explained how, by going behind the mere rules to the principles.

Jesus began with "Thou shalt not kill." He taught the people to look into their own inner attitudes about anger toward others instead of only focusing on outward actions. He taught them to recognize the source of their outward actions of hatred: the demand to be treated with respect. He taught them to value relationships with others more than their relationship with the letter of the Law: *"Ye have heard that it was said by them of old time, Thou shalt not kill; and whosoever shall kill shall be in danger of the judgment: But I say unto you, That whosoever is angry with his brother without a cause shall be in danger of the judgment: and whosoever shall say to his brother, Raca, shall be in danger of the council: but whosoever shall say, Thou fool, shall be in danger of hell fire. Therefore if thou bring thy gift to the altar, and there rememberest that thy brother hath ought against thee; Leave there thy gift before the altar, and go thy way; first be reconciled to thy brother, and then come and offer thy gift." Matthew 5:21-24.*

"Thou shalt not commit adultery." Jesus improved this to, "don't even look at a woman for the purpose of getting an image for your lust." The Pharisees had built a "seyag" around the command to say one should not look at a woman at all. The Bleeding Pharisees were the chief proponents of this fence rule. They walked with their eyes closed to keep from seeing women and thus hurt themselves often while walking down the street.[8] Jesus implied that a condition of the heart, not the eyes, causes adultery. That's why He didn't say, "close your eyes," but facetiously said, "pluck them out." Jesus knew that the problem with eyes is usually the operator:

"Ye have heard that it was said by them of old time, Thou shalt not commit adultery: But I say unto you, That whosoever looketh on a woman to lust after her hath committed adultery with her already in his heart. And if thy right eye offend thee, pluck it out, and cast it from thee: for it is profitable for thee that one of thy members should perish, and not that thy whole body should be cast into hell. And if thy right hand offend thee, cut it off, and cast it from thee: for it is profitable for thee that one of thy members should perish, and not that thy whole body should be cast into hell." Matthew 5:27-30.

"Thou shalt not forswear thyself, but perform unto the Lord thine oaths." The Pharisees measured a person's degree of seriousness by the object of his oath (Matthew 23:16). They used this system to back out of unwanted obligations (Matthew 15:5-6). But Jesus counseled them to make oaths unnecessary. He said, "Don't swear at all. Let your word be as good as your name. Let your yes mean yes and your no mean no. Don't verbally commit to anything you are not willing to actually do." He showed them how they should have let the Law of Moses make a change in their hearts and not just in their outward actions: *"Again, ye have heard that it hath been said by them of old time, Thou shalt not forswear thyself, but shalt perform unto the Lord thine oaths: But I say unto you, Swear not at all; neither by heaven; for it is God's throne: Nor by the earth; for it is his footstool: neither by Jerusalem; for it is the city of the great King. Neither shalt thou swear by thy head, because thou canst not make one hair white or black. But let your communication be, Yea, yea; Nay, nay: for whatsoever is more than these cometh of evil."* Matthew 5:33-37.

"An eye for an eye, and a tooth for a tooth." This was not a law to teach revenge, but to teach the Israelites to respect others: (Leviticus 24:19-20). Jesus pointed out that God does not take revenge when He is slighted, but shows mercy instead. If they had truly been seeking God in this, they would have followed His example. David the king meditated on this principle: *"The LORD is merciful and gracious, slow to anger, and plenteous in mercy. He will not always chide: neither will he keep his anger for ever. He hath not dealt with us after our sins; nor rewarded us according to our iniquities. For as the heaven is high above the earth, so great is his mercy toward them that fear him."* Psalms 103:8-11. David was able to see God's principles because he sought to have the heart of God in his own life (1 Samuel 13:14).

"Ye have heard that it hath been said, An eye for an eye, and a tooth for a tooth: But I say unto you, That ye resist not evil: but whosoever shall smite thee on thy right cheek, turn to him the other also. And if any man will sue

thee at the law, and take away thy coat, let him have thy cloke also. And whosoever shall compel thee to go a mile, go with him twain. Give to him that asketh thee, and from him that would borrow of thee turn not thou away." Matthew 5:38-42.

"Thou shalt love thy neighbor and hate thine enemy." The Old Testament reference to hating the enemy is Deuteronomy 23:3-6. The people were not to seek the peace or prosperity of the Ammonites or Moabites because they seduced the Israelites at Baal-Peor and they would have been a corrupting influence to the young nation. It was more of a warning against compromise. But the nation would not always be young and easily led astray. They were supposed to grow up and be strong (Ephesians 4:14-15). And spiritual strength allows us to love even when the other is wrong. God sends His rain on everyone. God shines His sun on everyone. So, we should learn to bless others to find the heart of God: *"Ye have heard that it hath been said, Thou shalt love thy neighbour, and hate thine enemy. But I say unto you, Love your enemies, bless them that curse you, do good to them that hate you, and pray for them which despitefully use you, and persecute you; That ye may be the children of your Father which is in heaven: for he maketh his sun to rise on the evil and on the good, and sendeth rain on the just and on the unjust. For if ye love them which love you, what reward have ye? do not even the publicans the same? And if ye salute your brethren only, what do ye more than others? do not even the publicans so? Be ye therefore perfect, even as your Father which is in heaven is perfect." Matthew 5:43-48.*

Christian in *Pilgrim's Progress* was also taught to rely on principles in preparation to fight against the enemy. At the top of the hill Difficulty, he rested at the palace Beautiful. There he communed with Discretion, Prudence, Piety, and Charity: virgins of the palace who embodied the principles needed to make it through the Valley of Humiliation. Discretion is the freedom or authority to make decisions and choices.[9] Prudence is the exercise of sound judgment in practical matters, esp. as concerns one's own interests.[10] Piety is devotion and duty to God in practice.[11] Charity is unconditional love for God and others. It's the kind of love Jesus spoke of as the greatest commandment.[12] These four principles armed Christian to go into the Valley of Humiliation, which in our scheme is spiritual adolescence.

Christian would have been unable to successfully engage the enemy without the armament of principles. He barely survived anyway. Rules are too limited to be effective against enemies ready to undermine, confuse, and go around the rules. Only principles provide a strong enough worldview to battle Satan and his representatives.

Understanding Cause and Effect in the Spiritual Realm

Moses reminded the children of Israel of their national experience of God to teach them cause and effect. Much of the book of Deuteronomy is devoted to this purpose (Deuteronomy 8:1-6; Deuteronomy 11:7-8). People learn cause and effect and make hypotheses based on multiple hands-on experiments.[13] We call it learning, the ability to apply old experience and knowledge to new situations.

Moses also taught them cause and effect through the testimonies of the patriarchs. Just as adolescents require good role models to admire and pattern themselves after, spiritual adolescents require heroes of faith. Adolescents also need to see the consequences of bad decisions, and negative examples to avoid. Moses wrote the first five books of the Bible, which included the stories of the patriarchs in Genesis (Deuteronomy 31:24-26). Before that, the people told the old stories by word of mouth. They had always been aware of God's dealing with individuals.

Abraham, the first patriarch, obeyed God and went to Canaan to become a great nation (Genesis 12:1-5; Hebrews 11:8-12). This was the demonstration of his faith. On the negative side, he took Lot, his nephew, with him, even though God had told him to get away from all his relatives. The result of Abraham's lack of complete obedience was Lot's sons, Moab and Ammon. These two sons Lot fathered by his own daughters (Genesis 19:29-38). The two sons became two nations that grieved Israel when they were preparing to enter the Promised Land. Moab and Ammon became noisy neighbors (Deuteronomy 23:3-6).

Isaac, the next patriarch, listened to God during the famine and went to Gerar instead of Egypt (Genesis 26:1-6). Therefore, God blessed him and gave him and hundredfold increase of crops during a year of famine (Genesis 26:12). Isaac became greater than the Philistines, his neighbors, and they acknowledged God's blessing on him (Genesis 26:16, 26-29).

Isaac's son Jacob wrestled with God and would not let go till he received a blessing (Genesis 32:24-30). And because of his determination to struggle with God, God named him Israel, the prince. But all this was after Jacob had much trouble because of his deception of his brother Esau (Genesis 27:41; 32:3-8).

Joseph, the last patriarch, was faithful to God in all his trials (Genesis 39). Consequently, God made him the second ruler over all Egypt (Genesis 41:37-43) and the salvation of his family (Genesis 45:4-8).

In addition to these testimonies, God's new covenant with the people as they entered the Promised Land, the Palestinian Covenant, was essentially a teaching on cause and effect. God initiated a series of covenants with His chosen people that correspond to the spiritual life cycle. God's original covenant with Abraham was the *birth* of the nation of Israel (Genesis 12:1-3; Genesis 15). The second covenant with Israel was at Sinai, the Ten Commandments. The second covenant signaled Israel's *childhood*. The Palestinian Covenant was the third, and it prepared Israel for *adolescence*.

The terms of the Palestinian Covenant are found in Deuteronomy 27-30. The people were commanded to gather on two mountains with a valley between after they passed over Jordan. Half would gather on Mt. Gerizim and half on Mt. Ebal. There they would hear the blessings of obedience to God, and the curses that accompany disobedience. Moses gave great detail about the blessings of listening to God and the consequences of rejecting His Word.

Moses made it clear that this was a new covenant in addition to the Ten Commandments: *"These are the words of the covenant, which the LORD commanded Moses to make with the children of Israel in the land of Moab, beside the covenant which he made with them in Horeb." Deuteronomy 29:1.* This new covenant was to be a guide for the people in the Promised Land (the land of spiritual adolescence). It was to be for all those born in the nation and for immigrants (Deuteronomy 29:14-15). The covenant was universal and perpetual so no one could claim exemption from its authority. Those that disregarded it would bring on themselves the curses (Deuteronomy 29:18-21).

The Palestinian Covenant warned the people that disobedience would result in expulsion from the land of promise. It also promised that if the people repented of their sins, God would bring them back to their land from captivity (Deuteronomy 30:1-5). Adolescence is a time of making choices and learning cause and effect. It is a time of experimentation with free will. Children must obey because they lack the knowledge and skill to survive on their own. But, adolescents gain strength and perspective by choosing. So God made a provision for them to choose to fail as well as succeed, hoping they would learn to choose success. Captivity to the consequences of wrong choices should bring adolescents to the point of repentance. At this stage, repentance is the way to build spiritual muscle.

Rich experience with cause and effect, blessings and cursings, builds strong spiritual character. Our hearts become knit together with God's heart as we learn His ways, so that our desires are the same as His (Deuteronomy 30:6; 1 Samuel 13:14): *"Delight thyself also in the LORD; and he shall give thee the desires of thine heart. Commit thy way unto the LORD; trust also in him; and he shall bring it to pass." Psalms 37:4,5.*

Moses taught that an understanding of the covenant was not far away and hard to get; they were ready to say it and believe it: *"For this commandment which I command thee this day, it is not hidden from thee, neither is it far off.*

It is not in heaven, that thou shouldest say, Who shall go up for us to heaven, and bring it unto us, that we may hear it, and do it? Neither is it beyond the sea, that thou shouldest say, Who shall go over the sea for us, and bring it unto us, that we may hear it, and do it? But the word is very nigh unto thee, in thy mouth, and in thy heart, that thou mayest do it." Deuteronomy 30:11-14.

The apostle Paul in his letter to the Romans explained it more fully. The word in their mouths and hearts was the word of faith in God's power to circumcise their hearts and cause them to love God's ways, even though they were unable to keep the commandments in their own power: *"But the righteousness which is of faith speaketh on this wise, Say not in thine heart, Who shall ascend into heaven? (that is, to bring Christ down from above:) Or, Who shall descend into the deep? (that is, to bring up Christ again from the dead.) But what saith it? The word is nigh thee, even in thy mouth, and in thy heart: that is, the word of faith, which we preach; That if thou shalt confess with thy mouth the Lord Jesus, and shalt believe in thine heart that God hath raised him from the dead, thou shalt be saved. For with the heart man believeth unto righteousness; and with the mouth confession is made unto salvation." Romans 10:6-10.*

It is only through failure by our own efforts do we become ripe to see God. This is an understanding of salvation appropriate to the stage of adolescence: *"The LORD is nigh unto them that are of a broken heart; and saveth such as be of a contrite spirit." Psalms 34:18.*

Moses summarized the covenant by emphasizing the choices of life/death, good/evil. He told the Israelites to follow God's plan if they wanted to prolong their time in the land. God wanted them to develop character through trials and survive the early choices of the spiritual life. These are tasks of adolescence. God wanted to give them strength through His character and example (Deuteronomy 30:15-20; Isaiah 57:15).

Our hero Christian was also given examples of those who had succeeded in the land of spiritual adolescence. Discretion, Prudence, Piety, and Charity took him to the study of the palace and "showed him the records of the greatest antiquity."[14] Those records included "some of the worthy acts that some of His servants had done." The records also showed how willing their Lord was to receive in His favor those who repented. So we see that John Bunyan recognized the combination of testimonies and repentance to build spiritual muscle. The armory was the next place the virgins took Christian.[15]

Satan wants us to fall down and quit fighting at the first sign of resistance. He wants us to become discouraged over the first negative consequence of our experimentation. But God wants us to be prepared to get up and keep fighting: *"For a just man falleth seven times, and riseth up again: but the wicked shall fall into mischief." Proverbs 24:16.*

Transition

Moses was the Israelites' nurturing guide through spiritual birth and childhood. God did not allow Moses to lead them into the Promised Land, but instead chose a military leader, Joshua, to help them through the transition into adolescence. Moses charged both the people and Joshua to "be strong and of good courage," and to remember that God would go with them: "he will not fail thee, nor forsake thee." (Deuteronomy 31:1-8). Moses also wrote a song as a testimony of the consequences of turning away from God and following their own hearts (Deuteronomy 32).

Vision

Although Moses was not allowed to enter into the Promised Land (Deuteronomy 32:48-52), yet he saw it before he died (Deuteronomy 34: 1-7). God told Moses to go up to the top of Mt. Nebo and there God gave Moses a vision of the land. Vision is very significant in the spiritual life. To every person who dedicates himself or herself to God, God gives a vision of the work that person can do for God. The fulfillment of the vision will not be immediate, but it will be a guide. The vision will be blurry at first, but it will come into focus as time goes by. The vision is the first hint of a person's full spiritual identity: *"When I was a child, I spake as a child, I understood as a child, I thought as a child: but when I became a man, I put away childish things. For now we see through a glass, darkly; but then face to face: now I know in part; but then shall I know even as also I am known." 1 Corinthians 13:11,12.*

I believe the vision of Moses was Israel at rest (Hebrews 4:8). He imagined them at a stage beyond adolescence. It was with this hope that he finished his work.

Christian was also given a vision before he left the Palace beautiful. The virgins showed him in the distance the Delectable Mountains. This vision would sustain him through his time of spiritual adolescence and young adulthood. They said the vision would comfort him because the mountains were nearer to his destination: "So he did, and behold at a great distance, he saw a most pleasant mountainous country, beautiful with woods, vineyards, fruits of all sorts, flowers also, with springs and fountains, very delectable to behold."[16]

Weapons of Warfare

The Israelites were now prepared to overcome the crisis of their childhood, entry into the Promised Land and a commitment to fight their enemies. God supplied Joshua with the weapons of warfare. He reminded Joshua of His faithfulness to Moses as a testimony (Joshua 1:5). He reminded Joshua of His promise of victory (Joshua 1:3-6; Deuteronomy 31:23). He reminded Joshua of the power of His word to give character and success (Joshua 1:7-8). Finally, He reminded Joshua of the power of His command (Joshua 1:9; Isaiah 55:11).

God had prepared the people since Kadesh-barnea. The people were young, strong, and willing to obey (Joshua 1:10-11,16). The enemies were prepared by God's spiritual armies to fail (Joshua 2:9-11; 5:1). The natural world was prepared to co-operate in their crossing (Joshua 3:15-17). This all shows us that in God's proper timing, everything is prepared to accomplish His will (Malachi 4:3).

The four virgins armed Christian with his spiritual weapons. They gave him the "whole armor of God" (Ephesians 6:13-18). They were the basic weapons brought from spiritual childhood. They had been exercised and practiced to be used at the right time: love of the truth, right standing with God, the good news that peace with God is available, faith and trust in God, salvation, the word of God, and prayer.[17]

Rites of Passage

Many cultures in the world have special ceremonies when children enter adolescence (In America, the entrance is not so clear, especially for boys). The ancient Israelites also had some rites of passage as a nation. When they crossed the barrier into the land of adolescence (the Jordan River), Joshua had them set up twelve stones in the river and twelve stones in the Promised Land as a memorial (Joshua 4:4-9). Joshua also had all the males circumcised as a rite of passage and as a reaffirmation of Abraham's covenant (Joshua 5:2-9; Genesis 17:9-14). God said this rolled away the reproach of Egypt from them (Joshua 5:9). In other words, they had matured to the point that the childish desires for the world were not a priority. The circumcision at this time symbolized their national commitment and dedication to God. Thus, they had passed the crisis of their childhood.

The manna ceased, another indication that something significant had occurred. The children had been fed baby food because they could not provide for themselves. When they finally committed themselves to God and crossed into adolescence, they were able to eat the fruit of Canaan (Joshua 5:12).

Crises

Finally, the time came for them to fight. Spiritual adolescence is a land where every foot of territory must be seized by warfare. The crises come immediately and together (Joshua 9:1-2; 11:1-5). The enemies of God attack whenever they see a new convert to commitment: *"But call to remembrance the former days, in which, after ye were illuminated, ye endured a great fight of afflictions; Partly, whilst ye were made a gazingstock both by reproaches and afflictions; and partly, whilst ye became companions of them that were so used." Hebrews 10:32,33.*

God reassured Joshua that spiritual armies were with him. Joshua and the people were on holy ground. It was the ground of complete separation from the world (the reproach of Egypt): *"And it came to pass, when Joshua was by Jericho, that he lifted up his eyes and looked, and, behold, there stood a man over against him with his sword drawn in his hand: and Joshua went unto him, and said unto him, Art thou for us, or for our adversaries? And he said, Nay; but as captain of the host of the LORD am I now come. And Joshua fell on his face to the earth, and did worship, and said unto him, What saith my lord unto his servant? And the captain of the LORD'S host said unto Joshua, Loose thy shoe from off thy foot; for the place whereon thou standest is holy. And Joshua did so." Joshua 5:13-15.*

The Israelites were no longer afraid of the giants of the land as they were at Kadesh (Chapter 8). Caleb himself expelled three of the sons of Anak (giants) from Hebron (Judges 1:20). The giants represented the crises of spiritual adolescence.

In the physical and psychological realms, a young person at puberty is faced with several giants. They are the challenges of life that must be mastered if a young person is to reach adulthood strong and intact. The advent of a more mature body heightens the awareness that adulthood in a physical, psychological, and social sense is not far away. The young person begins focusing on social skills and begins to use abstract and hypothetical reasoning. He or she begins to experiment with social and character roles. Decisions must be made about self, work, recreation, morals, spirituality, friends, dating relationships, money, etc. These decisions are difficult because of the exaggerated emotions of adolescence.

The giants of adolescence come at once and together. They are: self-image, authority, conscience, handling offenses, anger, morality, purpose, friendships, and finances. There may be more, but these are the main ones. Failure in any one of these areas can hamper a person's happiness for a lifetime.

Once the physical, social, emotional, and psychological conditions of adolescence are present, the giants must be wrestled. The giants cannot be eliminated, just as Israel never fully conquered the nations of Canaan or their giants (Judges 1:28), but a workable solution must be found for the conflicts they cause. The conflicts must be mastered or "brought under tribute."

The solutions to the giant conflicts can be thought of as ratios. Every person has the potential to answer the conflicts with wisdom or foolishness. Every person will have more than one solution to each conflict. Some will be effective and others will not be. The total experience of the answers to the conflict will be a mix of good and bad results. When the solutions that work are tapped into and used, they grow stronger than the ineffective answers. When the negative answers are used more often, the solutions themselves present problems.

Example:

$$\frac{\text{SELF IMAGE}}{\text{Poor self image}} = \frac{\text{positive solutions}}{\text{negative solutions}} >$$

$$\frac{\text{POOR SELF IMAGE}}{\text{Self image}} = \frac{\text{negative solutions}}{\text{positive solutions}} >$$

When Israel trusted in God, they overcame their enemies (Judges 2). When the Israelites stopped depending on God in the land, the enemies became stronger and put them under tribute.

The book of Proverbs, which was written for spiritual adolescents, presents many ratios of positive solutions v. negative solutions. A young person is wise to memorize and meditate on the entire book (Proverbs 1:1-8).

A few examples from Proverbs 10:

v. 4 He becometh poor that dealeth with a slack hand:	negative	Financial Bondage
but the hand of the diligent maketh rich.	positive	Financial Freedom
v. 7 The memory of the just is blessed:	positive	Clear Conscience
but the name of the wicked shall rot.	negative	Guilt
v. 8 The wise in heart will receive commandments:	positive	Respect for authority
but a prating fool shall fall.	negative	Rebellion
v. 12 Hatred stirreth up strifes:	negative	Anger
but love covereth all sins.	positive	Meekness
v. 14 Wise men lay up knowledge:	positive	Spiritual Purpose
but the mouth of the foolish is near destruction.	negative	Boredom and Depression
v. 20 The tongue of the just is as choice silver:	positive	Biblical Self-Image
the heart of the wicked is little worth.	negative	Poor Self-image
v. 23 It is as sport to a fool to do mischief:	negative	Moral Impurity
but a man of understanding hath wisdom.	positive	Moral Freedom

The crises of adolescence arise from natural processes of growth; nevertheless, they require spiritual solutions. People can never leave the problems adolescence causes without developing effective spiritual solutions. I'm talking about all people, not just believers; unbelievers are stuck. True spiritual solutions will not be sought until believers commit to God and cross over into spiritual adolescence.

Most Christians are afraid to commit to God because they don't want to fight these giants. They have ineffective ways of dealing with the crises, but they prefer the known and enslavement to the unknown and possible freedom in God's ways.

The Giant Crises and Their Ratios

1. Biblical Self-Image vs. Poor Self-Image
   "I will praise thee; for I am fearfully and wonderfully made: marvellous are thy works; and that my soul knoweth right well." Psalms 139:14.

2. Respect for Authority vs. Rebellion
   "Let every soul be subject unto the higher powers. For there is no power but of God: the powers that be are ordained of God. Whosoever therefore resisteth the power, resisteth the ordinance of God: and they that resist shall receive to themselves damnation." Romans 13:1,2.

3. Clear Conscience vs. Guilt
   "This charge I commit unto thee, son Timothy, according to the prophecies which went before on thee, that thou by them mightest war a good warfare; Holding faith, and a good conscience; which some having put away concerning faith have made shipwreck:" 1 Timothy 1:18,19.

4. Forgiveness vs. Bitterness
   "Then came Peter to him, and said, Lord, how oft shall my brother sin against me, and I forgive him? till seven times? Jesus saith unto him, I say not unto thee, Until seven times: but, Until seventy times seven." Matthew 18:21,22.

5. Meekness vs. Anger
   "The meek will he guide in judgment: and the meek will he teach his way." Psalms 25:9. "But sanctify the Lord God in your hearts: and be ready always to give an answer to every man that asketh you a reason of the hope that is in you with meekness and fear:" 1 Peter 3:15.

6. Moral Freedom vs. Moral Impurity
   "Flee also youthful lusts: but follow righteousness, faith, charity, peace, with them that call on the Lord out of a pure heart." 2 Timothy 2:22. "Now the end of the commandment is charity out of a pure heart, and of a good conscience, and of faith unfeigned:" 1 Timothy 1:5. "Blessed are the pure in heart: for they shall see God." Matthew 5:8.

7. Spiritual Purpose vs. Boredom and Depression
   "I beseech you therefore, brethren, by the mercies of God, that ye present your bodies a living sacrifice, holy, acceptable unto God, which is your reasonable service. And be not conformed to this world: but be ye transformed by the renewing of your mind, that ye may prove what is that good, and acceptable, and perfect, will of God." Romans 12:1,2.

8. Genuine Friendships vs. Using and Abusing People
   "A friend loveth at all times, and a brother is born for adversity." Proverbs 17:17.

9. Financial Freedom vs. Financial Bondage
   "Owe no man any thing, but to love one another: for he that loveth another hath fulfilled the law." Romans 13:8.

Joshua swiftly defeated most of the Canaanites in his wars, yet he was unable to conquer all the giants of the land (Joshua 11:16-23). God left some to prove Israel and to test them (Judges 2:21-23). In the same way, a zealous spiritual adolescent makes swift progress at first in subduing the giants, yet any one left can bring him or her to shame.

The Israelites were brought under bondage to particular tribes throughout the book of Judges, and when they repented, God freed them through military leaders. The Israelites could not live safely until all the opposing nations were held at bay. This did not happen until the time of David (2 Samuel 8). Similarly, a spiritual adolescent cannot rest or pass on to maturity without developing an effective answer to every one of these conflicts.

I will not attempt to give a complete treatment of these conflicts and their effective solutions. There are many good books about each one from a biblical perspective. Instead, I will attempt to show the foundational principle that underlies effective answers to the crises: each one has its answer in our relationship to God. For further study, the book of Proverbs has specific answers to the common situations of spiritual adolescence.

Effective Responses to the Crises

1. Biblical Self-Image vs. Poor Self-Image
    God made every one of us. This truth is the beginning of effective solutions to
    the crisis of self-image, because it puts us in a proper relationship to God.

    A. God made us with the qualities He wants us to have.

        *"Nay but, O man, who art thou that repliest against God? Shall
        the thing formed say to him that formed it, Why hast thou made
        me thus?" Romans 9:20. "For who maketh thee to differ from
        another? and what hast thou that thou didst not receive? now if
        thou didst receive it, why dost thou glory, as if thou hadst not
        received it?" 1 Corinthians 4:7. (also see Isaiah 45:9-10;
        Matthew 6:27-30).*

    B. God uses our outward qualities to develop inward character. That
        character reaches its zenith when we resemble Christ.

        *"And we know that all things work together for good to them that
        love God, to them who are the called according to his purpose. For
        whom he did foreknow, he also did predestinate to be conformed to
        the image of his Son, that he might be the firstborn among many
        brethren." Romans 8:28,29. (also see 2 Corinthians 12:9).*

    C. God is never finished making a Christian.

        *"Being confident of this very thing, that he which hath begun a
        good work in you will perform it until the day of Jesus Christ:"
        Philippians 1:6.*

        *"The LORD will perfect that which concerneth me: thy mercy, O
        LORD, endureth for ever: forsake not the works of thine own
        hands." Psalms 138:8.*

    D. God made us in a marvelous manner. We need to adopt the attitude that
        as image-bearers of God we are very special.

"For thou hast possessed my reins: thou hast covered me in my mother's womb. I will praise thee; for I am fearfully and wonderfully made: marvellous are thy works; and that my soul knoweth right well. My substance was not hid from thee, when I was made in secret, and curiously wrought in the lowest parts of the earth. Thine eyes did see my substance, yet being unperfect; and in thy book all my members were written, which in continuance were fashioned, when as yet there was none of them." Psalms 139:13-16.

2. Respect for Authority vs. Rebellion
    All authority belongs to God, and He uses it to accomplish His purposes: *"God hath spoken once; twice have I heard this; that power belongeth unto God." Psalms 62:11.*

    A. God delegates His authority to government to keep order and restrain evil.

        "For rulers are not a terror to good works, but to the evil. Wilt thou then not be afraid of the power? do that which is good, and thou shalt have praise of the same:" Romans 13:3.

    B. God makes authority for our good, to develop character in us.

        "For he is the minister of God to thee for good. But if thou do that which is evil, be afraid; for he beareth not the sword in vain: for he is the minister of God, a revenger to execute wrath upon him that doeth evil." Romans 13:4.

    C. God wants us to obey for two reasons: to escape punishment and to keep our relationship with God and others free of guilt.

        "Wherefore ye must needs be subject, not only for wrath, but also for conscience sake. For for this cause pay ye tribute also: for they are God's ministers, attending continually upon this very thing." Romans 13:5,6.

    D. God has given four structures of authority: family, government, the church, and business.

Family
Structure

God:

"But I would have you know, that the head of every man is Christ; and the head of the woman is the man; and the head of Christ is God." 1 Corinthians 11:3.

Father:

"For the husband is the head of the wife, even as Christ is the head of the church: and he is the saviour of the body." Ephesians 5:23. "And, ye fathers, provoke not your children to wrath: but bring them up in the nurture and admonition of the Lord." Ephesians 6:4.

Mother:

"Wives, submit yourselves unto your own husbands, as unto the Lord." Ephesians 5:22. "Therefore as the church is subject unto Christ, so let the wives be to their own husbands in every thing." Ephesians 5:24.

Children:

"Children, obey your parents in the Lord: for this is right." Ephesians 6:1. "Children, obey your parents in all things: for this is well pleasing unto the Lord." Colossians 3:20.

Government
Structure

God:

"The king's heart is in the hand of the LORD, as the rivers of water: he turneth it whithersoever he will." Proverbs 21:1.

National Leaders:

"Submit yourselves to every ordinance of man for the Lord's sake: whether it be to the king, as supreme;" 1 Peter 2:13.

Local Leaders:

"Or unto governors, as unto them that are sent by him for the punishment of evildoers, and for the praise of them that do well." 1 Peter 2:14.

Citizens:
"Let every soul be subject unto the higher powers. For there is no power but of God: the powers that be are ordained of God." Romans 13:1.

Church
Structure

Christ:
"For the husband is the head of the wife, even as Christ is the head of the church: and he is the saviour of the body." Ephesians 5:23.

Holy Spirit:
"These things have I spoken unto you, being yet present with you. But the Comforter, which is the Holy Ghost, whom the Father will send in my name, he shall teach you all things, and bring all things to your remembrance, whatsoever I have said unto you." John 14:25,26.

Church:
"And I say also unto thee, That thou art Peter, and upon this rock I will build my church; and the gates of hell shall not prevail against it. And I will give unto thee the keys of the kingdom of heaven: and whatsoever thou shalt bind on earth shall be bound in heaven: and whatsoever thou shalt loose on earth shall be loosed in heaven." Matthew 16:18,19.

"Moreover if thy brother shall trespass against thee, go and tell him his fault between thee and him alone: if he shall hear thee, thou hast gained thy brother. But if he will not hear thee, then take with thee one or two more, that in the mouth of two or three witnesses every word may be established. And if he shall neglect to hear them, tell it unto the church: but if he neglect to hear the church, let him be unto thee as an heathen man and a publican. Verily I say unto you, Whatsoever ye shall bind on earth shall be bound in heaven: and whatsoever ye shall loose on earth shall be loosed in heaven." Matthew 18:15-18.

Church Leaders:
"The elders which are among you I exhort, who am also an elder, and a witness of the sufferings of Christ, and also a

partaker of the glory that shall be revealed: Feed the flock of God which is among you, taking the oversight thereof, not by constraint, but willingly; not for filthy lucre, but of a ready mind; Neither as being lords over God's heritage, but being ensamples to the flock." 1 Peter 5:1-3.

Members:
"Obey them that have the rule over you, and submit yourselves: for they watch for your souls, as they that must give account, that they may do it with joy, and not with grief: for that is unprofitable for you." Hebrews 13:17.

Business Structure

God:
"With good will doing service, as to the Lord, and not to men: Knowing that whatsoever good thing any man doeth, the same shall he receive of the Lord, whether he be bond or free." Ephesians 6:7,8.

Employers:
"And, ye masters, do the same things unto them, forbearing threatening: knowing that your Master also is in heaven; neither is there respect of persons with him." Ephesians 6:9.

Employees:
"Servants, be obedient to them that are your masters according to the flesh, with fear and trembling, in singleness of your heart, as unto Christ; Not with eyeservice, as menpleasers; but as the servants of Christ, doing the will of God from the heart;" Ephesians 6:5,6.

E. God assures us that He is in charge of those in authority and is working His purposes through them (Proverbs 21:1). He also assures us that even the wrath of authority is under His control: *"Surely the wrath of man shall praise thee: the remainder of wrath shalt thou restrain." Psalms 76:10.*

F. God does not expect us to obey authority when they ask us to sin or rebel against God: *"And when they had brought them, they set them before the council: and the high priest asked them, Saying, Did not we straitly command you that ye should not teach in this name? and, behold, ye have filled Jerusalem with your doctrine, and intend to bring this man's blood upon us. Then Peter and the other apostles answered and said, We ought to obey God rather than men." Acts 5:27-29.*

G. Nevertheless, we are to pray for all those in authority, even if they do evil things: *"I exhort therefore, that, first of all, supplications, prayers, intercessions, and giving of thanks, be made for all men; For kings, and for all that are in authority; that we may lead a quiet and peaceable life in all godliness and honesty. For this is good and acceptable in the sight of God our Saviour;" 1 Timothy 2:1-3. "And seek the peace of the city whither I have caused you to be carried away captives, and pray unto the LORD for it: for in the peace thereof shall ye have peace." Jeremiah 29:7.*

3. Clear Conscience vs. Guilt

God puts within each person an innate sense of His ideal standards. When those standards are violated, our spiritual connection with God registers an injury and a response of spiritual pain. That pain is called guilt: *"For when the Gentiles, which have not the law, do by nature the things contained in the law, these, having not the law, are a law unto themselves: Which shew the work of the law written in their hearts, their conscience also bearing witness, and their thoughts the mean while accusing or else excusing one another;)" Romans 2:14,15. (also see Psalm 38:1-6).*

A. God uses conscience like a physician uses an X-ray machine. With it, He shows us where our spiritual arteries are blocked: *"The spirit of man is the candle of the LORD, searching all the inward parts of the belly." Proverbs 20:27.*

B. Only God can heal spiritual wounds and remove the pain of guilt. Guilt alerts us to spiritual illness and prompts us to call the Great Physician. David the king described the pain of guilt, the proper response (repentance), and the healing of God: *"Blessed is he whose transgression is forgiven, whose sin is covered. Blessed is the man unto whom the LORD imputeth not iniquity, and in whose spirit there is no guile. When I kept silence, my bones waxed old through my roaring all the day long. For day and night thy hand was heavy upon me: my moisture is turned into the drought of summer. Selah. I acknowledged my sin unto thee, and mine iniquity have I not hid. I said, I will confess my transgressions unto the LORD; and thou forgavest the iniquity of my sin. Selah." Psalms 32:1-5.*

C. Guilt requires us to seek God's forgiveness first, because sin is primarily an offense against God: *"Against thee, thee only, have I sinned, and done this evil in thy sight: that thou mightest be justified when thou speakest, and be clear when thou judgest." Psalms 51:4.* Psalm 51 is David's prayer after Nathan the prophet confronted him about his sin with Bathsheba. *(also see Joseph in Genesis 39:7-9).*

D. God's forgiveness first, then the forgiveness of others, cleanses the conscience of guilt. This order corresponds to the two great commandments: *"And Jesus answered him, The first of all the commandments is, Hear, O Israel; The Lord our God is one Lord: And thou shalt love the Lord thy God with all thy heart, and with all thy soul, and with all thy mind, and with all thy strength: this is the first commandment. And the second is like, namely this, Thou shalt love thy neighbour as thyself. There is none other commandment greater than these." Mark 12:29-31.*

E. God produces genuine love in us through a clear conscience. It is one of the three main components of a loving Christian life: *"Now the end of the commandment is charity out of a pure heart, and of a good conscience, and of faith unfeigned:" 1 Timothy 1:5.*

F. God equips us for spiritual warfare through a clear conscience, and at the same time a lack of good conscience makes us vulnerable: *"This charge I commit unto thee, son Timothy, according to the prophecies which went before on thee, that thou by them mightest war a good warfare; Holding faith, and a good conscience; which some having put away concerning faith have made shipwreck:" 1 Timothy 1:18,19.*

G. Our understanding of God's will is weakened by a guilty conscience. Paul taught that it is possible to cut the connection of our conscience with God like searing the skin nerves with an iron: *"Now the Spirit speaketh expressly, that in the latter times some shall depart from the faith, giving heed to seducing spirits, and doctrines of devils; Speaking lies in hypocrisy; having their conscience seared with a hot iron;" 1 Timothy 4:1,2.* Unbelievers routinely cauterize their consciences by habitually practicing certain sins. They disconnect God's influence over them (the conscience) and become "past feeling": *"This I say therefore, and testify in the Lord, that ye henceforth walk not as other Gentiles walk, in the vanity of their mind, Having the understanding darkened, being alienated from the life of God through the ignorance that is in them, because of the blindness of their heart: Who being past feeling have given themselves over unto lasciviousness, to work all uncleanness with greediness." Ephesians 4:17-19.*

H. Jesus taught that guilt is a huge burden that only He can lift: *"Come unto me, all ye that labour and are heavy laden, and I will give you rest. Take my yoke upon you, and learn of me; for I am meek and lowly in heart: and ye shall find rest unto your souls. For my yoke is easy, and my burden is light." Matthew 11:28-30.* Christian in *Pilgrim's Progress* had a great burden on his back that only rolled off at the foot of the cross.[18]

4. Forgiveness vs. Bitterness
    God is the source of all forgiveness. Since all sin is primarily an offense against God, forgiveness must first come from God. After God forgives us, we are free to forgive others: *"Let all bitterness, and wrath, and anger, and clamour, and evil speaking, be put away from you, with all malice: And be ye kind one to another, tenderhearted, forgiving one another, even as God for Christ's sake hath forgiven you." Ephesians 4:31,32. (also see Colossians 3:10-13).*

    A. God has made extraordinary provisions for our forgiveness: *"For God so loved the world, that he gave his only begotten Son, that whosoever believeth in him should not perish, but have everlasting life." John 3:16. "In whom we have redemption through his blood, the forgiveness of sins, according to the riches of his grace;" Ephesians 1:7.*

B. God provides the mechanism of forgiveness.

Our natural solution to the crisis of guilt is to balance our guilt with blame of others (I was raised that way, he or she offended me, etc.).[19] We don't allow ourselves to feel one more strongly than the other, and as a result we don't deal with either. Guilt and blame are the twin towers of the spiritual giants. They play on the court together. We fail to clear our conscience with God and others because we defend bitterness.

When we accept God's forgiveness, the guilt side of the seesaw comes down. This leaves the blame side to our full attention. The blame then feels like overkill. Relief of guilt diminishes the need to blame. Therefore, the seesaw becomes a child's toy to us, and we get off. We no longer defend our bitterness and become free to forgive: *"For we ourselves also were sometimes foolish, disobedient, deceived, serving divers lusts and pleasures, living in malice and envy, hateful, and hating one another. But after that the kindness and love of God our Saviour toward man appeared, Not by works of righteousness which we have done, but according to his mercy he saved us, by the washing of regeneration, and renewing of the Holy Ghost; Which he shed on us abundantly through Jesus Christ our Saviour; That being justified by his grace, we should be made heirs according to the hope of eternal life." Titus 3:3-7. (also see Luke 7:36-50).*

C. God's forgiveness takes away the domino effect of blame. In the Garden of Eden after the fall, Adam blamed Eve instead of accepting his guilt. Then Eve blamed the snake (Genesis3:8-13).They both balanced their guilt with blame. In the reverse, when the need for blame is taken away, when we are forgiven, the dominoes fall back the other way. Another metaphor for the process of blame is an infectious disease: you catch it from someone who has it. Another is the log and the splinter (Matthew 7:1-6).

D. God will not take away the torment of guilt until we forgive. Forgiveness by definition involves a triangle of ourselves, the other, and God: *"For if ye forgive men their trespasses, your heavenly Father will also forgive you: But if ye forgive not men their trespasses, neither will your Father forgive your trespasses." Matthew 6:14,15.* We can forgive others when we realize our forgiveness in Christ. But, when we refuse to forgive others, guilt must be kept at the same emotional level as the blame (the seesaw), and the pain of guilt remains. An example is the man who owed ten thousand talents and was forgiven (Matthew 18:23-35). When he would not forgive a debt of a hundred pence, his lord delivered him to the tormentors. I believe the tormentors are a symbol of emotional pain: *"Then his lord, after that he had called him, said unto him, O thou wicked servant, I forgave thee all that debt, because thou desiredst me: Shouldest not thou also have had compassion on thy fellowservant, even as I had pity on thee? And his lord was wroth, and delivered him to the tormentors, till he should pay all that was due unto him. So likewise shall my heavenly Father do also unto you, if ye from your hearts forgive not every one his brother their trespasses." Matthew 18:32-35.*

E. God wants us to focus on our own sins first so we can be free of guilt to help others overcome sin. Without that freedom, we will balance our guilt with blame of others: *"Judge not, that ye be not judged. For with what judgment ye judge, ye shall be judged: and with what measure ye mete, it shall be measured to you again. And why beholdest thou the mote that is in thy brother's eye, but considerest not the beam that is in thine own eye? Or how wilt thou say to thy brother, Let me pull out the mote out of thine eye; and, behold, a beam is in thine own eye? Thou hypocrite, first cast out the beam out of thine own eye; and then shalt thou see clearly to cast out the mote out of thy brother's eye." Matthew 7:1-5.*

F. Forgiveness is our top priority (Matthew 18:7-10). Forgiveness produces profound changes in the giver and receiver. "Will you forgive me?" is the second most powerful message next to "I love you."

• We are to sacrifice all to secure forgiveness: *"Ye have heard that it was said by them of old time, Thou shalt not kill; and whosoever shall kill shall be in danger of the judgment: But I say unto you, That whosoever is angry with his brother without a cause shall be in danger of the judgment: and whosoever shall say to his brother, Raca, shall be in danger of the council: but whosoever shall say, Thou fool, shall be in danger of hell fire. Therefore if thou bring thy gift to the altar, and there rememberest that thy brother hath ought against thee; Leave there thy gift before the altar, and go thy way; first be reconciled to thy brother, and then come and offer thy gift." Matthew 5:21-24.*

- Even our ministries aren't as important as receiving forgiveness and freeing others of blame, because unresolved bitterness corrupts the spirits   of those we are trying to help, and renders our efforts fruitless: *"Looking   diligently lest any man fail of the grace of God; lest any root of bitterness springing up trouble you, and thereby many be defiled;" Hebrews 12:15.*

5. Meekness vs. Anger
    God wants to be the focus of all our expectations. When we give our expectations to God, we take away the motivation for anger. The angry soul looks to self and others for rewards. The meek soul looks only to God: *"My soul, wait thou only upon God; for my expectation is from him." Psalms 62:5.*

    A. God is our only true hope of just, merciful, and considerate treatment. The Bible teaches us not to hope in self or others: *"Thus saith the LORD; Cursed be the man that trusteth in man, and maketh flesh his arm, and whose heart departeth from the LORD." Jeremiah 17:5.* Anger is the result of expecting others to be just, merciful, and considerate. When sinful people manage to be good, we should count it as a blessing. But, to demand holiness of others is God's prerogative (James 4:11-12).

        We get angry when others fail our expectations. We may expect to have privacy, or to be invited to a party, or to see a friend on a certain day; if those expectations are not met, anger has its motivation. Anger comes from being cut off from what we desire from others. In contrast, wisdom is focusing our desires on God*: "So shall the knowledge of wisdom be unto thy soul: when thou hast found it, then there shall be a reward, and thy expectation shall not be cut off." Proverbs 24:14.*

    B. God is sovereign in all affairs and He is working all things for our good (Romans 8:28-29). With that realization we can transfer our expectations to God and trust Him to fulfill our hopes in His way. Trust in God's sovereignty motivates us to be meek. Meekness is the opposite of anger. Meekness is waiting on God and refusing to take by force what He does not give (this could be emotional force as well).

    C. God gives special promises to the meek:

- The meek will inherit it all. The wicked will be missing persons. The meek will have peace. The wicked will be broken: *"Cease from anger, and forsake wrath: fret not thyself in any wise to do evil. For evildoers shall be cut off: but those that wait upon the LORD, they shall inherit the earth. For yet a little while, and the wicked shall not be: yea, thou shalt diligently consider his place, and it shall not be. But the meek shall inherit the earth; and shall delight themselves in the abundance of peace." Psalms 37:8-11.*

- The meek will have special guidance from God: *"The meek will he guide in judgment: and the meek will he teach his way." Psalms 25:9.*

- The meek will increase their joy. The angry may increase their possessions, but they will get no joy out of them: *"The meek also shall increase their joy in the LORD, and the poor among men shall rejoice in the Holy One of Israel." Isaiah 29:19.*

- The meek will have special beauty when their expectations are met. The angry will only be tired and spent: *"For the LORD taketh pleasure in his people: he will beautify the meek with salvation." Psalms 149:4. "But let it be the hidden man of the heart, in that which is not corruptible, even the ornament of a meek and quiet spirit, which is in the sight of God of great price." 1 Peter 3:4.*

D. The Spirit of God produces meekness in us: *"But the fruit of the Spirit is love, joy, peace, longsuffering, gentleness, goodness, faith, Meekness, temperance: against such there is no law." Galatians 5:22,23.*

E. Meekness is an essential character trait for witnessing and teaching: *"And the servant of the Lord must not strive; but be gentle unto all men, apt to teach, patient, In meekness instructing those that oppose themselves; if God peradventure will give them repentance to the acknowledging of the truth; And that they may recover themselves out of the snare of the devil, who are taken captive by him at his will." 2 Timothy 2:24-26. "But sanctify the Lord God in your hearts: and be ready always to give an answer to every man that asketh you a reason of the hope that is in you with meekness and fear:*

Having a good conscience; that, whereas they speak evil of you, as of evildoers, they may be ashamed that falsely accuse your good conversation in Christ." 1 Peter 3:15,16.

F. Meekness is the ultimate weapon in slaying the dragon of anger: *"Who is a wise man and endued with knowledge among you? let him shew out of a good conversation his works with meekness of wisdom. But if ye have bitter envying and strife in your hearts, glory not, and lie not against the truth. This wisdom descendeth not from above, but is earthly, sensual, devilish." James 3:13-15. "To speak evil of no man, to be no brawlers, but gentle, shewing all meekness unto all men." Titus 3:2.*

6. Moral Freedom vs. Moral Impurity
    God is the blessed addiction: *"And be not drunk with wine, wherein is excess; but be filled with the Spirit;" Ephesians 5:18.*

    "But wait a minute? I thought all addictions were bad." The verse makes a direct comparison between drunkenness and spirit fullness. "How can the comparison be made?" They are both solutions to an implied problem. "What is the problem?" Adversity - the principle of a fallen world that drives people to addictions or God.

    Since Adam and Eve, adversity has dogged us like Cujo. We were made for relationship and purpose, but adversity infiltrates and sabotages both. People don't treat us right. Things don't work right. So we seek diversion, amusements, and comfort. Addictions don't begin as a problem to be solved; at first they're an answer to an existing problem, adversity.

    Addictions are an extreme form of moral impurity. They are the result of looking to the pleasures of the body to satisfy spiritual longings. When I think of moral impurity, I think mainly of two pleasures: sexual and chemical. They are the sins listed in *1 Peter 4:3: "For the time past of our life may suffice us to have wrought the will of the Gentiles, when we walked in lasciviousness, lusts, excess of wine, revellings, banquetings, and abominable idolatries:"* These are the world's solutions to adversity and suffering.

    A. God's solution to adversity is His Spirit: *"In the last day, that great day of the feast, Jesus stood and cried, saying, If any man thirst, let him come unto me, and drink. He that believeth on me, as the*

206

scripture hath said, out of his belly shall flow rivers of living water." *John 7:37,38.* Jesus couldn't have been talking about a literal thirst. They were at a feast! He was referring to the thirst we have for perfection in relationships and purpose. Jesus promised that He could provide satisfaction to overflowing. Sex and chemicals never satisfy; instead they cause us to cry out for more. When not managed, they flood their banks and drown us. But the Spirit refreshes us and through us those around us.

B. God wants us to choose Him for our comfort. The name of the Holy Spirit is the Comforter (John 14.26-27). We can judge our morality by knowing where we go for comfort. Do we go to the refrigerator, the TV, the bottle, the pills, the club, or do we go to God and His word?

C. Moral purity allows us to have God's perspective, to see as God sees: *"Blessed are the pure in heart: for they shall see God." Matthew 5:8.*

7. Spiritual Purpose vs. Boredom and Depression
God's character is our ultimate goal: *"Be ye therefore followers of God, as dear children; And walk in love, as Christ also hath loved us, and hath given himself for us an offering and a sacrifice to God for a sweetsmelling savour." Ephesians 5:1,2.* Purpose overcomes boredom when we imitate God and love other people. Since the spiritual world precipitates into and dominates the natural world (Chapter 1), and since we are spiritual at our core, spiritual purpose is required to drive away boredom and depression. Otherwise, a large part of our potential goes unused, and we get bored.

A. God wants us to imitate Him in suffering. The apostle Paul said his purpose was to "fill up that which was left behind" of Christ's work. He defined the work as suffering: *"Who now rejoice in my sufferings for you, and fill up that which is behind of the afflictions of Christ in my flesh for his body's sake, which is the church:" Colossians 1:24.* Ephesians 5:2 also defines walking in love like Christ as suffering and sacrifice. Jesus came to sacrifice His own honor, position, wealth, etc. for us (2 Corinthians 8:9). He sends us to sacrifice for the sake of others.

We love others and minister to them through suffering, and often that suffering is at their hands because of their misunderstanding of our motives. There is so much self-serving in the world, that when a follower of Christ truly serves others, his motives are suspected: *"Forasmuch then as Christ hath suffered for us in the flesh, arm yourselves likewise with the same mind: for he that hath suffered in the flesh hath ceased from sin; …If ye be reproached for the name of Christ, happy are ye; for the spirit of glory and of God resteth upon you: on their part he is evil spoken of, but on your part he is glorified." 1 Peter 4:1, 14. "As thou hast sent me into the world, even so have I also sent them into the world." John 17:18.*

Suffering is one of the "hard sayings." The Hindus and Buddhists learn to ignore it and to wish it away, but God teaches us to live in it, appreciate it, and love through it: *"Saying, The Son of man must suffer many things, and be rejected of the elders and chief priests and scribes, and be slain, and be raised the third day. And he said to them all, If any man will come after me, let him deny himself, and take up his cross daily, and follow me. For whosoever will save his life shall lose it: but whosoever will lose his life for my sake, the same shall save it. For what is a man advantaged, if he gain the whole world, and lose himself, or be cast away?" Luke 9:22-25. "Be not thou therefore ashamed of the testimony of our Lord, nor of me his prisoner: but be thou partaker of the afflictions of the gospel according to the power of God; Who hath saved us, and called us with an holy calling, not according to our works, but according to his own purpose and grace, which was given us in Christ Jesus before the world began," 2 Timothy 1:8,9.*

B. God teaches us His character when we respond righteously to adversity and suffering: *"For which cause we faint not; but though our outward man perish, yet the inward man is renewed day by day. For our light affliction, which is but for a moment, worketh for us a far more exceeding and eternal weight of glory; While we look not at the things which are seen, but at the things which are not seen: for the things which are seen are temporal; but the things which are not seen are eternal." 2 Corinthians 4:16-18.*

8. Genuine Friendships vs. Using and Abusing People
The light of God is in every man and woman. We enjoy others to the extent we see God in them. It's not the evil traits and tendencies that attract, it's the

amiable hologram of God. We all display the image of God and have part of His light in us. Friendship is loving the Divine in others: *"So God created man in his own image, in the image of God created he him; male and female created he them." Genesis 1:27. "That was the true Light, which lighteth every man that cometh into the world." John 1:9.*

A. God is the source of all light. Fellowship depends on His light: *"This then is the message which we have heard of him, and declare unto you, that God is light, and in him is no darkness at all. If we say that we have fellowship with him, and walk in darkness, we lie, and do not the truth: But if we walk in the light, as he is in the light, we have fellowship one with another, and the blood of Jesus Christ his Son cleanseth us from all sin." 1 John 1:5-7.* If we love the light and live in it, we have fellowship with others who live in it. Without God's light, evil traits and tendencies dominate our interactions.

B. We show our love for God by loving others. Through friendship and fellowship we have an opportunity to love the characteristics of God in others: *"If a man say, I love God, and hateth his brother, he is a liar: for he that loveth not his brother whom he hath seen, how can he love God whom he hath not seen? And this commandment have we from him, That he who loveth God love his brother also." 1 John 4:20,21.* I am reminded of the Great Commandment and the second like unto it.

C. God wants us to turn on our lights. We let the light grow brighter to the extent we let God's Spirit control our life. We attract people to God by the light of God they see in us. Genuine friendships can only last in the light of God: *"Ye are the light of the world. A city that is set on an hill cannot be hid. Neither do men light a candle, and put it under a bushel, but on a candlestick; and it giveth light unto all that are in the house. Let your light so shine before men, that they may see your good works, and glorify your Father which is in heaven." Matthew 5:14-16.*

D. So why do people use and abuse others? Like the darkness that swallows a flashlight's beam, they have put out the light of God in themselves. They are past feeling. They have seared their consciences. Yet, just like the darkness, they aren't satisfied. They want fellowship, a benefit of the light, even in darkness. They try to steal the blessings of the light by worldly methods. They live a life characterized by deeds done in the dark: deception, injury, and misery: *"But evil men and seducers shall wax worse and worse, deceiving, and being deceived." 2 Timothy 3:13. "For every one that doeth evil hateth the light, neither cometh to the light, lest his deeds should be reproved." John 3:20.*

If a deed has to be done in the dark, without the knowledge or consent of the friend, it is abuse of genuine friendship: *"And have no fellowship with the unfruitful works of darkness, but rather reprove them." Ephesians 5:11.*

9. Financial Freedom vs. Financial Bondage
   God owns everything: *"In the beginning God created the heaven and the earth." Genesis 1:1.*

   A. God has entrusted part of what He owns to people: *"And God blessed them, and God said unto them, Be fruitful, and multiply, and replenish the earth, and subdue it: and have dominion over the fish of the sea, and over the fowl of the air, and over every living thing that moveth upon the earth." Genesis 1:28.* God wants us to use His creation to make things and increase its value.

   B. At the same time, God has placed limits on our stewardship of the earth.

   • Debt has a limit. We are to owe others our love, and that's all. Not that we should never give our love, but we should never feel we give enough love: *"Owe no man any thing, but to love one another: for he that loveth another hath fulfilled the law. For this, Thou shalt not commit adultery, Thou shalt not kill, Thou shalt not steal, Thou shalt not bear false witness, Thou shalt not covet; and if there be any other commandment, it is briefly comprehended in this saying, namely, Thou shalt love thy neighbour as thyself. Love worketh no ill to his neighbour: therefore love is the fulfilling of the law." Romans 13:8-10.*

   • Pressure to provide has a limit. When we put more pressure on ourselves than God has, we know we've gone too far: (Matthew 6:24-34).

- Love of money and things has a limit. God promises food and clothing. Everything else is extra: *"And having food and raiment let us be therewith content." 1 Timothy 6:8.*

  God instead wants us to focus on the eternal riches because we cannot haul our earthly riches to heaven: *"But godliness with contentment is great gain. For we brought nothing into this world, and it is certain we can carry nothing out." 1 Timothy 6:6,7.* The eternal riches are imitation of God's character (godliness), and meekness (contentment): *"But they that will be rich fall into temptation and a snare, and into many foolish and hurtful lusts, which drown men in destruction and perdition. For the love of money is the root of all evil: which while some coveted after, they have erred from the faith, and pierced themselves through with many sorrows." 1 Timothy 6:9,10.*

- Managing money has a limit. When the time invested in money management chokes our time for God's word, it's time to get out the weed eater: *"And some fell among thorns; and the thorns sprung up, and choked them: ...He also that received seed among the thorns is he that heareth the word; and the care of this world, and the deceitfulness of riches, choke the word, and he becometh unfruitful." Matthew 13:7, 22. (also see Luke 12:15-21).*

- Business duties have a limit. If they restrict our freedom to serve God and go where He leads, they are fetters on our feet: *"Thou therefore endure hardness, as a good soldier of Jesus Christ. No man that warreth entangleth himself with the affairs of this life; that he may please him who hath chosen him to be a soldier." 2 Timothy 2:3,4.*

- Employing others has a limit. Employees must be paid for their work and work for a living wage: *"Masters, give unto your servants that which is just and equal; knowing that ye also have a Master in heaven." Colossians 4:1. (also see Leviticus 19:13; Jeremiah 22:13; and James 5:4).*

C. God uses money to teach us His character, and character is more important than money: *"For ye know the grace of our Lord Jesus Christ, that, though he was rich, yet for your sakes he became poor, that ye through his poverty might be rich." 2 Corinthians 8:9. (also see Philippians 2:5-8).*

D. God uses poverty and prosperity as tests to teach us faith in Him: *"Not that I speak in respect of want: for I have learned, in whatsoever state I am, therewith to be content. I know both how to be abased, and I know how to abound: every where and in all things I am instructed both to be full and to be hungry, both to abound and to suffer need. I can do all things through Christ which strengtheneth me." Philippians 4:11-13. "Charge them that are rich in this world, that they be not highminded, nor trust in uncertain riches, but in the living God, who giveth us richly all things to enjoy;" 1 Timothy 6:17.*

E. Faith in God concerning wealth leads to exaltation. Jesus gave up the riches of heaven to do God's will, therefore God made him the rightful heir of the world: *"Wherefore God also hath highly exalted him, and given him a name which is above every name:" Philippians 2:9 "Hearken, my beloved brethren, Hath not God chosen the poor of this world rich in faith, and heirs of the kingdom which he hath promised to them that love him?" James 2:5.*

Subtleties and Stratagems of Giants

Avoid these mistakes when fighting your giants:

Avoid the false treasure guarded by the giant.

Every good gift comes from God, not from our own schemes (James 1:17). The first city Joshua and the people conquered was Jericho. God had given them orders to dedicate the city entirely, including people and possessions, to Him (Joshua 6:17-19). But Achan stealthily took the "goodly Babylonish garment, and two hundred shekels of silver, and a wedge of gold of fifty shekels weight." (Joshua 7:21). As a result, God did not help Israel at Ai, and they were turned back by a tiny city (Joshua 7:1-5).

Achan desired the treasure in Jericho and it betrayed him. Adolescents often pursue false methods to get treasure: anger, rebellion, moral impurity, revenge, extravagant spending, etc. Each seems to offer physical and psychological satisfaction,   212 but each leaves them weakened and vulnerable. Instead, spiritual growth requires humility, repentance, and repudiation of deceitful riches (1Timothy6:9).

Avoid giants wearing old garments.

After Ai, the other cities (giants) gathered to fight Israel. But Gibeon had a different plan. They disguised themselves as ambassadors from a far country and sued for peace. Joshua and the elders believed the Gibeonites because of their old sacks, old wine bottles, old shoes, old garments, and old bread (Joshua 9). Then Israel had to defend Gibeon as well as themselves (Joshua 10:1-11)

Israel made its first compromise with the giants at Gibeon. This led to more compromise. And eventually the people adopted religious practices of the Gibeonites and other Canaanites which led to defeat (Judges 2:1-3, 13-14).

Compromise with the giant conflicts of adolescence seems easy, but the result can be slavery. The conflicts will not go away nor shrink if we ignore them. They only grow stronger while we wait for them to sleep. We must be committed to attack and conquer every one of the giants: *"For though we walk in the flesh, we do not war after the flesh: (For the weapons of our warfare are not carnal, but mighty through God to the pulling down of strong holds;) Casting down imaginations, and every high thing that exalteth itself against the knowledge of God, and bringing into captivity every thought to the obedience of Christ; And having in a readiness to revenge all disobedience, when your obedience is fulfilled." 2 Corinthians 10:3-6.*

Avoid arguments with giants.

Christian went down into the Valley of Humiliation armed by the four virgins. Apollyon, the destroyer, came to greet him. Apollyon claimed lordship over Christian and offered mercy if Christian went back to the City of Destruction. Christian affirmed his new fealty to Christ. Apollyon offered protection for Christian if he went back, but threatened destruction if he continued. Christian asserted his faith in Christ. Apollyon then listed Christian's unfaithful acts already done (Guilt is the favorite subtlety of giants: 2 Corinthians 2:7-11). Christian claimed forgiveness in Christ. Finally Apollyon attacked Christian and wounded his head (understanding), his hand (faith),and his foot(way of life). Apollyon almost killed him except Christian struck back with his two-edged sword (the Word of God). [20]

Christian's physical wounds were mere symbols of the spiritual wounds he had already suffered by arguing with Apollyon. Apollyon wounded Christian's head by offering mercy, his hand by offering protection, and his foot by listing past sins. Our understanding is wounded when we listen to the ruler of this world (Ephesians 2:2). Our faith is wounded when we fear the hardships of the way (2 Timothy 1:7-8). And, our way of life is hampered when we remember and regret our past (Hebrews 10:3-4, 12-14, 19, 22).

Don't parley with giants; pierce them with the sword of the Spirit (Hebrews 4:11-13).

Jack the Giant Killer

We all know about Jack and the Beanstalk, but Jack killed other giants too. So much so that he was called Jack the Giant Killer. The stories about Jack illustrate the inclination toward giant-killing by adolescents.

Beanstalk Jack took back the valuable possessions (the hen, the gold, the enchanted harp) stolen by the giant. The giant had killed Jack's father and seized the treasures. Sometimes the son wins the battle where the father lost. The Israelites under Joshua conquered Canaan where their parents under Moses panicked and turned back: *"And they that shall be of thee shall build the old waste places: thou shalt raise up the foundations of many generations; and thou shalt be called, The repairer of the breach, The restorer of paths to dwell in." Isaiah 58:12.*

Giant-killer Jack made a career out of outsmarting ogres. He began in his own backyard and tricked Cormoran into a pit. Jack axed him there. Jack then traveled to the forest, a place of mystery, to battle Blunderbore. Jack hung Blunderbore and his friend from a beam. Jack went to Wales and duped a two-headed giant into doing himself in. With the power and confidence he had gained, Jack mocked another giant into a moat. Giant-killing becomes an obsession for youths. Overcoming the multiple crises of adolescence is their natural motivation. Joshua's charges overcame the grasshopper complex of their parents and annihilated the Anakims (Joshua 11:19-23).

Key - Strength

Moses' parting words to Israel were "be strong and very courageous" (Deuteronomy 31:6-8). Strength is necessary to defeat the giants of adolescence and develop a firm sense of integrity. Just as Joshua and the Israelites used their strength to drive out the Canaanites and inherit the land, so the spiritual adolescent uses strength to overcome life conflicts and develop a positive identity. "Strength" in Moses' charge means, "to seize."[21] "Good courage" means "to be alert."[22] The spiritual adolescent must seize his weapons and opportunities, and he must be alert to danger.

God also confirmed Joshua's charge with the same words: "be strong and very courageous" (Joshua 1:7). God's promises: 1. The inheritance of the land; 2. Prosperity; 3. Success: *"Be strong and of a good courage: for unto this people shalt thou divide for an inheritance the land, which I sware unto their fathers to give them. Only be thou strong and very courageous, that thou mayest observe to do according to all the law, which Moses my servant commanded thee: turn not from it to the right hand or to the left, that thou mayest prosper whithersoever thou goest. This book of the law shall not depart out of thy mouth, but thou shalt meditate therein day and night, that thou mayest observe to do according to all that is written therein: for then thou shalt make thy way prosperous, and then thou shalt have good success." Joshua 1:6-8.*

The inheritance represents the "rest of God" spoken of in Hebrews 4 and Chapter 8 of this book (Spiritual Childhood). Prosperity is the ongoing process of pushing forward.[23] Success is the ability to judge rightly again and again. It is the ability to consider all related circumstances before acting, judging, or deciding.[24] God uses words here to convey the growth of a person toward spiritual maturity. Strength is the key to continued growth: *"A wise man is strong; yea, a man of knowledge increaseth strength... If thou faint in the day of adversity, thy strength is small." Proverbs 24: 5,10.*

"And it came to pass, when Israel was strong, that they put the Canaanites to tribute, and did not utterly drive them out." Judges 1:28. This is the goal of spiritual adolescence. The life conflicts cannot be totally eliminated, only "put under tribute."

The New Testament also praises strength as a necessary ingredient for growth:

Strength and good soldiering lead to spiritual offspring: *"Thou therefore, my son, be strong in the grace that is in Christ Jesus. And the things that thou hast heard of me among many witnesses, the same commit thou to faithful men, who shall be able to teach others also. Thou therefore endure hardness, as a good soldier of Jesus Christ." 2 Timothy 2:1-3.*

Paul exhorts the Corinthians with military terms. Among them is "be strong,"[25] which means: 1. To increase in physical and mental force; 2. To grow actively and healthily. *"Watch ye, stand fast in the faith, quit you like men, be strong." 1 Corinthians 16:13.*

Ephesians 6:10-18 lists strength as the beginning of successful spiritual warfare: *"Finally, my brethren, be strong in the Lord, and in the power of his might." Ephesians 6:10.*

1 John shows strength to be the key to spiritual adolescence: *"I have written unto you, fathers, because ye have known him that is from the beginning. I have written unto you, young men, because ye are strong, and the word of God abideth in you, and ye have overcome the wicked one." 1 John 2:14.*

Symbol - Integrity

The symbol for spiritual adolescence is Thummim (integrity), as in Urim and Thummim. Urim and Thummim were objects the high priest of Israel used to determine God's will. They may have been two stones the same shape but different colors. One meant yes and the other meant no. The priest would draw one out of his pouch to find God's answer. The high priest kept these stones next to his heart when he went into the holy place. This signifies they were necessary to receive God's direction: *"And Aaron shall bear the names of the children of Israel in the breastplate of judgment upon his heart, when he goeth in unto the holy place, for a memorial before the LORD continually. And thou shalt put in the breastplate of judgment the Urim and the Thummim; and they shall be upon Aaron's heart, when he goeth in before the LORD: and Aaron shall bear the judgment of the children of Israel upon his heart before the LORD continually."* Exodus 28:29,30.

Urim And Thummim literally mean "lights and perfections."[26] Light is the symbol of spiritual childhood and perfection-Thummim-integrity is the symbol of spiritual adolescence. I prefer to use the word integrity.

There are two words for integrity in Hebrew. The masculine means "completeness, prosperity."[27] The children of Israel under Joshua were encouraged to become complete by inheriting the land and overcoming the giants. They were also urged to be prosperous, to keep pushing forward. The feminine integrity means "innocence."[28] This describes a purity of motives. The feminine integrity was used to explain Job's motives (Job 2:3; 27:5-6). It was also used in *Proverbs 11:3"The integrity of the upright shall guide them: but the perverseness of transgressors shall destroy them."* God and Moses counseled the people to be constantly alert to their own motives (Joshua 1:7; Deuteronomy 31, 32).

Thummin is the plural of integrity. It means integrities. The spiritual adolescent has several crises at once to be mastered. He or she needs integrities to overcome them. Just as the Israelites had to put down all the heathen nations at once to be safe, so the adolescent has to master every spiritual conflict to attain wholeness and maturity.

This integrity is the same as Erikson's identity. The adolescent becomes by about age 20 a complete person with a strong enough sense of identity to make independent decisions. These decisions involve thoughts, motives, and emotions. Notice that Thummim is in the breastplate of judgment over the high priest's heart - the seat of the thoughts, motives, and emotions. The Christian's armor from Ephesians 6:14 includes the "breastplate of righteousness." And inside the breastplate are Urim and Thummim.

The New Testament implies that integrity is a stage of spiritual development. But instead of integrity the New Testament uses the words "perfect and complete": *"Epaphras, who is one of you, a servant of Christ, saluteth you, always labouring fervently for you in prayers, that ye may stand perfect and complete in all the will of God." Colossians 4:12.*

Perfection (integrity) is part of a developmental process: *"Therefore leaving the principles of the doctrine of Christ, let us go on unto perfection; not laying again the foundation of repentance from dead works, and of faith toward God," Hebrews 6:1. "But when that which is perfect is come, then that which is in part shall be done away. When I was a child, I spake as a child, I understood as a child, I thought as a child: but when I became a man, I put away childish things." 1 Corinthians 13:10,11. "For the perfecting of the saints, for the work of the ministry, for the edifying of the body of Christ: Till we all come in the unity of the faith, and of the knowledge of the Son of God, unto a perfect man, unto the measure of the stature of the fulness of Christ: That we henceforth be no more children, tossed to and fro, and carried about with every wind of doctrine, by the sleight of men, and cunning craftiness, whereby they lie in wait to deceive; But speaking the truth in love, may grow up into him in all things, which is the head, even Christ:" Ephesians 4:12-15.*

Perfection (integrity) is achieved by spiritual warfare: *"Be sober, be vigilant; because your adversary the devil, as a roaring lion, walketh about, seeking whom he may devour: Whom resist stedfast in the faith, knowing that the same afflictions are accomplished in your brethren that are in the world. But the God of all grace, who hath called us unto his eternal glory by Christ Jesus, after that ye have suffered a while, make you perfect, stablish, strengthen, settle you." 1 Peter 5:8-10.*

This kind of perfection (integrity) is obtainable, otherwise the NewTestament would not refer to it as a stage of growth: *"Howbeit we speak wisdom among them that are perfect: yet not the wisdom of this world, nor of the princes of this world, that come to nought:" 1 Corinthians 2:6. "I press toward the mark for the prize of the high calling of God in Christ Jesus. Let us therefore, as many as be perfect, be thus minded: and if in any thing ye be otherwise minded, God shall reveal even this unto you. Nevertheless, whereto we have already attained, let us walk by the same rule, let us mind the same thing." Philippians 3:14-16. "For in many things we offend all. If any man offend not in word, the same is a perfect man, and able also to bridle the whole body." James 3:2.*

CHAPTER 10

Spiritual Young Adulthood

IN a good year, the latter rains fall in March-April (the first month of the Hebrew calendar). Because the harvest depends on them, these rains are more important to the farmer than the early rain and the violent rain.[1] If the latter rains fail, the crops can't mature, because it rarely rains in the summertime. Jeremiah laments: *"The harvest is past, the summer is ended, and we are not saved."* *Jeremiah 8:20.*

The prophet Joel describes rejoicing when the latter rains fall in the first month: *"Be glad then, ye children of Zion, and rejoice in the LORD your God: for he hath given you the former rain moderately, and he will cause to come down for you the rain, the former rain, and the latter rain in the first month. And the floors shall be full of wheat, and the fats shall overflow with wine and oil." Joel 2:23,24. (also see Job 29:23; Proverbs 16:15; Zech 10:1).*

The latter rains symbolize the advanced training required after adolescence to reach full maturity and to be fruitful. Just as the farmers wait expectantly for the spring showers to complete their crops, so spiritual cultivators must learn patience to wait on the Lord. Hosea hints at this symbolism and this stage by encouraging Israel to wait for the latter rain that will sustain them through the summer: *"Come, and let us return unto the LORD: for he hath torn, and he will heal us; he hath smitten, and he will bind us up. After two days will he revive us: in the third day he will raise us up, and we shall live in his sight. Then shall we know, if we follow on to know the LORD: his going forth is prepared as the morning; and he shall come unto us as the rain, as the latter and former rain unto the earth." Hosea 6:1-3. "Be patient therefore, brethren, unto the coming of the Lord. Behold, the husbandman waiteth for the precious fruit of the earth, and hath long patience for it, until he receive the early and latter rain.*

Be ye also patient; stablish your hearts: for the coming of the Lord draweth nigh." James 5:7,8.

Latter Rains

Young adulthood is a time of confirming life choices and proving integrity. It is the time between adolescence and before adulthood. Erik Erikson called this the psychosocial moratorium. He said this stage was for finding a niche, for delaying adult commitments like marriage, or parenting, and for being recognized as a unique and valuable member of the adult world.[2]

Spiritual young adulthood is the time to build a powerful life message. It is a time to become valuable to the progress of God's kingdom, and to prepare for spiritual children. Each pilgrim develops a unique solution to the challenges of the day. Only through testing and time does the solution become valid and reliable.

Maintaining integrity is essential to receiving the blessing of spiritual children. In spiritual young adulthood, any weakness in the answers of spiritual adolescence compromises development. Testing exposes flaws. Satan's greatest assault comes here to those who persevere: *"For many are called, but few are chosen."* Matthew 22:14. *"My brethren, count it all joy when ye fall into divers temptations; Knowing this, that the trying of your faith worketh patience. But let patience have her perfect work, that ye may be perfect and entire, wanting nothing." James 1:2-4.*

Erikson also said that this moratorium was especially pronounced in people of genius (people who even reach this stage of spiritual growth are rare). He said, "These trained minds of genius have a special identity and special identity problems often leading to a protracted crisis at the beginning of their careers."[3] Erikson taught that ideological leaders have an extended adolescence that adds to their charisma. They are "individuals with an uncommon depth of conflict, they also often have uncanny gifts and uncanny luck with which they offer to the crisis of a whole generation the solution of their own personal crisis."[4]

The hero offers his solution of the crisis to the whole community. The afflictions of each generation are common to all. Yet, the hero, not content with the standard answers, travels to the spiritual dimension. The time of obscurity, sacrifice, nothingness, and suffering gives the hero generative power: *"And he said unto me, My grace is sufficient for thee: for my strength is made perfect in weakness. Most gladly therefore will I rather glory in my infirmities, that the power of Christ may rest upon me. Therefore I take pleasure in infirmities, in reproaches, in necessities, in persecutions, in distresses for Christ's sake: for when I am weak, then am I strong." 2 Corinthians 12:9,10.*

Spiritual young adulthood is a delay of generativity for the purpose of greater fruitfulness. It is a time of darkness, waiting, refining, and sadness. Without the courage of some to take the journey, there is no spiritual progress. Spiritual young adults have something vital missing, usually in marriage or career or parenting. They are not content with the current processes of filling the void. They learn to trust in God and not their own resources. Waiting patiently for the missing part gives spiritual power. When the spiritual young adult is ready, God provides the missing part and the spiritual children follow: *"Humble yourselves therefore under the mighty hand of God, that he may exalt you in due time: Casting all your care upon him; for he careth for you. Be sober, be vigilant; because your adversary the devil, as a roaring lion, walketh about, seeking whom he may devour: Whom resist stedfast in the faith, knowing that the same afflictions are accomplished in your brethren that are in the world. But the God of all grace, who hath called us unto his eternal glory by Christ Jesus, after that ye have suffered a while, make you perfect, stablish, strengthen, settle you." 1 Peter 5:6-10. "A woman when she is in travail hath sorrow, because her hour is come: but as soon as she is delivered of the child, she remembereth no more the anguish, for joy that a man is born into the world." John 16:21.*

Erikson chose Martin Luther and Mahatma Gandhi to illustrate the protracted crisis of young adulthood and the heroics of their solutions. He also wanted to write about Jesus Christ (of whom the gospels say nothing from age 12 to 30). The connection among these men is their extraordinary spirituality and the gifts they gave to the world.

Martin Luther's father wanted him to marry at age 21. Instead, he became a monk, and put off career and marriage. Erikson implied that Luther's moratorium prepared him psychologically and spiritually to become the political/spiritual leader of the Reformation. Erikson said of this time: "he was less than somebody in any category; he was more nobody than at any other time."[5] Luther emerged from his young adulthood to begin lecturing at age 30. He nailed his ninety-five theses to the Wittenberg door at age 32. He finally married at 41 and had his first child at 42.

Mahatma Gandhi seemed to be on his way to a career in law when he left India for a case in South Africa at the age of 24. There he began to develop his philosophy of "Satyagraha": non-violent civil disobedience. Only after undoing several unfair restrictions against Indians did Gandhi return to India at 45. During this moratorium, Gandhi systematically concealed his aspirations to take over moral and philosophical leadership of India.[6] Finally, in 1919, in response to the Rowlett act, an anti-sedition law, Gandhi called for a day of fasting, prayer, and closing down of business and work. This "struck the religious imagination of an angry people and the whole of India observed a complete 'hartal' on that day."[7] Gandhi was 50 years old.

Learning Tasks

While the goal of spiritual adolescence is to be strong, have the word of God inside, and to overcome the wicked one; the goal of spiritual young adulthood is to "know him who is from the beginning." The spiritual fathers "have known" him that is from the beginning, so they must have passed through a stage of knowing (1 John 2:12-14). The spiritual young adult must learn by experience that God's solutions to life conflicts work. God draws a person through circumstances into the abyss where He reveals Himself at the moment of greatest need. The young adult learns the nature of God's grace and truth and how to imitate those qualities.

The Learning Task of Spiritual Young Adulthood

Understanding the Ways of God

Three Stages to the Ways of God[8]

1. Birth of the Vision - In adolescence, the spiritual traveler gains insight into a unique role he or she can fill in God's kingdom. *"He made known his ways unto Moses, his acts unto the children of Israel." Psalms 103:7. "Now faith is the substance of things hoped for, the evidence of things not seen." Hebrews 11:1.*

2. Death of the Vision - During young adulthood, the realization of that role is put off by unforeseen and seemingly insurmountable circumstances. *"Cast not away therefore your confidence, which hath great recompence of reward. For ye have need of patience, that, after ye have done the will of God, ye might receive the promise." Hebrews 10:35,36.*

3. God's Fulfillment of the Vision - The vision cannot be attained by human effort. God must intervene supernaturally to make it happen. The fulfillment marks the beginning of spiritual adulthood. *"And Jesus answered them,*

saying, The hour is come, that the Son of man should be glorified. Verily, verily, I say unto you, Except a corn of wheat fall into the ground and die, it abideth alone: but if it die, it bringeth forth much fruit. He that loveth his life shall lose it; and he that hateth his life in this world shall keep it unto life eternal." John 12:23-25.

The spiritual young adult must have faith in God's process and timing to endure the testing and waiting: *"Why sayest thou, O Jacob, and speakest, O Israel, My way is hid from the LORD, and my judgment is passed over from my God? Hast thou not known? hast thou not heard, that the everlasting God, the LORD, the Creator of the ends of the earth, fainteth not, neither is weary? there is no searching of his understanding. He giveth power to the faint; and to them that have no might he increaseth strength. Even the youths shall faint and be weary, and the young men shall utterly fall: But they that wait upon the LORD shall renew their strength; they shall mount up with wings as eagles; they shall run, and not be weary; and they shall walk, and not faint." Isaiah 40:27-31.*

Birth of the Vision

After Israel subdued their enemies they were no longer called "the children." They were called "Israel." They had been initiated as young adults by their victories. Now they would learn the Ways of God: *"And it came to pass, when Israel was strong, that they put the Canaanites to tribute, and did not utterly drive them out." Judges 1:28.*

Israel's initial vision was "the place God chooses." God would choose a place for the people to rally around as God's home. It would be the place of God's name. Yet, God put off the revelation of the Place because of the people's lack of integrity in fully conquering their giants (Judges 2:1-5, 20-23). This Place would only be revealed after Israel had defeated their enemies and lived safely, only after their "rest." (Deuteronomy 12:1-11a).

Much of the Old Testament revolves around this theme: finding and securing the place God chooses. The Place had significance because God would "put his name there." The Place would be the throne of God's son. This was hinted at even in Genesis: *"The sceptre shall not depart from Judah, nor a lawgiver from between his feet, until Shiloh come; and unto him shall the gathering of the people be." Genesis 49:10.* Shiloh was the early name for the Messiah. Shiloh was the place of the tabernacle in Canaan's land (Judges 18:31; Joshua 18:1,10).

The revelation would be complete only when the Place and the Person were together.

Mini Deaths of the Vision

The book of Judges illustrates Israel's lack of integrity in waiting for God's promise: "the place I will choose." The people were periodically put into bondage by the nations surrounding them. Their corporate bondage represents our individual bondage by the giant conflicts of spiritual adolescence. Incomplete integrity fails to master the giants.

God had promised that after rest from their enemies the Place would be revealed: *"But when ye go over Jordan, and dwell in the land which the LORD your God giveth you to inherit, and when he giveth you rest from all your enemies round about, so that ye dwell in safety; Then there shall be a place which the LORD your God shall choose to cause his name to dwell there; thither shall ye bring all that I command you; your burnt offerings, and your sacrifices, your tithes, and the heave offering of your hand, and all your choice vows which ye vow unto the LORD:" Deuteronomy 12:10,11.*

When the Place was not revealed right after Joshua gave them a little rest, they felt betrayed. They began to lose their trust in God and His promise of a central place. Israel showed their lack of patience by turning to the gods of the Canaanites and the pleasures of the Canaanite's worship. Because of their lack of faithfulness, God allowed them to be oppressed (Judges 2:7,10, 11-14; 3:5-7). *"And the children of Israel did evil in the sight of the LORD, and served Baalim: And they forsook the LORD God of their fathers, which brought them out of the land of Egypt, and followed other gods, of the gods of the people that were round about them, and bowed themselves unto them, and provoked the LORD to anger. And they forsook the LORD, and served Baal and Ashtaroth. And the anger of the LORD was hot against Israel, and he delivered them into the hands of spoilers that spoiled them, and he sold them into the hands of their enemies round about, so that they could not any longer stand before their enemies." Judges 2:11-14.*

Mini Saviors of the Vision

God provided judges to save the people when they repented. Judges were military leaders who led the Israelites to victory over oppressor nations. Each judge fought a particular giant of spiritual adolescence, and at the same time symbolized the nation's general struggles with the giants.

The need for judges represents different aspects of the corporate failure of integrity. I will show that Israel consistently worked on this problem of development presented by their initial vision. They were searching for the solution of their disjointedness, weakness, and lack of national integrity in a central place and person.

Israel's first effort to solve the problem of both the oppressors and the Place was with Gideon. Gideon apparently gathered a following from all the tribes because of his stunning upset of the Midianites. Before this judges only fought local oppressors (Othniel, Ehud, Shamgar, Deborah and Barak). Gideon and 300 men with trumpets and torches defeated the armies of the East, killing at least 120,000 (Judges 8:10). The people tried to make Gideon a hereditary ruler (Judges 8:22). But, Gideon refused, recognizing that God had placed Himself as their king. God ruled the people through His law and His Spirit: *"And Gideon said unto them, I will not rule over you, neither shall my son rule over you: the LORD shall rule over you." Judges 8:23.*

Nevertheless, Gideon used the opportunity to enrich himself: *"And Gideon said unto them, I would desire a request of you, that ye would give me every man the earrings of his prey. (For they had golden earrings, because they were Ishmaelites.) And they answered, We will willingly give them. And they spread a garment, and did cast therein every man the earrings of his prey." Judges 8:24,25.*

From the gold he collected, Gideon made an ephod and put it in his own city. The people, hoping that God was fulfilling His promise, came to Ophrah and the ephod as their central Place: *"And Gideon made an ephod thereof, and put it in his city, even in Ophrah: and all Israel went thither a whoring after it: which thing became a snare unto Gideon, and to his house." Judges 8:27.*

Gideon's weak point in integrity was in provisions. He failed in the crisis of financial freedom. Probably because of the long period of suffering he was especially distrustful of having enough. So, he asked the people for gold. There are hints all along that Gideon was fearful God would not provide for or protect him (Judges 6:12,13,17, 36-40). The primary hardship from the Midianites was financial: *"And so it was, when Israel had sown, that the Midianites came up, and the Amalekites, and the children of the east, even they came up against them; And they encamped against them, and destroyed the increase of the earth, till thou come unto Gaza, and left no sustenance for Israel, neither sheep, nor ox, nor ass. For they came up with their cattle and their tents, and they came as grasshoppers for multitude; for both they and their camels were without number: and they entered into the land to destroy it. And Israel was greatly impoverished because of the Midianites; and the children of Israel cried unto the LORD." Judges 6:3-6.*

Gideon's fearful attitude represented the attitude of all the people, who showed their lack of trust in God by asking Gideon to rule them and by making Ophrah their central Place without God's counsel.

"And it came to pass, as soon as Gideon was dead, that the children of Israel turned again, and went a whoring after Baalim, and made Baalberith their god." Judges 8:33. The people saw their great hope, Gideon, die, and they returned to their idols, feeling God had put them off again. This gave Abimelech, one of Gideon's sons, an opportunity to deceive the people and attempt to set himself up as king.

"And Gideon had threescore and ten sons of his body begotten: for he had many wives. And his concubine that was in Shechem, she also bare him a son, whose name he called Abimelech." Judges 8:30,31. Abimelech took advantage of the people of Shechem, who were his mother's relatives. Shechem had become the new central place where Baal-berith (the lord of the covenant) was worshipped. Abimelech presented himself as the obvious king because he was Gideon's son, and because he had roots in the central place of worship: *"And Abimelech the son of Jerubbaal went to Shechem unto his mother's brethren, and communed with them, and with all the family of the house of his mother's father, saying, Speak, I pray you, in the ears of all the men of Shechem, Whether is better for you, either that all the sons of Jerubbaal, which are threescore and ten persons, reign over you, or that one reign over you? remember also that I am your bone and your flesh." Judges 9:1,2.*

The men of Shechem supported Abimelech. He took their money, hired mercenaries and travelled to his father's home in Ophrah. There he executed sixty-nine of his seventy legitimate brothers. The men of Shechem then had a coronation for Abilmelech as the new king of Israel.

But one brother escaped! He went to Mount Gerizim (the mount of blessing and the place where the Palestinian Covenant was made) and pleaded Gideon's fate with a parable: *"And when they told it to Jotham, he went and stood in the top of mount Gerizim, and lifted up his voice, and cried, and said unto them, Hearken unto me, ye men of Shechem, that God may hearken unto you. The trees went forth on a time to anoint a king over them; and they said unto the olive tree, Reign thou over us. But the olive tree said unto them, Should I leave my fatness, wherewith by me they honour God and man, and go to be promoted over the trees? And the trees said to the fig tree, Come thou, and reign over us. But the fig tree said unto them, Should I forsake my sweetness, and my good fruit, and go to be promoted over the trees? Then said the trees unto the vine, Come thou, and reign over us. And the vine said unto them, Should I leave my wine, which cheereth God and man, and go to be promoted over the trees? Then said all the trees unto the bramble, Come thou, and reign over us. And the bramble said unto the trees, If in truth ye anoint me king over you, then come and put your trust in my shadow: and if not, let fire come out of the bramble, and devour the cedars of Lebanon."* Judges 9:7-15.

The parable illustrates the wisdom of Gideon's refusal to become king: he would make himself a judge of God's law rather than a follower of God's law (James 4:11-12); he would leave his natural place as a praiser of God to become a prince over God's people. The parable also shows the foolishness of the men of Shechem; Abimelech was unworthy to become king and would use his power to destroy rather than to build up.

Abimelech's downfall started when the fickle men of Shechem betrayed him. Abimelech destroyed the city and then went to Thebez to quell another rebellion. There he was killed by a woman from a tower with a piece of millstone (Judges 9:16-57).

Abimelech was representative of the people's failure to trust in God's authority. Through him, they attempted to do for themselves what God had delayed (to show the central Place and Shiloh).

After Abimelech, two more judges delivered the people and died. And yet, no Place had been established. Israel again lost heart and turned to the gods of Syria and Sidon: *"And the children of Israel did evil again in the sight of the LORD, and served Baalim, and Ashtaroth, and the gods of Syria, and the gods of Zidon, and the gods of Moab, and the gods of the children of Ammon, and the gods of the Philistines, and forsook the LORD, and served not him."* Judges 10:6.

God brought the giants of Ammon to afflict them because of their rebellion (Judges 10:8). The tribes of the east bank put away their gods and begged for Jehovah's intervention. He helped them because His "soul could no longer endure the misery of Israel" (Judges 10:15-16).

God raised up another judge to help them. Jepthah had a similar background to Abimelech. He was the illegitimate son of a harlot and was expelled from the house by his half-brothers (Judges 11:1-2). Jepthah became a bandit in the land of Tob, not bothering to visit his mother. But, when the eastern tribes, the Gileadites, needed a commander, they called him (Judges 11:5-6).

Jepthah lacked mastery over the crisis of self-image. Two events illustrate this: He made the Gileadites promise to make him their chief before he would help them: *"And Jephthah said unto the elders of Gilead, Did not ye hate me, and expel me out of my father's house? and why are ye come unto me now when ye are in distress? And the elders of Gilead said unto Jephthah, Therefore we turn again to thee now, that thou mayest go with us, and fight against the children of Ammon, and be our head over all the inhabitants of Gilead. And Jephthah said unto the elders of Gilead, If ye bring me home again to fight against the children of Ammon, and the LORD deliver them before me, shall I be your head? And the elders of Gilead said unto Jephthah, The LORD be witness between us, if we do not so according to thy words." Judges 11:7-10.*

He also vowed to sacrifice of his possessions a burnt offering in exchange for divine help. The method of choice would be the Lord's lot - the first thing to come out of the house after victory: *"And Jephthah vowed a vow unto the LORD, and said, If thou shalt without fail deliver the children of Ammon into mine hands, Then it shall be, that whatsoever cometh forth of the doors of my house to meet me, when I return in peace from the children of Ammon, shall surely be the LORD'S, and I will offer it up for a burnt offering." Judges 11:30,31.*

These actions reflected Jepthah's attitude about himself. He did not believe God would bless him because of his background. Unlike Gideon, whose chief concern seemed to be God's provision and protection, Jepthath's concentration was on God and other's perceptions of him. Jepthah required reassurance that he was accepted.

Jepthah and his army won the battle, but the Lord's lot fell on Jepthah's only child - his daughter. She became a burnt sacrifice. She is a terrible symbol of lack of self-acceptance, showing the self-mutilation involved in seeking to prove one's worthiness. We destroy the very best of ourselves when we give others power over our self-image. If Jepthah had only rested in God's acceptance, he would not have made the rash vow (Judges 11:34-40).

After this, the tribe of Ephraim came to battle the east bank tribes because they were not called to the war, saying, "You Gileadites are fugitives of Ephraim." The Ephraimites did not accept the Gileadites as true kinsmen and this infuriated Jepthah. Jepthah and his army killed 42,000 Ephraimites because they could not say "Shibboleth." They focused on a shallow difference to reinforce their prejudice. Jepthah represented the Israelites lack of self-acceptance and to his personal micro-mutilation (the daughter) was added the national macro-mutilation (the Ephraimites) at the fords of the Jordan (Judges 12:4-6).

"And the children of Israel did evil again in the sight of the LORD; and the LORD delivered them into the hand of the Philistines forty years." Judges 13:1. The Philistines had never been conquered in the first place (Joshua 13:1-2). They were different from the seven nations of Canaan. The Philistines were non-Semitic, uncircumcised people. They knew the secrets of iron, a weapon the Israelites did not have (Joshua 17:16; Judges 1:19; Judges 4:2-3). The Philistines stopped Israel from smelting iron: *"Now there was no smith found throughout all the land of Israel: for the Philistines said, Lest the Hebrews make them swords or spears:" 1 Samuel 13:19.*

The tribe of Dan was prevented from possessing its inheritance because of the Philistines and Amorites (Joshua 19:40-48; Judges 1:34). And the Philistines were advancing eastward into Israel's core. So, God raised up a Danite to resist them, Samson.

Samson was sent through the womb of a barren woman, and Samson was given special restrictions, the burden of a Nazarite. Even his mother ate non-alcoholic while he was an embryo (Judges 13:13-14). Samson was a Nazarite conceived and pre-conceived: *"For, lo, thou shalt conceive, and bear a son; and no razor shall come on his head: for the child shall be a Nazarite unto God from the womb: and he shall begin to deliver Israel out of the hand of the Philistines." Judges 13:5.*

A Nazarite was under a vow to God, and Samson's lifetime vow was made for him. Samson had three restrictions on his life: he could not cut his hair; he could not drink wine; and he could not touch the dead. All three signified his separation to God and his willingness to humble himself. Nevertheless, he had special blessings and great strength from God because of his separation (Judges 13:24-25).

Samson violated all three of his restrictions early and often. Remarkably, God used Samson to afflict the Philistines even through his scandals. In the adventure of Timnah, Samson touched the dead and drank wine (Judges 14:7-10). God used this occasion to cause slaughter, vexation, and loss to the Philistines. Samson killed thirty men for their clothes, caught three hundred foxes and put firebrands in their tails to burn down the fields, attacked them "hip and thigh" for firing his wife and father-in-law, and with the jawbone of an ass made a mountain of dead men (Judges 15).

"Then went Samson to Gaza, and saw there an harlot, and went in unto her." Judges 16:1. Thus Samson began to break his third restriction. This was the first incident in the progression to the loss of his hair. The Gazites surrounded him at night, hoping to kill him in the morning. But Samson arose at midnight and barged out of the city, taking gates and all (Judges 16:2-3).

Even after the rebukes of the past, Samson arrogantly loved Delilah, a woman who lived on the road to the Philistines. Apparently, Delilah enjoyed binding and afflicting Samson, and he agreed to the game: *"And Delilah said to Samson, Tell me, I pray thee, wherein thy great strength lieth, and wherewith thou mightest be bound to afflict thee. And Samson said unto her, If they bind me with seven green withs that were never dried, then shall I be weak, and be as another man." Judges 16:6,7.*

Delilah used the game as a way to turn over Samson to the Philistines. He avoided her "affliction" on three separate occasions and chased the Philistines away who were ready to capture him.

Finally, after Delilah continually pestered and pressed him, Samson provided the secret to his strength. Delilah cut off his hair and betrayed him to the Philistines. She left him to the lords of the Philistines who put out his eyes, took him to Gaza, bound him with bronze, and made him lord of the millstone (Judges 16:19-21).

Even in his humiliation, God used Samson to dishonor the Philistines. They brought him to the temple of Dagon to make fun of him. There, God allowed Samson to bring down the house. Three thousand Philistines died, as well as the five lords of the Philistines (Judges 16:25-30).

Although Samson defiled his separated life through moral failure, his greatest deficit was in genuine friendships. Samson never raised an army and never asked other Israelites to fight with him. He was the original rugged individualist. His best friends were harlots and Philistines. When he went to marry the Timnite, the Philistines took pity and produced thirty fake friends. Samson abused them with a riddle and then killed thirty others to pay his debt. Samson left in anger and the best man got his bride to be. Samson specialized in abuse, anger, self-gratification, and revenge. He had no friends or fellows, so the light of God over Israel went out with him in the temple of Dagon. Samson surely represented this saying: *"In those days there was no king in Israel, but every man did that which was right in his own eyes." Judges 17:6.*

Micah was not officially a judge, but his is the next story in the book of Judges. He was the first simoniac. He stole his mother's money and later gave it back because she put a curse on it. Yet, because she was so happy to recover it, she gave him part of the money to build a personal shrine. He had already made some gods and made one of his sons a priest (Judges 17:1-5).

His story illustrates the moral relativism and spiritual prostitution of the day. Morality and character were no longer required to be holy, only the right idol and magic words. Micah represented Israel's despair and boredom in spiritual progress. He was the symbol of their failure of spiritual purpose. They had not, after all this time, received God's promise of a central Place.

Micah improved his spiritual effort of the shrine and son-priest by hiring a wandering Levite in order to please God more (Judges 17:12-13). Nevermind that all this was outside God's design. It seemed and felt right, so it had to be. Apparently, the lessons of Nadab, Abihu, and Kerah had been forgotten (Leviticus 10:1-3; Numbers 16). It was nothing then to mix religions and beliefs in order to gain divine blessing, much like today.

About the same time the tribe of Dan went searching for a home. The Philistines and Amorites had pushed them up into the mountains. Their inheritance was supposed to be on the seacoast, but they never possessed it (Judges 1:34). Instead of following the faith of the Ephraimites, which said, "the hill is not enough for us" and fought for their place (Joshua 17:14-18; Judges 1:35), the Danites picked on a peaceful people and dispossessed the city of Laish (Judges 18). They searched the entire land before they discovered Laish and then easily destroyed it.

Micah's house was on the way. The Danites were ignorant of God's laws, because they stopped and asked the false priest to prophecy for them. Pleased with Jonathan's blessing, the Danites spied on the Sidonian outpost, Laish. They found the people vulnerable to attack. Later, six hundred Danites and their families went up to Laish to burn it with fire. On the way, they made Jonathan a better offer than Micah had. Apparently happy that his former advice was prosperous, the Danites asked him to be their tribal priest. They took Micah's gods. When Micah and his people tried to retrieve them, they were threatened with death.

This story shows the extent of the people's superstition and despair. The Danites refused to suffer the wait of God's promise, or the risk involved in fighting for their allotment. Even though the ark of God was at Shiloh, they knew that God had not yet revealed His Place. Micah's idols therefore became a snare for them: *"And the children of Dan set up the graven image: and Jonathan, the son of Gershom, the son of Manasseh, he and his sons were priests to the tribe of Dan until the day of the captivity of the land. And they set them up Micah's graven image, which he made, all the time that the house of God was in Shiloh." Judges 18:30,31.*

And the people were immoral also. The next section begins, "and it came to pass in those days, when there was no king in Israel," (Judges 19:1) and ends, "every man did that which was right in his own eyes (Judges 21:25)." Every person in the next tale lacked moral judgment. The story illustrates the consequences of moral relativism: permissiveness in the beginning, and violent reprisals in the end. When a person or society loses moral integrity, mayhem and mourning follow the pleasures of permissiveness.

The first offender was a Levite's concubine. She made him a cuckold and then ran away to her father in Bethlehem. Yet, the Levite loved her and went after her to fetch her back. The girl's father received him as a messenger of God and kept him there five days. On the fifth afternoon, the Levite, his servant, and his woman fled their overgracious host and went to Jebus, an unconquered city. The servant was for spending the night at Jebus, but the Levite looked for the hospitality of his own people (Judges 19:1-13).

"And they passed on and went their way; and the sun went down upon them when they were by Gibeah, which belongeth to Benjamin. And they turned aside thither, to go in and to lodge in Gibeah: and when he went in, he sat him down in a street of the city: for there was no man that took them into his house to lodging." Judges 19:14,15. The party at first found the hospitality of the place less than they had hoped. Then a sojourner from Ephraim (the Levite's home tribe) saw them and gave them a place to stay. He told them it wasn't safe to stay in the street (v.16-21).

The darkness weighed down on Gibeah, and the lovers of darkness came out. The evil men of the city wanted to abuse the Levite sexually. They weren't interested in providing hospitality to travelers, they were only interested in using whomever they could. The reprobates threatened the Levite and the sojourner, and their response was cowardly. The sojourner offered a virgin daughter and the Levite offered his concubine to the men (v.22-25).

The Levite showed his moral relativism in giving his girl to the evil men to save himself. He forgot that he had just spent four months and five days pining for her and proving his love to her. Perhaps he wasn't as loving to her and forgiving of her harlotry as he professed.

The concubine suffered the perversion of the men all night and in the morning lay dead at the sojourner's door. The Levite put her on a donkey and left Gibeah. At home, the Levite proved his own reprobation by dismembering her and sending her twelve pieces to the twelve tribes of Israel. Maybe he justified his butchery as presenting evidence of Gibeah's evil, or perhaps he did not know the difference between good and evil himself, having no conscience and no king to guide him (v.26-29).

"And it was so, that all that saw it said, There was no such deed done nor seen from the day that the children of Israel came up out of the land of Egypt unto this day: consider of it, take advice, and speak your minds." Judges 19:30. Finally, a deed dastardly enough to knock them from complacency. Sensuality causes a deep sleep in moral matters (1 Thessalonians 5:6-7). This sleep brings death to the soul, because morality is dormant, and Satan seeks and devours the unvigilant. An example is Simple, Sloth, and Presumption from *Pilgrims Progress.*

So the Israelites gathered at Mizpeh and said, "Tell us, how did this wicked deed happen?" The Levite was happy to answer: "I looked for hospitality from my people, but instead they tried to kill me. They raped my concubine and sadistically caused her death (he didn't mention his implicit consent), and I sent you her pieces only to show you their perversion (downplaying his part in the conflagration)," Judges 20:1-7.

The leaders said, "look," and they put the pieces together. Gibeah had become vile and reprobate (20: 7-10). The Israelites purposed to pay retribution. Awakened moral outrage becomes merely reactionary when it is not preceded by self-discipline. If the people had truly practiced morality, they would have been more merciful. But, because they were guilty of immorality also, they did not know where to stop: *"He that soweth iniquity shall reap vanity: and the rod of his anger shall fail." Proverbs 22:8.* At first they asked peacefully for Benjamin to give up the perverts, but this only activated the wayward tribe's arrogance, and they refused. Israel then raged against a generation of degenerates.

First, the people went twice to Bethel, the house of God, to see which tribe should fight first. Judah was chosen as the leader, foreshadowing their place as the home of God's future house. In the battle that followed, Benjamin's seven hundred selectmen did not miss often as they killed twenty-two thousand. Judah did not escape a bloody baptism into the executive role (Judges 1:1-2). Israel's despair increased the next day when Benjamin terminated eighteen thousand more.

The tribes of Israel went back to the house of God and wept, and they inquired at the Ark of the Covenant. God said, "go," because "tomorrow you will conquer." God had not allowed them to win without loss (20: 26-28; Hosea 6:1-2).

"And Israel set liers in wait round about Gibeah." Judges 20:29. The Israelites drew the Benjamites out of the city and then set it on fire. The Benjamites were routed and ran toward the wilderness. Only six hundred men survived and they stayed at the rock of Rimmon (20:30-47).

Like tame dogs who taste blood for the first time, Israel savagely struck the innocent with the guilty: *"And the men of Israel turned again upon the children of Benjamin, and smote them with the edge of the sword, as well the men of every city, as the beast, and all that came to hand: also they set on fire all the cities that they came to." Judges 20:48.*

When the army of Israel recovered from their acts of insanity, they wept at the house of God for their lost brother. Benjamin had become the holy sacrifice for national sin. Instead of each man judging his own morals, they collectively cut off Benjamin to purge the national soul (21:1-3). And so it came to pass when they had no principles or princes, they cured evil by evil methods. Unrestrained retribution usually follows unrestrained sin, and the last state is worse than the first. It is always better to heed conscience than to burn the bridges of self-control.

The Israelites had also made a rash vow at Mizpeh to deny marriage to the survivors. They later repented and looked for a way to secure women for their brethren. So they killed the people of Jabesh-Gilead, who failed to send representatives to the battle, and saved four hundred girls for the Benjamites (21: 4-13): *"And Benjamin came again at that time; and they gave them wives which they had saved alive of the women of Jabeshgilead: and yet so they sufficed them not. And the people repented them for Benjamin, because that the LORD had made a breach in the tribes of Israel." Judges 21:14,15.*

And yet, there were two hundred Benjamites left without wives. So they made another sacrifice for pragmatism, and gave the remaining Benjamites their pick of the dancers at Shiloh. The men of Benjamin were allowed to ambush their wives when the young women danced before the Lord (Judges 21:16-25).

Ruth is next in the story of Israel, and she seems at first to be inconsequential, without purpose in their quest for the central Place. Nevertheless, upon further investigation, we see that her story is the beginning of God's fulfillment of the vision. During the time of the judges, God chose the family line of the first Shiloh (David).

Ruth was a Moabite who followed her mother-in-law back to Bethlehem after the untimely death of all their men. She had seen the faith of Naomi and committed herself to both Naomi and the Lord. Ruth's integrity won the favor of a kinsman-redeemer, Boaz, who agreed to support both Naomi and Ruth in their inheritance. Ruth and Boaz had a child named Obed, who was the grandfather of David the king.

Ruth's story is notable in two ways. First, the main characters in the book acted with integrity, the needed ingredient to pass the tests of spiritual adolescence: *"And now, my daughter, fear not; I will do to thee all that thou requirest: for all the city of my people doth know that thou art a virtuous woman." Ruth 3:11.*

Second, Naomi made a hero journey that reflects the patience needed to inherit God's blessing. Every woman of Israel wanted to have a male child in hopes he would be the Messiah. Naomi had her vision crushed when both of her sons died. It would have been easy for her to stay in Moab and forget her inheritance and the Lord. She would not give up on God even though things looked bad. She purposed to return to her place in Bethlehem and turn over her fate to God. God then intervened on her behalf by leading Ruth to go to Israel with her and by leading Boaz to love and marry Ruth. God blessed Naomi's faith by making her family the line of David and later the Messiah.

The next heroine was a woman named Hannah. She also hoped for the Messiah to come from her, but she was barren. She went to the house of God at Shiloh every year to pray for a son, and one year she made a promise that she would dedicate that son to God. God heard her prayer and gave her Samuel (asked of God), who became the transition between the judges and the kings (1 Samuel 1).

Hannah's hero journey shows all the stages. She had a vision to raise a godly son. Her vision remained unfulfilled because of God's timing. She first had to endure the adversity of her rival and the years of hope in order to grow the needed character. She became emotionally and spiritually able to fully dedicate her child to God. At the right time, God gave her a son that would be the greatest judge of Israel. He also gave her three more sons and two daughters (1 Samuel 2:21). You can't outgive God.

Hannah's song to God in 1 Samuel 2:1-10 is very similar to the song of Mary in Matthew. She blessed God for His "salvation" to her through Samuel. Samuel also became the "salvation" of Israel over the Philistines. Her individual blessing became the blessing for the whole nation. This would not have been possible without her faith in the "ways of God."

The integrity of Samuel as judge became the turning point for Israel toward the fulfillment of their corporate vision. God was about to reveal the Place and to restore righteousness to Israel.

But first, as it happens so many times, God had to move the wicked out of the way. Even during the darkest time of Israel's history, God prepared for their salvation. Eli the priest had disgraced the office by allowing his evil sons to make light of God's sacrifices and to abuse the servants of God (1 Samuel 2:21-26). They were a reflection of the depravity of the people. God revealed to Samuel that the line of Eli as priest had been rejected (1 Samuel 3:11-13).

The Philistines invaded again. Israel was at first driven back and they had the idea that the Ark of God could save them. Eli's wicked sons agreed to the plan in order to receive glory. So they brought the Ark of God into the camp hoping God would favor them. He did not. Israel's army was defeated and the ark was captured. This is the result of thinking of God as a magic charm, of believing holy objects have power even though substance has been replaced with style, and of believing God will bless people without character and without faith (1 Samuel 4:1-11).

Eli's sons were killed in the battle. Eli died also when he heard the news of the lost ark. Eli's daughter in-law was giving birth at the same time, and she named the baby, "Ichabod" (no glory). There is no glory in attempting to force God's hand. The Israelites tried to use God instead of waiting on His timing.

Nevertheless, God judged the Philistines for taking the ark and the people of Bethshemesh for handling it wrong (1 Samuel 6). It finally rested at Kirjathjearim during Samuel's time for twenty years. Through the moving of the ark God signified that it had not come to its final place, and that the central Place had not yet been chosen. The people developed a sense of the temporary nature of its placement. Prior to its capture it had been at Shiloh for hundreds of years.

After the death of Eli, Samuel began his career as prophet and judge. God subdued the Philistines through his leadership and drove them from the borders of Israel. Samuel started a revival of true worship during his career that influenced the people for generations (1 Samuel 7). Samuel was the last judge and his integrity was never once questioned in the scripture. He truly was a forerunner to the next covenant just like John was a forerunner to Christ.

"And it came to pass, when Samuel was old, that he made his sons judges over Israel. Now the name of his firstborn was Joel; and the name of his second, Abiah: they were judges in Beersheba. And his sons walked not in his ways, but turned aside after lucre, and took bribes, and perverted judgment." 1 Samuel 8:1-3. The people naturally feared a repeat of Eli's sons, and they begged Samuel to appoint a king, like all the nations. This desire for an earthly king was the last phase of Israel's corporate failure of integrity. With the request, they demonstrated a defeated attitude toward the crises of spiritual adolescence*: "Then all the elders of Israel gathered themselves together, and came to Samuel unto Ramah, And said unto him, Behold, thou art old, and thy sons walk not in thy ways: now make us a king to judge us like all the nations. But the thing displeased Samuel, when they said, Give us a king to judge us. And Samuel prayed unto the LORD." 1 Samuel 8:4-6.*

Israel's request for a king showed a lack of victory over the crises of adolescence in the following ways:

1. Lack of self-acceptance - "make us a king, like all the nations." The Israelites felt inferior to other nations because they had no king. They didn't realize that God as their king made them better.

2. Lack of respect for God's authority - *"And the LORD said unto Samuel, Hearken unto the voice of the people in all that they say unto thee: for they have not rejected thee, but they have rejected me, that I should not reign over them." 1 Samuel 8:7.* Gideon had escaped this trap. He recognized that God Himself ruled over the people (Judges 8:22-23).

3. Lack of clear conscience, forgiveness, and meekness - "make us a king, to judge us." With God alone as the spiritual head, the people could not appeal to an earthly authority. Therefore, resolving problems required the exercise of

these disciplines of deference. With an earthly king, disputes could be handled in a more definite and yet less spiritual way.

4. Lack of moral purity - *"According to all the works which they have done since the day that I brought them up out of Egypt even unto this day, wherewith they have forsaken me, and served other gods, so do they also unto thee." 1 Samuel 8:8.* With an earthly king, the people could justify their sinfulness by comparison to him and his family. With God alone, the bar was set too high for fleshly appetites.

5. Lack of spiritual purpose - The people were tired of the long wait for the Place to be revealed, and for Shiloh to come. They tried to help God fulfill His promise. They did not acknowledge God's work in preparing them to appreciate His blessing. In this they failed to apply the key to young adulthood - patience.

6. Lack of genuine friendships - The people's request for a king and a government showed that they did not see themselves as a community. God gave them laws of community to help them have concern for the welfare of all. The people did not believe they could do this by themselves. The function of government is to enforce righteousness on diverse cultural norms and behaviors (1 Peter 2:13-14).

7. Lack of financial freedom - The people were required under the Law to give a tenth and also offerings to the Lord. They violated that by worshipping and giving to the false gods. The king would only increase their burden because he would require an additional tenth (1 Samuel 8:10-18).

   This corporate immaturity of Israel is similar to the corporate immaturity of many churches. We also long for someone to rule over us and tell us what to do. Many churches elevate the pastor to a position he was never intended to hold. His role is that of a teacher and an example, not as a lord (1 Peter 5:1-4). In this we lack understanding of God's will in a more serious way than the Israelites. They did not have the extended revelation of the church and its principles. Therefore, if we make the same mistake they did, we become twice the failure of them. The New Testament even more clearly than the Old shows the nature of God's intended community. Israel was one expression of His community and the church a more advanced expression of His community.

   "Now there was a man of Benjamin, whose name was Kish, the son of Abiel, the son of Zeror, the son of Bechorath, the son of Aphiah, a

Benjamite, a mighty man of power. And he had a son, whose name was Saul, a choice young man, and a goodly: and there was not among the children of Israel a goodlier person than he: from his shoulders and upward he was higher than any of the people." 1 Samuel 9:1,2. God gave the people what they wanted: a king they could admire because of his good looks and his height. God commissioned Samuel to anoint Saul as king (v.15-17). Samuel did so but made it clear that God's perfect will had been rejected (1 Samuel 10:18-19, also 12:16-19).

Saul was the people's choice: *"And on whom [is] all the desire of Israel? [Is it] not on thee, and on all thy father's house?"1 Samuel 9:20* (also 1 Samuel 12:13). He looked good to the flesh: he was attractive, honest in business, and morally upright. Nevertheless, he was not fully prepared in character to be the salvation of Israel. His reign became the individual expression of the people's lack of integrity. God would later have to replace him with a man of true integrity.

Saul's character revealed weaknesses in the following crises:

1.   The Early Burnt Offering (1 Samuel 13)

Jonathan, Saul's son, attacked a garrison of the Philistines and this led to Saul preparing for a defense against their reprisals. The men of Israel ran and hid from the thirty thousand iron chariots of the Philistines. Saul had the faithful few waiting with him in Gilgal for Samuel to come and sacrifice the offering. Saul grew impatient for the man of God and offered the burnt offering himself. Because of his lack of faith and patience Samuel declared for the first time that Saul was not fit to be king: *"And Samuel said to Saul, Thou hast done foolishly: thou hast not kept the commandment of the LORD thy God, which he commanded thee: for now would the LORD have established thy kingdom upon Israel for ever. But now thy kingdom shall not continue: the LORD hath sought him a man after his own heart, and the LORD hath commanded him to be captain over his people, because thou hast not kept that which the LORD commanded thee." 1 Samuel 13:13,14.*

Saul was drafted into the position of king. It was not something he was called of God to do. It was not the fulfillment of his vision for God. Therefore, he had not spent the years of preparation in trusting God. He was unfamiliar with the ways of God on a mature level. He did not know that God often saves "just in time." Saul was not ready in the area of Spiritual Purpose.

2.   The Bleating of the Sheep (1 Samuel 15)

God ordered Saul through Samuel to destroy the Amelekites, to avenge an old grievance. This was the first time Israel was strong enough to go on the offensive against their enemies. God wanted them to dedicate the Amelekites, but Saul did not obey completely: *"But Saul and the people spared Agag, and the best of the sheep, and of the oxen, and of the fatlings, and the lambs, and all that was good, and would not utterly destroy them: but every thing that was vile and refuse, that they destroyed utterly." 1 Samuel 15:9.*

God sent Samuel to investigate, and he found the "bleating of the sheep." Saul explained that he had a better plan than God because the sheep were to be a sacrifice (v.13-15). He felt that he had performed the word of the Lord. Samuel showed Saul the error of his incomplete obedience in these famous words: *"And Samuel said, Hath the LORD as great delight in burnt offerings and sacrifices, as in obeying the voice of the LORD? Behold, to obey is better than sacrifice, and to hearken than the fat of rams. For rebellion is as the sin of witchcraft, and stubbornness is as iniquity and idolatry. Because thou hast rejected the word of the LORD, he hath also rejected thee from being king." 1 Samuel 15:22,23.*

Saul was more concerned about his popularity with the people than with God's command. He had assembled an army of 210,000 instead of the 600 who remained faithful in the battle with the Philistines. If he completely destroyed the Amelekites, his army would have no reward. Therefore, Saul allowed the people to take the spoil. Samuel alluded to Saul's psychology in the matter: *"And Samuel said, When thou wast little in thine own sight, wast thou not made the head of the tribes of Israel, and the LORD anointed thee king over Israel?" 1 Samuel 15:17.* Saul had a continuing lack of self-confidence, and he felt the need to please people. In seeking to reward his army, Saul disparaged his role as the servant of God. His character did not reflect mastery over the area of Authority.

3.   An Evil Spirit From the Lord (1 Samuel 16:14-23)

"But the Spirit of the LORD departed from Saul, and an evil spirit from the LORD troubled him." 1 Samuel 16:14. Saul's repentance was incomplete; therefore God allowed a spirit to torment him (Matthew 18:34). Saul repented only with the necessary outward performance before Samuel. He did not go back and rebuild his relationship with God. He focused instead on ways to keep his power and position. Samuel prophesied twice that the Lord had rejected Saul as

king. Saul must have brooded about that. His "evil spirit" could have been a number of different feelings and attitudes. I choose to believe that it was Guilt and Shame.

4.   Retreat From the Giant (1 Samuel 17)

The Philistines came again to challenge the Israelites, except this time they selected a champion to fight with the mightiest of Israel. Saul had been chosen as king for this very reason, that he would lead the people and fight their battles (1 Samuel 8:19-20): *"And the Philistine said, I defy the armies of Israel this day; give me a man, that we may fight together. When Saul and all Israel heard those words of the Philistine, they were dismayed, and greatly afraid."* 1 Samuel 17:10,11.

Saul showed a lack of faith and leadership in this incident. He also showed a deficit in self-image. God had appointed him to be king. God was able to help him defeat Goliath (see Moses in Exodus 4). And yet, Saul could only see it as a matter of personal ability. The Philistine giant served as a metaphor for Saul's incomplete mastery for the crisis of Self-Image.

In contrast, David perceived the challenge as against God's power, and rightfully invoked God's reputation as the source of strength: *"Then said David to the Philistine, Thou comest to me with a sword, and with a spear, and with a shield: but I come to thee in the name of the LORD of hosts, the God of the armies of Israel, whom thou hast defied."* 1 Samuel 17:45.

5.   The Threat of David (remainder of 1 Samuel)

Samuel already told Saul that God had rejected him, and that God would replace him with a better prospect (1Samuel 15:28). When Saul perceived David symbolically take his place by killing the giant, and the people's praise of David, he became afraid and jealous: *"And the women answered one another as they played, and said, Saul hath slain his thousands, and David his ten thousands. And Saul was very wroth, and the saying displeased him; and he said, They have ascribed unto David ten thousands, and to me they have ascribed but thousands: and what can he have more but the kingdom?"* 1 Samuel 18:7,8.

Saul only looked at the politics and human perspective. And from these points of view he tried to stop David. At first he tried to kill David, then later he tried to demote him. The murder attempt didn't work because God was with David. The demotion didn't work because David gladly fulfilled his duties (1 Samuel 18:9- 15).

The rest of the book of 1 Samuel details how Saul continually tried to eliminate the threat of David to his kingdom. Saul could not acknowledge the eternal kingdom of God because he looked too much at the temporal kingdom. He became angry because he would not accept God's plan and will, and instead looked to others for praise. Saul at times repented of his jealousy at the words of Jonathan or the actions of David, yet the desire to kill David would arise again. By his jealousy and his murder attempts, Saul demonstrated a failure of Meekness vs. Anger.

6.   The Abuse of His Subjects (1 Samuel 18-31)

Saul demonstrated a lack of Genuine Friendship in his pursuit of David. It is recorded two times that Saul asked his subjects to kill David (1 Samuel 18:1; 20:28-31). Then later, Saul increased his error by killing the priests of Nob for helping David, even though they acted in good faith toward the king (1 Samuel 21:1-2; 22:11-19). Saul used his position to buy friendships that he could use to promote himself. He only considered others in light of their loyalty to him. He did not even mind asking them to violate the Law or their own consciences. He did not see them as individuals nor did he consider their rights (1 Samuel 23:19-21; 26:1). Saul showed his spirit by these words: *"Then Saul said unto his servants that stood about him, Hear now, ye Benjamites; will the son of Jesse give every one of you fields and vineyards, and make you all captains of thousands, and captains of hundreds; That all of you have conspired against me, and there is none that sheweth me that my son hath made a league with the son of Jesse, and there is none of you that is sorry for me, or sheweth unto me that my son hath stirred up my servant against me, to lie in wait, as at this day?" 1 Samuel 22:7,8.*

Partial Fulfillment

Saul died in battle just as the deceased Samuel prophesied through the witch of Endor: *"Moreover the LORD will also deliver Israel with thee into the hand of the Philistines: and to morrow shalt thou and thy sons be with me: the LORD also shall deliver the host of Israel into the hand of the Philistines." 1 Samuel 28:19. (1 Samuel 31:1-4).*

God had already prepared His choice to be king. God chose a man because of his character, one who sought to have the heart of God: *"the LORD hath sought him a man after his own heart, and the LORD hath commanded him to be captain over his people" 1Samuel 13:14. "But the LORD said unto Samuel,*

Look not on his countenance, or on the height of his stature; because I have refused him: for the LORD seeth not as man seeth; for man looketh on the outward appearance, but the LORD looketh on the heart." 1 Samuel 16:7.

In Samuel's prophesy from the grave, he named to Saul the replacement: *"And the LORD hath done to him, as he spake by me: for the LORD hath rent the kingdom out of thine hand, and given it to thy neighbour, even to David:" 1 Samuel 28:17.*

The scripture records events that show David's mastery of the crises of spiritual adolescence. God prepared David through many tests of character and he passed all of them. Even when he sinned, he was able to humble himself before God and correct his direction. He did not fully abolish the flesh, but he did demonstrate experience of God's ways to overcome it.

David's character revealed integrity in the following crises.

1. Is there not a cause? (1 Samuel 17)

    When Goliath defied the armies of Israel for forty days, David was tending his father's sheep. Jesse sent David to the battle site to deliver food to his brothers. David discovered the giant there and wondered out loud why no one had killed him. His eldest brother, perhaps feeling embarrassed about his own lack of faith, chided David like a child. He took the position that David was only lusting after some action in the battle (1 Samuel 17:28-29).

    David responded by declaring his confidence in God's purposes. He used that faith to defeat his first giant, which he had already defeated in his heart. Goliath served David as a literal giant and a metaphor for his mastery of the crisis of Spiritual Purpose: *"This day will the LORD deliver thee into mine hand; and I will smite thee, and take thine head from thee; and I will give the carcases of the host of the Philistines this day unto the fowls of the air, and to the wild beasts of the earth; that all the earth may know that there is a God in Israel." 1 Samuel 17:46.*

2. Better Than the Love of Women (1 Samuel 18: 1-4; 20:16-17, 41-42; 23:16-18; 1 Samuel 2:26-27)

    Jonathan, Saul's heir to the throne, developed a friendship with David that transcended their natural rivalry. David had been anointed by God to succeed Saul, whereas Jonathan was the accepted heir. David and Jonathan should have hated one another if they were following worldly principles. Saul alluded to this in a tirade against Jonathan: *"Then Saul's anger was kindled against Jonathan, and he said unto him, Thou son of the perverse rebellious woman, do not I know that thou hast chosen the son of Jesse to thine own confusion, and unto the confusion of thy mother's nakedness? For as long as the son of Jesse liveth upon the ground, thou shalt not be established, nor thy kingdom. Wherefore now send and fetch him unto me, for he shall surely die."* 1 Samuel 20:30,31.

Jonathan and David loved one another because of their shared love for God and they made a covenant to support one another. Jonathan agreed to be David's prince because he wanted God's will: *"And he said unto him, Fear not: for the hand of Saul my father shall not find thee; and thou shalt be king over Israel, and I shall be next unto thee; and that also Saul my father knoweth. And they two made a covenant before the LORD: and David abode in the wood, and Jonathan went to his house."* 1 Samuel 23:17,18.

David agreed to defend Jonathan and his heirs forever: *"And Jonathan said to David, Go in peace, forasmuch as we have sworn both of us in the name of the LORD, saying, The LORD be between me and thee, and between my seed and thy seed for ever. And he arose and departed: and Jonathan went into the city."* 1 Samuel 20:42. David honored this agreement after Jonathan's death with mercy toward his son Mephibosheth (2 Samuel 9:6-7).

David's Genuine Friendship toward Jonathan is evident in his lament after Jonathan's death: *"I am distressed for thee, my brother Jonathan: very pleasant hast thou been unto me: thy love to me was wonderful, passing the love of women."* 2 Samuel 1:26.

There are other incidents that show David's genuine love for others and his selflessness. Ziklag's spoil was shared by all of David's men, even those that could not go to the battle (1 Samuel 30:21-26).

3.   God's Anointed (1 Samuel 24:8-10)

David's mastery of the crisis of Authority was evidenced by his relationship to Saul. The scripture testifies that David was a loyal servant even though Saul was jealous and attempted to kill him. David understood that God is sovereign over all and that God would be his final judge, not any human. God would not allow an earthly authority to exceed His own will. It's easier to be under authority when you know that God is watching over your authority: *"The LORD judge between me and thee, and the LORD avenge me of thee: but mine hand shall not be upon thee."* 1 Samuel 24:12. *"And he said to David, Thou art more righteous than I: for thou hast rewarded me good, whereas I have rewarded thee evil… And now, behold, I know well that thou shalt surely be king, and that the kingdom of Israel shall be established in thine hand." 1 Samuel 24:17, 20.*

David had two opportunities to kill Saul and take over the kingdom by his own efforts, but he declined to do so. I believe he knew that God would not honor such a precedent and that he would be putting his own kingdom in jeopardy by setting such an example. Like all persons with integrity, David was constantly previewing the consequences of his decisions: *"And David said to Abishai, Destroy him not: for who can stretch forth his hand against the LORD'S anointed, and be guiltless? David said furthermore, As the LORD liveth, the LORD shall smite him; or his day shall come to die; or he shall descend into battle, and perish." 1 Samuel 26:9,10.*

4.   No Grief

David ensured a Clear Conscience and "no grief" by refusing to avenge himself. In the matter of Nabal, David submitted his case to God and turned away from vengeance. Abigail, the offender's wife, prophesied concerning David's integrity and his eye to the future: *"I pray thee, forgive the trespass of thine handmaid: for the LORD will certainly make my lord a sure house; because my lord fighteth the battles of the LORD, and evil hath not been found in thee all thy days…And it shall come to pass, when the LORD shall have done to my lord according to all the good that he hath spoken concerning thee, and shall have appointed thee ruler over Israel; That this shall be no grief unto thee, nor offence of heart unto my lord, either that thou hast shed blood causeless, or that my lord hath avenged himself: but when the LORD shall have dealt well with my lord, then remember thine handmaid." 1 Samuel 25:28,30,31.*

On several occasions, David spared those who made personal affronts toward him or who fought him. His conscience was such that he regularly left their judgment in God's hands: Abner (2 Samuel 3), Shimei (2 Samuel 16), Absalom (2 Samuel 18), Amasa (2 Samuel 19), etc.

David repented when his conscience provoked him. The most famous is his repentance over Bathsheba and Uriah. His attitude of repentance and clearing of conscience over this incident is found in Psalm 51: *"Against thee, thee only, have I sinned, and done this evil in thy sight: that thou mightest be justified when thou speakest, and be clear when thou judgest…Create in me a clean heart, O God; and renew a right spirit within me. Cast me not away from thy presence; and take not thy holy spirit from me. Restore unto me the joy of thy salvation; and uphold me with thy free spirit." Psalms 51:4, 10-12.* Another example is when he cut off the skirt of Saul (1 Samuel 24:5).

David's conscience was so delicate that he even cleared up an offense that didn't belong to him (Psalm 69:4). God allowed a famine in the land because Saul had broken the oath with the Gibeonites (Joshua 9:20). David knew that God would bless him for taking responsibility for the conscience of the nation. He delivered seven sons of Saul to the Gibeonites and God ended the famine. In this he preserved the integrity of Israel's word to the Gibeonites (2 Samuel 21:1-14).

5.   Let him curse. (2 Samuel 16:5-14)

One of Saul's relatives, Shimei, came out and cursed David as he retreated from Jerusalem duringAbsalom's rebellion. He also threw rocks and dust at David. Abishai wanted to kill Shimei, but David stopped him with the words of Meekness: *"And David said to Abishai, and to all his servants, Behold, my son, which came forth of my bowels, seeketh my life: how much more now may this Benjamite do it? let him alone, and let him curse; for the LORD hath bidden him. It may be that the LORD will look on mine affliction, and that the LORD will requite me good for his cursing this day." 2 Samuel 16:11,12.* David showed mastery of meekness by understanding that God uses the curses of others to demonstrate to the world His grace in us. Abishai was not given grace to endure David's cursing, but God enabled David through His grace to patiently wait on Him.

David showed meekness on many occasions, and quietly waited for God's salvation. He did not demand that Saul keep his promise to give him Merab, even after Saul promised. He did not demand his right to be king all the years that Saul chased him. After Absalom's rebellion, David meekly waited for the people to renew their commitment to him, and he did not take revenge on those that had insulted him (2 Samuel 19). David was so meek that Joab said: *"thou lovest thine enemies, and hatest thy friends. For thou hast declared this day, that thou regardest neither princes nor servants: for this day I perceive, that if Absalom had lived, and all we had died this day, then it had pleased thee well." 2 Samuel 19:6.*

David wrote the manual on meekness in Psalm 37. The attitude and perspective it teaches leads us to patiently wait on God for blessing: *"Delight thyself also in the LORD; and he shall give thee the desires of thine heart. Commit thy way unto the LORD; trust also in him; and he shall bring it to pass. And he shall bring forth thy righteousness as the light, and thy judgment as the noonday. Rest in the LORD, and wait patiently for him: fret not thyself because of him who prospereth in his way, because of the man who bringeth wicked devices to pass. Cease from anger, and forsake wrath: fret not thyself in any wise to do evil. For evildoers shall be cut off: but those that wait upon the LORD, they shall inherit the earth. For yet a little while, and the wicked shall not be: yea, thou shalt diligently consider his place, and it shall not be. But the meek shall inherit the earth; and shall delight themselves in the abundance of peace." Psalms 37:4-11.*

6. Fearfully and Wonderfully Made

David displayed a good Self-Image from the beginning. When he volunteered to fight Goliath, Saul tried to discourage him: *"And Saul said to David, Thou art not able to go against this Philistine to fight with him: for thou art but a youth, and he a man of war from his youth." 1 Samuel 17:33.* David showed his trust in God by comparing this battle to others in which the Lord had helped him: *"Thy servant slew both the lion and the bear: and this uncircumcised Philistine shall be as one of them, seeing he hath defied the armies of the living God." 1 Samuel 17:36.* David believed that God would enable him to accomplish any task to which he was called. In this attitude, he demonstrated a strong self-image.

When the Ark of the Covenant was brought into Jerusalem, David danced before the Lord in simple garments. He was not ashamed to let down his royal dignity in deference to the worship of God. Michal, David's wife, and Saul's daughter, despised this show of humility. I would guess that Saul never lowered himself so in the eyes of the common people. David had a strong enough sense of self-image to humble himself before God and others: *"And David danced before the LORD with all his might; and David was girded with a linen ephod… Then David returned to bless his household. And Michal the daughter of Saul came out to meet David, and said, How glorious was the king of Israel to day, who uncovered himself to day in the eyes of the handmaids of his servants, as one of the vain fellows shamelessly uncovereth himself! And David said unto Michal, It was before the LORD, which chose me before thy father, and before all his house, to appoint me ruler over the people of the LORD, over Israel: therefore will I play before the LORD. And I will yet be more vile than thus, and will be base in mine own sight: and of the maidservants which thou hast spoken of, of them shall I be had in honour." 2 Samuel 6:14, 20-22.*

David set the principles of self-image to poetry in the Psalms. Psalm 8 declares the greatness of God in two respects: 1. He created the moon and the stars; 2.

And He set lowly humans over His creation, in a higher position than the angels. Psalm 139 is the building code of self-image. David acknowledges God's omniscience (v.7) and the outgrowth of that, God's ever-present love and care for His creation: *"I will praise thee; for I am fearfully and wonderfully made: marvellous are thy works; and that my soul knoweth right well." Psalms 139:14.* The idea of "made" here is a "continous process." God is continually making us into His marvellous image.

7. Deal Gently

David practiced Forgiveness consistently throughout his life. He was never a vengeful or bitter person. He was forgiving toward Saul. He forgave Absalom's treachery and asked his men to "deal gently" with him (2 Samuel 18:5, 33). David forgave Shimei's cursing (2 Samuel 19). David also forgave the towns that tried to help Saul capture him (i.e. Ziph). He did not seek retribution after he became king.

David taught the principles of forgiveness in Psalm 51. The Psalm accurately ties clear conscience with the ability to forgive: *"Behold, I was shapen in iniquity; and in sin did my mother conceive me. Behold, thou desirest truth in the inward parts: and in the hidden part thou shalt make me to know wisdom. Purge me with hyssop, and I shall be clean: wash me, and I shall be whiter than snow. Make me to hear joy and gladness; that the bones which thou hast broken may rejoice. Hide thy face from my sins, and blot out all mine iniquities…then will I teach transgressors thy ways; and sinners shall be converted unto thee." Psalms 51:5-9,13.* He will teach transgressors God's ways by forgiving them the same way God forgives him. They will see the light of God in him and be drawn to that light (1 John 3:15-16; Ephesians 4:31-32).

8. I will make preparation.

David showed a mastery of money by his preparation for the Temple. He did not seek fame for himself by showing how great a house he could build for God in his lifetime. He wanted to build so excellent a house for God that he saved most of his career for his son to build it: *"And David said, Solomon my son is young and tender, and the house that is to be builded for the LORD must be exceeding magnifical, of fame and of glory throughout all countries: I will therefore now make preparation for it. So David prepared abundantly before his death…Now, behold, in my trouble I have prepared for the house of the LORD an hundred thousand talents of gold, and a thousand thousand talents of silver; and of brass and iron without weight; for it is in abundance: timber also and stone have I prepared; and thou mayest add thereto." 1 Chronicles 22:5,14.*

David did not use wealth to impress people nor was he impressed by it. I believe he was impervious to bribes and material corruption. When the king of Hamath sent a gift to David after Israel's defeat of Zobah, the scripture records that David dedicated it to the Lord like the other wealth he had accumulated (1 Chronicles 18:9-11).

David stated the essence of Financial Freedom in 2 Samuel 24. The death angel stopped short of Jerusalem in God's punishment of the numbering of the people. David knew this was the place God was choosing to build the Temple (1 Chronicles 22:1). Araunah, the Jebusite king, offered to give David oxen and wood for the burnt sacrifice. David refused the offer: *"And the king said unto Araunah, Nay; but I will surely buy it of thee at a price: neither will I offer burnt offerings unto the LORD my God of that which doth cost me nothing. So David bought the threshingfloor and the oxen for fifty shekels of silver." 2 Samuel 24:24.* When we give to God from sacrifice, that is true worship.

9.   Wash Me Thoroughly

Moral Freedom was David's weakest area of character. He committed adultery, murder, and deceit in the affair with Bathsheba. Because of this one failure in complete integrity David suffered the consequences of rape, murder, rebellion and conflict in his own family. Even a small chink in the armor can allow one of the giants of spiritual adolescence to get in their darts. David's career went well up to the incident with Bathsheba. After that, he had mostly sorrow. 2 Samuel after Chapter 11 is filled with the trials of David's failure. His poor example opened up the way for moral failure in his children. God declared that the "sword would never depart from his house" and that because of his sin "the enemies of the Lord would blaspheme" (2 Samuel 12:7-14). God took David's son by Bathsheba to repair His own reputation.

Nevertheless, David was strong in the principles of how to overcome moral failure. He immediately repented when Nathan confronted him (2 Samuel 12:13). He taught the principles of restoration in the Psalms: *"I acknowledged my sin unto thee, and mine iniquity have I not hid. I said, I will confess my transgressions unto the LORD; and thou forgavest the iniquity of my sin. Selah." Psalms 32:5"<<To the chief Musician, A Psalm of David, when Nathan the prophet came unto him, after he had gone in to Bathsheba.>> Have mercy upon me, O God, according to thy lovingkindness: according unto the multitude of thy tender mercies blot out my transgressions. Wash* *me throughly from mine iniquity, and cleanse me from my sin. For I acknowledge my transgressions: and my sin is ever before me. Against thee, thee only, have I sinned, and done this evil in thy sight: that thou mightest be justified when thou speakest, and be clear when thou judgest." Psalms 51:1- 4.*

David also knew how to take preventive steps against moral failure. He taught that meditation on God's word, a constant check of attitudes, and vigilance against presumption would prevent the build-up of immorality: *"Who can understand his errors? cleanse thou me from secret faults. Keep back thy servant also from presumptuous sins; let them not have dominion over me: then shall I be upright, and I shall be innocent from the great transgression. Let the words of my mouth, and the meditation of my heart, be acceptable In thy sight, O LORD, my strength, and my redeemer." Psalms 19:12-14.*

Israel Defeats the Giants

The last recorded battles of David highlight the defeat of the giants. The Philistines fought against Israel and brought Goliath's brothers. 2 Samuel 21:15- 22 records the deaths of the last four giants at the hands of David's mighty men. The placement here in the narrative of the Bible shows the symbolic defeat of the giants of spiritual adolescence. This marked the beginning of spiritual young adulthood for Israel. Israel did not have war anymore under David or Solomon and finally achieved the "rest" they had been promised. The ten spies of Moses declared the grasshopper complex toward the giants (Numbers 13:33). That was when Israel was in its childhood. Israel as a young adult had the character to overcome its fears.

David's song of deliverance comes right after the account of the giants in the narrative: *"And David spake unto the LORD the words of this song in the day that the LORD had delivered him out of the hand of all his enemies, and out of the hand of Saul:" 2 Samuel 22:1.* In it David emphasizes the importance of integrity and in trust in the ways of God, both of which are necessary to enter spiritual young adulthood. These are themes he amplifies many times in the Psalms, which is a book of comfort for the spiritual young adult.

Pilgrim's Progress

After Christian escaped Apollyon and the Valley of Humiliation, he entered the Valley of the Shadow of Death. This second valley corresponds to battles with the giants of spiritual adolescence. Christian first met two of the ten spies who brought an evil report of the land, and they advised him to go back. Apparently, they felt like grasshoppers in their own sight. The "discouraging clouds of confusion" frightened them.

The pathway through this valley was very narrow, just as the path to integrity is narrow. The Valley was full of "hobgoblins, satyrs, and dragons of the pit." Christian overcame his enemies with the weapons of "all-prayer" and confidence in God's strength: "I will walk in the strength of the Lord God." He was comforted by the words of Psalm 23:4: *"Yea, though I walk through the valley of the shadow of death, I will fear no evil: for thou art with me; thy rod and thy staff they comfort me."* On the second half of his walk through the Valley he had more light and could clearly see the "snares, traps, gins, nets, pits, deep holes, and slopes." This symbolizes how as a spiritual adolescent he had gained strength in the first part of the ordeal and had more skill to get through the second part.

At the end of the Valley, he passed by the cave of Pope and Pagan, which represent the dangers of false religion and secularism to a spiritual adolescent.

Finally, Christian came to a little hill, which was provided for pilgrims to see their way more clearly. The little hill represents the "rest" after the defeat of the giants. There Christian was joined by Faithful, his companion into spiritual young adulthood. Faithful and Christian went on their way and encouraged one another by sharing their stories of victory and growth.[9]

David's Psalm of Integrity: Psalm 15

v. 1 "LORD, who shall abide in thy tabernacle? who shall dwell in thy holy hill?" What are the requirements of the person who will live in God's Place that He chooses to put His name?

v. 2 "He that walketh uprightly, and worketh righteousness, and speaketh the truth in his heart." "Walketh uprightly" means "to have integrity." A man of integrity must put his beliefs into action (worketh righteousness), and he must possess the inner attitudes that motivate mature behavior.

v. 3 "He that backbiteth not with his tongue, nor doeth evil to his neighbour, nor taketh up a reproach against his neighbour." A man of integrity acts with a clear conscience toward others. He does not talk behind the back, but instead addresses concerns face to face. He does not seek to advance himself at the expense of tearing down another. He does not take up offenses based on hearsay.

v. 4 "In whose eyes a vile person is contemned; but he honoureth them that fear the LORD. He that sweareth to his own hurt, and changeth not." A man of integrity does not play politics. He stays with those who are true to God no matter what opinion is currently popular. He honors his word even if it is costly to keep it. He values his and God's reputation above every hardship.

v. 5 "He that putteth not out his money to usury, nor taketh reward against the innocent. He that doeth these things shall never be moved." A man of integrity does not profit from the poverty of others. He does not take advantage of others when they are down. A man of integrity who follows all these principles will have a portion in the Place God chooses because he has the character God chooses.

The Place

David conquered and possessed Jerusalem in his first act as the king over all Israel. Jerusalem was thought to be safe from attack, so much so that the Jebusites had a saying: "the blind and the lame can defend Jerusalem": *"Nevertheless David took the strong hold of Zion: the same is the city of David." 2 Samuel 5:7.*

Somehow God communicated to David that he had chosen Jerusalem or Zion as the Place. Zion is described as such in the Psalms: *"Yet have I set my king upon my holy hill of Zion." Psalms 2:6. "But chose the tribe of Judah, the mount Zion which he loved." Psalms 78:68. "For the LORD hath chosen Zion; he hath desired it for his habitation." Psalms 132:13.*

Shortly after the capture of Jerusalem, David prepared a tent in Jerusalem and brought the Ark of the Covenant into it (1 Chronicles 15:1, 28). David also purposed to build a permanent temple in Jerusalem to replace the tabernacle, and God blessed this desire: *"And it came to pass, when the king sat in his house, and the LORD had given him rest round about from all his enemies; That the king said unto Nathan the prophet, See now, I dwell in an house of cedar, but the ark of God dwelleth within curtains. And Nathan said to the king, Go, do all that is in thine heart; for the LORD is with thee." 2 Samuel 7:1-3.*

The Rest of God

God responded to David's desire to build the Temple by initiating a new covenant, the Davidic Covenant (1 Chronicles 28:4). In it God declared a new stage of Israel's development.

"And it came to pass the same night, that the word of God came to Nathan, saying, Go and tell David my servant, Thus saith the LORD, Thou shalt not build me an house to dwell in: For I have not dwelt in an house since the day that I brought up Israel unto this day; but have gone from tent to tent, and from one tabernacle to another. Wheresoever I have walked with all Israel, spake I a word to any of the judges of Israel, whom I commanded to feed my people, saying, Why have ye not built me an house of cedars? Now therefore thus shalt thou say unto my servant David, Thus saith the LORD of hosts, I took thee from the sheepcote, even from following the sheep, that thou shouldest be ruler over my people Israel: And I have been with thee whithersoever thou hast walked, and have cut off all thine enemies from before thee, and have made thee a name like the name of the great men that are in the earth. Also I will ordain a place for my people Israel, and will plant them, and they shall dwell in their place, and shall be moved no more; neither shall the children of wickedness waste them any more, as at the beginning, And since the time that I commanded judges to be over my people Israel. Moreover I will subdue all thine enemies" 1 Chronicles 17:3-10. In this passage God refers to the lack of "rest" in Israel during all the times of the judges. Then God brought David to power in order to give "rest" to Israel. Only after the "rest" is achieved does God choose the Place. This declaration marks the end of spiritual *adolescence* and the beginning of spiritual *young adulthood* for Israel.

The book of Hebrews describes the same "rest of God" as a desired level of spiritual growth (Hebrews 3 and 4).

In Chapter 3, the writer of Hebrews reminds us of the failure of the children of Israel to grow spiritually in the wilderness: *"Wherefore I was grieved with that generation, and said, They do alway err in their heart; and they have not known my ways. So I sware in my wrath, They shall not enter into my rest.)" Hebrews 3:10,11.* "Knowing God's ways," the learning task of spiritual young adulthood, is required to reach the level of "rest."

In Chapter 4, The writer encourages us to labor to "rest": *"Let us therefore fear, lest, a promise being left us of entering into his rest, any of you should seem to come short of it…Let us labour therefore to enter into that rest, lest any man fall after the same example of unbelief." Hebrews 4:1, 11.* The labor is in fighting and subduing the giant conflicts. The children of Israel at Kadesh failed because they saw themselves as grasshoppers and refused to fight.

The writer shows by example that David understood his covenant to be an opportunity for further spiritual growth for Israel: *"Again, he limiteth a certain day, saying in David, To day, after so long a time; as it is said, To day if ye will hear his voice, harden not your hearts. For if Jesus had given them rest, then would he not afterward have spoken of another day." Hebrews 4:7,8.* The reference is to Psalm 95. Joshua did not give them rest because he did not completely subdue the enemies. David gained the mastery over all neighboring countries and finished off the giants.

The Person

In addition to naming the Place, God named Shiloh, the Messiah. God promised that one of David's descendents would rule forever in Jerusalem: *"Furthermore I tell thee that the LORD will build thee an house. And it shall come to pass, when thy days be expired that thou must go to be with thy fathers, that I will raise up thy seed after thee, which shall be of thy sons; and I will establish his kingdom. He shall build me an house, and I will stablish his throne for ever. I will be his father, and he shall be my son: and I will not take my mercy away from him, as I took it from him that was before thee: But I will settle him in mine house and in my kingdom for ever: and his throne shall be established for evermore." 1Chronicles 17:10 c -14.*

The Psalms reveal David understood that God was promising the future king would have a divine nature (Psalm 2; 24; 72; 110): *"I will declare the decree: the LORD hath said unto me, Thou art my Son; this day have I begotten thee…Be wise now therefore, O ye kings: be instructed, ye judges of the earth. Serve the LORD with fear, and rejoice with trembling. Kiss the Son, lest he be angry, and ye perish from the way, when his wrath is kindled but a little. Blessed are all they that put their trust in him." Psalms 2:7, 10-12.*

A man of perfect character, of whom David was a forerunner, would build the true house of God. This man, the Messiah, would actually be the Lord: *"Who shall ascend into the hill of the LORD? or who shall stand in his holy place? He that hath clean hands, and a pure heart; who hath not lifted up his soul unto vanity, nor sworn deceitfully…Lift up your heads, O ye gates; and be ye lift up, ye everlasting doors; and the King of glory shall come in. Who is this King of glory? The LORD strong and mighty, the LORD mighty in battle." Psalms 24:3-4, 7-8.*

Jesus explained the nature of the Messiah. Jesus told the Pharisees that David understood the Messiah to be God in the flesh, that's why David called Him "Lord" (Psalm 110:1-2). Jesus also confirmed that He Himself was the ultimate fulfillment of the prophecy: *"While the Pharisees were gathered together, Jesus asked them, Saying, What think ye of Christ? whose son is he? They say unto him, The Son of David. He saith unto them, How then doth David in spirit call him Lord, saying, The LORD said unto my Lord, Sit thou on my right hand, till I make thine enemies thy footstool? If David then call him Lord, how is he his son? And no man was able to answer him a word, neither durst any man from that day forth ask him any more questions." Matthew 22:41-46.*

Crisis

David and Israel began to look for the promised one. Each new king and each son born in David's line would become a candidate. There was no way, however, for the people to know beforehand God's choice. They had to have patience and wait on God's timing. They had no ability to make it happen by human means, even though they wished to and tried to. Therefore the crisis of their spiritual young adulthood was *waiting on God vs. works of their own hands.*

After young adults have developed answers to the crises of adolescence, and choose their paths in relationships and purpose, then they can work toward their goals with confidence. Nevertheless, they are not in control of circumstances. Relationships sometimes go south because of unforeseen obstacles (extended family conflict, character flaws, affairs, lack of commitment, inability to have children). Jobs are dissolved because of takeovers, disasters, and financial problems. Young adults are not always able to accomplish their dreams even though their preparation is sound. That is why divine intervention is necessary for success.

The spiritual young adult has a vision of accomplishment for God's kingdom. He or she has overcome the wicked one and developed integrity. The only requirement to move on to adulthood is the fulfillment of the vision. Nevertheless, the spiritual young adult has no power to make it happen. *He or she must wait on God to be successful, no matter how long that takes.* David is a good example of waiting, first on the kingship, then on the Temple.

Attempts to fulfill God's vision by human effort dilute the desired treasure, and are violations of the ways of God. The fulfillment must be clearly seen to be by God's hand. That's why God allows time and circumstances to prevent success by human effort. He often allows the fulfillment to be blocked by seemingly permanent barriers. Then He intervenes supernaturally, which causes everyone to glorify God instead of human ingenuity.

And remember that the vision often involves something others take for granted (marriage, children, career, ministry, etc.), yet seems impossible to the hero. People must see the hero's life in that one area as an aberration, a curse: *"And lest I should be exalted above measure through the abundance of the revelations, there was given to me a thorn in the flesh, the messenger of Satan to buffet me, lest I should be exalted above measure. For this thing I besought the Lord thrice, that it might depart from me. And he said unto me, My grace is sufficient for thee: for my strength is made perfect in weakness. Most gladly therefore will I rather glory in my infirmities, that the power of Christ may rest upon me. Therefore I take pleasure in infirmities, in reproaches, in necessities, in persecutions, in distresses for Christ's sake: for when I am weak, then am I strong." 2 Corinthians 12:7-10.*

Look at Abraham. God had changed his name from Abram to Abraham (father of a multitude, Genesis 17: 5) Yet Abraham had no children. His wife had passed the age where she could have children. His faith in God's promise must have seemed strange to his neighbors, doubly so because he had left his home country and their religion in pursuit of God. God seemed to be a traitor from a human perspective, but God honored His word eventually through supernatural intervention: *"(As it is written, I have made thee a father of many nations,) before him whom he believed, even God, who quickeneth the dead, and calleth those things which be not as though they were. Who against hope believed in hope, that he might become the father of many nations, according to that which was spoken, So shall thy seed be. And being not weak in faith, he considered not his own body now dead, when he was about an hundred years old, neither yet the deadness of Sara's womb: He staggered not at the promise of God through unbelief; but was strong in faith, giving glory to God; And being fully persuaded that, what he had promised, he was able also to perform. And therefore it was imputed to him for righteousness." Romans 4:17-22.*

FromAbraham we learn that belief in God's ability to do the impossible is the basis of our relationship with God: *"And the scripture was fulfilled which saith, Abraham believed God, and it was imputed unto him for righteousness: and he was called the Friend of God." James 2:23.*

Nevertheless, because Abraham and Sarah did not fully wait on the promised child, but instead used their own human ingenuity in an attempt to complete the vision, Ishmael was born. Ishmael became the father of the Arab nations, and thus we have the Arab-Israeli conflict. Partial waiting brings heartaches.

Boredom is another danger of spiritual young adulthood. Even though the crises of adolescence have been mastered, the spiritual young adult may justify lapses because of the long wait: "I have been faithful so long, so what if I indulge myself a little. It will not change the person I am."

Sin in the spiritual young adult is different from sin in the spiritual adolescent, because the young adult knows better. God judges these lapses very seriously, just as He did with David (Bathsheba, the counting of the people). The consequences of sin are serious for the spiritual young adult because of his or her reputation and example: *"Howbeit, because by this deed thou hast given great occasion to the enemies of the LORD to blaspheme, the child also that is born unto thee shall surely die." 2 Samuel 12:14. "So the LORD sent a pestilence upon Israel from the morning even to the time appointed: and there died of the people from Dan even to Beersheba seventy thousand men." 2 Samuel 24:15. "And that servant, which knew his lord's will, and prepared not himself, neither did according to his will, shall be beaten with many stripes. But he that knew not, and did commit things worthy of stripes, shall be beaten with few stripes. For unto whomsoever much is given, of him shall be much required: and to whom men have committed much, of him they will ask the more." Luke 12:47,48.*

Another danger is despair. Giving up on God. Not a repudiation of faith, but a resigned attitude that God will not deliver His promise. This leads to a lack of power. David gave up and went over to the Philistines. The scripture even hints that David would have gone to war against Israel had not God prevented him through the lords of the Philistines: *"And David said in his heart, I shall now perish one day by the hand of Saul: there is nothing better for me than that I should speedily escape into the land of the Philistines; and Saul shall despair of me, to seek me any more in any coast of Israel: so shall I escape out of his hand." 1 Samuel 27:1. (also see 1 Samuel 28:1-2).*

David was even more in despair when the Amalekites invaded Ziklag his home and burned it with fire. Yet, this was a turning point because he "encouraged his heart in the Lord." In other words, he reminded himself of God's promise and His power to keep it, even if circumstances look bad: *"For God is not unrighteous to forget your work and labour of love, which ye have shewed toward his name, in that ye have ministered to the saints, and do minister." Hebrews 6:10. "Cast not away therefore your confidence, which hath great recompence of reward." Hebrews 10:35.*

Persecution is strongest toward the spiritual young adult. By young adulthood, character is mostly formed, a person's life choices are made, and very few change their path. The person who lives for God at this stage has developed a different lifestyle from the world that is less subject to peer pressure and worldly values. Therefore, he or she lives in contrast to the world. And since the worldly young adult is likewise fully committed to worldliness, and is not likely to change, there is conflict. The two grow farther apart because each must justify the path that has been chosen. The difference is that the spiritual person has a more solid foundation, and presents a stronger challenge to worldliness than vice versa. Therefore, the worldly person becomes more violent to protect his or her interests. In our day, the violence is not usually in the physical realm. It is subtler, but it is real: *"But call to remembrance the former days, in which, after ye were illuminated, ye endured a great fight of afflictions; Partly, whilst ye were made a gazingstock both by reproaches and afflictions; and partly, whilst ye became companions of them that were so used." Hebrews 10:32,33. "Yea, and all that will live godly in Christ Jesus shall suffer persecution." 2 Timothy 3:12.*

Loneliness is a constant ache in spiritual young adulthood. The spiritual traveler takes an individual journey for the benefit of all. He or she goes into the spiritual realm to bring back its treasure. Because other people are naturally accomplishing their life tasks of marriage, children, job success, houses, retirement, etc. and the spiritual traveler is first concentrating on supernatural goals, there is a rift, a misunderstanding. The spiritual young adult may be seen as naive, selfish, silly, or foolish. The spiritual traveler understands worldly goals, but doesn't live by them. The worldly person does not perceive the return on investment for taking a hero's journey: *"For what man knoweth the things of a man, save the spirit of man which is in him? even so the things of God knoweth no man, but the Spirit of God. Now we have received, not the spirit of the world, but the spirit which is of God; that we might know the things that are freely given to us of God…But the natural man receiveth not the things of the Spirit of God: for they are foolishness unto him: neither can he know them, because they are spiritually discerned. But he that is spiritual judgeth all things, yet he himself is judged of no man." 1 Corinthians 2:11-12, 14-15.*

David expresses this emotion to God in the Psalms, and for the very reason discussed here, misunderstanding from people: *"I looked on my right hand, and beheld, but there was no man that would know me: refuge failed me; no man cared for my soul. I cried unto thee, O LORD: I said, Thou art my refuge and my portion in the land of the living." Psalms 142:4,5. "But I am a worm, and no man; a reproach of men, and despised of the people. All they that see me laugh me to scorn: they shoot out the lip, they shake the head, saying, He trusted on the LORD that he would deliver him: let him deliver him, seeing he delighted in him." Psalms 22:6-8. "I was a reproach among all mine enemies, but especially among my neighbours, and a fear to mine acquaintance: they that did see me without fled from me. I am forgotten as a dead man out of mind: I am like a broken vessel. For I have heard the slander of many: fear was on every side: while they took counsel together against me, they devised to take away my life. But I trusted in thee, O LORD: I said, Thou art my God." Psalms 31:11-14.*

Waiting On The Eternal King

Solomon was the first candidate. He built the Temple, established peace, and led Israel into economic dominance of the Middle East. To the people of Israel, if he wasn't the "one," then the "one" must be soon coming. It was a time of continual improvement in their fortunes: *"And David said to Solomon, My son, as for me, it was in my mind to build an house unto the name of the LORD my God: But the word of the LORD came to me, saying, Thou hast shed blood abundantly, and hast made great wars: thou shalt not build an house unto my name, because thou hast shed much blood upon the earth in my sight. Behold, a son shall be born to thee, who shall be a man of rest; and I will give him rest from all his enemies round about: for his name shall be Solomon, and I will give peace and quietness unto Israel in his days. He shall build an house for my name; and he shall be my son, and I will be his father; and I will establish the throne of his kingdom over Israel for ever. Now, my son, the LORD be with thee; and prosper thou, and build the house of the LORD thy God, as he hath said of thee."* 1 Chronicles 22:7-11.

David charged Israel to keep God's commandments: *"Now therefore in the sight of all Israel the congregation of the LORD, and in the audience of our God, keep and seek for all the commandments of the LORD your God: that ye may possess this good land, and leave it for an inheritance for your children after you for ever."* 1 Chronicles 28:8.

David charged and prayed for Solomon to have a "perfect heart," knowing that the chosen one would have to be a man of perfect character: *"And thou, Solomon my son, know thou the God of thy father, and serve him with a perfect heart and with a willing mind: for the LORD searcheth all hearts, and understandeth all the imaginations of the thoughts: if thou seek him, he will be found of thee; but if thou forsake him, he will cast thee off for ever."* 1 Chronicles 28:9. *"And give unto Solomon my son a perfect heart, to keep thy commandments, thy testimonies, and thy statutes, and to do all these things, and to build the palace, for the which I have made provision."* 1 Chronicles 29:19.

God made two covenants with Solomon, the first was personal, but the second applied also to future kings.

In the first covenant, God honored Solomon's request for wisdom by granting him wisdom, honor, and long life (1 Kings 3:5-13). God also granted a conditional promise to lengthen his days: *"And if thou wilt walk in my ways, to keep my statutes and my commandments, as thy father David did walk, then I will lengthen thy days."* 1 Kings 3:14.

In the second covenant, God revealed more of His qualifications for the "person" and of the generation to which He would come. God initiated the second covenant after Solomon's prayer of dedication of the Temple. God emphasized that "integrity of heart" would be the prime qualification for the Messiah and His people. The king would always be a reflection of the people because of his life task as the hero. God warned that Israel and the king could lose their Place because of moral and spiritual corruption: *"And it came to pass, when Solomon had finished the building of the house of the LORD, and the king's house, and all Solomon's desire which he was pleased to do, That the LORD appeared to Solomon the second time, as he had appeared unto him at Gibeon. And the LORD said unto him, I have heard thy prayer and thy supplication, that thou hast made before me: I have hallowed this house, which thou hast built, to put my name there for ever; and mine eyes and mine heart shall be there perpetually. And if thou wilt walk before me, as David thy father walked, in integrity of heart, and in uprightness, to do according to all that I have commanded thee, and wilt keep my statutes and my judgments: Then I will establish the throne of thy kingdom upon Israel for ever, as I promised to David thy father, saying, There shall not fail thee a man upon the throne of Israel. But if ye shall at all turn from following me, ye or your children, and will not keep my commandments and my statutes which I have set before you, but go and serve other gods, and worship them: Then will I cut off Israel out of the land which I have given them; and this house, which I have hallowed for my name, will I cast out of my sight; and Israel shall be a proverb and a byword among all people:"* 1 Kings 9:1-7.

Solomon completed David's victory over the giants by making the remaining Canaanites bondservants: *"And all the people that were left of the Amorites, Hittites, Perizzites, Hivites, and Jebusites, which were not of the children of Israel, Their children that were left after them in the land, whom the children of Israel also were not able utterly to destroy, upon those did Solomon levy a tribute of bondservice unto this day."* 1 Kings 9:20,21.

Nevertheless, Solomon failed the test of integrity. Even with all the momentum from David's reign and with the building of the Temple, Solomon got bored and sinned. His heart was compared to David's, which became the high standard, even though David himself prophesied of the perfect character of a future king. None of the kings even lived up to the mere human standard of David. *"But king Solomon loved many strange women, together with the daughter of Pharaoh, women of the Moabites, Ammonites, Edomites, Zidonians, and Hittites; Of the nations concerning which the LORD said unto the children of Israel, Ye shall not go in to them, neither shall they come in unto you: for surely they will turn away your heart after their gods: Solomon clave unto these in love. And he had seven hundred wives, princesses, and three hundred concubines: and his wives turned away his heart. For it came to pass, when Solomon was old, that his wives turned away his heart after other gods: and his heart was not perfect with the LORD his God, as was the heart of David his father. For Solomon went after Ashtoreth the goddess of the Zidonians, and after Milcom the abomination of the Ammonites. And Solomon did evil in the sight of the LORD, and went not fully after the LORD, as did David his father." 1 Kings 11:1-6.*

Because of Solomon's sin, God allowed the nation to be divided. In this, God pushed the dream of the Messiah further away. The Messiah would now have to find a way to reunite Israel: *"Wherefore the LORD said unto Solomon, Forasmuch as this is done of thee, and thou hast not kept my covenant and my statutes, which I have commanded thee, I will surely rend the kingdom from thee, and will give it to thy servant. Notwithstanding in thy days I will not do it for David thy father's sake: but I will rend it out of the hand of thy son. Howbeit I will not rend away all the kingdom; but will give one tribe to thy son for David my servant's sake, and for Jerusalem's sake which I have chosen." 1 Kings 11:11-13.*

Rehoboam, Solomon's son, distinguished himself by his lack of wisdom. Instead of making the people's burden of public works lighter, he pledged to make it more grievous (1 Kings 12:12-15). This became the pretext for the rebellion of the ten northern tribes. They renounced their inheritance in David and at the same time in the Messiah: *"So when all Israel saw that the king hearkened not unto them, the people answered the king, saying, What portion have we in David? neither have we inheritance in the son of Jesse: to your tents, O Israel: now see to thine own house, David. So Israel departed unto their tents." 1 Kings 12:16.*

Judah and Benjamin were the only tribes left that still hoped for the dream of Shiloh. Nevertheless, they were declared unfit to receive Him (1 Kings 14:22-24). The people under Rehoboam did not keep their pledge of worshipping only in Jerusalem, God's chosen place. Instead they built the high places, copying the customs of the Canaanites, who worshipped their gods in the open air on hills with pillars and trees surrounding the sacred spots. This practice led to worshipping pagan deities along with the Lord (why not have the favor of all the gods of any locality?). The people also allowed immorality to grow unchallenged as evidenced by the proliferation of sodomites in the land. For all this, God judged them as an evil generation, and the Messiah could only come to a generation prepared to receive Him (1 Chronicles 29:18; Luke 19:41-44; Zechariah 12:10).

The high places, the erosion of their commitment to the Place, and moral laxness, the erosion of their commitment to the character of the Person, became the yardsticks to measure Judah's fitness throughout the time of the kings. Both lapses of national integrity showed their boredom and despair in waiting on God. They knew God's will; it was just too inconvenient and difficult to remain diligent.

Rehoboam served God for three years in strengthening Judah and Benjamin against Israel and in welcoming the true worshippers of the Lord who fled from Israel (2 Chronicles 11). After that, Rehoboam and Israel relaxed in their worship of God: *"And it came to pass, when Rehoboam had established the kingdom, and had strengthened himself, he forsook the law of the LORD, and all Israel with him." 2 Chronicles 12:1.*

Because of their sin, God humbled Judah by sending Shishak, king of Egypt, to take their treasures out of the house of the Lord and the king's house. Rehoboam made shields of brass to replace the shields of gold that were taken as tribute. In this, God demonstrated His willingness to discipline His people, even at this stage of their maturity. God also showed them that sin reduces the glory of God's blessing. The shields of brass symbolized the backsliding of the king and people (2 Chronicles 12:2-10).

The scripture says plainly that Rehoboam failed because of a lack of integrity. He was unprepared to lead the people to further maturity because he did not seek it for himself: *"And he did evil, because he prepared not his heart to seek the LORD." 2 Chronicles 12:14.*

Nevertheless, there was still hope and many good things left to comfort the people's dream: *"And when he humbled himself, the wrath of the LORD turned from him, that he would not destroy him altogether: and also in Judah things went well." 2 Chronicles 12:12.*

Jeroboam was the leader of the rebellion of the northern tribes and became their king. Solomon had made Jeroboam the ruler over public works in Israel. Apparently, he had felt that the work should be less grievous, even in Solomon's time. When Solomon didn't listen to him he rebelled (1 Kings 11:26-28). Solomon tried to kill him, so Jeroboam ran to Egypt for the remainder of Solomon's reign (1 Kings 11:40).

Ahijah met Jeroboam as he fled from Solomon and prophesied of the division of Israel (1 Kings 11:30-36). He told Jeroboam that God would afflict the house of David because of Solomon's idolatry. But, even in this affliction the prophet reaffirmed God's commitment to Jerusalem and to the house of David: *"And unto his son will I give one tribe, that David my servant may have a light alway before me in Jerusalem, the city which I have chosen me to put my name there." 1 Kings 11:36.*

Ahijah also instructed Jeroboam in the nature of God's covenant with the northern kings and their purpose in the history of Israel. God would hold the northern kings responsible to model themselves after David's worship and to cherish integrity. Their lineage would never lead to the Messiah but their purpose was to set a good example for the kings of Judah and provoke them to serve the Lord: *"And I will take thee, and thou shalt reign according to all that thy soul desireth, and shalt be king over Israel. And it shall be, if thou wilt hearken unto all that I command thee, and wilt walk in my ways, and do that is right in my sight, to keep my statutes and my commandments, as David my servant did; that I will be with thee, and build thee a sure house, as I built for David, and will give Israel unto thee. And I will for this afflict the seed of David, but not for ever." 1 Kings 11:37-39.*

Jeroboam led the revolt against Rehoboam. The people of the northern tribes sent for him to be present at the coronation of Rehoboam. Jeroboam challenged him to make the people's burden lighter in the public works. When Rehoboam refused the counsel of the old men and spoke roughly to the people, Israel made Jeroboam their king and stoned Rehoboam's conscriptionist: *"And it came to pass, when all Israel heard that Jeroboam was come again, that they sent and called him unto the congregation, and made him king over all Israel: there was none that followed the house of David, but the tribe of Judah only." 1 Kings 12:20.*

Rehoboam gathered an army to fight Israel but God prevented him: *"Thus saith the LORD, Ye shall not go up, nor fight against your brethren the children of Israel: return every man to his house; for this thing is from me. They hearkened therefore to the word of the LORD, and returned to depart, according to the word of the LORD." 1 Kings 12:24.*

Jeroboam did not know the reason Rehoboam turned back but he did not take chances. He fortified cities in Ephraim in preparation for an attack and began to think politically instead of honoring the covenant of God to him. He became more concerned about his own place of honor than the worship of God. God had promised him the kingdom if he continued in true worship. Jeroboam showed his lack of trust by fearing the people's loyalty to the sacrifices at Jerusalem: *"And Jeroboam said in his heart, Now shall the kingdom return to the house of David: If this people go up to do sacrifice in the house of the LORD at Jerusalem, then shall the heart of this people turn again unto their lord, even unto Rehoboam king of Judah, and they shall kill me, and go again to Rehoboam king of Judah." 1 Kings 12:26,27.*

Therefore, Jeroboam devised a three-pronged plan to keep the people at home and away from Jerusalem. First, he replaced the Temple: he took the precedent

Of Aaron's golden calf (Exodus 32:4) and made two images of calves to represent Jehovah (the people understood that the images did not contain Jehovah but that He was present with them). He set them in two strategic places in Israel to give everyone an opportunity to worship. Second, he replaced the priests: he ousted the priests and Levites because of their loyalty to the true worship of God and substituted priests of his own choosing. Third, he replaced the feasts: he made up a feast at Bethel for the eighth month like the Feast of Tabernacles at Jerusalem. This satisfied the people's habit of gathering as a nation for worship (1 Kings 12:28-33). Jeroboam also encouraged the use of high places for worship of God, which was heresy (2 Chronicles 11:15).

Jeroboam's plan succeeded. The majority of the people accepted his substitute religion The minority left Israel to live in Judah: many priests and Levites who could not conscience the apostasy and lay people who desired the true worship of God (2 Chronicles 11:13-17).

Israel as a whole never repented from the apostasy and the Lord gave them up. They rejected the Place and the Person and believed they could worship God on their own terms. The attitudes of their kings were a reflection of the attitudes of the people. They let politics and worldly values decide their unhappy destiny. God's summary of His judgment of Israel showed the apostasy was a corporate decision, and not just in obedience to Jeroboam (2 Kings 17).

The Lord prophesied two times against Jeroboam and his acts. The first prophet condemned the altar at Bethel and named the king of Judah who would desecrate it after Israel's demise: *"And he cried against the altar in the word of the LORD, and said, O altar, altar, thus saith the LORD; Behold, a child shall be born unto the house of David, Josiah by name; and upon thee shall he offer the priests of the high places that burn incense upon thee, and men's bones shall be burnt upon thee." 1 Kings 13:2.* In this, Jeroboam was warned that his plan to replace true worship would ultimately fail. The prophet even gave him a sign: the altar rent and Jeroboam's hand withered. Jeroboam begged God and received physical restoration, yet he later went back and rebuilt the altar (1 Kings 13:1-10, 33-34).

The second prophecy came from Ahijah. Jeroboam had sent his wife with his sick son to be healed. Instead, Ahijah pronounced the death of the child, the end of Jeroboam's line as king, and Israel's captivity. Ahijah listed God's charges: 1. Thou hast not been as my servant David 2. Thou hast gone and made thee other gods. Ahijah prophesied that Israel would never turn back from their sin and that God had already judged them as a nation: *"For the LORD shall smite Israel, as a reed is shaken in the water, and he shall root up Israel out of this good land, which he gave to their fathers, and shall scatter them beyond the river, because they have made their groves, provoking the LORD to anger. And he shall give Israel up because of the sins of Jeroboam, who did sin, and who made Israel to sin." 1 Kings 14:15,16.*

Jeroboam at his end gathered a huge army and fought against Abijah, Solomon's grandson, and was defeated. 2 Chronicles 13 summarizes Judah's position regarding the new religion of Jeroboam. Judah had confidence that God would honor their steadfastness with victory in battle, and so He did: Abijah and his people slew them with a great slaughter: *"so there fell down slain of Israel five hundred thousand chosen men. Thus the children of Israel were brought under at that time, and the children of Judah prevailed, because they relied upon the LORD God of their fathers...Neither did Jeroboam recover strength again in the days of Abijah: and the LORD struck him, and he died." 2 Chronicles 13:17-18, 20.*

Jeroboam's son was assassinated and the assassin, Baasha, became king. After this, the crown in Israel was transferred mainly through violence. Politics and worldly values invaded every area of life, and the new religion became profane. The nation had no uniting principles except for expediency (sounds a lot like our day). Eventually, Israel accepted the worship of Baal from its kings without protest.

Kings didn't last long in Israel. Eight of the nineteen were assassinated. Jehu's dynasty was the longest, four generations (2 Kings 10:30).

None of the northern kings were like God's servant David, and none turned back from Jeroboam's sin, wherewith he made Israel to sin. Jeroboam was the only northern king to be compared to David, and that unfavorably. Ezra in the Chronicles rarely discussed the northern kings because they could not be in the line of the Messiah. All of the northern kings were judged as apostates because of the golden calves, even Zimri, who only reigned for seven days (1Kings 16:15-20). None of the northern kings would risk allowing the people to truly worship God in Jerusalem.

Some of the northern kings were better than others. Ahab was the worst because he sanctioned Baal worship in Israel: *"And Ahab the son of Omri did evil in the sight of the LORD above all that were before him. And it came to pass, as if it had been a light thing for him to walk in the sins of Jeroboam the son of Nebat, that he took to wife Jezebel the daughter of Ethbaal king of the Zidonians, and went and served Baal, and worshipped him." 1 Kings 16:30,31.* Ahaziah sent to Baalzebub for healing (2 Kings 1:1-18). Therefore God allowed Ahaziah, Ahab's son, to die from the effects of a fall. Ahaziah's brother Jehoram, was one of the better kings because he put away the image of Baal (2 Kings 3:2-3). Jehu, the executioner, was the best of the northern kings because he did God's will in destroying the house of Ahab and the worship of

Baal. The worship of Baal was never sanctioned again in Israel: *"And they brake down the image of Baal, and brake down the house of Baal, and made it a draught house unto this day. Thus Jehu destroyed Baal out of Israel…And the LORD said unto Jehu, Because thou hast done well in executing that which is right in mine eyes, and hast done unto the house of Ahab according to all that was in mine heart, thy children of the fourth generation shall sit on the throne of Israel. But Jehu took no heed to walk in the law of the LORD God of Israel with all his heart: for he departed not from the sins of Jeroboam, which made Israel to sin."* 2 Kings 10:27-28, 30-31.

During the two hundred years of the Northern Kingdom, the people became increasingly profane in their outlook. They only responded politically and worship became a mere political tool. Elijah's challenge to the prophets of Baal at Mt. Carmel serves as a poignant example of the people's view of religion. They would not choose between the Lord and Baal but waited to see which side would become politically correct. They were not true believers in either. They only responded after the Lord intervened supernaturally: *"And Elijah came unto all the people, and said, How long halt ye between two opinions? if the LORD be God, follow him: but if Baal, then follow him. And the people answered him not a word…Then the fire of the LORD fell, and consumed the burnt sacrifice, and the wood, and the stones, and the dust, and licked up the water that was in the trench. And when all the people saw it, they fell on their faces: and they said, The LORD, he is the God; the LORD, he is the God."* 1 Kings 18:21, 38-39.

Yet there were still true followers of the Lord even during the apostasy. The Lord sent prophets to the Northern Kingdom. God declared to Elijah that even during the time of Baal worship there were still seven thousand faithful Israelites. This was after Elijah complained that he was the only true believer left: *"And he said, I have been very jealous for the LORD God of hosts: for the children of Israel have forsaken thy covenant, thrown down thine altars, and slain thy prophets with the sword; and I, even I only, am left; and they seek my life, to take it away…Yet I have left me seven thousand in Israel, all the knees which have not bowed unto Baal, and every mouth which hath not kissed him."* 1 Kings 19:10, 18.

God continued to work in Israel even during the apostasy. He continually bore witness to Himself. God's purpose in His mercy was for the people to "know that I am the Lord" (1 Kings 20:13). God saved them from their oppressors even though the people did not repent (2 Kings 13:22-23, Jehoahaz; 14:22-27, Jeroboam 2). God even performed miracles by the hands of Elijah and Elisha in order to lead the people back. No prophets of Judah performed miracles. God went the extra mile to show Himself faithful to His people.

"In the ninth year of Hoshea the king of Assyria took Samaria, and carried Israel away into Assyria, and placed them in Halah and in Habor by the river of Gozan, and in the cities of the Medes." 2 Kings 17:6. The prophecy of Ahijah was fulfilled and the apostasy was totally condemned (2 Kings 17:20- 23). The northern tribes lost their place and their identity and still remain scattered. Only Jesus at His return can give their place back. 2 Kings 17:7-18 summarizes the process of their downfall and God's judgment of them:

1. They forgot God's mercy in giving them freedom from the world: *"For so it was, that the children of Israel had sinned against the LORD their God, which had brought them up out of the land of Egypt, from under the hand of Pharaoh king of Egypt, and had feared other gods," 2 Kings 17:7.*

2. They lived by worldly principles: *"And walked in the statutes of the heathen, whom the LORD cast out from before the children of Israel, and of the kings of Israel, which they had made." 2 Kings 17:8.*

3. They secretly committed heresy in using the high places to worship: *"And the children of Israel did secretly those things that were not right against the LORD their God, and they built them high places in all their cities, from the tower of the watchmen to the fenced city." 2 Kings 17:9. (also v.10- 12).*

4. They rejected God's warning to repent. They stopped their spiritual progress through unbelief: *"Yet the LORD testified against Israel, and against Judah, by all the prophets, and by all the seers, saying, Turn ye from your evil ways, and keep my commandments and my statutes, according to all the law which I commanded your fathers, and which I sent to you by my servants the prophets. Notwithstanding they would not hear, but hardened their necks, like to the neck of their fathers, that did not believe in the LORD their God." 2 Kings 17:13,14.*

5. They became profane and political. They used religion only to endear themselves to others: *"And they rejected his statutes, and his covenant that he made with their fathers, and his testimonies which he testified against them; and they followed vanity, and became vain, and went after the heathen that were round about them, concerning whom the LORD had charged them, that they should not do like them." 2 Kings 17:15.*

6. They embraced apostasy: *"And they left all the commandments of the LORD their God, and made them molten images, even two calves, and made a grove, and worshipped all the host of heaven, and served Baal."* 2 Kings 17:16.

7. Finally, they sold themselves to do evil; they became reprobate. They could no longer tell good from evil; they could only relate to expediency: *"And they caused their sons and their daughters to pass through the fire, and used divination and enchantments, and sold themselves to do evil in the sight of the LORD, to provoke him to anger."* 2 Kings 17:17.

8. God gave them up: *"Therefore the LORD was very angry with Israel, and removed them out of his sight: there was none left but the tribe of Judah only."* 2 Kings 17:18.

Ezra retold the story of the kings in the Chronicles from the perspective of looking for the Messiah. His commentary gives spiritual insight into the history of the kings. He only mentions the Northern Kingdom in its relation to Judah because the Northern Kingdom repudiated the Messiah and Jerusalem.

The Southern Kingdom retained its hope of the Messiah. The faithful ones from Israel immigrated to Judah to worship the Lord during the time of Rehoboam and Jeroboam (2 Chronicles 11:13-17). There were still many good things in Judah during Rehoboam's time, and when Abijah began his rule.

Abijah condemned the apostasy of Israel and defeated Jeroboam on the battlefield (2 Chronicles 13). Yet, God did not commend him: *"And he walked in all the sins of his father, which he had done before him: and his heart was not perfect with the LORD his God, as the heart of David his father. Nevertheless for David's sake did the LORD his God give him a lamp in Jerusalem, to set up his son after him, and to establish Jerusalem:"* 1 Kings 15:3,4.

Asa, the next king, received a commendation from the Lord because of his faith and his reforms. Asa condemned immorality and idolatry (1 Kings 15:12). He took away many of the high places (2 Chronicles 14:3-5). He even publicly condemned the idolatry of the queen, Maacah, his grandmother (1 Kings 15:13; 2 Chronicles 15:16).

Asa's revival began, like all revivals, with the Lord's intervention. The Lord answered Asa's prayer in the defeat of the million-man army of the Ethiopians. God Himself fought for Judah (2 Chronicles 14:9-15). Afterward, the Lord confirmed His moving with a prophet sent to Asa (2 Chronicles 15:1-7): *"Be ye strong therefore, and let not your hands be weak: for your work shall be rewarded." 2 Chronicles 15:7.* These are words of comfort to those in spiritual young adulthood.

Then Asa instituted his reforms. There were also converts from the Northern Kingdom during this time. Perhaps they felt that Asa might be the "one" or the beginning of better things. The people's hope was renewed under Asa: *"And he gathered all Judah and Benjamin, and the strangers with them out of Ephraim and Manasseh, and out of Simeon: for they fell to him out of Israel in abundance, when they saw that the LORD his God was with him…And they entered into a covenant to seek the LORD God of their fathers with all their heart and with all their soul;" 2 Chronicles 15: 9,12.*

But Asa's fervor for the Lord waned, and when he was tested in his old age, he blinked. Baasha the king of Israel declared war on him, and instead of trusting God like in the war with the Ethiopians; he hired the Syrians to help him. This underscored two principles of spiritual young adulthood: *"And at that time Hanani the seer came to Asa king of Judah, and said unto him, Because thou hast relied on the king of Syria, and not relied on the LORD thy God, therefore is the host of the king of Syria escaped out of thine hand. Were not the Ethiopians and the Lubims a huge host, with very many chariots and horsemen? yet, because thou didst rely on the LORD, he delivered them into thine hand. For the eyes of the LORD run to and fro throughout the whole earth, to shew himself strong in the behalf of them whose heart is perfect toward him. Herein thou hast done foolishly: therefore from henceforth thou shalt have wars." 2 Chronicles 16:7-9.*

Principle 1: God often brings conflict and tribulation into our lives in order to expand our influence. Perhaps Israel would have hired the Syrians in God's plan to have Asa defeat them both. But Asa's fear precluded his victory over the Syrians. God may have also planned to renew Israel to the king of Judah, as had been prophesied (1 Kings 11:39). Asa's focus was too narrow. He defeated the Israelites in battle, but did not seek to bring them back into the kingdom. The true son of David would have been concerned with reconciliation.

Principle 2: God is constantly seeking to reward integrity of character and faith in Him. But that integrity has to be unwavering. Asa became complacent and unwatchful. He let his spiritual muscles atrophy and was not courageous at the time of his potential triumph. Perhaps he was only waiting to pass on in peace. He may have given up on any more gains for God's kingdom. It is necessary that the spiritual young adult stay ready even when many years pass and the dream seems impossible.

At the end of his life, Asa became diseased in his feet. He did not seek the Lord but only the physicians, and was not healed (2 Chronicles 16:12). This attitude shows the difficulty of repentance when one has fallen from such great spiritual heights.

Asa was close to God's ideal, and he showed great character during his life, but he was not Shiloh: *"And Asa did that which was good and right in the eyes of the LORD his God:"* 2 Chronicles 14:2.

Jehoshaphat, Asa's son, was also zealous for the Lord, and received high praise in the scriptures (2 Chronicles 17:3-6). He sent out teaching princes of the scriptures into all the land (v. 7-9). He continued moral reform by banishing the sodomites (1 Kings 22:46). He brought the Philistines and Arabians under tribute (v.10-11). He also had an army of 1,160,000 soldiers.

Jehoshaphat determined that Israel would not be won back through war, so instead he sought to bring them back to the Lord through peaceful means. He chose Solomon's method of making alliances through marriage. He arranged for his heir, Jehoram, to marry Ahab's daughter, Athaliah.

This strategy led to unwise compromises with the wicked northern kings. Jehoshaphat agreed to go with Ahab to recapture lost Israeli territory from the Syrians (2 Chronicles 18). Before leaving for the battle, Jehoshaphat tried to be a good role model to Ahab by asking for a prophecy from the Lord. Ahab ignored the true prophecy of Micaiah and was killed by an archer whose arrow accidentally slipped.

Upon Jehoshaphat's return to Judah, he was rebuked by the prophet for compromising with the apostates: *"And Jehu the son of Hanani the seer went out to meet him, and said to king Jehoshaphat, Shouldest thou help the ungodly, and love them that hate the LORD? therefore is wrath upon thee from before the LORD. Nevertheless there are good things found in thee, in that thou hast taken away the groves out of the land, and hast prepared thine heart to seek God."* 2 Chronicles 19:2,3.

Jehoshaphat's attempt at reconciliation seemed to be wise, but it led to evil. Instead of waiting on God's intervention, he chose one that made sense in human terms. This is a common mistake in spiritual young adulthood. Because of Jehoshaphat's error, the preparation for the Messiah was derailed for four generations. Instead of winning Israel back, the kings of Judah were influenced by evil.

After Jehoshaphat's rebuke, he instituted further reforms. He went out himself as an ambassador of the Lord to the people (2 Chronicles 19:4). He set up a civil government in every city (v.5-7). He also set up an ecclesiastical court in Jerusalem to judge spiritual matters (v. 8).

Jehoshaphat relied on the Lord when attacked by the Moabites, Ammonites, and Edomites. He appealed to God's revealed will concerning the holy place and holy people. God heard his prayer and caused the invaders to turn on one another. In this Jehoshaphat corrected the precedent of his father, who hired mercenaries to help him against Israel: *"O our God, wilt thou not judge them? for we have no might against this great company that cometh against us; neither know we what to do: but our eyes are upon thee...And he said, Hearken ye, all Judah, and ye inhabitants of Jerusalem, and thou king Jehoshaphat, Thus saith the LORD unto you, Be not afraid nor dismayed by reason of this great multitude; for the battle is not yours, but God's...Ye shall not need to fight in this battle: set yourselves, stand ye still, and see the salvation of the LORD with you, O Judah and Jerusalem: fear not, nor be dismayed; to morrow go out against them: for the LORD will be with you."* 2 Chronicles 20:12, 15, 17.

Jehoshaphat appeared to have second thoughts about his alliance with the kings of Israel. Nevertheless, Ahab's son persuaded him to join together and build ships with which to trade. God condemned the league again and caused the ships to founder at Eziongeber (1 Kings 22:48-49; 2 Chronicles 20:35-37): *"Then Eliezer the son of Dodavah of Mareshah prophesied against Jehoshaphat, saying, Because thou hast joined thyself with Ahaziah, the LORD hath broken thy works. And the ships were broken, that they were not able to go to Tarshish."* 2 Chronicles 20:37.

Even though Judah had two great kings in a row, they still persisted in their sins. Both Asa and Jehoshaphat condemned the high places, and yet there were some left. The people were not ready for the Messiah: *"Howbeit the high places were not taken away: for as yet the people had not prepared their hearts unto the God of their fathers."* 2 Chronicles 20:33.

Jehoram, son-in-law to Ahab, husband of Athaliah, and lastly king of Judah, became an apostate through the influence of his wife. Her queen mother Jezebel had been a good teacher of how to turn the followers of the Lord to Baal. Jehoram was prepared to betray the Lord, Jehoshaphat, and Judah even before his father's death.

Jehoshaphat had given Jehoram a double portion and the kingdom because he was the firstborn, but he had also given other sons riches and cities in Judah. Jehoram's first act was to murder his brothers and the teaching princes. In this he prevented the voice of dissent against his apostasy (2 Chronicles 21:1-4).

After the teaching princes had been quashed, Jehoram introduced Baal worship into Judah and compelled the people to follow: *"And he walked in the way of the kings of Israel, like as did the house of Ahab: for he had the daughter of Ahab to wife: and he wrought that which was evil in the eyes of the*

LORD...Moreover he made high places in the mountains of Judah, and caused the inhabitants of Jerusalem to commit fornication, and compelled Judah thereto." 2 Chronicles 21:6, 11.

Jehoram's apostasy led to revolt against Judah and weakened the positioning of his father and grandfather. Edom revolted and made themselves a king (v.8). The Philistines and Arabians, who had been under tribute to Jehoshaphat, broke into Jerusalem and looted the king's house, taking away his wives and every son except the youngest (v.16, 17). Libnah, the strongest of Judah's fortified cities and the home of the true priests of the Lord (1 Chronicles 6:54-57), revolted because of the apostasy (v.10).

Elijah the prophet sent a letter to Jehoram predicting evil on him and his kingdom because of the apostasy: *"And there came a writing to him from Elijah the prophet, saying, Thus saith the LORD God of David thy father, Because thou hast not walked in the ways of Jehoshaphat thy father, nor in the ways of Asa king of Judah, But hast walked in the way of the kings of Israel, and hast made Judah and the inhabitants of Jerusalem to go a whoring, like to the whoredoms of the house of Ahab, and also hast slain thy brethren of thy father's house, which were better than thyself: Behold, with a great plague will the LORD smite thy people, and thy children, and thy wives, and all thy goods: And thou shalt have great sickness by disease of thy bowels, until thy bowels fall out by reason of the sickness day by day." 2 Chronicles 21:12-15.*

The people did not mourn for him nor did they bury him with the other kings (v.20).

In short, Jehoram was a disaster. He moved Judah back away from the Messiah, but not irrevocably: *"Howbeit the LORD would not destroy the house of David, because of the covenant that he had made with David, and as he promised to give a light to him and to his sons for ever." 2 Chronicles 21:7.*

After Jehoram's death, Athaliah in effect ruled as queen. Ahaziah, their remaining son, became king in name only. Athaliah counseled him to continue the conversion of the people to Baal worship (2 Chronicles 22:1-4).

Ahaziah's alliance with the house of Ahab became his downfall, because of God's judgment against Ahab. Ahaziah helped his cousin Joram the king of Israel to war against Syria. When Joram was injured, Ahaziah went with him to Jezreel, and was killed by Jehu the executioner (2 Chronicles 22:5-9): *"And the destruction of Ahaziah was of God by coming to Joram: for when he was come, he went out with Jehoram against Jehu the son of Nimshi, whom the LORD had anointed to cut off the house of Ahab." 2 Chronicles 22:7.*

Athaliah was determined to rule even after Ahaziah's death and to enforce the worship of Baal. She must have been angered by Jehu's slaughter of her mother

Jezebel and her family, so she killed all of her grandsons who would be natural heirs to the throne of David: *"But when Athaliah the mother of Ahaziah saw that her son was dead, she arose and destroyed all the seed royal of the house of Judah." 2 Chronicles 22:10.*

The dream of the Messiah would have been lost except that Athaliah's daughter Jehoshabeath, the wife of the high priest, hid Joash, the king's son, in the Temple (2 Chronicles 22:11-12). Apparently, her priest husband Jehoiada had converted Jehoshabeath to the worship of God. Most likely, their marriage was meant to confirm the conversion to Baal through the house of Ahab, and to legitimize it through the high priest, but Jehoiada used it as an opportunity to win the people back to God.

Athaliah ruled over Judah for six years as the queen. And in the seventh year, in one day, she was dethroned and Baal worship was overthrown. Jehoiada the priest arranged a coup. He had not dismissed the courses of the Levites, which served the Temple (2 Chronicles 23:8). They must have seemed a mere window dressing toAthaliah, with no real significance. Jehoiada used the courses of Temple service to bring men to the Temple to protect Joash in the coup. He armed the men with David's old instruments of war that were in the Temple (v.9). *"Then they brought out the king's son, and put upon him the crown, and gave him the testimony, and made him king. And Jehoiada and his sons anointed him, and said, God save the king." 2 Chronicles 23:11.*

Athaliah said "Treason, treason," but she was executed, along with all who followed her (v.12-15). Athaliah had learned by the example of the Northern Kingdom that assassination was an acceptable way to gain the throne, but in Judah they still believed that God would only honor a descendent of David: *"And all the congregation made a covenant with the king in the house of God. And he said unto them, Behold, the king's son shall reign, as the LORD hath said of the sons of David." 2 Chronicles 23:3.*

On the same day Jehoiada condemned Baal worship and re-established the official worship of God: *"And Jehoiada made a covenant between him, and between all the people, and between the king, that they should be the LORD'S people. Then all the people went to the house of Baal, and brake it down, and brake his altars and his images in pieces, and slew Mattan the priest of Baal before the altars." 2 Chronicles 23:16,17.*

Joash was only seven years old when his reign began, and he had Jehoiada the high priest for his counselor. Joash and Jehoiada repaired the Temple that had been damaged and pilfered during the time of Baal (2 Chronicles 24:7). They used the collection for the tabernacle required by the Law of Moses (Exodus 30:11-16). The collection money was used to make new vessels and instruments for the sacrifices, which were kept up continually during the time of Jehoiada (2 Chronicles 24:13-14).

But Jehoiada died in the middle of Joash's reign at the age of 130. The people honored him as God's representative and defender of the hope of Israel by burying him among the kings (2 Chronicles 24:16).

Afterward, Joash gave in to political pressure from the former Baal worshippers and allowed them to resume their practices (2 Chronicles 24:17-18). God testified against this lapse and compromise, but the king and people did not perceive its seriousness (v.19).

At last, the new high priest, Zechariah, Joash's cousin, denounced the compromise (v.20). Joash refused to go back on his word and instead condemned Zechariah as a seditionist. Zechariah was stoned in the court of the Lord's house (v.21), an event recalled by Jesus Christ (Matthew 23:35): *"Thus Joash the king remembered not the kindness which Jehoiada his father had done to him, but slew his son. And when he died, he said, The LORD look upon it, and require it." 2 Chronicles 24:22.*

God did require it. The Syrians came and destroyed the Baal worshipping princes and spoiled the country (v.23-24). Joash was assassinated by his own servants because of his betrayal of the Lord and because of his violence against Jehoiada's son. Joash was not buried with the kings as Jehoiada had been (v.25).

Amaziah, the next king, tried to repair some of the damage to the dream of the Messiah, but the influence of the past few generations hampered him. He was unable to rise above the bad examples of the recent past: *"And he did that which was right in the sight of the LORD, yet not like David his father: he did according to all things as Joash his father did." 2 Kings 14:3. "And he did that which was right in the sight of the LORD, but not with a perfect heart." 2 Chronicles 25:2.*

Amaziah followed David's example by executing the conspirators who had killed the Lord's anointed (2 Samuel 1:13-16; 2 Chronicles 25:3-4). He then gathered an army to put Edom back under tribute, which had rebelled against Jehoram. His mistake was that he hired mercenaries from Israel to help him (2 Chronicles 25:6). Apparently, he felt this wasn't the same mistake as joining in league with them as Jehoshaphat had done. Amaziah was rebuked by the Lord's prophet for this and warned that he would lose if Israel helped. He then reluctantly released the mercenaries (v. 7-10).

Amaziah defeated the Edomites with his own forces, but then brought back the idol gods of the Edomites as a trophy (v.14). He had been taught by his recent family history to think of gods as Baalim: that each god ruled over a certain territory and that if you defeated an enemy you defeated the god also, and as a corollary that you had power over a territory if you had its god. The Philistines practiced this principle when they captured the Ark of the Covenant and put it in the house of Dagon (1 Samuel 5:2).

God sent a prophet to Amaziah to teach him that the Lord rules over all, and is not like Baalim. The prophet attempted to persuade Amaziah of his error: *"Wherefore the anger of the LORD was kindled against Amaziah, and he sent unto him a prophet, which said unto him, Why hast thou sought after the gods of the people, which could not deliver their own people out of thine hand?" 2 Chronicles 25:15.*

Amaziah then recalled his father's ways by threatening the prophet: *"And it came to pass, as he talked with him, that the king said unto him, Art thou made of the king's counsel? forbear; why shouldest thou be smitten? Then the prophet forbare, and said, I know that God hath determined to destroy thee, because thou hast done this, and hast not hearkened unto my counsel." 2 Chronicles 25:16.*

By now, Amaziah was way off track, and he was embarrassed and angry about the Israeli mercenary fiasco. They took the opportunity after he released them to spoil the unprotected cities of Judah (v.13). He gathered his army to war against Israel. The king of Israel (Joash) declined at first to fight but Amaziah insisted: *"But Amaziah would not hear; for it came of God, that he might deliver them into the hand of their enemies, because they sought after the gods of Edom." 2 Chronicles 25:20.*

Judah was put to the worse before Israel (v.22). Joash broke down 600 feet of the wall of Jerusalem, stole from the house of God and the king's house, and took hostages (v.22-24).

Amaziah did not repent from his errors, and drifted from God's design. Finally, the people rose up against him and executed him (v.25-28).

The people made Uzziah king when he was only sixteen. Uzziah saw the results of the backsliding of his father. He emulated the first part of Amaziah's reign in following the Lord and listened to a godly counselor, a prophet named Zechariah (2 Chronicles 26:4-5).

Uzziah followed up on his father's subjugation of Edom by building Eloth on the site of former Eziongeber at the end of the Sinai Peninsula. Then he colonized the land of the Philistines (he accomplished this by breaking down the walls of fortified Philistine cities), and put theAmmonites under tribute (v.6-8).

Uzziah became a great military king. He fortified Jerusalem, built towers in the desert, and manufactured catapults and arrow throwers. Uzziah developed a professional standing army of 2600 officers and 307,500 soldiers. The king armed his soldiers by continuously manufacturing weapons. Apparently, he was always in search of better and more efficient armaments (v. 9-15).

"But when he was strong, his heart was lifted up to his destruction: for he transgressed against the LORD his God, and went into the temple of the LORD to burn incense upon the altar of incense." 2 Chronicles 26:16. Uzziah had rest from his enemies and perfected his role as civil king over many years. He may have even felt he was a candidate to be God's chosen one. Perhaps Uzziah understood from David's prophecies about the Messiah that God would accept him as a priest even though he was of the tribe of Judah. The relevant scripture is Psalm 110: *"<<A Psalm of David.>> The LORD said unto my Lord, Sit thou at my right hand, until I make thine enemies thy footstool. The LORD shall send the rod of thy strength out of Zion: rule thou in the midst of thine enemies." Psalms 110:1,2.* Uzziah must have felt he had already accomplished this prophecy. *"The LORD hath sworn, and will not repent, Thou art a priest for ever after the order of Melchizedek." Psalms 110:4.* Uzziah went into the Temple to test God's acceptance of him as a priest.

His answer came in two parts. The first was a rebuke by the high priest and eighty others. They told him that he did not have the right to offer incense and that God would not honor his attempt: *"And they withstood Uzziah the king, and said unto him, It appertaineth not unto thee, Uzziah, to burn incense unto the LORD, but to the priests the sons of Aaron, that are consecrated to burn incense: go out of the sanctuary; for thou hast trespassed; neither shall it be for thine honour from the LORD God." 2 Chronicles 26:18.*

The second was a sudden case of leprosy in Uzziah's forehead. The leprosy signified that God had put Uzziah back under the ecclesiastical authority of the priests, for it was their job to rule on leprosy (Leviticus 13-14). The lifelong leprosy also left him outside the congregation. He became unclean. He did not become a priest after the order of Melchizedek, and he could not even worship at the house of the Lord: *"Then Uzziah was wroth, and had a censer in his hand to burn incense: and while he was wroth with the priests, the leprosy even rose up in his forehead before the priests in the house of the LORD, from beside the incense altar. And Azariah the chief priest, and all the priests, looked upon him, and, behold, he was leprous in his forehead, and they thrust him out from thence; yea, himself hasted also to go out, because the LORD had smitten him. And Uzziah the king was a leper unto the day of his death, and dwelt in a several house, being a leper; for he was cut off from the house of the LORD: and Jotham his son was over the king's house, judging the people of the land." 2 Chronicles 26:19-21.*

They did not bury Uzziah in the honored sepulchres of the kings because of his leprosy (v.23). The results of his presumption are another warning against trying to help God fulfill the vision in spiritual young adulthood. Notice that it was in Uzziah's young adulthood that he went into the Temple: *"But when he was strong, his heart was lifted up to his destruction."*

Jotham had the benefit of a living testimony of humility in his father Uzziah after the trespass. He was required to rule in the place of his Uzziah while he still lived. The scriptures give Jotham high marks in integrity and righteousness: *"So Jotham became mighty, because he prepared his ways before the LORD his God." 2 Chronicles 27:6.*

Jotham continued the fortification building of his father. He built towers in the mountains and in the forests to go with the previous ones in the desert. Jotham also defeated the Ammonites after they rebelled and forced them to pay tribute (v.3- 5). And even though he strengthened Judah militarily he did not make his father's error of exalting himself by intruding on the priesthood. Instead he waited on God's judgment: *"And he did that which was right in the sight of the LORD, according to all that his father Uzziah did: howbeit he entered not into the temple of the LORD" 2 Chronicles 27:2a, b.*

"And the people did yet corruptly." 2 Chronicles 27:2c. Although Judah had some good kings, and a succession of two very godly kings, they still fell farther in their backsliding. The people were confident in their hope of the Messiah and they felt little need to live exactly by the letter of God's will. They believed God would honor them anyway. They continued to use the high places even after repeated warnings and they were lax in their morals (2 Kings 15:35). They did not remember that the honor of God's promise would only come to a prepared people.

Isaiah described their state in his first chapter: *"Thy princes are rebellious, and companions of thieves: every one loveth gifts, and followeth after rewards: they judge not the fatherless, neither doth the cause of the widow come unto them." Isaiah 1:23.* He also prescribed the cure for their corruption and the consequences of further rebellion: *"Wash you, make you clean; put away the evil of your doings from before mine eyes; cease to do evil; Learn to do well; seek judgment, relieve the oppressed, judge the fatherless, plead for the widow. Come now, and let us reason together, saith the LORD: though your sins be as scarlet, they shall be as white as snow; though they be red like crimson, they shall be as wool. If ye be willing and obedient, ye shall eat the good of the land: But if ye refuse and rebel, ye shall be devoured with the sword: for the mouth of the LORD hath spoken it." Isaiah 1:16-20.*

Ahaz, the next king, followed the lead of the people instead of leading them to greater righteousness. He is condemned in the scriptures for following the ways of paganism and Baalim. Ahaz increased the number of high places and worship centers outside of Jerusalem. He even went so far as to sacrifice his own children in false worship. Ahaz apparently believed in pleasing as many gods as possible; as if worshipping an enemies' god would win him favor over them in battle (2 Chronicles 28:1-4). He worshipped the gods of Syria and Assyria, as well as the Lord (2 Chronicles 28:23; 2 Kings 16:10-16).

During the time of Ahaz, Assyria became a threat to the entire region. Israel and Syria made a league and hoped to bring Judah into it to defend the region (2 Kings 16:5). Ahaz apparently refused to join the league but instead showed deference to Assyria (2 Kings 16:7). Therefore, Israel and Syria spoiled Judah to finance their wars and tried to set up a puppet king favorable to them (Isaiah 7.1-7). The two kings were unsuccessful in capturing Jerusalem and this allowed Ahaz time to appeal to Assyria (2 Kings 16:5-8). The king of Israel, seeing he could not capture Jerusalem, slaughtered 120,000 soldiers in Judah and captured 200,000 people. Nevertheless, a prophet of the Lord shamed the Israelites into letting the captives return (2 Chronicles 28:6-15).

Meanwhile, Ahaz's appeal to Tiglathpileser, king of Assyria, was partially successful. Assyria conquered Damascus, killed Rezin the king, and deported the Syrians to a place called Kir (2 Kings 16:9). Tiglathpileser also annexed the eastern and northern portions of Israel into his empire and carried many away as captives (2 Kings 15:29).

The success ended there. Ahaz, in order to buy Assyria's help, and to keep them from taking Judah also, gave Tiglathpileser presents from the king's house and from the Lord's house (2 Chronicles 28:20-21). Ahaz then changed worship procedures in Israel and closed the Temple in order to show deference to the king of Assyria. In effect, he surrendered to Assyria's gods (2 Chronicles 28:24-25; 2 Kings 16:17-18).

At the same time, because of Ahaz's weakened position, the Edomites and Philistines rebelled and attacked Judah (2 Chronicles 28: 17-18). *"For the LORD brought Judah low because of Ahaz king of Israel; for he made Judah naked, and transgressed sore against the LORD." 2 Chronicles 28:19.*

Even during all these negative events, God through Isaiah revealed more about the coming Messiah to unbelieving Ahaz. Perhaps this was to lead him to repentance and to keep the people's focus on the treasure and not on present circumstances. Isaiah's prophecy's to Ahaz lodged deeply in the consciousness of Judah and influenced events far into the future.

First of all, Isaiah told Ahaz to not be afraid of Israel and Syria, since God was preparing to destroy them as kingdoms: *"For the head of Syria is Damascus, and the head of Damascus is Rezin; and within threescore and five years shall Ephraim be broken, that it be not a people." Isaiah 7:8. (also Isaiah 7:16*).

Secondly, Isaiah prophesied that God Himself, in person (Immanuel = God with us), would save them and give them a preview of the Messiah's work. The "virgin birth" in this first fulfillment signified that human agency would not be required: *"And he said, Hear ye now, O house of David; Is it a small thing for you to weary men, but will ye weary my God also? Therefore the Lord himself shall give you a sign; Behold, a virgin shall conceive, and bear a son, and shall call his name Immanuel. Butter and honey shall he eat, that he may know to refuse the evil, and choose the good. For before the child shall know to refuse the evil, and choose the good, the land that thou abhorrest shall be forsaken of both her kings." Isaiah 7:13-16.*

He warned Ahaz and the people to not make any confederacy, but trust in Immanuel, God with us (Isaiah 8:10): *"Say ye not, A confederacy, to all them to whom this people shall say, A confederacy; neither fear ye their fear, nor be afraid. Sanctify the LORD of hosts himself; and let him be your fear, and let him be your dread. And he shall be for a sanctuary; but for a stone of stumbling and for a rock of offence to both the houses of Israel, for a gin and for a snare to the inhabitants of Jerusalem. And many among them shall stumble, and fall, and be broken, and be snared, and be taken. Bind up the testimony, seal the law among my disciples. And I will wait upon the LORD, that hideth his face from the house of Jacob, and I will look for him. Behold, I and the children whom the LORD hath given me are for signs and for wonders in Israel from the LORD of hosts, which dwelleth in mount Zion." Isaiah 8:12-18.*

Thirdly, Assyria would indeed invade Judah as God's purifier of the people but would not be able to conquer Jerusalem: *"The LORD shall bring upon thee, and upon thy people, and upon thy father's house, days that have not come, from the day that Ephraim departed from Judah; even the king of Assyria." Isaiah 7:17. "And he shall pass through Judah; he shall overflow and go over, he shall reach even to the neck; and the stretching out of his wings shall fill the breadth of thy land, O Immanuel." Isaiah 8:8. "Therefore thus saith the Lord GOD of hosts, O my people that dwellest in Zion, be not afraid of the Assyrian: he shall smite thee with a rod, and shall lift up his staff against thee, after the manner of Egypt. For yet a very little while, and the indignation shall cease, and mine anger in their destruction." Isaiah 10:24,25.*

Finally, Isaiah prophesied that the Messiah would take the remnant of Israel and Judah, unite them in one purpose, and conquer the world: *"And in that day there shall be a root of Jesse, which shall stand for an ensign of the people;*

to it shall the Gentiles seek: and his rest shall be glorious. And it shall come to pass in that day, that the Lord shall set his hand again the second time to recover the remnant of his people, which shall be left, from Assyria, and from Egypt, and from Pathros, and from Cush, and from Elam, and from Shinar, and from Hamath, and from the islands of the sea. And he shall set up an ensign for the nations, and shall assemble the outcasts of Israel, and gather together the dispersed of Judah from the four corners of the earth. The envy also of Ephraim shall depart, and the adversaries of Judah shall be cut off: Ephraim shall not envy Judah, and Judah shall not vex Ephraim. But they shall fly upon the shoulders of the Philistines toward the west; they shall spoil them of the east together: they shall lay their hand upon Edom and Moab; and the children of Ammon shall obey them." Isaiah 11:10-14.

Isaiah gives the strongest prophecy yet of the Messiah in the light of these events. He would recover the lost portions of Israel that Assyria would take: *"Nevertheless the dimness shall not be such as was in her vexation, when at the first he lightly afflicted the land of Zebulun and the land of Naphtali, and afterward did more grievously afflict her by the way of the sea, beyond Jordan, in Galilee of the nations. The people that walked in darkness have seen a great light: they that dwell in the land of the shadow of death, upon them hath the light shined." Isaiah 9:1,2. (2 Kings 15:29).*

Then He would become the eternal prince upon David's throne: *"For unto us a child is born, unto us a son is given: and the government shall be upon his shoulder: and his name shall be called Wonderful, Counsellor, The mighty God, The everlasting Father, The Prince of Peace. Of the increase of his government and peace there shall be no end, upon the throne of David, and upon his kingdom, to order it, and to establish it with judgment and with justice from henceforth even for ever. The zeal of the LORD of hosts will perform this." Isaiah 9:6,7.*

"And Ahaz slept with his fathers, and they buried him in the city, even in Jerusalem: but they brought him not into the sepulchres of the kings of Israel: and Hezekiah his son reigned in his stead." 2 Chronicles 28:27.

Hezekiah believed Isaiah and purposed in his heart to have faith in the promise of Immanuel. He ordered his actions according to God's prophecy through Isaiah. He became the greatest king since David: *"And he did that which was right in the sight of the LORD, according to all that David his father did…He trusted in the LORD God of Israel; so that after him was none like him among all the kings of Judah, nor any that were before him." 2 Kings 18:3, 5.*

Hezekiah's first act was to reopen and cleanse the Temple (2 Chronicles 29:3-19). His explanation was that he purposed to make a new covenant to God:

"Now it is in mine heart to make a covenant with the LORD God of Israel, that his fierce wrath may turn away from us." 2 Chronicles 29:10.

Next, Hezekiah called all of Israel to dedicate themselves to God with offerings at the Temple. He started with the sin offering, which symbolizes repentance, for Judah and all Israel (2 Chronicles 29:23-24). By including Israel he followed Isaiah's word that they would be joined together. Then he offered the burnt offering, which symbolizes dedication to God, and encouraged the people to do so also (v.27-31). Finally, Hezekiah and the people gave thank offerings and peace offerings, which symbolize the renewed relationship with God (v.31, 35).

"And Hezekiah rejoiced, and all the people, that God had prepared the people: for the thing was done suddenly." 2 Chronicles 29:36. Like Asa's revival, this one started with the Lord's intervention, and seemed to occur spontaneously. The Lord's intervention was the work of grace in Hezekiah and the people. No amount of human effort can start a revival, only people who humbly submit to God's grace.

The king and the people then worked to observe a nationwide Passover that included Israel (the last northern king, Hoshea, had no power to prevent the Israelites from worshipping in Jerusalem, as he was busy resisting the Assyrians): *"And Hezekiah sent to all Israel and Judah, and wrote letters also to Ephraim and Manasseh, that they should come to the house of the LORD at Jerusalem, to keep the passover unto the LORD God of Israel." 2 Chronicles 30:1.*

Hezekiah rightly saw that God could reverse His judgment against Israel and bring them again into a united nation if they would repent. He also showed faith in the prophecy that the lost portions would be recovered: *"So the posts went with the letters from the king and his princes throughout all Israel and Judah, and according to the commandment of the king, saying, Ye children of Israel, turn again unto the LORD God of Abraham, Isaac, and Israel, and he will return to the remnant of you, that are escaped out of the hand of the kings of Assyria…For if ye turn again unto the LORD, your brethren and your children shall find compassion before them that lead them captive, so that they shall come again into this land: for the LORD your God is gracious and merciful, and will not turn away his face from you, if ye return unto him." 2 Chronicles 30:6, 9.*

Hezekiah received a partial response to his invitation: many laughed at the messengers, but many also went to the Passover: *"So the posts passed from city to city through the country of Ephraim and Manasseh even unto Zebulun: but they laughed them to scorn, and mocked them. Nevertheless divers of Asher and Manasseh and of Zebulun humbled themselves, and came to Jerusalem." 2 Chronicles 30:10,11.*

The Passover was kept the right way, with all Israel present (v. 5), and the people rejoiced. It seemed God might finally be prepared to fulfill His promises to Israel: *"So there was great joy in Jerusalem: for since the time of Solomon the son of David king of Israel there was not the like in Jerusalem." 2 Chronicles 30:26.*

"Now when all this was finished, all Israel that were present went out to the cities of Judah, and brake the images in pieces, and cut down the groves, and threw down the high places and the altars out of all Judah and Benjamin, in Ephraim also and Manasseh, until they had utterly destroyed them all. Then all the children of Israel returned, every man to his possession, into their own cities." 2 Chronicles 31:1. The people renounced and purged the high places, which represented heresy. By this they continued their push toward revival. Hezekiah even destroyed the brazen serpent of Moses and called it Nehushtan, "just a piece of brass" (2 Kings 18:4). The Assyrian king gave testimony to the completeness of his reforms (2 Chronicles 32:12).

Hezekiah had a long list of accomplishments. He restored the priesthood and the work of the Levites (2 Chronicles 31). He expanded the book of Proverbs (Proverbs 25:1). He fought back against the Philistines and reached as far as Gaza (2 Kings 18:8). He successfully rebelled against the king of Assyria (2Kings18:7), and Hezekiah became the richest king since Solomon (2 Chronicles 32:27-30).

A big test came in his fourteenth year, eight years after Israel was carried away by Shalmaneser, king of Assyria: *"Now in the fourteenth year of king Hezekiah did Sennacherib king of Assyria come up against all the fenced cities of Judah, and took them." 2 Kings 18:13.* The Bible gives these events great significance, as the story was told three times: in 2 Kings, 2 Chronicles, and Isaiah. The Assyrians continued their westward campaign. They had already taken Syria and Israel. Now they desired Judah as a base to proceed against Egypt. They were able to conquer every fortress in Judah except Jerusalem, as Isaiah had predicted (Isaiah 8:8; 10:24-34).

Hezekiah feigned submission by agreeing to pay tribute again. Sennacherib accepted the bribe but treacherously looked to attack anyway (2 Kings 18:14-15). He sent his officer, Rabshakeh, to Jerusalem for psychological warfare while he fought against Lachish.

The Rabshekah spoke in the Jews language so the civilian people could understand also, and he used the prophesies of Isaiah against them. His three charges were these:

1. You are trusting in Egypt to help you (Isaiah 36:6). TheAssyrians learned that Isaiah had condemned help from Egypt: *"For the Egyptians shall help in*

vain, and to no purpose: therefore have I cried concerning this, Their strength is to sit still." Isaiah 30:7.

2. You have offended the Lord by taking down the high places (Isaiah 36:7; 2 Chronicles 31:1). Although the removal of the high places and the re-establishment of Jerusalem as the place of worship was definitely God's will, the people had believed for generations that the local high places were honoring to God. The Rabshekah took advantage of the heresy that had been allowed to go on. He hoped to make them believe they had made a mistake, and he may have actually felt they had dishonored their gods, since he was a believer in local Baalim.

3. You are disobeying God by not yielding, because He has commissioned me to conquer this land (Isaiah 36:10). Isaiah had indeed spoken of the commission of the Assyrians (Isaiah 7:17-20; 10:5), but he had also made it clear that Jerusalem would not fall: *"As birds flying, so will the LORD of hosts defend Jerusalem; defending also he will deliver it; and passing over he will preserve it." Isaiah 31:5.*

The Rabshekah concluded by offering the people an opportunity to surrender and be deported (Isaiah 36:16-17). He also warned them not to trust in God since no people's gods were able to resist the Assyrians (v.18-20). *"But they held their peace, and answered him not a word: for the king's commandment was, saying, Answer him not." Isaiah 36:21.*

Hezekiah, upon hearing all this, sent a delegation to Isaiah with an odd proverb: *"And they said unto him, Thus saith Hezekiah, This day is a day of trouble, and of rebuke, and of blasphemy: for the children are come to the birth, and there is not strength to bring forth." Isaiah 37:3.* In this Hezekiah reminded Isaiah of the prophecy that the Assyrians would be turned back, a remnant would survive, and to that remnant the Messiah would come. Hezekiah was saying that he still believed but was afraid: *"wherefore lift up thy prayer for the remnant that is left." Isaiah 37:4b. (also Isaiah 10:21).*

Isaiah answered by reassuring Hezekiah and prophesying that Sennacherib would hear a rumour of an approaching army, become afraid, return to Assyria, and be killed in his own land: all of which came to pass (Isaiah 37:6-7).

Sennacherib heard that the Ethiopians were coming against him, and as a last effort to secure Jerusalem as a base to defend himself, he magnified his psychological warfare and blasphemy against God: *"And he heard say concerning Tirhakah king of Ethiopia, He is come forth to make war with thee. And when he heard it, he sent messengers to Hezekiah, saying, Thus shall ye speak to Hezekiah king of Judah, saying, Let not thy God, in whom thou trustest, deceive thee, saying, Jerusalem shall not be given into the hand of the king of Assyria." Isaiah 37:9,10.*

This time, with more assurance, Hezekiah prayed directly to God. He took Sennacherib's letter to the Temple, spread it before the Lord, and prayed. He acknowledged God as ruler of all the earth, not just a local god like the Baalim. He acknowledged God's use of theAssyrians as punishment against idolatry. Then he asked God to save Jerusalem as a testimony to His sovereignty over the earth (Isaiah 37:16-20). Perhaps he was also expressing faith through this in God's Messiah, who would begin His kingdom at Jerusalem and extend it to the entire world (Isaiah 9:6-7; Isaiah 11).

Isaiah responded with God's message. Hezekiah sent for Isaiah the first time, but with his demonstration of increased faith, God sent Isaiah to him. God responded by saying that indeed the Assyrians were used as an instrument of His wrath, but now their time was up (Isaiah 37: 21-29). The people of Jerusalem would escape and once again prosper. God Himself, Immanuel, God with us, would defend and save Jerusalem: *"And this shall be a sign unto thee, Ye shall eat this year such as groweth of itself; and the second year that which springeth of the same: and in the third year sow ye, and reap, and plant vineyards, and eat the fruit thereof. And the remnant that is escaped of the house of Judah shall again take root downward, and bear fruit upward: For out of Jerusalem shall go forth a remnant, and they that escape out of mount Zion: the zeal of the LORD of hosts shall do this. Therefore thus saith the LORD concerning the king of Assyria, He shall not come into this city, nor shoot an arrow there, nor come before it with shields, nor cast a bank against it. By the way that he came, by the same shall he return, and shall not come into this city, saith the LORD. For I will defend this city to save it for mine own sake, and for my servant David's sake." Isaiah 37:30-35.*

"Then the angel of the LORD went forth, and smote in the camp of the Assyrians a hundred and fourscore and five thousand: and when they arose early in the morning, behold, they were all dead corpses." Isaiah 37:36. Immanuel did His work. The people were saved without human agency or intervention. Sennacherib returned to Nineveh in shame, where he was assassinated by two of his sons (v.37-38).

Vanity Fair

After successfully navigating the Valley of the Shadow of Death, Christian and Faithful made their way to Vanity Fair, where they were examined by the world and judged to be troublemakers. They would not buy anything at the fair but instead said, "We buy the truth."

With this Bunyan shows that a Christian in this stage of maturity (young adulthood) begins to look very strange to the world. He has rejected the world's values and doesn't fit in anymore. The people of the world become confused because their purpose is tied up in getting for themselves.

Christian and Faithful were put into a cage and made a spectacle to the people at the fair. They were accused by Envy, Superstition, and Pickthank (a flatterer). Faithful was condemned to death but Christian escaped by God's grace and power.[10]

Hezekiah's stand against theAssyrians was also a trial unto death. Judah lost every stronghold but Jerusalem. TheAssyrians ridiculed the people's faith in God and their strange customs. Yet, Hezekiah remained faithful and God caused the Assyrian army to leave off its siege of Jerusalem.

Pre Death of the Vision

Isaiah's prophecy to Ahaz had now been fulfilled except for the part about the Messiah and His kingdom. I imagine Hezekiah was expecting that soon. So it was a great shock when he was told he would die childless: *"In those days was Hezekiah sick unto death. And Isaiah the prophet the son of Amoz came unto him, and said unto him, Thus saith the LORD, Set thine house in order: for thou shalt die, and not live." Isaiah 38:1.* In other words, "make your will." Isaiah implies in a later statement that Hezekiah had no heirs at the time: *"And of thy sons that shall issue from thee, which thou shalt beget" Isaiah 39:7.*

Hezekiah was apparently stunned that God would cut him off because the Messiah had to come from the lineage of David the king. Up until this time, there was always hope with the Davidic Covenant that the Messiah could be the very next king. The idea that David's line would be wiped out, especially by God Himself, was unthinkable to Hezekiah and the people. He was not prepared to let himself go through the death of the vision. He forgot that Isaiah's prophecy to Ahaz that Immanuel would be born of a virgin: *"And he said, Hear ye now, O house of David; Is it a small thing for you to weary men, but will ye weary my God also? Therefore the Lord himself shall give you a sign; Behold, a virgin shall conceive, and bear a son, and shall call his name Immanuel." Isaiah 7:13,14.* God had just defeated the Assyrians without human agency; He could also produce an heir of David without human help.

Hezekiah blinked when he should have been watching. He was the greatest hope of Israel to fulfill the Davidic Covenant. Nevertheless, He failed at the crisis point of spiritual young adulthood. He did not look for God's supernatural intervention to overcome a seemingly impossible barrier. He reasoned that God would only send the Messiah through him, and so could not understand the new prophecy of his death. He forgot that God wants to show Himself strong through overcoming the impossible. The Messiah, like all treasures of spiritual young adulthood, could only be a gift of God, not a wage for human effort.

Therefore Hezekiah begged God for his life; I believe not so much because he was afraid to die, but because he was afraid that the dream and hope of Israel would die with him. The Messiah was not a notion at the back of his mind, but was the driving motivation of his life. He hoped to see the Messiah, his son or grandson: *"I said, I shall not see the LORD, even the LORD, in the land of the living: I shall behold man no more with the inhabitants of the world." Isaiah 38:11.*

To see his and Israel's dream cut down at the moment of fulfillment must have been excruciating, especially because he tried so hard. Hezekiah reminded God that he had faithfully followed the plan for the Davidic Covenant: *"I beseech thee, O LORD, remember now how I have walked before thee in truth and with a perfect heart, and have done that which is good in thy sight. And Hezekiah wept sore." 2 Kings 20:3.*

God granted Hezekiah's request to live. Not only that, but He gave Hezekiah the date of his death, fifteen years later. God promised that the Assyrians would never take Jerusalem. He also gave Hezekiah the sign of turning back time, which showed God's ability to reverse or overcome any obstacle to His will. Thus God shamed Hezekiah's lack of faith with a miracle (2 Kings 20:4-11).

The fifteen years gave Hezekiah time to father and partially raise sons. The guaranteed protection against the Assyrians gave Hezekiah confidence to devote his full attention to fathering. The sign gave Hezekiah a reminder of his lack of patience with God's ways. In effect, God was saying, "we'll do it your way. I'm giving you a chance to prepare the Messiah yourself": *"God left him, to try him, that he might know all that was in his heart." 2 Chronicles 32:31.*

The scripture records Hezekiah's performance: *"But Hezekiah rendered not again according to the benefit done unto him; for his heart was lifted up: therefore there was wrath upon him, and upon Judah and Jerusalem." 2 Chronicles 32:25.* Hezekiah's pride was not without basis: He had successfully put down heresy and re-established the central place of worship; he was the only king to successfully resist the Assyrians; and God had performed two miracles on his behalf (the defeat of the Assyrians and the sun-dial of Ahaz). From a human perspective, there was no reason to think he would not usher in the Messiah.

Hezekiah's new test came in the form of ambassadors from Babylon (2 Chronicles 32:31). The king of Babylon heard of Hezekiah's two miracles and wished to form an alliance with him (Merodach-baladan had been trying unsuccessfully to rebel against Assyria). Hezekiah agreed to ally himself with Babylon by receiving and giving presents. Hezekiah also showed the ambassadors his wealth and military preparedness (Isaiah 39:1-2).

Isaiah heard of this and confronted Hezekiah. He condemned the alliance because it violated the spirit of Immanuel. Isaiah's original prophecy to Ahaz, which Hezekiah had followed up to this point, warned against alliances (Isaiah 8: 9-18). God Himself would save the people and exalt His Messiah without help from other nations: *"Say ye not, A confederacy, to all them to whom this people shall say, A confederacy; neither fear ye their fear, nor be afraid. Sanctify the LORD of hosts himself; and let him be your fear, and let him be your dread." Isaiah 8:12,13.*

Isaiah announced the results of God's experiment with Hezekiah. Hezekiah failed to properly prepare for the Messiah (his son or grandson) by trusting in human strategy to strengthen his position. This announcement not only ended the dream of the Messiah (for the moment) but foretold of Judah's coming captivity: *"Then said Isaiah to Hezekiah, Hear the word of the LORD of hosts: Behold, the days come, that all that is in thine house, and that which thy fathers have laid up in store until this day, shall be carried to Babylon: nothing shall be left, saith the LORD. And of thy sons that shall issue from thee, which thou shalt beget, shall they take away; and they shall be eunuchs in the palace of the king of Babylon." Isaiah 39:5-7.*

Hezekiah responded with repentance and acceptance of God's judgment. Therefore, God put off the evil to come until after Hezekiah's death: *"Notwithstanding Hezekiah humbled himself for the pride of his heart, both he and the inhabitants of Jerusalem, so that the wrath of the LORD came not upon them in the days of Hezekiah." 2 Chronicles 32:26. (also see Isaiah 39:8).*

"And Hezekiah slept with his fathers, and they buried him in the chiefest of the sepulchres of the sons of David: and all Judah and the inhabitants of Jerusalem did him honour at his death. And Manasseh his son reigned in his stead." 2 Chronicles 32:33.

Manasseh acted more like the antichrist than the Christ (Messiah). As strongly as Hezekiah served the Lord, Manasseh served everyone but the Lord. The reason for this is unclear. He was only twelve when he inherited the throne. He wasn't old enough to really have a teenage rebellion against his father. Perhaps his advisors were waiting for Hezekiah to pass on so they could resurrect the pagan ways of

Ahaz. For whatever reason, his zeal for rebellion against the Lord was unmatched by anyone before or after.

Hezekiah and Judah's dream of raising the Messiah was cruelly crushed by Manasseh's life. God had been prepared to reveal the Messiah after Hezekiah's childless death. Yet when Hezekiah's request for more time was granted, and he raised Manasseh, the fulfillment of the Davidic Covenant became impossible through human means. God gave up on Judah's effort. Up until that time, hope was always on the rise. After Manasseh, Judah's hope steadily declined.

Every spiritual quest has its point of failure: the failure of fleshly effort. Only God can initiate the spiritual young adult into adulthood by supernaturally intervening to grant the desired treasure. Judah had to learn, like all spiritual young adults, that without a full understanding by experience of waiting on God, they would not be ready for the blessing.

Manasseh seduced the people into idolatry, Baal worship, astrology, and human sacrifice. He rebuilt the high places that Hezekiah had torn down and set up an idol in the Temple (2 Kings 21: 3-7). On top of the idolatry, Manasseh made a sport of tracking down and killing those who opposed him. Josephus tells of Manasseh: "for by setting out from a contempt of God, he barbarously slew all the righteous men that were among the Hebrews; nor would he spare the prophets, for he every day slew some of them, till Jerusalem was overflown with blood."[11] (2 Kings 21:16). According to tradition, Isaiah was ordered to be sawn in half in the presence of Manasseh (Hebrews 11:37).

The scripture gives this judgment of Manasseh and Judah at that time: *"And he did that which was evil in the sight of the LORD, after the abominations of the heathen, whom the LORD cast out before the children of Israel." 2 Kings 21:2. "But they hearkened not: and Manasseh seduced them to do more evil than did the nations whom the LORD destroyed before the children of Israel." 2 Kings 21:9.*

As a result of Manasseh's wickedness, God pronounced the imminent death of the vision: *"Because Manasseh king of Judah hath done these abominations, and hath done wickedly above all that the Amorites did, which were before him, and hath made Judah also to sin with his idols: Therefore thus saith the LORD God of Israel, Behold, I am bringing such evil upon Jerusalem and Judah, that whosoever heareth of it, both his ears shall tingle. And I will stretch over Jerusalem the line of Samaria, and the plummet of the house of Ahab: and I will wipe Jerusalem as a man wipeth a dish, wiping it, and turning it upside down. And I will forsake the remnant of mine inheritance, and deliver them into the hand of their enemies; and they shall become a prey and a spoil to all their enemies; Because they have done that which was evil in my sight, and have provoked me to anger, since the day their fathers came forth out of Egypt, even unto this day." 2 Kings 21:11-15.* Jeremiah confirmed that Manasseh was the last straw for God (Jeremiah 15:4).

Nevertheless, Manasseh repented and reversed the evil he had done with good works. God allowed the Assyrian king to take Manasseh to Babylon with hooks and fetters. This was the "hook in the nose" practice that was mentioned in 2 Kings 19:28. The Assyrians did this to humiliate conquered peoples. Manasseh prayed to God in his prison and asked forgiveness for his rebellion. He had behaved as a child who delights in wrongdoing, daring the parent to correct, but secretly desires to be put under authority.

God restored him and then provided him an opportunity to prove his loyalty (2 Chronicles 33:10-13). Manasseh responded by strengthening Judah militarily, by renouncing idolatry, by removing false worship, by repairing the altar of God, and by sacrificing to God only (2 Chronicles 33:14-17). I imagine Manasseh was as zealous in restoring Jehovah worship as he had been in ridiculing it, as converts usually don't change in their basic personalities but merely redirect their energies (see the apostle Paul). Manasseh's repentance was genuine, and he served the Lord the remainder of his life, but the consequences of his idolatry could not be undone.

The next king, Amon, began his reign by fetching the carved images that Manasseh had cast out of the city (2 Chronicles 33:22). Amon began to re-establish the false worship in Judah. The royal servants, who had endured Manasseh's idolatry and then rejoiced in his conversion, could not submit to another apostasy. They conspired against Amon and assassinated him (v.24). Perhaps they still retained hope that Hezekiah's Messiah would soon arrive, even though his son and grandson were worse than disappointing. They thus tried to help God raise up a godly king.

"But the people of the land slew all them that had conspired against king Amon; and the people of the land made Josiah his son king in his stead." 2 Chronicles 33:25.

Josiah was the best candidate ever to fulfill the requirements of the Messiah, yet the people were too corrupt and unprepared to receive Him. It was too late. The list of his accomplishments is impressive. When he was 20 years old, he abolished the Baalim and their places of sacrifice. He polluted their altars by burning the bones of their priests on them. He did this throughout Judah and Israel. He fulfilled the prophecy about the altar at Bethel by burning the priests' bones on it (1 Kings 13:2; 2 Kings 23:16).

When he was 26, Josiah repaired the Temple. He also kept a national Passover, including the northern tribes, the largest since the days of Samuel (2 Chronicles 35:18-19).

During the repairs of the Temple, the priests found the Law of Moses (2 Chronicles 34:14). They brought it to Josiah, who grieved over hearing its words. He sent to Huldah the prophetess to see what God would do to them for forsaking His law. She said that God would indeed judge the nation but that He would spare Josiah from seeing it (2 Chronicles 34: 27-28). Josiah then made a covenant with the people to obey the Law, which they did outwardly all of his life (2 Chronicles 34: 31-33).

Josiah died when he challenged Pharaoh-Neco as the Pharaoh went to capture territory from the weakened Assyrians. Perhaps Josiah still hoped that God would repent and usher in the age of the Messiah. There is evidence that Josiah reigned over a period of unprecedented expansion of Judah's political power as well as religious reform.

Jeremiah, who began his ministry during the height of the revival (the revival started in the twelfth year, Jeremiah started in the thirteenth year of Josiah), gave the reasons why Josiah did not become the promised one. All of the reasons revolved around the people's lack of heartfelt commitment to the Lord. Perhaps the years of idolatry and moral laxness were too much to overcome.

The people were only feigning loyalty to God during the time of Josiah's reform. Perhaps that brought about the vehemence of their destruction of the idols, to make up for their lack of inward commitment: *"And yet for all this her treacherous sister Judah hath not turned unto me with her whole heart, but feignedly, saith the LORD." Jeremiah 3:10.*

Instead, the Lord was looking for inward conversions: *"Circumcise yourselves to the LORD, and take away the foreskins of your heart" Jeremiah 4:4. "O Jerusalem, wash thine heart from wickedness, that thou mayest be saved. How long shall thy vain thoughts lodge within thee?" Jeremiah 4:14.*

They did not learn the lessons of spiritual young adulthood and therefore were not able overcome its crisis: *"Therefore I said, Surely these are poor; they are foolish: **for they know not the way of the LORD**, nor the judgment of their God." Jeremiah 5:4.* They had not learned about the death, burial, and resurrection of the vision. Specifically, they did not understand that God must fulfill the vision supernaturally.

The people of Judah became profane and political in their outlook, just like the Israelites before them. They forgot their spiritual purpose: *"A wonderful and horrible thing is committed in the land; The prophets prophesy falsely, and the priests bear rule by their means; and my people love to have it so: and what will ye do in the end thereof?" Jeremiah 5:30,31.*

Jeremiah 9:1- 6 describes their descent into a politically driven nation rather than a spiritually driven nation:

v. 1 "Oh that my head were waters, and mine eyes a fountain of tears, that I might weep day and night for the slain of the daughter of my people!" A purely political society not informed by absolutes produces injustice.

v. 2 "Oh that I had in the wilderness a lodging place of wayfaring men; that I might leave my people, and go from them! for they be all adulterers, an assembly of treacherous men." It seems that adultery is common for the politically minded.

v. 3 "And they bend their tongues like their bow for lies: but they are not valiant for the truth upon the earth; for they proceed from evil to evil, and they know not me, saith the LORD." Political people are not valiant for the truth, but for expediency.

v. 4 "Take ye heed every one of his neighbour, and trust ye not in any brother: for every brother will utterly supplant, and every neighbour will walk with slanders." This verse teaches they were greedy and litigious, just like our society. They looked for opportunities to catch others and take from them, and they looked for chances to slander. Just like our society today, they delighted in the downfall of others.

v. 5 "And they will deceive every one his neighbour, and will not speak the truth: they have taught their tongue to speak lies, and weary themselves to commit iniquity." They learned how to sear their consciences so they would not feel guilt. In profane and political societies a quiet conscience is considered a mark of maturity. Then their quiet conscience allows them to live by expediency. A side effect of that is a loss of moral integrity. Iniquity is the process of moral corruption. It is the energy that leads toward reprobation.

v. 6 "Thine habitation is in the midst of deceit; through deceit they refuse to know me, saith the LORD." The result of all of this was a suppression of the knowledge of God, the power behind absolute values. They did this because absolute rights and wrongs do not yield to political pressure.

Jeremiah 6:13-17 lists their sins, a list remarkably similar to the one outlining the offences of the Northern Kingdom before them:

1. They lived by the worldly principles of covetousness and deceit in business: *"For from the least of them even unto the greatest of them every one is*

given to covetousness; and from the prophet even unto the priest every one dealeth falsely." v.13.

2. They allowed politics to influence their teaching, and were only willing to listen to pleasing words, words that did not require a change of lifestyle: *"They have healed also the hurt of the daughter of my people slightly, saying, Peace, peace; when there is no peace."* v. 14.

3. They seared their consciences with sin and became reprobate: *"Were they ashamed when they had committed abomination? nay, they were not at all ashamed, neither could they blush: therefore they shall fall among them that fall. at the time that I visit them they shall be cast down, saith the LORD."* v. 15.

4. They rejected God's warnings to repent: *"Thus saith the LORD, Stand ye in the ways, and see, and ask for the old paths, where is the good way, and walk therein, and ye shall find rest for your souls. But they said, We will not walk therein. Also I set watchmen over you, saying, Hearken to the sound of the trumpet. But they said, We will not hearken."* v. 16-17.

Finally, Jeremiah declared their condition in terms of the spiritual life cycle: *"The harvest is past, the summer is ended, and we are not saved." Jeremiah 8:20.* It was the right time for them to receive their harvest, the Messiah, but they were not ready.

Death of the Vision

Three of Josiah's sons and one grandson reigned as kings in Jerusalem, but the fate of the kingdom was already sealed. All four of the new kings rebelled against Jeremiah and God. Their rule was a descent into captivity. The people still hoped that the warring parties of Egypt and Babylon would be distracted by one another and leave them alone, but instead they used Judah as a trophy in their conflict. Babylon became stronger and prevailed.

Jehoahaz was king for three months before Pharoah-Neco deposed him and set up Jehoiakim his brother (2 Chronicles 36:1-4).

Jehoiakim was bound in chains and taken to Babylon along with the vessels of the house of the Lord (2 Chronicles 36:5-7).

Jehoiakim's eight year old son Jehoiachin lasted three months and ten days before Nebuchadnezzar sent for him also to be brought to Babylon, along with all the skilled workers in Jerusalem (2 Chronicles 36:9-10).

Zedekiah, the last son of Josiah to reign, rebelled against the king of Babylon: *"For through the anger of the LORD it came to pass in Jerusalem and Judah, until he had cast them out from his presence, that Zedekiah rebelled against the king of Babylon." 2 Kings 24:20.* Zedekiah saw his sons die before his eyes and then was marched to Babylon in chains (2 Kings 25:7).

The Babylonians finished their work by burning the Temple, the king's house, and Jerusalem. They also broke down the walls of the city (2 Kings 25:8-10).

With the Temple destroyed, and the line of David ended, the Israelites truly experienced the death of their vision of a God chosen Place and Person. God left no human way for the vision to be accomplished. He would have to work a miracle. Hezekiah failed to believe in God's power to supernaturally produce the Messiah; now God would leave no doubt.

Jeremiah declared plainly the death of the vision. First of all, he said that Manasseh, Hezekiah's project, was so miserable God could not allow the process go on (2 Kings 24:3-4; Jeremiah 15:4). Jeremiah also reported that Moses (the lawgiver), and Samuel (the king maker), could not change God's mind (Jeremiah 15:1).

Jeremiah confirmed the end of both the Place and the Person. *"But go ye now unto my place which was in Shiloh, where I set my name at the first, and see what I did to it for the wickedness of my people Israel." Jeremiah 7:12. "Then will I make this house like Shiloh, and will make this city a curse to all the nations of the earth." Jeremiah 26:6. (1 Samuel 4).* Shiloh was rejected as the final resting place of the Ark of the Covenant and Jerusalem was rejected also. But unlike Shiloh, there was no other place left in Israel for the tabernacle of God.

Jeconiah (Jehoiachin), the last heir to the throne, had his kingdom taken away, signaling the end of David's line, and seemingly contradicting God's promise of the Messiah: *"O earth, earth, earth, hear the word of the LORD. Thus saith the LORD, Write ye this man childless, a man that shall not prosper in his days: for no man of his seed shall prosper, sitting upon the throne of David, and ruling any more in Judah." Jeremiah 22:29,30.*

Key - Patience

"For ye have need of patience, that, after ye have done the will of God, ye might receive the promise." Hebrews 10:36. Patience is the key to spiritual

young adulthood. After we have done the will of God, we must wait on Him to provide the promised treasure.

"Be patient therefore, brethren, unto the coming of the Lord. Behold, the husbandman waiteth for the precious fruit of the earth, and hath long patience for it, until he receive the early and latter rain. Be ye also patient; stablish your hearts: for the coming of the Lord draweth nigh. Grudge not one against another, brethren, lest ye be condemned: behold, the judge standeth before the door. Take, my brethren, the prophets, who have spoken in the name of the Lord, for an example of suffering affliction, and of patience. Behold, we count them happy which endure. Ye have heard of the patience of Job, and have seen the end of the Lord; that the Lord is very pitiful, and of tender mercy." James 5:7-11. God must prepare us and those we serve for the treasure He wants to give. We are to allow the fruit of His Spirit to grow within us so that our spiritual offspring will be strong.

Job was a great example of patient waiting on God's timing. He believed throughout his ordeal that God would bless him: *"Though he slay me, yet will I trust in him: but I will maintain mine own ways before him." Job 13:15.* Job knew that he had lived with integrity: *"Let me be weighed in an even balance, that God may know mine integrity." Job 31:6.* Job even declared that God could supernaturally restore him from death to bless him if needed: *"For I know that my redeemer liveth, and that he shall stand at the latter day upon the earth: And though after my skin worms destroy this body, yet in my flesh shall I see God: Whom I shall see for myself, and mine eyes shall behold, and not another; though my reins be consumed within me." Job 19:25-27.* The kind of patience I'm talking about is a supernatural patience based on hope, one of the spiritual gifts. *"For we are saved by hope: but hope that is seen is not hope: for what a man seeth, why doth he yet hope for? But if we hope for that we see not, then do we with patience wait for it." Romans 8:24,25.*

Isaiah describes an example from nature of patience and the possibilities of renewal after a long wait: *"Even the youths shall faint and be weary, and the young men shall utterly fall: But they that wait upon the LORD shall renew their strength; they shall mount up with wings as eagles; they shall run, and not be weary; and they shall walk, and not faint." Isaiah 40:30,31. (Psalm 103:4-5).* Eagles renew their strength in a strange and instructive way for the spiritual young adult. Barbara Bowen describes this process in her book *Strange Scriptures That Perplex the Western Mind*: "The eagle lives to a very great age. As he grows old his beak becomes so long that he can no longer eat; then he flies away by himself to the top of a cliff and pecks and pecks on a rock until his bill falls off, after which a new bill grows in its place. While without the use of his bill, the bird also loses his feathers because of fasting. After the new bill grows and he again takes food, new feathers start growing, so that he looks and appears like a young eagle, going forth in a new covering with youthful beauty and strength."[12] God says that it's always too soon to quit, and it's never too late for Him to fulfill the dreams He has given His children. He can renew us like the eagle, so that even when we are old we can be young again from the thrill of His blessing.

Symbol - Treasure

The symbol of spiritual young adulthood is treasure. The young adult waits patiently for God to reveal His treasure. The treasure represents the goal of the individual's spiritual journey. It must be given by God and is impossible to secure with human effort. Each person has a different treasure, based on his or her vision of God's will. For some it will be a spouse, for some it will be children, for others it will be a special place of service. For each person, the treasure will mark a shift from the growing stages to the generative stages. The treasure enables the spiritual traveler to bless others. It marks the transition into adulthood in a spiritual sense.

The treasures of the children of Israel are the Place and the Person, the Temple and the Messiah. When both are together, then their dream will be realized. The people looked to the Temple as partial fulfillment of God's promise to them, and they looked forward to the Messiah's coming to the Temple as complete fulfillment: *"Behold, I will send my messenger, and he shall prepare the way before me: and the Lord, whom ye seek, shall suddenly come to his temple, even the messenger of the covenant, whom ye delight in: behold, he shall come, saith the LORD of hosts." Malachi 3:1.*

The writer of Hebrews stresses the importance and significance of the treasure. In Chapter 11 he lists the heroes of faith that patiently waited on God for their treasure and the ensuing ministry to others. Abel waited on the knowledge of the proper sacrifice. Enoch waited on wisdom in walking with God. Noah waited on the salvation of his family and a new beginning in a new world. Abraham waited on the promised child. Isaac waited on the preparation of his sons to keep God's covenant. Jacob waited on the dream of his people returning to Canaan. Moses waited on freedom for his people and the re-establishment of their relationship with God. Joshua waited on the conquest of Canaan. Rahab waited on a new hope for her country and family. *"And what shall I more say? for the time would fail me to tell of Gedeon, and of Barak, and of Samson, and of Jephthae; of David also, and Samuel, and of the prophets:" Hebrews 11:32.*

The writer reports the attitude of all these heroes of faith and patience: *"These all died in faith, not having received the promises, but having seen them afar off, and were persuaded of them, and embraced them, and confessed that they were strangers and pilgrims on the earth.*

v. 14 *For they that say such things declare plainly that they seek a country.*

v. 15 *And truly, if they had been mindful of that country from whence they came out, they might have had opportunity to have returned.*

v. 16 *But now they desire a better country, that is, an heavenly: wherefore God is not ashamed to be called their God: for he hath prepared for them a city." Hebrews 11:13-16.*

In v. 13 he shows that the actual receiving of the treasure is not as important as being convinced of its reality. God's goal for the spiritual traveler is to have faith in Him. He accomplishes this with the trials and rewards of believing Him. Our ultimate reward is knowing God.

In v. 14-16 he shows that spiritual young adults desire better things than this corrupt world has to offer, therefore they are willing to risk the loss of worldly treasures for heavenly treasures (v. 24-26).

"And these all, having obtained a good report through faith, received not the promise: God having provided some better thing for us, that they without us should not be made perfect." Hebrews 11:39,40. The writer to the Hebrews explains that all of these heroes were working toward the ultimate goal, the redemption of mankind through the Messiah. His generation of Jews saw the ultimate treasure, the Savior of the world.

Doubting Castle and Giant Despair

As soon as Christian was delivered from Vanity Fair he was joined by Hopeful. The spiritual young adult develops hope as a result of his experience with God: (Romans 5:3-4).

Christian and Hopeful had some times of Ease and pleasantness just as a Christian life has times of rest and ease. They followed a pleasant path by the river until the river and path separated. They were afraid to leave the path so they stayed on it. Then the path became rough so they looked for an easier way.

After Hezekiah, the Jews believed God would save them and Jerusalem no matter what. They became complacent in their faith and practice. They looked for easy ways to secure their treasure. They did not stop to consider that God could fulfill his promises in unthought of ways. God did not have to save the present Jerusalem to bring His Messiah to it.

Christian and Hopeful found By-path Meadow and left the path for an easier terrain. They were soon captured by Giant Despair and thrown into his Doubting Castle. The giant at first "beat them without mercy," and later counseled them to kill themselves. Then he showed them the bones of other Christians he had killed. Christian and Faithful stayed in the dungeon from Wednesday morning to Saturday night (showing that it was a symbol of the death/tomb/grave). Hopeful on more than one occasion encouraged Christian to "have patience" through the ordeal. The pilgrims escaped on Sunday morning with the key of Promise.[13]

The Babylonians were Judah's Giant Despair and the captivity was their Doubting Castle. The prophets encouraged them to look ahead to God's blessings because of His promises.

All spiritual young adults go through a time of deep doubt and despair, usually right before the realization of their vision. God uses this time to purify motives and get attention firmly on Him. David the king left the ashes of Ziklag to inherit the kingdom.

In the next chapter, we will see how God moved to give Israel their treasure and how God works to bless those who wait on Him.

CHAPTER 11

Spiritual Adulthood

THE latter rains prepare the crops for the next phase of their growth. There is no rain in the last few months of their development. They must depend on the stored supply of water to keep them refreshed until they are fully-grown and able either to reproduce seed or be harvested.

In the same way, the spiritual young adult depends on faith and hope to nourish him until God fulfills the vision. The time of drought comes right before the blessing. God seems to be far away and stingy with His presence. Nevertheless, this time of drought allows the Christian to become mature enough to lead others to spiritual maturity, which requires one to trust in God regardless of circumstances. Spiritual adulthood is achieved when one can become a spiritual parent, not just to lead people to Christ, but also to lead them to maturity in Christ.

Harvest

Adulthood is a time of productivity in career choices and generativity toward the next generation.[1]Healthy adults work to share their insights and love to a new generation. Their care is shown in many different ways, whether by building families, institutions, philosophies, or actual buildings. Loving adults want to achieve something lasting and beneficial to others.

Spiritual adulthood is reached when God fulfills the vision that started with the crisis of spiritual childhood - commitment or dedication. Then the spiritual children follow. The spiritual adult's unique solution to the problem presented at the vision stage becomes an attractive alternative to the community. This solution may not have been seriously considered before, but now because of the life of the spiritual adult is seen as achievable.

In God's timetable fruitfulness many take many generations. One person's work can influence the whole course of history, and God's blessing of a life can go on forever: *"Know therefore that the LORD thy God, he is God, the faithful God, which keepeth covenant and mercy with them that love him and keep his commandments to a thousand generations;"* Deuteronomy 7:9.

Abraham's vision was to have children who would carry on the revolution for belief in God. Today there are billions who believe in God because of his vision: *"Who against hope believed in hope, that he might become the father of many nations, according to that which was spoken, So shall thy seed be."* Romans 4:18. *"Know ye therefore that they which are of faith, the same are the children of Abraham."* Galatians 3:7.

David's vision was to establish Jerusalem as the Place God would choose. Today the world is still engaged in a titanic battle over Jerusalem as the most holy place on earth. Yet, we know that David's vision will become a reality and Jesus will one day rule from Jerusalem.

Paul's vision was to provoke Israel to jealousy to receive the gospel by the salvation of the Gentiles, a process which is still going today and will ultimately be achieved at the end of time: *"For I speak to you Gentiles, inasmuch as I am the apostle of the Gentiles, I magnify mine office: If by any means I may provoke to emulation them which are my flesh, and might save some of them."* Romans 11:13,14. *"And so all Israel shall be saved: as it is written, There shall come out of Sion the Deliverer, and shall turn away ungodliness from Jacob:"* Romans 11:26.

Learning Tasks

Spiritual fathers "have known him that is from the beginning." Therefore, in order for spiritual adults to become fathers they must have first hand experience of God's supernatural blessing and intervention into their lives. Spiritual adults understand that trust and faith in God pays off and they become willing to lead others to trust God; not on an immature level, but on a level that is informed by experience. *"I write unto you, fathers, because ye have known him that is from the beginning"* 1 John 2:13.

The Learning Task of Spiritual Adulthood

Knowing God on a Mature Level, by Experience

The desire of the spiritual young adult is to be resurrected. The spiritual young adult puts his faith in God to fulfill the vision when nothing else can be done from a human standpoint. The confident expectation of fulfillment of the vision marks the transition into adulthood. This is the power of the resurrection: to do God's will, then to wait on God to work a miracle when all seems lost. This is what Jesus Christ did (Philippians 2:5-11).

Paul related his desire to share in the experience of the resurrection: *"That I may know him, and the power of his resurrection, and the fellowship of his sufferings, being made conformable unto his death; If by any means I might attain unto the resurrection of the dead. Not as though I had already attained, either were already perfect: but I follow after, if that I may apprehend that for which also I am apprehended of Christ Jesus. Brethren, I count not myself to have apprehended: but this one thing I do, forgetting those things which are behind, and reaching forth unto those things which are before, I press toward the mark for the prize of the high calling of God in Christ Jesus."* Philippians 3:10-14.

The "resurrection" here is not just a literal resurrection, but an active striving of life according to the context. Otherwise he wouldn't have to "press toward the mark." He knew the literal resurrection would come even if he were passive. Paul wanted to apprehend that level of spiritual development that sees a resurrection of the vision after defeat. We know he was speaking in developmental terms because of the next two verses: *"Let us therefore, as many as be perfect, be thus minded: and if in any thing ye be otherwise minded, God shall reveal even this unto you. Nevertheless, whereto we have already attained, let us walk by the same rule, let us mind the same thing." Philippians 3:15,16.*

How fitting that Paul rejoiced over the Philippians even from the Roman prison and knew that his labor was not lost, because he had confidence they would continue to grow and develop spiritually: *"Being confident of this very thing, that he which hath begun a good work in you will perform it until the day of Jesus Christ:" Philippians 1:6. "Therefore, my brethren dearly beloved and longed for, my joy and crown, so stand fast in the Lord, my dearly beloved." Philippians 4:1.*

The spiritual young adult wants to know God and to see as God sees, so that he can become more like God in character. He knows that his work will be unfruitful if he cannot demonstrate the type of character that will be admired and followed by others: *"Be ye followers of me, even as I also am of Christ." 1 Corinthians 11:1. "For if these things be in you, and abound, they make you that ye shall neither be barren nor unfruitful in the knowledge of our Lord Jesus Christ." 2 Peter 1:8.*

When God reveals Himself through the resurrection of the vision, then the spiritual young adult gets a true picture of God's love, and thus is able to pass into spiritual adulthood: *"Beloved, now are we the sons of God, and it doth not yet appear what we shall be: but we know that, when he shall appear, we shall be like him; for we shall see him as he is." 1 John 3:2. "But we all, with open face beholding as in a glass the glory of the Lord, are changed into the same image from glory to glory, even as by the Spirit of the Lord." 2 Corinthians 3:18. (Romans 5:2-5).*

History of Israel

Even before the captivity of Judah, God promised through Jeremiah that the vision of the Place and Person would be fulfilled. Jeremiah predicted this even after he said that Jeconiah would have no heir to sit on the throne at Jerusalem. In Chapter 22 he predicted that Jeconiah would be childless in regard to the kingdom and in Chapter 23 he said that God would raise up the Messiah Himself: *"Behold, the days come, saith the LORD, that I will raise unto David a righteous Branch, and a King shall reign and prosper, and shall execute judgment and justice in the earth. In his days Judah shall be saved, and Israel shall dwell safely: and this is his name whereby he shall be called, THE LORD OUR RIGHTEOUSNESS." Jeremiah 23:5,6.* The future Messiah would not need an earthly father because God would raise Him up. Hezekiah did not believe that God would raise up the Messiah supernaturally, but God made it so there would be no other way. *"Thus saith the LORD; Behold, I will bring again the captivity of Jacob's tents, and have mercy on his dwellingplaces; and the city shall be builded upon her own heap, and the palace shall remain after the manner thereof." Jeremiah 30:18.*

Zephaniah, a contemporary of Jeremiah, also predicted both the captivity and the return. He prophesied that the Place and the Person would become a reality: *"Sing, O daughter of Zion; shout, O Israel; be glad and rejoice with all the heart, O daughter of Jerusalem. The LORD hath taken away thy judgments, he hath cast out thine enemy: the king of Israel, even the LORD, is in the midst of thee: thou shalt not see evil any more." Zephaniah 3:14,15. "At that time will I bring you again, even in the time that I gather you: for I will make you a name and a praise among all people of the earth, when I turn back your captivity before your eyes, saith the LORD." Zephaniah 3:20.*

When the captivity of Judah was imminent, Jeremiah introduced a new covenant to the people. The Davidic Covenant had apparently failed because of the people's lack of patience and integrity. Even though God would still honor the Davidic Covenant (Jeremiah 33:17-21), He provided a new covenant to prepare the people for the Messiah: *"Behold, the days come, saith the LORD, that I will make a new covenant with the house of Israel, and with the house of Judah: Not according to the covenant that I made with their fathers in the day that I took them by the hand to bring them out of the land of Egypt; which my covenant they brake, although I was an husband unto them, saith the LORD: But this shall be the covenant that I will make with the house of Israel; After those days, saith the LORD, I will put my law in their inward parts, and write it in their hearts; and will be their God, and they shall be my people. And they shall teach no more every man his neighbour, and every man his brother, saying, Know the LORD: for they shall all know me, from the least of them unto the greatest of them, saith the LORD: for I will forgive their iniquity, and I will remember their sin no more." Jeremiah 31:31-34.*

The writer of Hebrews explains that Jesus Christ became the mediator of this New Covenant, and His blood sealed the testament (Hebrews 8:6-13; 9:15-16). The New Covenant marks the preparation for *spiritual adulthood*. The New Covenant would solve the problem of sin and prepare the people to receive the Messiah: *"And she shall bring forth a son, and thou shalt call his name JESUS: for he shall save his people from their sins." Matthew 1:21.*

Reflections on the Death of the Vision

Ezekiel was called to prophesy in the fifth year of Jeconiah's (Jehoiachin) captivity. By dating his ministry in relation to Jeconiah, the childless son of David, the Holy Sprit signified that Ezekiel was to prophesy about the death of the vision (Ezekiel 1:2).

God's word came to Ezekiel in the land of the Chaldeans, Babylon, the place of the captivity. In this, the Holy Spirit showed His prophet and people to be in the belly of the whale, in the pit, at the place of defeat (Ezekiel 1:3).

God gave Ezekiel a roll of lamentations, mourning and woe (Ezekiel 2:9). Ezekiel incorporated it into his life, he ate it, so he could deliver the message of the death of the vision. The message was to the captivity in Babylon (Ezekiel 3:11). They were the ones God chose to renew the vision. God took them out of Israel to cleanse them and make them fit to receive His blessings. Ezekiel's hard message was meant to heal their backslidings (Ezekiel 6:8-10). It was God's will to return a people of integrity to the land of Israel.

Ezekiel was struck mute at the beginning of his ministry. Until the destruction of Jerusalem he could not speak except when prophesying in the name of the Lord (Ezekiel 33:21-22). The people of the captivity came to him often to see if the Lord had a word for them (Ezekiel 8:1; 14:1; 20:1; 33:30-32). The people watched the events happening at Jerusalem through Ezekiel's prophecies and through his metaphorical enactments. His ministry became a reflection on the death of a vision.

The people who were left in Jerusalem believed that God had judged the captivity and had given the land to those that remained. Nevertheless, God took Ezekiel there in a vision and showed the captivity the truth through him. God had marked the remaining Jews for destruction because He deemed them incorrigible (Ezekiel 11:1-13; 33: 23-29). Pelatiah the son of Benaiah, one of the princes, died in Jerusalem as Ezekiel watched from Babylon. Ezekiel reported this to the captivity. Ezekiel saw God's presence move away from Jerusalem to rest on a nearby mountain as if to watch the end: *"And the glory of the LORD went up from the midst of the city, and stood upon the mountain which is on the east side of the city." Ezekiel 11:23.*

During this vision, Ezekiel also prophesied that the captivity would restore the dream to Israel. He followed up on Jeremiah's promise of the New Covenant, which was that God Himself would prepare the people to receive Him: *"Therefore say, Thus saith the Lord GOD; I will even gather you from the people, and assemble you out of the countries where ye have been scattered, and I will give you the land of Israel. And they shall come thither, and they shall take away all the detestable things thereof and all the abominations thereof from thence. And I will give them one heart, and I will put a new spirit within you; and I will take the stony heart out of their flesh, and will give them an heart of flesh: That they may walk in my statutes, and keep mine ordinances, and do them: and they shall be my people, and I will be their God." Ezekiel 11:17-20.*

The captivity had grown so tired of waiting on God that they could not believe something decisive would shortly happen. This is the crisis of spiritual young adulthood. God was about to be decisive. He was about to end hope based on human effort. God was preparing to allow Jerusalem and the Temple to be destroyed: *"Son of man, what is that proverb that ye have in the land of Israel, saying, The days are prolonged, and every vision faileth?"* *Ezekiel 12:22.* *"Son of man, behold, they of the house of Israel say, The vision that he seeth is for many days to come, and he prophesieth of the times that are far off. Therefore say unto them, Thus saith the Lord GOD; There shall none of my words be prolonged any more, but the word which I have spoken shall be done, saith the Lord GOD."* *Ezekiel 12:27,28.*

Ezekiel identified "idols of the heart" as a barrier to the cleansing of the captivity: *"Son of man, these men have set up their idols in their heart, and put the stumblingblock of their iniquity before their face: should I be enquired of at all by them?"* *Ezekiel 14:3.* The Jews usually thought only in terms of actual Idolatry as being sin, but God was working to put them on a higher level of conscience. The New Covenant would require not only outward actions, but also inward transformation. Jesus completed the explanation of this in the Sermon on the Mount (Matthew 6). The "stumblingblock of iniquity" refers to habitual sins that keep their power through sensuality. Idol worship often revolved around the use of intoxicants and sex to hold the people.

God's solution was a repentance that would produce a new heart, a clearing of conscience: *"Therefore say unto the house of Israel, Thus saith the Lord GOD; Repent, and turn yourselves from your idols; and turn away your faces from all your abominations…That the house of Israel may go no more astray from me, neither be polluted any more with all their transgressions; but that they may be my people, and I may be their God, saith the Lord GOD."* *Ezekiel 14:6,11.*

This repentance would be easier for the captivity than the people left in Jerusalem because of their daily reminder in Babylon of the outward results of their inward captivity: *"By the rivers of Babylon, there we sat down, yea, we wept, when we remembered Zion. We hanged our harps upon the willows in the midst thereof. For there they that carried us away captive required of us a song; and they that wasted us required of us mirth, saying, Sing us one of the songs of Zion. How shall we sing the LORD'S song in a strange land? If I forget thee, O Jerusalem, let my right hand forget her cunning. If I do not remember thee, let my tongue cleave to the roof of my mouth; if I prefer not Jerusalem above my chief joy. Psalms 137:1-6.*

God promised the captivity that their children would revive the vision and would renew their hope in God's promises: *"Yet, behold, therein shall be left a remnant that shall be brought forth, both sons and daughters: behold, they shall come forth unto you, and ye shall see their way and their doings: and ye shall be comforted concerning the evil that I have brought upon Jerusalem, even concerning all that I have brought upon it. And they shall comfort you, when ye see their ways and their doings: and ye shall know that I have not done without cause all that I have done in it, saith the Lord GOD." Ezekiel 14:22,23.*

The children would grow up to live with integrity. Sometimes the fulfillment of the vision is shown to the young adult but the completion is for another time: *"These all died in faith, not having received the promises, but having seen them afar off, and were persuaded of them, and embraced them, and confessed that they were strangers and pilgrims on the earth." Hebrews 11:13.*

"The word of the LORD came unto me again, saying, What mean ye, that ye use this proverb concerning the land of Israel, saying, The fathers have eaten sour grapes, and the children's teeth are set on edge?" Ezekiel 18:1,2. The people had a tendency to blame their failure on past generations, as if the deck was stacked against them. Nevertheless, God corrected this notion. He was building in them a sense of responsibility that would be necessary for them to raise a generation with integrity. He ended the chapter with a plea for repentance and a restating of the New Covenant: *"Cast away from you all your transgressions, whereby ye have transgressed; and make you a new heart and a new spirit: for why will ye die, O house of Israel?" Ezekiel 18:31.*

Ezekiel prophesied that there would be no more kings of Israel until the Messiah. Although there would be kings in Jerusalem during the days of the Greeks and Romans, they would not be of the lineage of David. There has still been no king of Israel since the captivity and there will not be until Jesus begins His millennial reign: *"And thou, profane wicked prince of Israel, whose day is come, when iniquity shall have an end, Thus saith the Lord GOD; Remove the diadem, and take off the crown: this shall not be the same: exalt him that is low, and abase him that is high. I will overturn, overturn, overturn, it: and it shall be no more, until he come whose right it is; and I will give it him." Ezekiel 21:25-27.*

Ezekiel himself became a sign to the captivity of the death of the vision. God told Ezekiel that the "desire of his eyes" would be taken from him. His wife died the next day. The scripture makes the parallel between Ezekiel's desire and the desire of Israel toward the Temple. A personal vision is often related to spouse, children, etc. The vision of Israel was to have the Place and Person together. Ezekiel's loss became the metaphor of Israel's loss. God promised to end their desire by allowing the Temple to be destroyed. God allowed Ezekiel's speech to return after news of the Temple's demise: *"Also the word of the LORD came unto me, saying, Son of man, behold, I take away from thee the desire of thine eyes with a stroke: yet neither shalt thou mourn nor weep, neither shall thy tears run down. Forbear to cry, make no mourning for the dead, bind the tire of thine head upon thee, and put on thy shoes upon thy feet, and cover not thy lips, and eat not the bread of men. So I spake unto the people in the morning: and at even my wife died; and I did in the morning as I was commanded. And the people said unto me, Wilt thou not tell us what these things are to us, that thou doest so? Then I answered them, The word of the LORD came unto me, saying, Speak unto the house of Israel, Thus saith the Lord GOD; Behold, I will profane my sanctuary, the excellency of your strength, the desire of your eyes, and that which your soul pitieth; and your sons and your daughters whom ye have left shall fall by the sword. And ye shall do as I have done: ye shall not cover your lips, nor eat the bread of men. And your tires shall be upon your heads, and your shoes upon your feet: ye shall not mourn nor weep; but ye shall pine away for your iniquities, and mourn one toward another. Thus Ezekiel is unto you a sign: according to all that he hath done shall ye do: and when this cometh, ye shall know that I am the Lord GOD. Also, thou son of man, shall it not be in the day when I take from them their strength, the joy of their glory, the desire of their eyes, and that whereupon they set their minds, their sons and their daughters, That he that escapeth in that day shall come unto thee, to cause thee to hear it with thine ears? In that day shall thy mouth be opened to him which is escaped, and thou shalt speak, and be no more dumb: and thou shalt be a sign unto them; and they shall know that I am the LORD." Ezekiel 24:15-27.*

Rebirth of the Vision

The latter chapters of Ezekiel confirm God's promise to restore Israel, to establish a new covenant, and to place the Messiah on the throne at Jerusalem.

In Chapter 34, God condemned the past leaders of Israel as being self-serving. He promised to lead them Himself: *"For thus saith the Lord GOD; Behold, I, even I, will both search my sheep, and seek them out." Ezekiel 34:11.* He specifically mentioned David (the descendent of David) as the chosen one to lead them (v. 23-24). There is a hint in this chapter that God and David (the Messiah) are linked in a more than human way. Finally, God made clear the parable in the last verse: *"And ye my flock, the flock of my pasture, are men, and I am your God, saith the Lord GOD." Ezekiel 34:31.*

In Chapter 36, God restated the New Covenant and explained it in detail: *"For I will take you from among the heathen, and gather you out of all countries, and will bring you into your own land. Then will I sprinkle clean water upon you, and ye shall be clean: from all your filthiness, and from all your idols, will I cleanse you. A new heart also will I give you, and a new spirit will I put within you: and I will take away the stony heart out of your flesh, and I will give you an heart of flesh. And I will put my spirit within you, and cause you to walk in my statutes, and ye shall keep my judgments, and do them. And ye shall dwell in the land that I gave to your fathers; and ye shall be my people, and I will be your God." Ezekiel 36:24-28.*

Chapter 37 gives a metaphorical description of the rebirth of the vision. It is so dramatic and colorful that it should serve as the hope of every Christian pilgrim seeking to "apprehend that for which we are apprehended" (the resurrection of the vision): *"The hand of the LORD was upon me, and carried me out in the spirit of the LORD, and set me down in the midst of the valley which was full of bones, And caused me to pass by them round about: and, behold, there were very many in the open valley; and, lo, they were very dry. And he said unto me, Son of man, can these bones live? And I answered, O Lord GOD, thou knowest. Again he said unto me, Prophesy upon these bones, and say unto them, O ye dry bones, hear the word of the LORD." Ezekiel 37:1-4.* "Can these bones live"; when there is a death of the vision with the spiritual young adult, it is complete. There seems to be no hope of reviving it. All the better for God to work a miracle so all can see His power. God wants to prove Himself strong. He can do it when we trust in Him despite the circumstances: *"For the eyes of the LORD run to and fro throughout the whole earth, to shew himself strong in the behalf of them whose heart is perfect toward him" 2 Chronicles 16:9.*

"So I prophesied as he commanded me, and the breath came into them, and they lived, and stood up upon their feet, an exceeding great army. Then he said unto me, Son of man, these bones are the whole house of Israel: behold, they say, Our bones are dried, and our hope is lost: we are cut off for our parts. Therefore prophesy and say unto them, Thus saith the Lord GOD; Behold, O my people, I will open your graves, and cause you to come up out of your graves, and bring you into the land of Israel. And ye shall know that I am the LORD, when I have opened your graves, O my people, and brought you up out of your graves, And shall put my spirit in you, and ye shall live, and I shall place you in your own land: then shall ye know that I the LORD have spoken it, and performed it, saith the LORD." Ezekiel 37:10-14. "I will open your graves"; God is able to perform any miracle necessary to accomplish the vision of His people (John11:40). "I will bring you into your own land"; the fulfillment of the vision will not be a substitute but the real thing. "I will put my spirit within you"; the fulfillment of the vision produces love-the Spirit of God (Romans 5: 3-5).

As part of the rebirth of the vision, God promised that the divided nation would be brought together again. Ephraim and his companions and Judah and his companions would join together under the Messiah. They would never give in to pagan religion again after the captivity: *"And I will make them one nation in the land upon the mountains of Israel; and one king shall be king to them all: and they shall be no more two nations, neither shall they be divided into two kingdoms any more at all: Neither shall they defile themselves any more with their idols, nor with their detestable things, nor with any of their transgressions: but I will save them out of all their dwellingplaces, wherein they have sinned, and will cleanse them: so shall they be my people, and I will be their God." Ezekiel 37:22,23.*

Finally, as the ultimate promise of fulfillment, Ezekiel told the captivity that the Place and the Person would still one day be together, that the royal line of David would be resurrected and the Temple rebuilt: *"And David my servant shall be king over them; and they all shall have one shepherd: they shall also walk in my judgments, and observe my statutes, and do them. And they shall dwell in the land that I have given unto Jacob my servant, wherein your fathers have dwelt; and they shall dwell therein, even they, and their children, and their children's children for ever: and my servant David shall be their prince for ever. Moreover I will make a covenant of peace with them; it shall be an everlasting covenant with them: and I will place them, and multiply them, and will set my sanctuary in the midst of them for evermore. My tabernacle also shall be with them: yea, I will be their God, and they shall be my people. And the heathen shall know that I the LORD do sanctify Israel, when my sanctuary shall be in the midst of them for evermore." Ezekiel 37:24-28.*

In chapters 38 - 39 Ezekiel prophesied that the Israelites would be invaded after the final end of the captivity and that God would destroy the invaders. This prophecy has never been realized but it is clearly connected to the fulfillment of the vision. The purpose of God's intervention is twofold: to prove to the world that God still chooses Israel, and to turn the Jews' hearts to God: *"When I have brought them again from the people, and gathered them out of their enemies' lands, and am sanctified in them in the sight of many nations; Then shall they know that I am the LORD their God, which caused them to be led into captivity among the heathen: but I have gathered them unto their own land, and have left none of them any more there." Ezekiel 39:27,28.*

Chapters 40-48 describe a new Temple to be built in Jerusalem where the Messiah will reign. This also has never been fulfilled. It represents the ultimate realization of the people's dreams. To this Temple only the Shekinah glory will return, signifying God's presence: *"Afterward he brought me to the gate, even the gate that looketh toward the east: And, behold, the glory of the God of Israel came from the way of the east: and his voice was like a noise of many waters: and the earth shined with his glory. And it was according to the appearance of the vision which I saw, even according to the vision that I saw when I came to destroy the city: and the visions were like the vision that I saw by the river Chebar; and I fell upon my face. And the glory of the LORD came into the house by the way of the gate whose prospect is toward the east." Ezekiel 43:1-4.* There is also a hint that God Himself will enter the Temple, a theme that would be developed by later prophets (Chapter 44:1-2; 48:35).

The book of Daniel records the renewed hope of Israel. Daniel was one of the children taken captive to Babylon. A primary theme of the book is the integrity of Daniel and the Hebrew children (Shadrach, Meshach, Abednego). Ezekiel had promised that the captives would be comforted by the unwavering faith of their children. Daniel and his friends became the symbols of the new generation. The book recounts incidents where the Hebrew children would not compromise their integrity, as had the people before the captivity. That's the purpose of including the accounts of the king's meat, the fiery furnace, and the lions den: *"But Daniel purposed in his heart that he would not defile himself with the portion of the king's meat, nor with the wine which he drank: therefore he requested of the prince of the eunuchs that he might not defile himself." Daniel 1:8.*

Daniel prophesied the order of historical events leading up to the revelation of the Messiah, and even gave the time frame. The most significant passage is from Chapter 9: *"Seventy weeks are determined upon thy people and upon thy holy city, to finish the transgression, and to make an end of sins, and to make reconciliation for iniquity, and to bring in everlasting righteousness, and to seal up the vision and prophecy, and to anoint the most Holy. Know therefore and understand, that from the going forth of the commandment to restore and to build Jerusalem unto the Messiah the Prince shall be seven weeks, and threescore and two weeks: the street shall be built again, and the wall, even in troublous times. And after threescore and two weeks shall Messiah be cut off, but not for himself: and the people of the prince that shall come shall destroy the city and the sanctuary; and the end thereof shall be with a flood, and unto the end of the war desolations are determined. And he shall confirm the covenant with many for one week: and in the midst of the week he shall cause the sacrifice and the oblation to cease, and for the overspreading of abominations he shall make it desolate, even until the consummation, and that determined shall be poured upon the desolate." Daniel 9:24-27.* The weeks are weeks of years, 490 years. Daniel predicted that a second death of the vision would occur in the 483rd year. This time both the Messiah and the Temple would be cut off. Yet, Daniel consistently showed that God would eventually triumph and set up an everlasting kingdom: *"And the kingdom and dominion, and the greatness of the kingdom under the whole heaven, shall be given to the people of the saints of the most High, whose kingdom is an everlasting kingdom, and all dominions shall serve and obey him." Daniel 7:27.* Daniel went on to expand this prophecy in the latter chapters.

The Persian king made the decree after 70 years of captivity (Jeremiah 29:10) for the Jews to return to Jerusalem and rebuild the Temple (Ezra 1:1-3). Jeconiah's descendent, Zerubbabel, became the governor, and Joshua became the high priest. There were about 50,000 of the remnant that returned.

They quickly laid the foundation of the new Temple in the second year of their return. This new Temple was inferior in size and workmanship to the first. There was joy over the rebirth of the vision but sadness that it had lost some of its splendor: *"But many of the priests and Levites and chief of the fathers, who were ancient men, that had seen the first house, when the foundation of this house was laid before their eyes, wept with a loud voice; and many shouted aloud for joy: So that the people could not discern the noise of the shout of joy from the noise of the weeping of the people: for the people shouted with a loud shout, and the noise was heard afar off." Ezra 3:12,13.*

Haggai the prophet warned the people to not despise it, because he prophesied it would become greater that the first. It would be greater because "the desire of all nations shall come." In other words, it would be greater because the Messiah would come to it, at last joining the Place and Person: *"Who is left among you that saw this house in her first glory? and how do ye see it now? is it not in your eyes in comparison of it as nothing? Yet now be strong, O Zerubbabel, saith the LORD; and be strong, O Joshua, son of Josedech, the high priest; and be strong, all ye people of the land, saith the LORD, and work: for I am with you, saith the LORD of hosts: According to the word that I covenanted with you when ye came out of Egypt, so my spirit remaineth among you: fear ye not. For thus saith the LORD of hosts; Yet once, it is a little while, and I will shake the heavens, and the earth, and the sea, and the dry land; And I will shake all nations, and the desire of all nations shall come: and I will fill this house with glory, saith the LORD of hosts. The silver is mine, and the gold is mine, saith the LORD of hosts. The glory of this latter house shall be greater than of the former, saith the LORD of hosts: and in this place will I give peace, saith the LORD of hosts." Haggai 2:3-9.*

The people who lived in Israel during the time of the captivity opposed the rebuilding of the Temple and successfully petitioned to halt it for many years (Ezra 4:24). Then two events spurred the completion of the Temple. The first was a successful petition to Darius to allow the resumption of the work. The second was the prophecies of Haggai and Zechariah that inspired the people (Ezra 5:1). The Temple was finished in 516 B.C., about 20 years after the foundation was laid.[2]

Haggai argued that the Jews had not been blessed in the return because they neglected to finish the Temple.They gave up too easily when they faced opposition. Often, when a dream has been thwarted for so long it's easy for the dreamer to give up and be satisfied with less. The Jews had been content to live in their own land and build houses for themselves. But, God's heroes never give up on God's best: *"Ye looked for much, and, lo, it came to little; and when ye brought it home, I did blow upon it. Why? saith the LORD of hosts. Because of mine house that is waste, and ye run every man unto his own house." Haggai 1:9.*

Haggai later praised the people for their quick obedience at God's word and promised them they would receive God's blessings: *"Consider now from this day and upward, from the four and twentieth day of the ninth month, even from the day that the foundation of the LORD'S temple was laid, consider it. Is the seed yet in the barn? yea, as yet the vine, and the fig tree, and the pomegranate, and the olive tree, hath not brought forth: from this day will I bless you." Haggai 2:18,19.*

Zechariah inspired the people by sharing God's promises to fulfill the vision. The first was the completion of the Temple and the renewal of the promise to choose Jerusalem as the Place: *"Therefore thus saith the LORD; I am returned to Jerusalem with mercies: my house shall be built in it, saith the LORD of hosts, and a line shall be stretched forth upon Jerusalem. Cry yet, saying, Thus saith the LORD of hosts; My cities through prosperity shall yet be spread abroad; and the LORD shall yet comfort Zion, and shall yet choose Jerusalem." Zechariah 1:16,17.*

The second promise was that God's glory would return and that God Himself would live in Jerusalem. The hint is that the Messiah would come in addition to the return of the Shekinah: *"And said unto him, Run, speak to this young man, saying, Jerusalem shall be inhabited as towns without walls for the multitude of men and cattle therein: For I, saith the LORD, will be unto her a wall of fire round about, and will be the glory in the midst of her." Zechariah 2:4,5."Sing and rejoice, O daughter of Zion: for, lo, I come, and I will dwell in the midst of thee, saith the LORD." Zechariah 2:10.*

The third was that the Messiah, the BRANCH, would complete the work of the priesthood by removing iniquity in one day: *"Hear now, O Joshua the high priest, thou, and thy fellows that sit before thee: for they are men wondered at: for, behold, I will bring forth my servant the BRANCH. For behold the stone that I have laid before Joshua; upon one stone shall be seven eyes:*

behold, I will engrave the graving thereof, saith the LORD of hosts, and I will remove the iniquity of that land in one day." Zechariah 3:8,9. "In that day there shall be a fountain opened to the house of David and to the inhabitants of Jerusalem for sin and for uncleanness. And it shall come to pass in that day, saith the LORD of hosts, that I will cut off the names of the idols out of the land, and they shall no more be remembered: and also I will cause the prophets and the unclean spirit to pass out of the land." Zechariah 13:1,2._

The fourth was that God would raise up the Messiah through Zerubbabel's line, who had been reduced to a governor's status at that time: _"The hands of Zerubbabel have laid the foundation of this house; his hands shall also finish it; and thou shalt know that the LORD of hosts hath sent me unto you. For who hath despised the day of small things? for they shall rejoice, and shall see the plummet in the hand of Zerubbabel with those seven; they are the eyes of the LORD, which run to and fro through the whole earth." Zechariah 4:9,10._

The fifth was that the kingdom and the priesthood would be joined in one person, the Messiah: _"And speak unto him, saying, Thus speaketh the LORD of hosts, saying, Behold the man whose name is The BRANCH; and he shall grow up out of his place, and he shall build the temple of the LORD: Even he shall build the temple of the LORD; and he shall bear the glory, and shall sit and rule upon his throne; and he shall be a priest upon his throne: and the counsel of peace shall be between them both." Zechariah 6:12,13_.

The sixth was that God would bless them in a gracious way, that God would write a new chapter in their history: _"But now I will not be unto the residue of this people as in the former days, saith the LORD of hosts. For the seed shall be prosperous; the vine shall give her fruit, and the ground shall give her increase, and the heavens shall give their dew; and I will cause the remnant of this people to possess all these things. And it shall come to pass, that as ye were a curse among the heathen, O house of Judah, and house of Israel; so will I save you, and ye shall be a blessing: fear not, but let your hands be strong. For thus saith the LORD of hosts; As I thought to punish you, when your fathers provoked me to wrath, saith the LORD of hosts, and I repented not: So again have I thought in these days to do well unto Jerusalem and to the house of Judah: fear ye not." Zechariah 8:11-15._

The seventh was that the Messiah would establish peace and prosperity, and that His covenant would be a blood covenant, a permanent commitment by God: _"Rejoice greatly, O daughter of Zion; shout, O daughter of Jerusalem: behold, thy King cometh unto thee: he is just, and having salvation; lowly, and riding_ *upon an ass, and upon a colt the foal of an ass. And I will cut off the chariot from Ephraim, and the horse from Jerusalem, and the battle bow shall be cut off: and he shall speak peace unto the heathen: and his dominion shall be from sea even to sea, and from the river even to the ends of the earth. As for thee also, by the blood of thy covenant I have sent forth thy prisoners out of the pit wherein is no water." Zechariah 9:9-11.*

The eighth was that God would replay the time of the latter rain and prepare the people again for a harvest of their vision. In other words, God would turn back the seasonal clock and give them another chance: *"Ask ye of the LORD rain in the time of the latter rain; so the LORD shall make bright clouds, and give them showers of rain, to every one grass in the field." Zechariah 10:1. "Who satisfieth thy mouth with good things; so that thy youth is renewed like the eagle's." Psalms 103:5.*

The ninth was that God would defend Israel and Jerusalem from its enemies: *"Behold, the day of the LORD cometh, and thy spoil shall be divided in the midst of thee. For I will gather all nations against Jerusalem to battle; and the city shall be taken, and the houses rifled, and the women ravished; and half of the city shall go forth into captivity, and the residue of the people shall not be cut off from the city. Then shall the LORD go forth, and fight against those nations, as when he fought in the day of battle. And his feet shall stand in that day upon the mount of Olives, which is before Jerusalem on the east, and the mount of Olives shall cleave in the midst thereof toward the east and toward the west, and there shall be a very great valley; and half of the mountain shall remove toward the north, and half of it toward the south." Zechariah 14:1-4.*

Nehemiah, the cupbearer to the Persian king, obtained permission to travel to Jerusalem and build the walls. This occurred in 445 B.C. Nehemiah was distressed by the news that the Jews had not progressed further in the vision. He, like others left behind in Babylon and Persia, hoped for the restoration of Israel and the fulfillment of God's promises. When he heard the report of stagnation, he mourned: *"And they said unto me, The remnant that are left of the captivity there in the province are in great affliction and reproach: the wall of Jerusalem also is broken down, and the gates thereof are burned with fire." Nehemiah 1:3.*

Nehemiah went to Jerusalem with a mission, to take away the reproach of God's people in the eyes of the world. The reproach was that the people's vision had not grown past the completion of the Temple. He exhorted the people to work with him to rebuild God's reputation: *"Then said I unto them, Ye see the distress that we are in, how Jerusalem lieth waste, and the gates thereof are burned with fire: come, and let us build up the wall of Jerusalem, that we be no more a reproach." Nehemiah 2:17.*

The wall was finished in fifty-two days under adverse conditions with the threat of armed conflict with the neighbors (Nehemiah 6:15): *"And it came to pass, that when all our enemies heard thereof, and all the heathen that were about us saw these things, they were much cast down in their own eyes: for they perceived that this work was wrought of our God." Nehemiah 6:16.*

Nehemiah not only rebuilt the wall, but also continued in his dedication by restoring the people's sense of purpose. He urged and cajoled and ordered them to follow God's law and not compromise. He instituted reforms to clarify the purposes of the return.

There were some of the children of the captivity that had grown callous in their dealings with fellow Jews and adopted oppressive practices. They held mortgages on their fellows and exacted labor in the form of indentured servitude as payment (Nehemiah 5:1-5). But, Nehemiah and his people in Persia and Babylon had spent their wealth to redeem Jews in hope of the restoration. He was angry because the Jews at Jerusalem had lost the vision and had thought of themselves in secular terms: *"And I said unto them, We after our ability have redeemed our brethren the Jews, which were sold unto the heathen; and will ye even sell your brethren? or shall they be sold unto us? Then held they their peace, and found nothing to answer. Also I said, It is not good that ye do: ought ye not to walk in the fear of our God because of the reproach of the heathen our enemies?" Nehemiah 5:8,9.*

Nehemiah had the people separate themselves from foreigners in order to maintain their religious identity (Nehemiah 13:1-3). He overturned the use of politics in the service of the Lord. He did not want the children of the captivity to make the mistakes of their ancestors (Nehemiah 13:4-14). He was zealous for keeping the Sabbath, which the people had grown lax toward. They formerly traded with foreign merchants from Tyre on the Sabbath (Nehemiah 13:15-22). Finally, Nehemiah condemned the practice of marriage to people of other religions. He demanded that the people keep themselves pure (Nehemiah 13:23-31).

All of these reforms were good and necessary; however, the subsequent overreaction of the people against compromise led to the Pharisee sect, and a multiplication of rules of conduct without regard to the spirit of the Law. We see the results of Nehemiah's reforms run amok in the New Testament.

When the wall was finished, the Jews had a great celebration and a renewal of their commitment to God. Nehemiah and Ezra, a priest who had returned to Jerusalem ten years before, led the revival meeting.

The people gathered together to hear Ezra and the priests read from the Law of Moses. They set aside an entire week to do nothing but hear the word of God. The people wept when they learned how far their ancestors and they themselves had strayed from the covenant with God. This was the first recorded revival meeting that is similar to ours: *"So they read in the book in the law of God distinctly, and gave the sense, and caused them to understand the reading. And Nehemiah, which is the Tirshatha, and Ezra the priest the scribe, and the Levites that taught the people, said unto all the people, This day is holy unto the LORD your God; mourn not, nor weep. For all the people wept, when they heard the words of the law." Nehemiah 8:8,9.*

The Jews decided to renew their commitment to God and their covenant with Him as a result of this revival meeting. They recounted their journey so far and determined to follow God till they received His blessing: *"And the seed of Israel separated themselves from all strangers, and stood and confessed their sins, and the iniquities of their fathers." Nehemiah 9:2. "And because of all this we make a sure covenant, and write it; and our princes, Levites, and priests, seal unto it." Nehemiah 9:38.*

Malachi is the last book of the Old Testament and also the last in historical order. It describes the state of the Jews several years after the revival of Nehemiah and Ezra, perhaps decades. Malachi addressed several problems that grew over time to taint the spiritual atmosphere into which Jesus was born. The people quickly backslid from their heartfelt repentance of the great revival and instead relied on the formality of their religious activities. They never again became involved in idols but they did not take the next step of entering into the New Covenant, which required a cleansing of the heart.

The first practice Malachi condemned was the use of the office of the priesthood for personal gain. The priests no longer demanded acceptable sacrifices from the people but instead took the ill and lame as offerings to God. They also took bribes in judgment and altered their applications of the scripture to appease the mighty. Because of these practices, the priests set the stage for the complete co-option of the priesthood by the politicians during the intertestamental period (Malachi 1:6 - 2:9).

The second practice was the liberal interpretation of divorce laws. The people were allowed to divorce their Hebrew wives and even marry women of other religions. This was a detestable practice to God because it showed the people's unwillingness to abide by their covenant. If they couldn't keep the marriage covenant holy, how would they keep the covenant with God (Malachi 2:10-17)?

The Lord promised to reform the priesthood Himself with the Messiah. In this famous passage we see the most clearly in the Old Testament the identity of the Messiah: *"Behold, I will send my messenger, and he shall prepare the way before me: and the Lord, whom ye seek, shall suddenly come to his temple, even the messenger of the covenant, whom ye delight in: behold, he shall come, saith the LORD of hosts." Malachi 3:1.*

The third practice Malachi condemned was the holding back of tithes and offerings by the people. Because of the lenience of the priests, the people soon saw no need to give at all. A high standard and expectation usually produces faith. A low standard produces lowered expectations (Malachi 3:7-12).

The last issue Malachi addressed was an attitude rather than a practice. The people were weary of serving the Lord without the completion of the vision. They grew discontented in following the Lord: *"Ye have said, It is vain to serve God: and what profit is it that we have kept his ordinance, and that we have walked mournfully before the LORD of hosts?" Malachi 3:14.*

The fourth chapter of Malachi contains two references to God's ultimate fulfillment of His promises to Israel and warnings about the wait. *"But unto you that fear my name shall the Sun of righteousness arise with healing in his wings; and ye shall go forth, and grow up as calves of the stall." Malachi 4:2. "Behold, I will send you Elijah the prophet before the coming of the great and dreadful day of the LORD: And he shall turn the heart of the fathers to the children, and the heart of the children to their fathers, lest I come and smite the earth with a curse." Malachi 4:5,6.*

Compromise of the Vision

During the four hundred years between Malachi and the birth of Jesus, politics and corruption caused the loss of the inherited priesthood. The children of the return gave up hope of waiting on God and instead tried to help God with their militancy. A false spirit of the Messiah developed. The principles that they adopted during this time prevented them from recognizing God's Messiah when He arrived: *"He came unto his own, and his own received him not." John 1:11.*

While there are no scriptures to describe this time between the testaments, we do have some reliable sources of the key events of history that relate to the vision of the Messiah. I will draw mostly from 1 Maccabees for the details of this time.

The children of the captivity returned to Jerusalem with the blessings of the Persians, who generally left each culture to itself and did not try to impose its ways and values on the people. Nevertheless, Alexander the Great conquered the Persian Empire by about 330 B.C. The Greeks, the kingdom of brass (Daniel 2), sought to assimilate their empire through cultural means.

The drama of the four hundred "silent years" revolved around the acceptance or rejection of Greek ways by the Jews. There were many who believed they should compromise with the Greeks. This party eventually became the Sadducees. Another group was for holding fast to the tradition and the hope of Israel. This party became the Pharisees of Jesus' day. Jesus entered into a Jewish world where the correct vision of Him had been mostly lost because of compromise and extreme reaction.

1 Maccabees does not mention any Greek ruler until Antiochus Epiphanes, in the one hundred thirty seventh year of the Greeks. It was under this Seleucid ruler that singular events affecting Israel's vision took place. The author laments that during his reign the party of the compromisers, the Hellenizers, gained the high priesthood. Antiochus set aside the hereditary high priest and placed Joshua, a leader of the Hellenizers, in his place. Joshua promised to do all he could to make the people Greeks culturally and religiously. (1 Maccabees 1:11-15).[3]

With the goal of assimilating the Jews by force, Antiochus attacked Jerusalem. He killed tens of thousands, destroyed their walls and houses, and stole the treasures of the Temple. (1 Maccabees 1:20-32)[4] Then he declared the Act of Uniformity (1 Maccabees 1:41-49),[5] which compelled the people to adopt Greek religion and customs on the pain of death. The Greeks tortured and killed those who would not conform, and the Hellenizers supported them. Antiochus also commanded the people to sacrifice to the Greek gods in every city (1 Maccabees 1:51).

"Now the fifteenth day of the month Casleu, in the hundred forty and fifth year, they set up the abomination of desolation upon the altar, and builded idol altars throughout the cities of Juda on every side;" I Maccabees 1:54. The abomination of desolation is defined as an idol altar built on top of the altar of God (I Maccabees 1:59). This was the first fulfillment of Daniel's prophecy and Antiochus was the first antichrist or anti-messiah.

The traditionalists were horrified of this threat to the dream and hope of Israel. They refused to sacrifice and give up their worship of God. These ancestors of the Pharisees were noble in their adherence to the law of God: *"Wherefore they chose rather to die, that they might not be defiled with meats, and that they might not profane the holy covenant: so they died." 1 Maccabees 1:63.*

The Hellenizers eventually came to Modin, where Mattathias lived with his five sons. Mattathias mourned the tragedy of the victory of the Hellenizers and purposed in his heart that he would not forsake the covenant with God. The king's officers asked Mattathias to be the first to sacrifice to the Greek gods since he was a leader in the town: *"Then Mattathias answered and spake with a loud voice, Though all the nations that are under the king's dominion obey him, and fall away every one from the religion of their fathers, and give consent to his commandments: Yet will I and my sons and my brethren walk in the covenant of our fathers. God forbid that we should forsake the law and the ordinances. We will not hearken to the king's words, to go from our religion, either on the right hand, or on the left." 1 Maccabees 2:19-22.*

One Jew from Modin, however, offered to please the Hellenizers and be the first to sacrifice. When Mattathias saw this, he rushed the traitor and killed him at the altar. Then, not yet content, he killed the king's officer and tore down the idol altar (1 Maccabees 2:24-25).

The author of 1 Maccabees comments: *"Thus dealt he zealously for the law of God, like as Phinees did unto Zambri the son of Salom (v.26)."* From the acceptance and praise of this rash action by Mattathias, the future Pharisees began to make decisions that would lead them away from Christ. *"And Mattathias cried throughout the city with a loud voice, saying, Whosoever is zealous of the law, and maintaineth the covenant, let him follow me (v.27)."*

Many patriotic and zealous Jews took him at his word and left the towns to form guerilla groups in the wilderness. Yet, their inflexible dedication to the Law of Moses hindered their militant stand. They were attacked on the Sabbath day and refused to fight; therefore they were slaughtered (v. 31-38).

The first harmful decision, based on this massacre, was to compromise the Law and fight on the Sabbath: *"At that time they decreed, saying, Whosoever shall come to make battle with us on the Sabbath day, we will fight against him; neither will we all die, as our brethren that were murdered in the secret places (v.41)."* In this they showed more of a spirit of self-sufficiency than trust in God. They took matters in their own hands, a tendency which later caused them to ignore God's provision in Jesus Christ.

These zealous forerunners of the Pharisees forcibly circumcised children (v.46) and adopted the principle of righteousness by arms: *"So they recovered the law out of the hand of the Gentiles, and out of the hand of kings, neither suffered they the sinner to triumph (v. 48)."*

Mattathias died about a year after the abomination of desolation, but he appointed his son Judas Maccabeus, the hammer of God, to be his successor in the revolution. He taught his followers to be militant instead of meek: *"Take also unto you all those that observe the law, and avenge ye the wrong of your people (v. 67)."*

The *Hammer of God* became the leader of a real army in time as more and more zealous Jews joined him. They went through the cities tearing down the idols and circumcising the infants. Judas was so successful that the generals of Antiochus took notice and desired to conquer the rebels to win the favor of the king (1 Maccabees 3:10-15). Nevertheless, Judas defeated these generals and enraged the king.

Antiochus went into Persia to raise money for the war. His goal was that Judah and its people should be destroyed, and that strangers should be brought in from other countries to live there (v. 31-36, 42)

Judas was successful in turning back the forces of Antiochus. He then went to Jerusalem and restored the Temple (1 Maccabees 4:36-61). This was the first time that Daniel's prophecy was fulfilled about the abomination of desolation and the restoration (Daniel 12:11-12).[6] It will be fulfilled again in the tribulation.

After this, Judas fought against Israel's ancient enemies and won many victories (1 Maccabees 5). He was so successful that the people began to see him and his family as a new type of Messiah. Their confidence that the Maccabees were God's chosen was confirmed by the failure of other would be leaders. Joseph and Azarias attempted to lead like Judas but were defeated. The author of 1 Maccabees gives this editorial on the event: *"Thus there was a great overthrow among the children of Israel, because they were not obedient unto Judas and his brethren, but thought to do some valiant act. Moreover these men came not of the seed of those, by whose hand deliverance was given unto Israel." 1 Maccabees 5:61-62.*

He was a new type of Messiah because he was not of the lineage of David, but was instead of the family of priests. The people began to change their thinking and to look primarily for a military leader instead of a descendant of David. Jeconiah had indeed been childless as far as the kingdom was concerned. Jeremiah's prophecy had come true and the people could see no restoration of God's promise to David.

Judas made a league with the Romans to help against the power of the Seleucids (1 Maccabees 8). It seemed like a good idea at the time but led to the incorporation of Judea into the Roman Empire. The true Messiah would not need to make alliances to usher in God's kingdom. This was still another compromise in Israel's quest for the Place and Person. The actions of the Maccabees and the people's belief in them demonstrate the folly of compromise while waiting on the vision to be fulfilled. Because of the shift in focus the true blessing is overlooked when it comes.

After Judas' death in a battle the people asked Jonathan his brother to lead them (1 Maccabees 9:31). The succession of the Maccabees had been established and the people looked to them as the new royal line. Jonathan went on to repel the Seleucids and end their attempt to resubjugate Judea: *"Thus the sword ceased from Israel: but Jonathan dwelt at Machmas, and began to govern the people; and he destroyed the ungodly men out of Israel." 1 Maccabees 9:73.*

Jonathan Maccabees accepted the office of the high priesthood in a political move by one of the Seleucid contenders (1 Maccabees 10:20). By this, the

Maccabees joined the offices of ruler and high priest into one person. It seemed as though the promise of the Messiah was given an unexpected turn and new hope through the Maccabees.

Jonathan was killed by the treachery of Tryphon and the people asked Simon, Jonathan's brother, to take his place (1 Maccabees 13:8-9). Under Simon, the Seleucids officially released Judea and gave them independence. This occurred in the one hundred and seventieth year of the Greeks, or 143B.C.

During the time of peace afterward, Judea was rebuilt and the people's hope grew. They named Simon and the Maccabees the hereditary rulers and high priests forever. The intention was to replace David's line with the Maccabees and hope that God would send the Messiah through them. The evidence for this is in *1 Maccabees 14:41, 47: "Also that the Jews and priests were well pleased that Simon should be their governor and high priest forever, until there should arise a faithful prophet... Then Simon accepted hereof, and was well pleased to be high priest, and captain and governor of the Jews and priests, and to defend them all."* The "faithful prophet" they looked for was the Messiah (Deuteronomy 18:15).

The Seleucids reneged on their promise of independence and one party tried to reconquer Judea. Simon and his sons resisted and won the battle. Nevertheless, Simon and two of his sons were assassinated shortly after. Simon became the last of the sons of Mattathias to die for his country in 135 B.C.

The people made Simon's son, John Hyrcanus, ruler and high priest in the place of his father. This is where the book of 1 Maccabees ends. Its purpose is to show new direction in the quest for the Place and Person and to affirm the Maccabees as the successors to David's covenant. This, however, proved to be a false hope.

John Hyrcanus took a page from the Greek playbook and forced conquered peoples to become Jews. He ordered that they be circumcised. Militancy was established as the path to the fulfilled vision. This plan would eventually backfire.

During his time the parties of the Hellenizers and the reactionaries became known as the Sadducees and Pharisees. The Maccabees had always been Pharisees but John Hyrcanus turned on them because they refused to severely punish someone who defamed him. After that, the Maccabees were generally Sadducees.[7]

John Hyrcanus lost favor with the people after his break with the Pharisees. At his death, he appointed his wife to be his successor. Nevertheless, John's son Aristobulus imprisoned and starved her.

Aristobulus assumed the title of king of the Jews. So he officially joined the roles of king and high priest, showing that the Maccabees were the family of the coming Messiah. Aristobulus only lasted one year.

The later Maccabees were Sadducees but they still forced conquered peoples to submit to circumcision or be put to death. In this way, the Edomites technically became Jews, which provided a way for an Edomite to eventually claim the throne legitimately (Antipater and Herod).

The last two Maccabees to hold any real power were Hyrcanus and another Aristobulus. Hyrcanus was the high priest and a puppet of the Pharisees, and Aristobulus was the leader of the Sadducees. It was the rivalry between the two that allowed the Edomites and Romans to take control of the country. Through intrigues and bribes, enough confusion was generated that the Roman armies took notice. In order to restore peace, they took over Judea in their larger effort to tame the former Seleucid Empire.

The Romans saw Antipater the Edomite as the liaison to the Jews. Julius Caesar eventually made him Procurator of Judea. Antipater and his sons were nominally Pharisees because it served their political ends. One of his sons, Herod, became the governor of Judea. Hyrcanus remained the high priest.

The intrigues and bribes continued, but Herod was victorious. Caesar Augustus declared him king of Judea in 40 B.C. He succeeded in killing the last of the Maccabees, both male and female. One of them, Mariamne, was his beloved wife, whom he murdered in a rage of jealousy. The finalAristobulus, the last male Maccabee, was made high priest for a day or so over Herod's objections, but then was "accidentally" drowned in one of the king's fishponds. Herod's sister, to secure the throne for an Edomite heir, killed Herod's two sons by Mariamne, who were half Maccabee, in a plot.

The last two Maccabees were murdered in the year 6 B.C. just two years before the birth of Jesus Christ. The new hope of the Jews proved to be a false hope. God did not honor their militancy or their effort to name a new family as the inheritors of David's covenant. Their league with Rome proved to be the avenue of their servitude.

Crisis

The death of Herod's Maccabee sons ended the hope of the Messiah through the new chosen family. Nevertheless, God intended all along to keep His promise to David literally. The Messiah would be of David's lineage and sit on the throne of Israel. That's why the book of Matthew begins with the lineage of Jesus by His earthly father, Joseph. Matthew traces His descent throughAbraham, David, and Zerubbabel. In addition, Luke shows that Jesus was of the house of David through Mary (Luke 3:23-38).

The people did not understand how God could any longer fulfill His promises literally. They forgot that God is full of surprises and delights to show Himself strong in supernatural and unexpected ways. The first chapter of Matthew is elegant in its statement of God's fulfillment of the vision: *"The book of the generation of Jesus Christ, the son of David, the son of Abraham...Now the birth of Jesus Christ was on this wise: When as his mother Mary was espoused to Joseph, before they came together, she was found with child of the Holy Ghost." Matthew 1:1,18.* Jesus was the son of God Himself. He didn't need an earthly father. Yet he was also of the house of David.

The crisis of the Jews was whether to accept God's long awaited Messiah or reject Him. If they accepted Him, they would enter into the endless glory they had hoped for. Instead, God knew that the problem of sin had to be dealt with first: *"And she shall bring forth a son, and thou shalt call his name JESUS: for he shall save his people from their sins." Matthew 1:21.*

The crisis of spiritual adulthood is the *meeting with God.* At last God delivers the fulfillment of the vision. The challenge is to recognize it and have the faith to accept it.

The spiritual traveler often doesn't recognize the fulfillment because he has given up or has lowered his standards to accept substitutes. Only a person afraid to miss God's best will be able to recognize God's hand in the first fulfillment. Such a person will not likely reject a possibility, especially one that seems to have overcome the impossible, because faith looks for God to do the improbable and the impossible. That was the kind of faith of Abraham, the father of faith: *"Who against hope believed in hope, that he might become the father of many nations, according to that which was spoken, So shall thy seed be. And being not weak in faith, he considered not his own body now dead, when he was about an hundred years old, neither yet the deadness of Sara's womb: He staggered not at the promise of God through unbelief; but was strong in faith, giving glory to God; And being fully persuaded that, what he had promised, he was able also to perform. And therefore it was imputed to him for righteousness." Romans 4:18-22.*

The book of Matthew tells the story of Jesus from a Jewish perspective, so it is an appropriate book to study the Jew's response to their meeting with God, which was the life and ministry of Jesus. I will also refer to other gospels to help illuminate events.

Herod heard the wise men were looking for one born King of the Jews. That would be impossible in many people's eyes because the house of David had never ruled since the captivity and Herod had wiped out the would-be replacements, the Maccabees. There were no others who could lay claim to the title. Herod rightly judged that this new king would have to be the Messiah: *"When Herod the king had heard these things, he was troubled, and all Jerusalem with him. And when he had gathered all the chief priests and scribes of the people together, he demanded of them where Christ should be born." Matthew 2:3,4.*

The chief priests said "Bethlehem," but they didn't tell Herod the complete prophecy. Matthew records that they only told Herod part of the verse: *"And they said unto him, In Bethlehem of Judaea: for thus it is written by the prophet, And thou Bethlehem, in the land of Juda, art not the least among the princes of Juda: for out of thee shall come a Governor, that shall rule my people Israel." Matthew 2:5,6.* The original is much stronger. Micah implies that this governor is God Himself: *"But thou, Bethlehem Ephratah, though thou be little among the thousands of Judah, yet out of thee shall he come forth unto me that is to be ruler in Israel; whose goings forth have been from of old, from everlasting." Micah 5:2.*

There were others besides the wise men and Herod with the spiritual insight to recognize God's fulfillment of the vision. Simeon andAnna had earnestly prayed and waited for the Lord's Messiah. They saw through eyes of faith even though it looked impossible. Both were present at Jesus' circumcision and both blessed Him as the Savior of Israel. The Holy Spirit had revealed to Simeon that he would not die until he saw the Lord's Christ. Anna had waited the entire eighty-four years of her widowhood. Those two saints are pure examples of the faith to accept and receive God's best, not only for themselves, but also for their people. The personal solution can become the solution for the people if they also have faith (Luke 2:25-38).

Herod tried to destroy the young Messiah but was unsuccessful because of God's intervention (Matthew 2). God told Joseph to take his family to Egypt to protect the new king. Herod gave orders to kill all the children in Bethlehem to eliminate the rival. After Herod's death, God told Joseph to return to Israel.

Matthew moved forward in time about thirty years later for the direct declaration of the fulfillment. First, John the Baptist, the Messiah's forerunner, announced it: *"In those days came John the Baptist, preaching in the wilderness of Judaea, And saying, Repent ye: for the kingdom of heaven is at hand." Matthew 3:1,2.* The scripture says that everyone was curious, even the Pharisees and Sadducees. The Maccabees had been gone only a few years and there did not seem to be any hope of restoring the vision. It was astounding to hear someone say that God's blessing was upon them.

Some of the Pharisees and Sadducees were so intrigued that they applied for John's baptism, not wanting to miss anything. John warned them not to trust in their national identity (children of Abraham). He let them know that the new kingdom would be based on individual spiritual relationship (Matthew 3:7-12).

Then, Jesus Himself began to publicly declare Himself: *"From that time Jesus began to preach, and to say, Repent: for the kingdom of heaven is at hand." Matthew 4:17.* In effect, he was saying, "It's time, the Messiah is here, and the fulfillment of the vision has come." Jesus preached the gospel, the good news of the kingdom, that the hope of Israel was upon them: *"And Jesus went about all Galilee, teaching in their synagogues, and preaching the gospel of the kingdom, and healing all manner of sickness and all manner of disease among the people." Matthew 4:23.*

Jesus established His legitimacy primarily by two methods: speaking with authority and with miracles.

Jesus did not speak like the religious leaders of the day, merely making commentary on the scriptures; He spoke as one with intimate knowledge of the meaning behind the scriptures and their proper application. He even spoke as one with authority to change the direction of thought on scriptural interpretations: *"And it came to pass, when Jesus had ended these sayings, the people were astonished at his doctrine: For he taught them as one having authority, and not as the scribes." Matthew 7:28,29.*

On one occasion the Pharisees sent officers to arrest Jesus, but the officers were so enthralled by His authority that they did not approach Him: *"Then said some of them of Jerusalem, Is not this he, whom they seek to kill? But, lo, he speaketh boldly, and they say nothing unto him. Do the rulers know indeed that this is the very Christ? Howbeit we know this man whence he is: but when Christ cometh, no man knoweth whence he is. Then cried Jesus in the temple as he taught, saying, Ye both know me, and ye know whence I am: and I am not come of myself, but he that sent me is true, whom ye know not. But I know him: for I am from him, and he hath sent me. Then they sought to take him: but no man laid hands on him, because his hour was not yet come. And many of the people believed on him, and said, When Christ cometh, will he do more miracles than these which this man hath done? The Pharisees heard that the people murmured such things concerning him; and the Pharisees and the chief priests sent officers to take him." John 7:25-32. "Then came the officers to the chief priests and Pharisees; and they said unto them, Why have ye not brought him? The officers answered, Never man spake like this man." John 7:45,46.*

When Jesus overturned the table of the money changers, He demonstrated both His authority to apply scripture to current events and the power His presence had on those who heard Him: *"And he taught, saying unto them, Is it not written, My house shall be called of all nations the house of prayer? but ye have made it a den of thieves. And the scribes and chief priests heard it, and sought how they might destroy him: for they feared him, because all the people was astonished at his doctrine. And when even was come, he went out of the city." Mark 11:17-19.*

Matthew follows his observation of Jesus' authoritative style with a narrative describing Jesus' miracles in Matthew 8. In verse 27, we see the response of the people: *"But the men marvelled, saying, What manner of man is this, that even the winds and the sea obey him!" Matthew 8:27.*

Jesus' miracle produced a similar response in the people at the would-be funeral of the widow of Nain's son: *"And there came a fear on all: and they glorified God, saying, That a great prophet is risen up among us; and, That God hath visited his people." Luke 7:16.*

John records Jesus' first miracle and says that it showed His glory and position with God: *"This beginning of miracles did Jesus in Cana of Galilee, and manifested forth his glory; and his disciples believed on him." John 2:11.*

It was not long after Jesus began to prove His claims of the kingdom that the Pharisees and religious leaders began to show skepticism and question Him. The Pharisees prided themselves as the true believers in the Law. They wanted to lead the nation by example to scrupulously uphold every jot and tittle, so much so that they developed laws around the Law. Their purpose was to build a fence around the Law to keep from getting close to violations. The Pharisees believed that by upholding the scriptures, they would gain God's favor and He would bless the nation. Jesus did not follow their fence rules around the Law so they began to reject Him.

Jesus' ministry reflected the views of the Pharisees closer than other sects. Yet, He focused His strongest words against their errors. Perhaps Jesus worked the hardest to convince them since they were the orthodox most likely to accept Him. Indeed, the people who accepted Jesus were allied to the Pharisees more than other sects.[8]

Jesus had some support among the Pharisees. Luke says that it was a Pharisee who warned Jesus to stay away from Jerusalem because of Herod's threats (Luke 13:31). John writes that Jesus' miracles caused a division among the Pharisees (John 9:16).

Matthew begins to record in Chapter 9 the Pharisees'response to Jesus. At the first incident Jesus showed the true focus of His ministry, when He healed the man sick of the palsy. Jesus forgave the man's sins first and his healing was a secondary blessing. He was not trying to make an outward show of power as much as trying to change men's hearts. His focus was not on changing people's circumstances as much as healing them of sin. The victory over sin was Jesus' primary mission. Because only with a change of heart would people be able to benefit from His kingdom (Matthew 9:1-8).

When Jesus openly associated with the "impure," the Pharisees, or separated ones, could not reconcile that with their view of holiness: *"And it came to pass, as Jesus sat at meat in the house, behold, many publicans and sinners came and sat down with him and his disciples. And when the Pharisees saw it, they said unto his disciples, Why eateth your Master with publicans and sinners?" Matthew 9:10,11.* Jesus told them that His ministry was to sinners, not to those already righteous, implying that they were wrong for completely cutting themselves off from the unenlightened.

Then John's disciples, who were seen as part of the Pharisee movement, questioned Jesus' lack of fasting. Jesus responded by giving them the metaphor of the wineskins, indicating that He was building something entirely new and that their effort to see Him conforming to traditional expectations was misguided: *"Then came to him the disciples of John, saying, Why do we and the Pharisees fast oft, but thy disciples fast not? And Jesus said unto them, Can the children of the bridechamber mourn, as long as the bridegroom is with them? but the days will come, when the bridegroom shall be taken from them, and then shall they fast. No man putteth a piece of new cloth unto an old garment, for that which is put in to fill it up taketh from the garment, and the rent is made worse. Neither do men put new wine into old bottles: else the bottles break, and the wine runneth out, and the bottles perish: but they put new wine into new bottles, and both are preserved." Matthew 9:14-17.*

John himself questioned Jesus' legitimacy from prison, anxious that he had performed his ministry in vain. Jesus sent word back to him with a combination of quotations from Isaiah confirming His identity to John (Matthew 11:1-6). The passage I like to think John understood from Jesus' message is Isaiah 29:18-24. In it Isaiah prophesies of the ministry of the Messiah, that He would not only open the people's understanding but that He would put an end to petty bickering over the details of piety. The decisive blow to pettiness would be "the work of his hands, the children": the meek and poor who would come to have faith in God: *"And in that day shall the deaf hear the words of the book, and the eyes of the blind shall see out of obscurity, and out of darkness. The meek also shall increase their joy in the LORD, and the poor among men shall rejoice in the Holy One of Israel. For the terrible one is brought to nought, and the scorner is consumed, and all that watch for iniquity are cut off: That make a man an offender for a word, and lay a snare for him that reproveth in the gate, and turn aside the just for a thing of nought. Therefore thus saith the LORD, who redeemed Abraham, concerning the house of Jacob, Jacob shall not now be ashamed, neither shall his face now wax pale. But when he seeth his children, the work of mine hands, in the midst of him, they shall sanctify my name, and sanctify the Holy One of Jacob, and shall fear the God of Israel. They also that erred in spirit shall come to understanding, and they that murmured shall learn doctrine." Isaiah 29:18-24.*

Jesus stated His attitude in Matthew 11:16-19. He anticipated the Pharisees rejection of Him and their reasons. They were immature in their faith. They believed that the Messiah had to act like them to be legitimate. They did not acknowledge the deeper issues of faith, hope, and love. In essence, Jesus said, "They will reject me because I don't play their games": *"But whereunto shall I liken this generation? It is like unto children sitting in the markets, and calling unto their fellows, And saying, We have piped unto you, and ye have not danced; we have mourned unto you, and ye have not lamented. For John came neither eating nor drinking, and they say, He hath a devil. The Son of man came eating and drinking, and they say, Behold a man gluttonous, and a winebibber, a friend of publicans and sinners. But wisdom is justified of her children." Matthew 11:16-19.*

The next two incidents were a direct violation by Jesus and His disciples of the fence rules constructed by the Pharisees. The Pharisees had a list of acceptable and unacceptable work on the Sabbath days. They did not take into account special circumstances and had no flexibility, although God showed flexibility even in the original Law of Moses. Jesus' disciples picked corn and ate it, which was their right to do under the Law (Deuteronomy 23:25), even if they did not grow the corn. The Pharisees, however, objected because it was done on the Sabbath. Jesus also healed a man on that same Sabbath, and the Pharisees made up a new rule on the spot that the healing constituted forbidden work. Jesus gave a strong response regarding both incidents, affirming that God does not forbid doing good on the Sabbath under special circumstances (Matthew 12:1-13).

As a result of Jesus' belittling the Pharisees' fence rules, they determined that He was too great a threat to their spiritual hegemony over the people. They had a meeting and decided to kill Him if possible: *"Then the Pharisees went out, and held a council against him, how they might destroy him." Matthew 12:14.* Mark says that they invited the Herodians (supporters of Herod's line of kings) to their council. The Pharisees proved their willingness to use violence to accomplish their agenda, forgetting the very basics of the Law in favor of their own interpretations and applications: *"Thou shalt not kill." Exodus 20:13.*

After the council of the Pharisees, Jesus healed a deaf and blind man, and the people began to regard Him as the Messiah, the Son of David (Matthew 12:22-23). But the Pharisees accused Him of using satanic power to accomplish His goals: *"But when the Pharisees heard it, they said, This fellow doth not cast out devils, but by Beelzebub the prince of the devils." Matthew 12:24.* Jesus' response is instructive to all those that try to minimize the Spirit's work in other groups or churches out of jealousy. Jesus told them that it is impossible to do the Lord's work with Satan's power, otherwise Satan would be working against himself. He also warned them to beware speaking against the work of the Holy Spirit, the unpardonable sin (Matthew 12:25-37).

The Pharisees grew more confrontational with Him and demanded that He show a supernatural sign that He was the Messiah, even after all He had done. Jesus rebuked their desire to see a sign. He told them that the desire to see a sign is like the sin of adultery. They are the same because they both reflect dissatisfaction with God's provision and evidence of His grace. Jesus had already given them enough signs. The greatest sign was the conviction in their own hearts (Luke 24:32). Nevertheless, Jesus told them the sign. He would be like Jonah in the belly of the whale. Jonah spent three days in there and God brought him out. Jesus would be in the grave for three days and would be resurrected by God: *"But he answered and said unto them, An evil and adulterous generation seeketh after a sign; and there shall no sign be given to it, but the sign of the prophet Jonas: For as Jonas was three days and three nights in the whale's belly; so shall the Son of man be three days and three nights in the heart of the earth." Matthew 12:39,40.*

Apparently, Jesus gave the sign of Jonah every time He was asked for a sign, because the gospels record His response in other contexts (Matthew 15:1-4). In John He says it a little differently: *"Jesus answered and said unto them, Destroy this temple, and in three days I will raise it up." John 2:19.* By this He signified that His body was the Temple of the Lord.

John wrote of an incident where the Pharisees rejected Him on two grounds: that they, as spiritual masters of Israel, did not believe in Him and that the Prophet could not come from Galilee (John 7:46-53). They were wrong on both counts. Nicodemus, a Pharisee who believed in Him, was present when they said it, and Isaiah prophesied that the Messiah would have a ministry in Galilee (Isaiah 9:1-7; Matthew 4:12-17). The incident showed their true loyalties: *"How can ye believe, which receive honour one of another, and seek not the honour that cometh from God only?" John 5:44.*

Principles of the Kingdom

In Matthew 13, Jesus explained the mysteries of the kingdom to His disciples and to the people. Nevertheless, He did so in parables, so that the disciples understood, and the people, because of their hardness of heart, did not: *"Who hath ears to hear, let him hear. And the disciples came, and said unto him, Why speakest thou unto them in parables? He answered and said unto them, Because it is given unto you to know the mysteries of the kingdom of heaven, but to them it is not given. For whosoever hath, to him shall be given, and he shall have more abundance: but whosoever hath not, from him shall be taken away even that he hath. Therefore speak I to them in parables: because they seeing see not; and hearing they hear not, neither do they understand. And in them is fulfilled the prophecy of Esaias, which saith, By hearing ye shall hear, and shall not understand; and seeing ye shall see, and shall not perceive: For this people's heart is waxed gross, and their ears are dull of hearing, and their eyes they have closed; lest at any time they should see with their eyes, and hear with their ears, and should understand with their heart, and should be converted, and I should heal them." Matthew 13:9-15.*

1. It will be individual hearts that are conquered in the first stage, not countries, kingdoms or empires. This was in the parable of the sower (Matthew 13:1-23). Luke records that the Pharisees asked when the kingdom would be observable, and Jesus replied that it would not: *"And when he was demanded of the Pharisees, when the kingdom of God should come, he answered them and said, The kingdom of God cometh not with observation: Neither shall they say, Lo here! or, lo there! for, behold, the kingdom of God is within you." Luke 17:20,21. "Jesus answered and said unto him, Verily, verily, I say unto thee, Except a man be born again, he cannot see the kingdom of God." John 3:3.*

2. There will be evil and hypocrisy present in the kingdom in its present form. The kingdom will grow and evil will grow alongside it until God comes and separates the elements of the kingdom from falsehood. The parables of the tares, the mustard seed, and the leaven all represent this principle (Matthew 13:24-43). Jesus instituted His kingdom while He was here on earth. The world has worked to enter His kingdom since that time, but many have tried to use unapproved methods: *"The law and the prophets were until John:*

since that time the kingdom of God is preached, and every man presseth into it." Luke 16:16.

3. Jesus' kingdom will grow inexorably until He comes back, but it will have many problems due to the influence of worldliness. Another way to say this is that Jesus' kingdom will infect the world system, but it will not completely eliminate it. Jesus Himself will have to do that. Many people say that at the second coming of Christ, there will only be a few Christians left huddled together in a corner, but that's not accurate according to Matthew 13: *"Another parable spake he unto them; The kingdom of heaven is like unto leaven, which a woman took, and hid in three measures of meal, till the whole was leavened." Matthew 13:33.* The kingdom of heaven will grow in power, number, and influence until the end of time. It has already happened and will continue. They say that people will get worse and worse till the end, but the Bible tells us which people will get worse and worse: *"But evil men and seducers shall wax worse and worse, deceiving, and being deceived." 2 Timothy 3:13.*

4. The kingdom will be priceless to those who find it. It will be hidden from the eyes of the world until it is revealed in all its splendor: *"When he shall come to be glorified in his saints, and to be admired in all them that believe (because our testimony among you was believed) in that day." 2 Thessalonians 1:10.* This principle is found in the parables of the treasure and the pearl of great price (Mathew 13:44-46).

5. Finally, the kingdom will be revealed at the second coming, when Christ will separate His kingdom from the world. This principle is reflected in the parable of the net (Matthew 13:47-50).

Decision Time

Then Jesus went into His own country and was rejected by His town on the grounds that He couldn't be the Messiah because they knew Him, an apparently common if silly reason for rejecting a prophet (Matthew 13:53-56; John 7:26-27): *"And they were offended in him. But Jesus said unto them, A prophet is not without honour, save in his own country, and in his own house. And he did not many mighty works there because of their unbelief." Matthew 13:57,58.*

Matthew records in Chapter 14 the incident of the five loaves and two fishes; John, however, in Chapter 6 shows the significance as far as the people's acceptance of Jesus'Messiahship. In John's account, after the feeding of the five thousand, Jesus leaves the place and crosses the Sea of Galilee: *"Then those men, when they had seen the miracle that Jesus did, said, This is of a truth that prophet that should come into the world. When Jesus therefore perceived that they would come and take him by force, to make him a king, he departed again into a mountain himself alone." John 6:14,15.*

Jesus knew that the people wanted to accept Him only because of what He could do for them materially, and not for spiritual reasons. Their view of the Messiah didn't include spiritual transformation. And yet, that was the always-missing ingredient in Old Testament revivals (Isaiah 1:10-20). God had determined to save His people, but in the proper order. The spirit first, then the psychological and material life (1 Thessalonians. 5:23): *"Jesus answered them and said, Verily, verily, I say unto you, Ye seek me, not because ye saw the miracles, but because ye did eat of the loaves, and were filled. Labour not for the meat which perisheth, but for that meat which endureth unto everlasting life, which the Son of man shall give unto you: for him hath God the Father sealed." John 6:26,27.*

Jesus rebuked them for their shallow materialism and encouraged them to accept His offer of spiritual regeneration through Him. The fulfillment of the vision is never primarily a material blessing but an affirmation of the champion's faith: *"They said therefore unto him, What sign shewest thou then, that we may see, and believe thee? what dost thou work? Our fathers did eat manna in the desert; as it is written, He gave them bread from heaven to eat. Then Jesus said unto them, Verily, verily, I say unto you, Moses gave you not that bread from heaven; but my Father giveth you the true bread from heaven. For the bread of God is he which cometh down from heaven, and giveth life unto the world. Then said they unto him, Lord, evermore give us this bread. And Jesus said unto them, I am the bread of life: he that cometh to me shall never hunger; and he that believeth on me shall never thirst." John 6:30-35.*

John records that many of Jesus' would-be disciples stopped following Him after this incident. They wanted an outward show of God's power and weren't content with the true inner deliverance that He was offering them. It's the same today with many people, and many religious leaders feel constrained to give the people material manna instead of the true manna: *"It is the spirit that quickeneth; the flesh profiteth nothing: the words that I speak unto you, they are spirit, and they are life.... From that time many of his disciples went back, and walked no more with him. Then said Jesus unto the twelve, Will ye also go away? Then Simon Peter answered him, Lord, to whom shall we go? thou hast the words of eternal life. And we believe and are sure that thou art that Christ, the Son of the living God." John 6:63, 66-69.*

"Then came to Jesus scribes and Pharisees, which were of Jerusalem, saying, Why do thy disciples transgress the tradition of the elders? for they wash not their hands when they eat bread. But he answered and said unto them, Why do ye also transgress the commandment of God by your tradition?" Matthew 15:1-3. Jesus used this incident to address the fence rules. He showed the danger of putting tradition and applications on the same level with scripture. He used the example of the Pharisees refusing to help their parents financially by saying their property is a gift to the Lord. In doing so, they violated the commandment to honor their parents (Matthew 15:4-6): *"Ye hypocrites, well did Esaias prophesy of you, saying, This people draweth nigh unto me with their mouth, and honoureth me with their lips; but their heart is far from me. But in vain they do worship me, teaching for doctrines the commandments of men." Matthew 15:7-9.* (This is a quotation from Isaiah 29:13, the same chapter Jesus used to show John the nature of His work.).

The disciples themselves had difficulty breaking away from the teachings of the Pharisees; just as people today have a hard time seeing the radical nature of Jesus' teaching because of the nice traditions our churches make to tame Him. They did not yet understand completely that Jesus was making a distinction from their tradition: *"Then came his disciples, and said unto him, Knowest thou that the Pharisees were offended, after they heard this saying?" Matthew 15:12.* Later, Jesus told them to beware the "leaven," or teachings, of the Pharisees and Sadducees (Matthew 16:5-12).

The disciples had their questions too. They believed that Jesus was the Messiah but they did not always know how to harmonize His reality with their expectations: *"And his disciples asked him, saying, Why then say the scribes that Elias must first come?" Matthew 17:10.* They had read the prophecy from Malachi that Elijah would come before the kingdom (Malachi 4:5-6). Jesus explained to them that John the Baptist accomplished the ministry of Elijah (Matthew 17:11-13).

The disciples believed that the kingdom was for adults only. They chased away children who came to Him. They thought he was only concerned with adult matters (Matthew 19:13-15). But, Jesus consistently taught that the attitude of a child would be necessary to gain entrance to the kingdom: faith, hope, and love are all stronger naturally in children than in adults: *"At the same time came the disciples unto Jesus, saying, Who is the greatest in the kingdom of heaven? And Jesus called a little child unto him, and set him in the midst of them, And said, Verily I say unto you, Except ye be converted, and become as little children, ye shall not enter into the kingdom of heaven. Whosoever therefore shall humble himself as this little child, the same is greatest in the kingdom of heaven." Matthew 18:1-4.*

The disciples believed that material success was the evidence of right relationship with God. Jesus disabused them of that notion in His encounter with the rich young ruler (Matthew 19:16-22). *"Then said Jesus unto his disciples, Verily I say unto you, That a rich man shall hardly enter into the kingdom of heaven. And again I say unto you, It is easier for a camel to go through the eye of a needle, than for a rich man to enter into the kingdom of God. When his disciples heard it, they were exceedingly amazed, saying, Who then can be saved?" Matthew 19:23-25.* Jesus convinced them that only trust and faith in Him would get them into the kingdom, not riches. Riches are neither a ticket into, nor evidence of the kingdom of heaven. He told them the parable of the householder who showed grace to all his laborers, even those that only labored one hour. The grace was based on his goodness, and the heart of the laborers, not the amount of their work (Matthew 19:26 - 20:16).

The disciples also thought of the kingdom as a hierarchy, with some people over others. The mother of James and John asked that her sons be given the highest rank. Jesus took the occasion to show them that the kingdom is about serving others and God, not about advancing in a hierarchy (Matthew 20:20-28).

The irony is that many church groups today teach the very principles that Jesus corrected with His disciples: they do not allow Christian children to be included in the membership; they equate material success with spirituality; and they see the church as a hierarchy of righteousness, with each person in his rank.

When Jesus actually approached Jerusalem for His showdown with the religious leaders, the Pharisees had already rejected His claim. They worked hard to embarrass and trip Him up on legal, scriptural, and political controversies. Their aim was to alienate Him from different groups who would otherwise support Him. At Jerusalem, the Sadducees and other groups who were even more predisposed to reject Jesus joined them.

Of all the Jewish groups, the Pharisees were the closest to the truth. The Sadducees had already given up on ancient Judaism and had chosen politics instead. They only accepted the material aspects of the Law of Moses as legitimate. Many of the leaders of the nation were Sadducees. They were more intent on using their own political power than in seeking God's power. They were interested in protecting their positions and in preserving what was left of Israel's independence at all costs.

The Zealots advocated militancy. They wanted to follow the example of the Maccabees and throw off Roman rule by force. Their way resulted in the destruction of Israel and the Temple by the Romans in 70 A.D.

The Herodians were followers of Herod. They believed Herod's family was the new royal family and the nation's best hope for continued independence. Mark put the Herodians in league with the Pharisees at Jerusalem in their attacks on Jesus (Mark 12:13).

"The Pharisees also came unto him, tempting him, and saying unto him, Is it lawful for a man to put away his wife for every cause?" Matthew 19:3. The Pharisees knew that there were competing views on the subject and that a clear position by Jesus would alienate some groups. Jesus put the question in a bigger perspective by stating that God intends for marriage to be permanent. Jesus consistently answered people's controversies by showing God's perspective, which is always wider and clearer (Matthew 19:4-9).

When Jesus drove out the moneychangers from the Temple, the religious leaders of Jerusalem asked Him about His authority. The leaders truly believed in a hierarchy in which their authority was necessary to do spiritual things. They weren't ready to give ground to anyone, including the Messiah. His response implied that His authority came from God just like John's authority. The leaders did not challenge His answer because the people believed John was a prophet sent from God. (Matthew 21:12-17, 23-32).

Then Jesus told the parable of the vineyard in which the servants schemed to take away the vineyard by force by killing the lord's representatives and finally the heir. The leaders rightly judged that Jesus was condemning them (Matthew 21:33-41). Jesus ended this particular discourse by announcing that their rejection of His kingdom had become final and that God was going to carry out plan B, the church: *"Jesus saith unto them, Did ye never read in the scriptures, The stone which the builders rejected, the same is become the head of the corner: this is the Lord's doing, and it is marvellous in our eyes? Therefore say I unto you, The kingdom of God shall be taken from you, and given to a nation bringing forth the fruits thereof." Matthew 21:42,43.*

After Jesus' announcement that the kingdom would be taken away from them, the religious leaders continued their baiting in earnest: *"Then went the Pharisees, and took counsel how they might entangle him in his talk." Matthew 22:15.* They sent some of their representatives with the Herodians and asked Him about paying taxes to the Romans, an issue bound to divide His following, because many people believed it was disloyal to Israel and its vision to pay taxes to a foreign government. There was also support in the Old Testament for this idea (Deuteronomy 28). The Herodians instead advocated cooperation with Rome as the only way to save the nation. Jesus again took a larger perspective, one from God's point of view. People should honor their rulers as representatives of God but they should not give them the honor that only God deserves. No one could find fault with His answer: *"They say unto him, Caesar's. Then saith he unto them, Render therefore unto Caesar the things which are Caesar's; and unto God the things that are God's. When they had heard these words, they marvelled, and left him, and went their way." Matthew 22:21,22.*

The Sadducees took their turn. Their big issue was the denial of the supernatural. They were the liberals of their day. Yet, they claimed to believe the Law of Moses to the letter. Paul explained their philosophy of religion: *"For Moses describeth the righteousness which is of the law, That the man which doeth those things shall live by them." Romans 10:5.* They believed the Law was the best way to live but had no promise of an afterlife (1 Corinthians 15:19).

The Sadducees presented Jesus with a made up scenario of the levirate law: that a widow should be allowed to have children by the deceased's brother or brothers if possible. They implied that if there were a resurrection then because of the levirate law there would be confusion about marriage bonds in heaven. Jesus responded that former relationships wouldn't be as important as our relationship to God in heaven: *"Jesus answered and said unto them, Ye do err, not knowing the scriptures, nor the power of God. For in the resurrection they neither marry, nor are given in marriage, but are as the angels of God in heaven." Matthew 22:29,30.*

Jesus went further than their little hypothetical exercise and utterly destroyed their central tenet, that there is no resurrection. He reasoned that if the very scriptures the Sadducees claimed to believe showed the resurrection, then they would be speechless. If God addressed Himself in present tense as the God of dead patriarchs, then they must be alive also. They must have been resurrected: *"But as touching the resurrection of the dead, have ye not read that which was spoken unto you by God, saying, I am the God of Abraham, and the God of Isaac, and the God of Jacob? God is not the God of the dead, but of the living. And when the multitude heard this, they were astonished at his doctrine." Matthew 22:31-33.*

"But when the Pharisees had heard that he had put the Sadducees to silence, they were gathered together. Then one of them, which was a lawyer, asked him a question, tempting him, and saying, Master, which is the great commandment in the law?" Matthew 22:34-36. If Jesus had chosen any other commandments than He did, He would have given an occasion for them to pick His theology apart, just like religious debaters today look for minor doctrines of their opponents to criticize. Jesus sidestepped their assault and at the same time answered the question elegantly. God's law is about loving Him and others. Doctrines that get in the way of those goals are of less magnitude. Once again,

Jesus showed the pettiness of the religious leaders of His day and what their true priorities should be (Matthew 22:37-40).

Then, Jesus went straight to the heart of the matter, the question of His claim to be the Messiah, and the true nature of the Messiah. The Messiah would be God in the flesh, a thought that had not developed in the minds of the Jews (John 10:22-36). They thought only in terms of a great man blessed by God who proved his claim by exploits of battle and politics. He asked them how David could address the Messiah, his son, as his Lord. There is only one correct answer; the promised one would be God Himself (Matthew 22:41-45): *"And no man was able to answer him a word, neither durst any man from that day forth ask him any more questions." Matthew 22:46.*

Jesus' challenge to them reveals the reason why the Jews failed to recognize Him. They had a small view of God's power. They could only accept a Messiah that made sense to them. Even after God's many miracles in their past, they still looked for human solutions. The fulfillment of the vision is a task only God can do. Everyone must see that it could not be achieved by human ingenuity.

Matthew 23 is Jesus' scathing denouncement of the Pharisees. At the end of it He prophesies of the destruction of Jerusalem as a result of their rejection of Him. The Jews acceptance of their Messiah would have to wait for another time: *"O Jerusalem, Jerusalem, thou that killest the prophets, and stonest them which are sent unto thee, how often would I have gathered thy children together, even as a hen gathereth her chickens under her wings, and ye would not! Behold, your house is left unto you desolate. For I say unto you, Ye shall not see me henceforth, till ye shall say, Blessed is he that cometh in the name of the Lord." Matthew 23:37-39.*

Luke described Jesus'words at this incident a different way. Jesus gave more details in Luke's version. He says their destruction is the result of not knowing "the time of your visitation." This is another way of saying that they could not recognize God's fulfillment of their vision of the Place and Person. Jesus prophesied that the stones would not be left one on top of another. This literally happened approximately forty years later (A.D. 70) when the Roman general Titus destroyed Jerusalem and the Temple. Josephus gave a blow-by-blow description of how it happened.[9] *"For the days shall come upon thee, that thine enemies shall cast a trench about thee, and compass thee round, and keep thee in on every side, And shall lay thee even with the ground, and thy children within thee; and they shall not leave in thee one stone upon another; because thou knewest not the time of thy visitation." Luke 19:43,44.*

Matthew recorded Jesus' prophecies of His second coming in chapters 24-25. Then in Chapter 26 He picked up his narrative again about Jesus' encounters with the religious leaders. By this time, the leaders had put a bounty on Jesus, looking for someone to betray Him in such a way as not to incite the crowds, who still looked at Jesus with hope (Matthew 26:3-5).

John gave a detailed account of the leaders proceedings and their reasoning: *"If we let him thus alone, all men will believe on him: and the Romans shall come and take away both our place and nation." John 11:48.* They feared the Roman response. The Romans wanted peace at all costs in their empire and looked with suspicion upon any popular movement as a threat to order. The chief priests rightly judged this, and forty years later the Romans did come and take away their nation because of popular rebellion: *"And one of them, named Caiaphas, being the high priest that same year, said unto them, Ye know nothing at all, Nor consider that it is expedient for us, that one man should die for the people, and that the whole nation perish not…Then from that day forth they took counsel together for to put him to death." John 11:49-50, 53*. The justification for killing Jesus was for political reasons. But the motivation was for spiritual reasons. They did not accept Him as the Messiah.

The leaders found one to betray Him, Judas. Judas, like many others, had hoped that Jesus was the Messiah, but for some reason became disillusioned and gave up. He looked at Jesus with worldly eyes, not through the eyes of faith. In a way, his individual response to Jesus reflected the nation's response (Matthew 26:14-16).

The leaders followed Judas to Jesus and arrested Him. The high priest got right to the point in examining Him: *"But Jesus held his peace. And the high priest answered and said unto him, I adjure thee by the living God, that thou tell us whether thou be the Christ, the Son of God. Jesus saith unto him, Thou hast said: nevertheless I say unto you, Hereafter shall ye see the Son of man sitting on the right hand of power, and coming in the clouds of heaven." Matthew 26:63,64*. Jesus confessed that He was the Messiah, but already knowing His present fate, prophesied to them of His second coming. They termed His confession as blasphemy, because they did not believe anyone could be the son of God. They sentenced Him to death at that moment (Matthew 26: 65-66).

The chief priests took Jesus to the Roman governor, Pilate, to have Him condemned. They accused Him of sedition (John 19:12; Luke 23:2). But Pilate knew the real reason they hated Him: *"For he knew that for envy they had delivered him." Matthew 27:18;* (John 12:19). The leaders were not about to give up their political power, even for the Lord's Messiah.

John wrote a fascinating account of Jesus' dialogue with Pilate. Pilate asked Him if He called Himself a king. Jesus responded that He was not a political king at the present, but that He was king of those that hear the truth. Pilate declared his allegiance to politics instead of truth by questioning the very existence of truth. It was after this that Pilate wanted to release Jesus because he perceived that He was not a political threat: *"Jesus answered, My kingdom is not of this world: if my kingdom were of this world, then would my servants fight, that I should not be delivered to the Jews: but now is my kingdom not from hence. Pilate therefore said unto him, Art thou a king then? Jesus answered, Thou sayest that I am a king. To this end was I born, and for this cause came I into the world, that I should bear witness unto the truth. Every one that is of the truth heareth my voice. Pilate saith unto him, What is truth? And when he had said this, he went out again unto the Jews, and saith unto them, I find in him no fault at all." John 18:36-38.*

Even at His crucifixion, the Jews were still testing Him. They did not believe that the Messiah could be defeated, and His voluntary death was proof to them that Jesus was not the one. They wanted Him to come down from the cross and destroy His enemies, but He would not: *"Likewise also the chief priests mocking him, with the scribes and elders, said, He saved others; himself he cannot save. If he be the King of Israel, let him now come down from the cross, and we will believe him. He trusted in God; let him deliver him now, if he will have him: for he said, I am the Son of God." Matthew 27:41-43.*

Another Death of the Vision

And so, another hope had died for Israel, they thought. Jesus rose from the grave on the third day and explained to His disciples the nature of His present kingdom; that they would be witnesses of Him and the world would be conquered heart by heart until His return. Then He would establish His political kingdom (Matthew 28:18-20).

Luke records details of Jesus' explanation of His resurrection to the disciples. Two disciples were walking on the road to Emmaus when Jesus joined them. They did not recognize Him because they thought He was dead. Jesus used the occasion to ask them what had happened in Jerusalem and hear their explanation. They told Him that Jesus was a promising Messiah but that the religious leaders had Him crucified, ending the hope. They also believed that a true Messiah could never be defeated (Luke 24:13-20): *"But we trusted that it had been he which should have redeemed Israel: and beside all this, to day is the third day since these things were done." Luke 24:21.*

Then Jesus explained to them the meaning of the suffering Messiah and reassured them that His mission was not over: *"Then he said unto them, O fools, and slow of heart to believe all that the prophets have spoken: Ought not Christ to have suffered these things, and to enter into his glory? And beginning at Moses and all the prophets, he expounded unto them in all the scriptures the things concerning himself." Luke 24:25-27.*

Even then, the disciples expected Jesus to immediately start His earthly kingdom: *"When they therefore were come together, they asked of him, saying, Lord, wilt thou at this time restore again the kingdom to Israel?" Acts 1:6.* Jesus responded that it was their mission to be a witness of Him till He returns (Acts 1:7-11); that only God knew the time of His political kingdom.

"And he said unto them, Verily I say unto you, That there be some of them that stand here, which shall not taste of death, till they have seen the kingdom of God come with power." Mark 9:1. On the day of Pentecost, Jesus' prophecy to His disciples was fulfilled: the Holy Spirit energized the church to accomplish the Great Commission, a work that goes on still today.

Many Jews accepted Jesus as the Messiah, some while He was alive. John wrote that even many of the Council believed in Jesus while He was still alive, but were afraid to let their faith be known: *"Nevertheless among the chief rulers also many believed on him; but because of the Pharisees they did not confess him, lest they should be put out of the synagogue: For they loved the praise of men more than the praise of God." John 12:42,43.*

Many more Jews accepted Jesus after His death. The disciples, finally understanding the mystery of His death and resurrection and of the kingdom, became essential witnesses of His claims: *"Therefore let all the house of Israel know assuredly, that God hath made that same Jesus, whom ye have crucified, both Lord and Christ." Acts 2:36.* The disciples eventually understood Jesus' mission on His first advent: *"Unto you first God, having raised up his Son Jesus, sent him to bless you, in turning away every one of you from his iniquities." Acts 3:26.* On one occasion three thousand were converted and on another five thousand (Acts 2:41; 4:4). There were many more besides those that became Christians.

Nevertheless, the Jews as a nation still rejected Jesus. The Jewish leaders, especially the Sadducees, according to the book of Acts, persecuted the believers because they taught the resurrection of the dead (Acts 4:1-2), and that the leaders had killed the Messiah (Acts 5:17-28).

The controversy came to a head when one disciple, Stephen, was accused before the religious leaders. The accusation was he preached that Jesus would change their traditions: *"For we have heard him say, that this Jesus of Nazareth shall destroy this place, and shall change the customs which Moses delivered us." Acts 6:14.*

The Jewish high priest asked for Stephen's defense. Stephen's defense consisted of a recounting of the history of Israel: that the people consistently refused to hear God through His prophets (Acts 7); they were slow to accept changes in God's program; and they persecuted His leaders. As for the Temple, he quoted Solomon himself that God was bigger than the Temple and that no Temple could contain Him (2 Chronicles 2:6). Stephen also applied Moses' words about the coming Prophet to Jesus. He implied that the coming Prophet would be like Moses because He would be rejected at first, but God would still choose Him (Acts 7:35-37). Stephen directly accused the Council at the end of his speech and reaffirmed the place of Jesus: *"Ye stiffnecked and uncircumcised in heart and ears, ye do always resist the Holy Ghost: as your fathers did, so do ye. Which of the prophets have not your fathers persecuted? and they have slain them which shewed before of the coming of the Just One; of whom ye have been now the betrayers and murderers:" Acts 7:51,52.*

Then the Council had Stephen stoned. After that, the Jewish believers were scattered from Jerusalem because of organized persecution from the Council (Acts 8:1-3). The Council's man was Saul, later to become the apostle Paul.

The Jewish church did not die, but they were unable to convert the masses of Jews. The Jewish state ended a generation later, and the Jews were dispersed throughout the world.

Saul was converted to Christianity through a powerful experience with Jesus Himself according to Acts 9. His name was changed to Paul to show his humility from that time forth. Paul went on to write most of the books of the New Testament.

He articulated the mystery of the church (Ephesians 3); that the Jews had rejected Jesus but God would use that as an opportunity to convert the Gentiles first, and then convert the Jews at the end. Paul's explanation in Romans is that the Gentiles are being grafted into the holy tree and that the Jews will be grafted in again as the last branch: *"For if thou wert cut out of the olive tree which is wild by nature, and wert graffed contrary to nature into a good olive tree: how much more shall these, which be the natural branches, be graffed into their own olive tree? For I would not, brethren, that ye should be ignorant of this mystery, lest ye should be wise in your own conceits; that blindness in part is happened to Israel, until the fulness of the Gentiles be come in. And so all Israel shall be saved: as it is written, There shall come out of Sion the Deliverer, and shall turn away ungodliness from Jacob:" Romans 11:24-26.*

Paul stated his motivation in preaching Jesus to the Gentiles was to provoke to jealousy the Jews and have them accept the Messiah also: *"For I speak to you Gentiles, inasmuch as I am the apostle of the Gentiles, I magnify mine office:*

If by any means I may provoke to emulation them which are my flesh, and might save some of them." Romans 11:13,14.

Paul and the writers of the New Testament explained that the Jews would be given another chance to pass their crisis of the meeting with God. Jesus Christ will return the second time to save them from their enemies. He will come as a military figure, just as they have expected all along (Revelation 19:11-21). He will defeat their enemies and establish a worldwide kingdom from Jerusalem. The Place and the Person will be joined together at last.

And so, Jesus is the only Messiah that the Jews will accept after all. Some people believe they will accept the Antichrist, but that is not possible according to the scriptures. Instead, the Jews will reject theAntichrist when he sits in the Temple and shows himself to be God (2 Thessalonians 2:3-4; Matthew 24:15-22; Daniel 11:21-12:1). This is the abomination that makes desolate. It is then that the Jews as a nation will accept the suffering Messiah and look for His swift return (Zechariah 12-14). They will be given a second chance just as Zechariah had prophesied (Zechariah 10:1). The Antichrist will fight against them but will be destroyed by the second coming of Christ (Zechariah 14:2-4).

Jesus Himself prophesied that the Jews would accept Him before His second coming: *"For I say unto you, Ye shall not see me henceforth, till ye shall say, Blessed is he that cometh in the name of the Lord." Matthew 23:39.* Jesus knew that this phrase was from the 118th Psalm, a prophecy of the salvation of Israel from its enemies. The phrase is from verse 26, but four verses before is a phrase that Jesus had already used to accuse the religious leaders: *"The stone which the builders refused is become the head stone of the corner." Psalms 118:22.* So their acceptance of Him comes before His return just as verse 22 comes before verse 26 in Psalm 118.

At the meeting with God, God does for us what we cannot do ourselves. When Israel first met God, He died for their sins (and for the whole world) and gave them an opportunity to be right with God again. He dealt with the sin problem first. Although they as a nation did not accept it at the time, the opportunity has always been there because of the mystery of the church (Romans 11:23). At their second meeting, He will deliver them from their enemies and establish the kingdom they have been looking for.

The Jews missed their opportunity at the first meeting with God, and have endured much suffering the two thousand years since then. The world has also endured suffering. Nevertheless, God in His grace has turned it to good, in giving the Gentiles a place in His kingdom. God will give the Jews a second chance and they will take it. God will make all things work together for good and the result will be glorious: *"Now if the fall of them be the riches of the world, and the*

diminishing of them the riches of the Gentiles; how much more their fulness?"
Romans 11:12.

God wants us to succeed so much in this journey that He works to give us another chance to see His goodness (Psalm 27:13-14). The crisis will present itself again, but we must have spiritual eyes to see it. God has to work the circumstances over to give it to us again and we have to allow Him to prepare our hearts to accept His grace at our second meeting: *"And we know that all things work together for good to them that love God, to them who are the called according to his purpose." Romans 8:28.*

Nevertheless, it is best to avoid the suffering of mistakes by accepting God's offer at the first meeting. Let's use the examples God has given us to avoid those mistakes (1 Corinthians 10:11).

Key - Love

The key to becoming a spiritual adult is love. We receive God's love in such abundance when He fulfills our vision that it overflows and we are compelled to share with others. We know the goodness of God by experience. Our cup truly runs over. A spiritual adult must be capable of raising the next generation to spiritual maturity, and this requires knowing God's love in a sure way: *"I have written unto you, fathers, because ye have known him that is from the beginning" 1 John 2:14.* It's not a mistake that John referred to spiritual maturity as fatherhood.

John explained that this kind of love comes from God and is passed on to others. When we truly comprehend the love that God has for us then we lose our fear of helping others in their spiritual journey. The fear is present because of our continuing doubts of God's goodness. How can we ask others to trust God when we don't fully trust Him? But, when we see His blessings in the fulfillment, we can then approach others with confidence and the testimony of God's blessing: *"Herein is our love made perfect, that we may have boldness in the day of judgment: because as he is, so are we in this world. There is no fear in love; but perfect love casteth out fear: because fear hath torment. He that feareth is not made perfect in love. We love him, because he first loved us...And this commandment have we from him, That he who loveth God love his brother also." 1 John 4:17-19,21.*

Paul taught that love was the end result of the spiritual journey: *"Therefore being justified by faith, we have peace with God through our Lord Jesus Christ: By whom also we have access by faith into this grace wherein we stand, and rejoice in hope of the glory of God. And not only so, but we glory in tribulations also: knowing that tribulation worketh patience; And patience, experience; and experience, hope: And hope maketh not ashamed; because the love of God is shed abroad in our hearts by the Holy Ghost which is given unto us." Romans 5:1-5.*

The course is presented. The keys are all there. We are first made right with God by grace through *faith* (Ephesians 2:8). We have access to God's power through His grace. We *trust* God to develop us spiritually so that we can become like Him. We see something wonderful that God can do through us just as He did through Jesus (John 14:12). We are presented with crises, with tribulations. We must learn to have *strength* to overcome them. We glory in our tribulations because we trust in God to deliver us. We learn *patience* during the long wait for God's blessings (Hebrews 10:36), for the harvest. We experience His love in a mature way when He blesses us with the answer to our hope. His *love* cannot be contained within us, so we share it with others.

Symbol - Children

The symbol of spiritual adulthood is children. They come after receiving the treasure. Not children in a physical sense, although some people may receive children as their long sought after treasure, but children in a spiritual sense. When the spiritual adult receives the treasure, he or she is ready to teach others how to advance to spiritual maturity, having fully learned the ways of God and having passed through the stages: *"I will declare thy name unto my brethren, in the midst of the church will I sing praise unto thee. And again, I will put my trust in him. And again, Behold I and the children which God hath given me." Hebrews 2:12,13.*

Paul as a spiritual adult described his efforts to bring others to spiritual maturity and he called them his children: *"My little children, of whom I travail in birth again until Christ be formed in you," Galatians 4:19.*

John addressed his first letter to his "little children." He used the term nine times in the brief letter called 1 John. John was qualified as a spiritual adult who had known by experience the love that God had for him. He called himself after all, "the disciple whom Jesus loved." He wrote his letter to encourage the children to trust God for eternity: *"These things have I written unto you that believe on the name of the Son of God; that ye may know that ye have eternal life, and that ye may believe on the name of the Son of God." 1 John 5:13.*

And so the full expression of our ministry comes after the treasure. Then we are witnesses capable of showing with our lives the power of God, having witnessed the power of His resurrection, the fulfillment of the vision after all human effort had failed (Philippians 3:10-11).

The disciples received their treasure when Jesus rose from the dead. Their vision of the kingdom, which Jesus gave to them, became clear: *"But ye shall receive power, after that the Holy Ghost is come upon you: and ye shall be witnesses unto me both in Jerusalem, and in all Judaea, and in Samaria, and unto the uttermost part of the earth." Acts 1:8. "The God of our fathers raised up Jesus, whom ye slew and hanged on a tree. Him hath God exalted with his right hand to be a Prince and a Saviour, for to give repentance to Israel, and forgiveness of sins. And we are his witnesses of these things; and so is also the Holy Ghost, whom God hath given to them that obey him."* Acts 5:30-32. The disciples saw thousands of their countrymen accept Jesus and they saw the beginning of the worldwide acceptance by the Gentiles (Acts 15).

Israel's children will follow their treasure also. When Jesus the Messiah comes the second time to save them from their enemies He will establish His millennial kingdom (Revelation 20:4). Jerusalem will be His throne and the Jewish people will be the rulers of the world, just as the Old Testament prophets predicted (Isaiah 9:6-7; Daniel 7:27; Zechariah 9:9-10; 14:9,16). The Jews will become the teachers of the world in the ways of His kingdom, even though they will be the last to accept Him. Their long experience in the ways of God will equip them at last to provide insights for the rest of the world: *"But in the last days it shall come to pass, that the mountain of the house of the LORD shall be established in the top of the mountains, and it shall be exalted above the hills; and people shall flow unto it. And many nations shall come, and say, Come, and let us go up to the mountain of the LORD, and to the house of the God of Jacob; and he will teach us of his ways, and we will walk in his paths: for the law shall go forth of Zion, and the word of the LORD from Jerusalem." Micah 4:1,2. "The children which thou shalt have, after thou hast lost the other, shall say again in thine ears, The place is too strait for me: give place to me that I may dwell. Then shalt thou say in thine heart, Who hath begotten me these, seeing I have lost my children, and am desolate, a captive, and removing to and fro? and who hath brought up these? Behold, I was left alone; these, where had they been? Thus saith the Lord GOD, Behold, I will lift up mine hand to the Gentiles, and set up my standard to the people: and they shall bring thy sons in their arms, and thy daughters shall be carried upon their shoulders. And kings shall be thy nursing fathers, and their queens thy nursing mothers: they shall bow down to thee with their face toward the earth, and lick up the dust of thy feet; and thou shalt know that I am the LORD: for they shall not be ashamed that wait for me." Isaiah 49:20-23. "Sing and rejoice, O daughter of Zion: for, lo, I come, and I will dwell in the midst of thee, saith the LORD. And many nations shall be joined to the LORD in that day, and shall be my people: and I will dwell in the midst of thee, and thou shalt know that the LORD of hosts hath sent me unto thee." Zechariah 2:10,11. "Thus saith the LORD of hosts; It shall yet come to pass, that there shall come people, and the inhabitants of many cities: And the inhabitants of one city shall go to another, saying, Let us go speedily to pray before the LORD, and to seek the LORD of hosts: I will go also. Yea, many people and strong nations shall come to seek the LORD of hosts in Jerusalem, and to pray before the LORD. Thus saith the LORD of hosts; In those days it shall come to pass, that ten men shall take hold out of all languages of the nations, even shall take hold of the skirt of him that is a Jew, saying, We will go with you: for we have heard that God is with you." Zechariah 8:20-23. "But ye shall be named the Priests of the LORD: men shall call you the Ministers of our God: ye shall eat the riches of the Gentiles, and in their glory shall ye boast yourselves." Isaiah 61:6.*

Pilgrim's Progress - Delectable Mountains

Christian and Hopeful passed their ordeal of the Doubting Castle, which required faith and their use of the key of Promise. These are perfect metaphors for the victory of spiritual young adulthood. The spiritual young adult must overcome the doubts of God's long delayed blessings and still look at the fulfillment of the vision through the eyes of faith even when it seems impossible. He or she must maintain hope in the face of discouragement. The key of Promise opens the gate to the way toward maturity.[10]

The Jews passed through their Doubting Castle and looked for the promised one. At the first meeting with God, they rejected Him because they added their own expectations to God's promise. At the second meeting, the second chance, Jesus will unmistakably display His power and the Jews will receive their promise.

Christian and Hopeful soon arrived at the Delectable Mountains, in Immanuel's Land, the symbol of spiritual maturity. Christian had seen the mountains from afar when he stood at the top of the hill Difficulty, which represented the beginning of spiritual adolescence. God gives us a vision of what we can do for His kingdom when we commit our lives to Him. That vision sustains us through the long and difficult time it takes for God to build His message in us. Then when we have fully experienced the ways of God, He will bring us to the Delectable Mountains, the vision we saw at the beginning.

Christian and Hopeful met the shepherds of the hills, whose names were Knowledge, Experience, Watchful, and Sincere. All of these are qualities of spiritual adulthood. They told the pilgrims "few of those who begin the journey to this place ever show their faces on these mountains."[11] In other words, few Christians who pass the crisis of commitment will endure to see the fulfillment of their vision: *"For many are called, but few are chosen." Matthew 22:14.*

The pilgrims went to the top of the hill Clear and got a view of the Celestial City, heaven. From the Delectable Mountains, or spiritual adulthood, we get a clear vision of eternity. Life with God becomes the new goal.

Before Christian and Hopeful resumed their journey, the shepherds gave them two warnings, to beware the Flatterer and the Enchanted Ground. Both are dangers in spiritual adulthood. Pride is an ever-present snare to those who have overcome and flatterers are those who prepare a net for the feet (Proverbs 29:5). The Enchanted Ground represents laziness. Spiritual adulthood is not a time to rest but a time to be fruitful and raise the next generation to spiritual maturity: *"Therefore let us not sleep, as do others; but let us watch and be sober." 1 Thessalonians 5:6.*

CHAPTER 12

Spiritual Parenthood

THE harvest is a time of rejoicing, especially if the latter rains were good and the crops developed to their fullest. The farmer even calls in extra help if the season has produced an exceptional yield (Matthew 20). After the harvest is the time of rest until the next year's time of plowing (Luke 12:16-21). The time of rest allows the farmer time to reflect on non-mundane matters, like his relationships with God and others.

Spiritual parenthood is the final stage of the journey. The spiritual adult has proved what is that good and acceptable and perfect will of God by his life, often through trials and heartaches, and enjoys the time of harvest - the time of bringing others to maturity in Christ: *"They that sow in tears shall reap in joy. He that goeth forth and weepeth, bearing precious seed, shall doubtless come again with rejoicing, bringing his sheaves with him." Psalms 126:5,6.*

If the response to her message is more than she can handle alone, the spiritual parent seeks help in taking that message to others. Books, tapes, recordings, internet, television, magazines, and other methods are used to get the story to all who want to hear it. But, still today, the most effective method is by word of mouth from those who have understood that a life has been changed by God's power: *"Therefore said he unto them, The harvest truly is great, but the labourers are few: pray ye therefore the Lord of the harvest, that he would send forth labourers into his harvest." Luke 10:2.*

The spiritual parent, while rejoicing in the faith he has inspired in others, and thankful to God for the opportunity to be a vessel fit for use, still wants to grow. Erikson taught that psychosocial growth is a continual process till death, and I believe spiritual growth is as well. The last chapter of spiritual growth is to understand the nature of God. This understanding is not fully possible until spiritual fatherhood or motherhood, and then we can perceive the heart of God as Father. God encourages us to "know him" as the end result of spiritual quest: *"I have written unto you, fathers, because ye have known him that is from the beginning" 1 John 2:14. "Thus saith the LORD, Let not the wise man glory in his wisdom, neither let the mighty man glory in his might, let not the rich man glory in his riches: But let him that glorieth glory in this, that he understandeth and knoweth me, that I am the LORD which exercise lovingkindness, judgment, and righteousness, in the earth: for in these things I delight, saith the LORD."* Jeremiah 9:23,24.

Harvest Celebration

Spiritual parenthood is a time of celebration. The long journey is almost over and now there are others starting their journey because of the example of faith. The spiritual parent gets an opportunity to tell often the story of how God finished the work and overcame all obstacles to bless in the end. Hebrews 11 is an example of telling the stories of heroes. All of the heroes mentioned overcame adversity to claim God's promises, or at least be convinced of their coming reality.

The Jews have their Feast of Tabernacles after the harvest to rest and rejoice in the goodness of God (Deuteronomy 16:13-15). It was originally made to celebrate their deliverance from Egypt. It lasts eight days. Solomon's dedication of the Temple was during this time (1 Kings 8). The Jews were commanded to use this time to share the goodness of God with the immigrants, the poor, and the grief-stricken. Jesus used the occasion to offer Himself as the living water (John 7:37-38). It is a wonderful time to tell stories of triumph.

The thousand-year reign of Christ will be a time of rejoicing and continual celebration. Israel will have its children, the people of the entire world. Zechariah predicted that all peoples would join the Jews in their Feast of Tabernacles (Zechariah 8:20-23): *"And it shall come to pass, that every one that is left of all the nations which came against Jerusalem shall even go up from year to year to worship the King, the LORD of hosts, and to keep the feast of tabernacles." Zechariah 14:16.*

Learning Tasks

Spiritual parents have overcome adversity to take God's *treasure*. They have been resurrected by God's power and have inspired others to begin their journey. The world has asked them to *return* and give an account of their experience with

God. Now their task is to encourage others toward maturity (Galatians 4:19). They understand the learning tasks and crises of each stage, and the keys to open doors to new levels. They must learn the best ways to motivate their children to stay on the path.

The great example for spiritual parents is God Himself. After all, He chose the title of Father to define His role in the incarnation. By studying the attributes of God, and by remembering His dealing with them, spiritual parents find the wisdom to mentor the next generation: *"Be ye followers of me, even as I also am of Christ." 1 Corinthians 11:1. "For though ye have ten thousand instructors in Christ, yet have ye not many fathers: for in Christ Jesus I have begotten you through the gospel. Wherefore I beseech you, be ye followers of me." 1 Corinthians 4:15,16.*

The Learning Task of Spiritual Parenthood

Motivating and Mentoring the Next Generation

Paul listed the methods of raising the next generation as a spiritual parent: *v.7 "But we were gentle among you, even as a nurse cherisheth her children: v.8 So being affectionately desirous of you, we were willing to have imparted unto you, not the gospel of God only, but also our own souls, because ye were dear unto us. v.9 For ye remember, brethren, our labour and travail: for labouring night and day, because we would not be chargeable unto any of you, we preached unto you the gospel of God. v.10 Ye are witnesses, and God also, how holily and justly and unblameably we behaved ourselves among you that believe: v.11 As ye know how we exhorted and comforted and charged every one of you, as a father doth his children, v.12 That ye would walk worthy of God, who hath called you unto his kingdom and glory." 1 Thessalonians 2:7-12.*

The first method is gentleness, like a nursing mother, who shows patience and determination to feed her child the necessary nutrition for growth (v.7).

The second is affectionate desire for the good of the children, so much so that the spiritual parent is willing to suffer physically and psychologically from the children's misunderstanding rather than give up leading (v.8). Paul reminded the Thessalonians that he had worked two jobs, secular and spiritual, to provide for them the necessary provisions for growth (v.9).

The third method is holiness. Spiritual parents must love God and others so much that they will not compromise standards, because they know that would be discouraging to those who are following them (Psalms 73:15).

The fourth method is encouragement (v.11 - exhorted, comforted). Spiritual parents counsel their children on the dangers and opportunities in front of them, and comfort them when they slip. Spiritual parents don't give up on their children but continue to love. They also don't do for the children what the children can do for themselves. Spiritual parents know they must get out of the way sometimes to see growth. Even if the parents can do better, the children need to develop their skills and muscles. By this, spiritual parents prepare for their own deaths and turn over leadership to others.

The fifth method is testifying. The word "charged" here means "to bear witness."[1] Spiritual parents continue to bear witness of God's faithfulness in their own lives as they lead their children. They tell the stories of God's triumph in their lives. Paul emphasizes that encouragement and testifying should be handled like loving fathers. The final result of these methods is to see the children get their treasure and become spiritually mature (v. 12).

History of Israel

The children of Israel will receive their treasure at the second coming of Jesus. The Place and the Person will be secured at last. The Bible says He will rule from His throne for a thousand years and that the Jews will be priests of the Lord (Revelation 20:4; Isaiah 61:6).

The people of the world who survive the tribulation period will look to the Jews for leadership in the new kingdom (Zechariah 2:10,11; 8:20-23). Because of their long relationship with God and their new maturity as a people, the Jews will be the best prepared to teach the ways of God. In addition, they will have Jesus Himself living among them as a teacher and an example. The Bible predicts those days both in the Old and New Testaments: *"For this is the covenant that I will make with the house of Israel after those days, saith the Lord; I will put my laws into their mind, and write them in their hearts: and I will be to them a God, and they shall be to me a people: And they shall not teach every man his neighbour, and every man his brother, saying, Know the Lord: for all shall know me, from the least to the greatest." Hebrews 8:10,11. (Jeremiah 31:33-34; Ezekiel 36:25-28).*

Paul gives more insight into the passage about the New Covenant and changes the term God to Father: *"And will be a Father unto you, and ye shall be my sons and daughters, saith the Lord Almighty." 2 Corinthians 6:18.* Jeremiah mentioned the Jews'children also. I believe it's their spiritual children: *"And they shall be my people, and I will be their God: And I will give them one heart, and one way, that they may fear me for ever, for the good of them, and of their children after them:" Jeremiah 32:38,39.*

Crisis

The thousand-year kingdom will close with the defeat of rebellious nations who come to Jerusalem to fight against Jesus and His people. Satan will be loosed from his prison and will succeed in convincing all unbelievers in the world to rebel. John says in the Revelation that God will send fire down from heaven to consume them, and will cast Satan into the lake of fire. With this, the last threat to the people of God will be dissolved (Revelation 20:5-10). Only believers will be left in the world.

After the defeat of Satan and the living unbelievers, who will have more evidence than any in history of God's goodness since Jesus will live among them, and thus will have no excuse, God will proceed to judge the dead unbelievers at the Great White Throne. The Bible says that their works will judge them, which will be insufficient for all of them. They too will perish because their names will not be found in the book of life (Revelation 20:11-15).

With the defeat of Satan and his followers the Messiah's kingdom will be close to the end. The end will be the destruction of the last enemy - death: *"And death and hell were cast into the lake of fire. This is the second death." Revelation 20:14.*

Paul predicted the span of the Messiah's kingdom: *"For he must reign, till he hath put all enemies under his feet. The last enemy that shall be destroyed is death." 1 Corinthians 15:25,26.*

Death is the last crisis. For Israel, and the world, death will be defeated at the end of the millennial kingdom. Then Jesus will deliver up the kingdom to the father and complete His work: *"Then cometh the end, when he shall have delivered up the kingdom to God, even the Father; when he shall have put down all rule and all authority and power." 1 Corinthians 15:24.*

Transcendence

Transcendence is the best word to describe what happens next. God will gather up everyone into Himself. Those who remain will truly become one with God, the goal of every mystic who has ever sought God: *"And when all things shall be subdued unto him, then shall the Son also himself be subject unto him that put all things under him, that God may be all in all." 1 Corinthians 15:28.*

Paul explained that this was the ultimate goal all along: *"Having made known unto us the mystery of his will, according to his good pleasure which he hath purposed in himself: That in the dispensation of the fulness of times he might gather together in one all things in Christ, both which are in heaven, and which are on earth; even in him:" Ephesians 1:9,10.*

The individual spiritual parent must pass through the crisis of death to transcend self (2 Corinthians 5:1-2), both metaphorically and literally. Even though death is a fearful thing, God gives us assurances that He has paved the way and taken away its sting. The other side of death for the believer is the presence of God (2 Corinthians 5:8). Paul rhapsodized about the defeat of death: *"For this corruptible must put on incorruption, and this mortal must put on immortality. So when this corruptible shall have put on incorruption, and this mortal shall have put on immortality, then shall be brought to pass the saying that is written, Death is swallowed up in victory. O death, where is thy sting? O grave, where is thy victory? The sting of death is sin; and the strength of sin is the law. But thanks be to God, which giveth us the victory through our Lord Jesus Christ." 1 Corinthians 15:53-57.*

The writer of Hebrews explained that Jesus voluntarily went through death in order to take away its power: *"Thou hast put all things in subjection under his feet. For in that he put all in subjection under him, he left nothing that is not put under him. But now we see not yet all things put under him. But we see Jesus, who was made a little lower than the angels for the suffering of death, crowned with glory and honour; that he by the grace of God should taste death for every man…Forasmuch then as the children are partakers of flesh and blood, he also himself likewise took part of the same; that through death he might destroy him that had the power of death, that is, the devil; And deliver them who through fear of death were all their lifetime subject to bondage." Hebrews 2:8-9, 14-15.*

The mystics have always been wrong. It does not take striving and suffering to transcend this world and reach God. God is so gracious that He has done it for us. All we have to do is trust in the finished work of Jesus.

Key - Confidence

The key to transcendence is confidence. The spiritual parent ready for transcendence needs confidence to make the ride less bumpy. In this case confidence is the opposite of fear. Without confidence fear is allowed to creep back in and cause torment. We have confidence because we know the love that God has shown to us: *"Herein is our love made perfect, that we may have boldness in the day of judgment: because as he is, so are we in this world. There is no fear in love; but perfect love casteth out fear: because fear hath torment. He that feareth is not made perfect in love. We love him, because he first loved us."* 1 John 4:17-19.

The words "confidence, persuaded, assure, etc." are used in several contexts in the New Testament regarding transcendence.[2] God in His love does not want His people to fear death, but to look forward to being with Him: *"Therefore we are always confident, knowing that, whilst we are at home in the body, we are absent from the Lord: (For we walk by faith, not by sight:) We are confident, I say, and willing rather to be absent from the body, and to be present with the Lord."* 2 Corinthians 5:6-8.

"Persuaded" is used in 2 Timothy to show assurance of salvation: *"For the which cause I also suffer these things: nevertheless I am not ashamed: for I know whom I have believed, and am persuaded that he is able to keep that which I have committed unto him against that day."* 2 Timothy 1:12.

John explained that God puts confidence into the heart of the believer: *"And hereby we know that we are of the truth, and shall assure our hearts before him. For if our heart condemn us, God is greater than our heart, and knoweth all things. Beloved, if our heart condemn us not, then have we confidence toward God."* 1 John 3:19-21.

John also said that confidence would keep us from shame if the Lord comes back before our death: *"And now, little children, abide in him; that, when he shall appear, we may have confidence, and not be ashamed before him at his coming."* 1 John 2:28.

Symbol - Heaven

Heaven is the symbol of transcendence. Heaven is the final reward for spiritual pilgrims. It is their abiding city: *"For here have we no continuing city, but we seek one to come."* Hebrews 13:14. *"But now they desire a better country, that is, an heavenly: wherefore God is not ashamed to be called their God: for he hath prepared for them a city."* Hebrews 11:16.

John the Revelator described heaven in chapters 21 and 22. Heaven comes after the defeat of all enemies, even death. It is the New Jerusalem that comes down from God (Revelation 21:1-2). It signals the beginning of God's final covenant, the Eternal Covenant. John described the key elements of the covenant that are a comfort for those seeking transcendence.

The first is the presence of God. God Himself will be with us (Revelation 21:3).

The second is the elimination of suffering. God will wipe all tears from the eyes (Revelation 21:4).

The third is the inheritance of the meek: *"He that overcometh shall inherit all things; and I will be his God, and he shall be my son." Revelation 21:7.*

The fourth is eternal life, represented by the water of life and the tree of life (Revelation 22:1-2).

Finally, God will end the curse, the negative entropy of the universe: *"And there shall be no more curse: but the throne of God and of the Lamb shall be in it; and his servants shall serve him: And they shall see his face; and his name shall be in their foreheads. And there shall be no night there; and they need no candle, neither light of the sun; for the Lord God giveth them light: and they shall reign for ever and ever." Revelation 22:3-5.*

Pilgrim's Progress - Celestial City

Christian and Hopeful walked on toward the Celestial City, stirred by their view of it from atop the hill Clear: "They crossed the Enchanted Ground and entered the country of Beulah, where the air was very sweet and pleasant."Beulah land represents the borders of transcendence, or heaven: "This was beyond the Valley of Shadow of Death and out of reach of Giant Despair, in fact, they could not even see Doubting Castle from this place."[3]

From Beulah land, the pilgrims had a "more perfect view" of the city. They became "sick with desire" at seeing it. They talked more in their sleep than usual. Bunyan used the imagery from Song of Solomon to describe the traveler's feelings in this place. Song is often applied as an expression of love between God and man. The name Beulah means "married." Their feelings were like those of the engaged. The transcendent are ready to be with God (2 Corinthians 5:6-8).

Before the gate of the city was a river with no bridge across it. This is the imagery of death in *Pilgrim's Progress*. The task of the pilgrims was to cross. Angels told them that the river would be deep or shallow according to their faith *(or confidence)* in the King of the city. Those with more confidence would find it shallow; those with less would find it deep.

Christian almost drowned but Hopeful encouraged him while he waded across. Hopeful quoted Psalm 73:4-5, which describes the death of the wicked as not troubled. Hopeful implied it's because they have no sense of their standing with God. Christian's difficulty was only because he knew of God's reality.

Their entrance into the city was anticlimactic, because they had already walked there in their hearts.

ENDNOTES

Chapter 1

1   Bettelheim, Bruno, *Freud and Man's Soul* (NewYork: Vintage Books, 1984), pp.11-12.
2   Vine, W.E., *An Expository Dictionary of New Testament Words* (Nashville, TN: Thomas Nelson, Inc., 1983), "heart, soul."
3   Bettleheim, *Freud and Man's Soul,* p. 77. Freud understood that psyche stood for the mind and the emotions.
4   Vine, *Expository Dictionary...* "mind."
5   Ibid., "heart."
6   Ibid., "sword."
7   Bettleheim, *Freud and Man's Soul*, pp. 53-62, 72.
8   Lewis, C.S., *Miracles* (NewYork, NY: Collier Books, Macmillan Publishing Co., 1947), p.82.
9   Ibid., p. 83.
10   Goethe, Johann Wolfgang von, *Faust, First Part,* trans. by Peter Salm (New York: Bantam Books, 1985), p. 21.
11   Ibid., p. 69.
12   Ibid., p. 83.
13   Goethe, Johann Wolfgang von, *Faust, Part Two,* trans. by Philip Wayne (New York: Viking Penguin, Inc., 1959), p. 220.
14   Simonton, Stephanie Matthews, Robert L. Shook, *The Healing Family: The Simonton Approach for Families Facing Illness* (New York: Bantam Books, 1984), pp.1-9.
15   McMillen, S.I., M.D., *None of These Diseases: A Famous Doctor's Christian Prescription for a Healthier and Happier Life* (Old Tappan, New Jersey: Fleming H. Revell Company, 1963), p. 63.
16   Ibid., p. 68.

17   *Arkansas Democrat*, May 2, 1990.
18   Schaeffer, Franky, Ed., *Is Capitalism Christian? Toward a Christian Perspective on Economics* (Westchester, Ill: Crossway Books, 1985), p. 19.
19   Ibid., p. 20.
20   *Arkansas Democrat*, December 12, 1990, Front Page.
21   *The Washington Post*, November 15, 1986, Front Page.
22   *Arkansas Gazette*, November 2, 1990, Front Page.

Chapter 2

1   Erikson, Erik, *Identity: Youth and Crisis* (New York, NY: W.W. Norton & Co., 1968), p.96.
2   Pinker, Steven, *The Language Instinct: How the Mind Creates Language* (New York, NY: W. Morrow and Co., 1994).
3   Erikson, Erik, *Life History and the Historical Moment* (New York, NY: W.W. Norton & Co., 1975), p.19.
4   Ibid., p.19.
5   *Webster's New Collegiate Dictionary* (Springfield, Mass: G & C. Merriam Co., 1979), p.267.
6   Erikson, Erik, *The Life Cycle Completed* (New York, NY: W.W. Norton & Co., 1982), p.59.
7   Ibid., p.67.

Chapter 4

1   *Pine Bluff Commercial,* June 9, 1990.
2   Blackaby, Henry T, and King, Claude V., *Experiencing God: Knowing and Doing the Will of God* (Nashville, TN: Lifeway Press, 1990).
3   *Merriam-Webster Collegiate Dictionary - Tenth Edition* (1994).
4   Campbell, Joseph, with Moyers, Bill, *The Power of Myth* (New York, NY: Doubleday, 1988), pp. xvi and xvii.
5   Lewis, C.S., *Miracles* (New York, NY: Collier Books, Macmillan Publishing Co., 1947), p. 134, footnote.
6   Lewis, C.S., "Myth Became Fact", *World Dominion, 22* (1944), reprinted in *God in the Dock: Essays on Theology and Ethics,* ed. Walter Hooper (Grand Rapids, MI: Eerdmans, 1970), p. 66.
7   Ibid., p. 66.
8   Ibid., p. 66.

9   Ibid., p. 64.

10   Yancey, Philip, *What's So Amazing About Grace* (Grand Rapids, MI: Zondervan, 1997).

11   Wangerin, Walter Jr., *The Book of God: The Bible as a Novel* (Grand Rapids, MI: Zondervan, 1996).

12   Jung, C.G., *Symbols of Transformation* (Princeton, NJ: Princeton University Press, 1956).

13   Campbell, *The Power of Myth*, p.11.

14   Campbell, Joseph, *Transformations of Myth Through Time* (New York, NY: Harper and Row, 1990), pp. 30 & 31.

15   Lewis, *Miracles*, p. 82.

16   Lewis, C.S., *Surprised By Joy: The Shape of My Early Life* (New York, NY: Harcourt Brace Jovanovich, 1956), p. 235.

17   Campbell, *The Power of Myth*, p. 207.

18   Lewis, *Miracles*, p. 81.

19   Campbell, *The Power of Myth*, p.53.

20   Lewis, "Myth Became Fact," pp.66 & 67.

21   Apuleius, *The Golden Ass*.

22   Bulfinch, Thomas, *Mythology,* "Cupid and Psyche."

Chapter 5

1   Yancey, Philip, *Soul Survivor: How My Faith Survived the Church* (New York, NY: Doubleday, 2001), pp. 121,122.

2   *"I have more understanding than all my teachers: for thy testimonies are my meditation." Psalms 119:99.* God's testimonies of how He has dealt with people in the past will enable you to become wiser than your teachers.

3   Jung, Carl G., Ed., *Man and His Symbols* (New York: Dell Publishing, 1964), p. 101.

4   "Elpenor." "A Drunkards Progress: AA and the Sobering Strength of Myth." *Harpers* (October 1986), pp. 43-48.

5   Kilpatrick, William K., *Psychological Seduction: The Failure of Modern Psychology* (Nashville, TN: Thomas Nelson, Inc., 1983), Chapters on "Moral Education," pp.102-121.

6   Campbell, Joseph, *The Hero With a Thousand Faces* (Princeton, NJ: Princeton University Press, 1949), p. 59.

7   Ibid., p. 69.

8   Ibid., p. 71.

9   Campbell, *Hero...* p. 109.

10   Nietzsche, Friedrich, *Thus Spoke Zarathustra* (NewYork: Viking Penguin, Inc., 1969). Nietzsche, in my opinion, was the forerunner of the modern existentialists and one of the wisest of the secular philosophers. He taught that people are imperfect and need saving; "Man is something that should be overcome. What have you done to overcome him?" p.41. He also taught that even our virtues are insufficient for salvation; "Man is something that must be overcome: and for that reason you must love your virtues-for you will perish by them." p.65. Nevertheless, Nietzsche didn't reach the level of understanding the need for divine sacrifice.

11   Campbell, *Hero...*p. 217.

12   *The Little Mermaid* (New York: Scholastic, Inc., 1989), p.18.

13   Anderson, Hans Christian, *Hans Anderson: His Classic Fairy Tales* (Garden City, New York: Doubleday and Company, Inc., 1978), p. 150.

14   Ibid., p. 156.

15   Ibid., p.160.

16   *The Little Mermaid*, p. 32.

17   Anderson, *His Classic Fairy Tales*, p. 160.

18   Ibid., p. 160.

19   Ibid., pp. 160 & 161.

20   Ibid., p. 161.

Chapter 6

1   *In Quest of the Hero* (Princeton, New Jersey: Princeton University Press, 1990), p.57.

2   Ibid., p. 195.

3   Ibid., p. 192.

4   Ibid., p. xxiv, pp. 188-189.

5   Strong, James, *Dictionary of the Greek Testament* (James Strong, 1890), 3402, "follower."

Chapter 7

1   Unger, Merrill F., *Unger's Bible Dictionary* (Chicago, Ill: Moody Press, 1966), p.909, "rain."

2   Ibid., p.263, "dew."

3   Yamamoto, Kaoru, Ed., *Death in the Life of Children* (Kappa Delta Pi, 1978), p.45.

4   Piaget, Jean, *The Language and Thought of the Child* (New York: The Humanities Press, Inc., 1959), p. 206.

5   Ibid., p. 178.

6   Chapter 1, "God vs. Satan"

7   Bunyan, John, *Pilgrims Progress: First Part* (1678).

8   Revelation 8:20.

9   Hosea 4:12-14.

10   *The Epic of Gilgamesh* (New York; NY: Penguin Books, 1972), p. 97.

11   Coles, Robert, *The Spiritual Life of Children* (Boston, Mass: Houghton Mifflin Company, 1990), p. 110.

12   Ibid., p. 109.

13   Ibid., p. 107.

14   Ibid., p. 107.

15   Colson, Charles, *Born Again* (Old Tappan, New Jersey: Fleming H. Revell Company, 1976). The information in this section is drawn from this book.

16   Ibid., pp. 113-114.

17   Lewis, C.S., *Mere Christianity* (New York, NY: Macmillan Publishing Company, 1952), p. 111.

18   Ibid., p. 112.

19   My emphasis on these last two sentences.

20   Lewis, C.S., *Surprised By Joy* (New York, NY: Harcourt Brace Jovanovich, 1956), pp. 16-17.

21   Ibid., pp. 17-18.

22   Lewis, C.S., *The Weight of Glory and Other Addresses* (New York, NY: Macmillan Publishing Company, 1949), p.7.

23   Lewis, C.S., *Surprised By Joy*, p. 169.

24   Ibid., p. 172.

25   Ibid., p. 191.

26   Ibid., p. 228.

27   Ibid., p. 231.

28   Bunyan, John, *Grace Abounding: To the Chief of Sinners* (Springdale, PA: Whitaker House, 1993), all quotes in this section are from pages 1-65.

29   Defoe, Daniel, *Robinson Crusoe* (New York, NY: NAL Penguin, Inc., 1961), all quotes in this section are from pages 89-97.

30   Lewis, C.S., *The Pilgrim's Regress* (Grand Rapids, Michigan: Wm B. Eerdmans Publishing Company, 1958), p.168.

31   Colson, Charles, *Born Again*: all quotes in this section are from pages 126-130.

32   Only in Judges 3:25 is "key" used literally.

33   Titus 1:4 "common faith": Acts 14:27 "door of faith."

34   Jung, Carl G., Ed., *Man and His Symbols* (New York: Dell Publishing, 1964), p. 4.

35   *"This Moses whom they refused, saying, Who made thee a ruler and a judge? the same did God send to be a ruler and a deliverer by the hand of the angel which appeared to him in the bush." Acts 7:35.*

Chapter 8

1   Unger, Merrill F., *Unger's Bible Dictionary* (Chicago, Ill: Moody Press, 1966), p.909, "rain." Wight, Fred H., *Manners and Customs of Bible Lands* (Chicago, Ill: Moody Bible Institute, 1953), p.169.

2   Unger, Merrill F., *Unger's Bible Dictionary*, p. 463.

3   Piaget, Jean, and Inhelder, Barbel, *Psychology of the Child* (New York: Basic Books, 1969), p.100.

4   Piaget and Inhelder, *Psychology of the Child*, p.119.

5   Gilligan, Carol, *In a Different Voice* (Cambridge, Mass: Harvard University Press, 1982), p.9-11.

6   Piaget and Inhelder, *Psychology of the Child*, p.121-122.

7   Erikson, Erik, *Identity: Youth and Crisis* (New York, NY: W.W. Norton & Co., 1968), p.122.

8   Erikson, Erik, *The Life Cycle Completed* (New York, NY: W.W. Norton & Co., 1982), p.75.

9   Bunyan, John, *Pilgrim's Progress: First Part* (1678).

10   Erikson, *The Life Cycle Completed*, p. 56.

11   Jung, Carl G., Ed., *Man and His Symbols* (New York: Dell Publishing, 1964), pp.152, 161, 163-66.

12   *Merriam-Webster Collegiate Dictionary - Tenth Edition* (1994), "psychic," definition 3.

13   *"Blessed is the man that trusteth in the LORD, and whose hope the LORD is. For he shall be as a tree planted by the waters, and that spreadeth out her roots by the river, and shall not see when heat cometh, but her leaf shall be green; and shall not be careful in the year of drought, neither shall cease from yielding fruit." Jeremiah 17:7,8. "I am the true vine, and my Father is the husbandman. Every branch in me that beareth not fruit he taketh away: and every branch that beareth fruit, he purgeth it, that it may bring forth more fruit. Now ye are*

clean through the word which I have spoken unto you." John 15:1-3. "Son of man, What is the vine tree more than any tree, or than a branch which is among the trees of the forest?" Ezekiel 15:2.

14 Vine, W.E., *An Expository Dictionary of New Testament Words* (Nashville, TN: Thomas Nelson, Inc., 1983), "rock."

15 *Webster's New World Dictionary of the American Language* (New York: Simon and Schuster, 1986), "worship," definition 2.

16 Allen, Charles L., *God's Psychiatry* (Grand Rapids, MI: Fleming H. Revell Company, 1953), p.45.

17 Ibid., p.47.

18 Strong, James, *Dictionary of the Hebrew Bible* (James Strong, 1890), 6754, "image."

19 Rank, Otto, *The Double: A Psychoanalytic Study* (Originally published in 1925. Translated and edited by Harry Tucker Jr., Chapel Hill, NC: University of North Carolina Press, 1971), p.57.

20 Ibid., p.62.

21 Ibid., p.65.

22 Ibid., p.60.

23 Vine, *Expository Dictionary...* "image."

24 *International Children's Bible: New Century Version* (Dallas, TX: Word Publishing Co., 1988).

25 Unger, Merrill F., *Unger's Bible Dictionary,* p. 940, "Sabbath."

26 Strong, *Dictionary of the Hebrew Bible,* 4397, 4399, "work."

27 Swindoll, Charles, *Sanctity of Life,* p.xiv.

28 *Arkansas Democrat,* August 5, 1990.

29 Ibid., October 27, 1991.

30 Ibid., December 8, 1991.

31 Ibid., November 17, 1991.

32 *Pine Bluff Commercial,* August 12, 1990.

33 *Webster's New World Dictionary*, "adulterate."

34 Crain, Gary S., "Ghosts of First Sex Break Marriages," *Arkansas Democrat,* June 22, 1985: "The memories of premarital sex often begin to 'haunt'a marriage after 10 or 15 years when a couple in their 30's have teenagers. The marital bond, says Dr. Donald M. Joy, tends to weaken and often break because either the husband or the wife or both are double-bonded - to each other and to that person of the first sexual experience...

"A marriage can survive the double bond, but won't be as strong or as able to withstand the pressures of life until the individual faces and deals with the past relationship.

"We imagine we can put away those relationships without consequences, but the fact is those early memories - of a relationship that should have been permanent - tend to harm a marriage."

35   Strong, James, *Dictionary of the Greek Testament* (James Strong, 1890), 4202, "fornication."

36   Ibid., 4122, "defraud."

37   Ibid., 2932, "possess." 4632, "vessel." 38, "sanctification." 5092, "honour." 3806, "lust." 1939, "concupiscence." 1492, "know." 167, "uncleanness." 38, "holiness."

38   Strong, *Dictionary of the Hebrew Bible*, 1589, "steal."

39   Allen, *God's Psychiatry,* pp.72-75.

40   Vine, *Expository Dictionary…* "kill."

41   Ibid., "destroy."

42   Strong, *Dictionary of the Hebrew Bible,* 6030, "bear." 8267, "false." 5707, "witness." 5921, "against." 7453, "neighbor."

43   Ibid., 2530, "covet."

44   Piaget and Inhelder, *Psychology of the Child*, pp.132-136.

45   Gromacki, Robert G., *Stand Bold in Grace: An Exposition of Hebrews* (Grand Rapids, MI: Baker Book House, 1984), p. 104.

46   Ibid., p. 106.

47   Strong, *Dictionary of the Greek Testament*, 4731, "strong meat." *Webster's New World Dictionary*, "stereo."

48   Ibid., "stereophonic."

49   Ibid., "monophonic."

50   Epanchin, Betty C., Paul, James L., *Emotional Problems of Childhood and Adolescence* (New York, NY: Macmillan, 1987), p.56.

51   Strong, *Dictionary of the Greek Testament*, 5046, "full age."

52   Ibid., 1223, "reason." 1838, "use."

53   Ibid., 145, "senses."

54   Vine, *Expository Dictionary…* "senses."

55   Strong, *Dictionary of the Greek Testament*, 1128, "exercise."

56   Wight, *Manners and Customs of Bible Lands,* p. 294.

57   *Webster's New World Dictionary,* "Gymnasium."

58   Piaget and Inhelder, *Psychology of the Child*, pp. 93-109.

59   Ibid., pp. 71,77,79.

60   Strong, *Dictionary of the Greek Testament*, 1252,1253, "discern." *Webster's New World Dictionary,* "discern," definition 5.

61   Strong, *Dictionary of the Greek Testament*, 2570, "good." 2556, "evil."

62   Vine, *Expository Dictionary...* "experience."

63   Strong, *Dictionary of the Greek Testament*, 3056, "word."

64   Ibid., 1343, "righteousness." Vine, *Expository Dictionary...* "righteousness."

65   Strong, *Dictionary of the Greek Testament*, 3516, "babe." Vine, *Expository Dictionary...* "babe."

66   Strong, *Dictionary of the Greek Testament*, 5550, "time." 1320, "teachers." 746, "first." 4747,4748, "principles." Vine, *Expository Dictionary...* "elements." Strong, *Dictionary of the Greek Testament*, 3051, "oracles."

67   Bunyan, *Pilgrim's Progress: First Part.*

68   Strong, *Dictionary of the Greek Testament*, 3576, "dull."

69   Ibid., 1421, "hard." 3004, "uttered."

70   Erikson, Erik, *Dimensions of a New Identity* (New York, NY: W.W. Norton & Co., 1974), p.72.

71   Strong, *Dictionary of the Greek Testament*, 3870, "exhort."

72   Vine, *Expository Dictionary...* "holy."

73   Strong, *Dictionary of the Greek Testament*, 8549, "without blemish."

74   Vine, *Expository Dictionary...* "milk."

75   *Encyclopaedia Britannica: Micropaedia, Volume 9* (Chicago, Il: Encyclopaedia Britannica, Inc. Fifteenth Edition), p.19.

76   Mack, Sara, *Ovid* (New Haven: Yale University Press, 1988), pp. 35-39.

77   Ovid, *Metamorphosis: translated by Rolphe Humphries* (Bloomington, IN: Indiana University press, 1955), p.3.

78   Ibid., p.10.

79   Ibid., pp. 16-20.

80   Ibid., p.39.

81   Ibid., pp.48,49.

82   Ibid.,pp. 67-69.

83   Ibid.,pp. 69-73.

84   Ibid.,pp. 83-86.

85   Ibid., pp. 89,90.

86   Ibid., pp. 116-128.

87   Strong, *Dictionary of the Greek Testament*, 4964, "conform."

88   Vine, *Expository Dictionary...* "conformed, conformable."

89   Ibid., "transfigure."

90   *Webster's New World Dictionary,* "renew."

91   Strong, *Dictionary of the Greek Testament*, 3563, "mind."

92   Vine, *Expository Dictionary...* "transfigure": "the present continuous tenses indicate a process."

93   *Webster's New World Dictionary,* "metamorphosis."

94   Strong, *Dictionary of the Greek Testament*, 1381, "prove."

95   Thanks to Tim Montgomery for his help on this.

96   Strong, *Dictionary of the Hebrew Bible*, 7130, "among": the word can literally be translated "inward parts or thoughts."

97   Ibid., 7725, "turned."

98   Ibid., 3807, "discomfit."

99   Green, Jay P., Sr., *Pocket Interlinear New Testament* (Grand Rapids, MI: Baker Book House, 1988), Hebrews 6:3.

100   Strong, *Dictionary of the Greek Testament*, 5461, "enlightened."

101   Vine, *Expository Dictionary...* "fall," definition B7.

102   *Webster's New World Dictionary,* "renew," definition 2.

103   Vine, *Expository Dictionary...* "repentance," definition C.

104   Strong, *Dictionary of the Greek Testament*, 2192, "echo." *Webster's New World Dictionary,* "echo," definition 3.

105   Strong, *Dictionary of the Greek Testament*, 4360, "grieved." 4105, "err." 2588, "heart." 3598, "my ways."

106   Ibid., 991, "take heed." 570, "unbelief." 868, "departing."

107   Vine, *Expository Dictionary...* "confidence," definition A2.

108   Strong, *Dictionary of the Greek Testament*, 620, "remaineth."

109   Ibid., 4704, "labor."

110   Ibid., 3901, "let them slip."

111   Ibid., 272, "neglect."

112   Bunyan, *Pilgrim's Progress: First Part.*

113   Ibid.

114   Ibid.

115   Ibid.

116   Ibid.

117   Strong, *Dictionary of the Hebrew Bible,* 7114, "discouraged."

118   Strong, *Dictionary of the Greek Testament*, 1111, "to grumble."

119   Strong, *Dictionary of the Hebrew Bible,* 3885, "murmur, murmured."

120   Vine, *Expository Dictionary...* "destroy," definition A1.

121   Strong, *Dictionary of the Greek Testament*, 623, "Apollyon."

122   Ibid., 3644, "destroyer."

123   Ibid., 5056, "end." Vine, *Expository Dictionary...* "come," definition 28b.

Chapter 9

1   Wight, Fred H., *Manners and Customs of Bible Lands* (Chicago, Ill: Moody Bible Institute, 1953), pp. 178-179. Unger, Merrill F., *Unger's Bible Dictionary* (Chicago, Ill: Moody Press, 1966), p.909, "rain."

2   Strong, James, *Dictionary of the Hebrew Bible* (James Strong, 1890), 1652, 1653, "rain." Wight, *Manners and Customs of Bible Lands,* pp.178, 179.

3   Piaget, Jean, and Inhelder, Barbel, *The Psychology of the Child* (New York: Basic Books, 1969), pp. 149-51.

4   Ibid., pp. 130-132.

5   Although Levinson says that such crises are the rule during certain times of adulthood rather than the exception. Levinson, Daniel J., *The Seasons of a Man's Life* (New York: Basic Books, 1979).

6   Coleman, William L., *The Pharisees Guide to Total Holiness* (Minneapolis, MN: Bethany House Publishers, 1977), pp. 8-10.

7   Bork, Robert H., *The Tempting of America* (New York: The Free Press, 1990).

8   Unger, *Unger's Bible Dictionary,* p. 855, "Pharisees."

9   *Webster's New World Dictionary of the American Language* (New York: Simon and Schuster, 1986), p. 403 "discretion," def. 1.

10   *Webster's New World Dictionary*, p. 1145, "prudent," def. 1.

11   *Webster's New World Dictionary,* p. 1078, "piety," def. 1.

12   The word translated "love" in Matt. 22:37-40 is "agapao," which is often translated into "charity."

13   Piaget and Inhelder, *The Psychology of the Child*, p. 155.

14   Bunyan, John, *Pilgrim's Progress: First Part* (1678).

15   Ibid.

16   Ibid.

17   Ibid.

18   Bowen, Barbara M., *Strange Scriptures that Perplex the Western Mind* (Grand Rapids, MI: Wm. B. Eerdman's Publishing, 1944), pp. 66-67.

19   Gothard, Bill, *Institute In Basic Life Principles.*

20   Bunyan, *Pilgrim's Progress: First Part.*

21   Strong, *Dictionary of the Hebrew Bible*, 2388, "strong."

22   Ibid., 553, "good courage."
23   Ibid., 6743, "prosperous."
24   Ibid., 7919, "prosper."
25   Strong, James, *Dictionary of the Greek Testament* (James Strong, 1890), 2901, "strong."
26   Strong, *Dictionary of the Hebrew Bible*, 224, "Urim"; 8550, "Thummim"- plural of 8537, "perfections."
27   Ibid., 8537, "integrity."
28   Ibid., 8538, "integrity."

Chapter 10

1   Unger, Merrill F., *Unger's Bible Dictionary* (Chicago, Ill: Moody Press, 1966), p.909, "rain."
2   Erikson, Erik, *Identity: Youth and Crisis* (New York, NY: W.W. Norton & Co., 1968), pp.156,157.
3   Ibid., p. 21.
4   Ibid., p. 258.
5   Erikson, Erik, *Young Man Luther* (New York, NY: W.W. Norton & Co., 1962), p.98.
6   Erikson, Erik, *Gandhi's Truth* (New York, NY: W.W. Norton & Co., 1969), p.188.
7   Ibid., pp. 383,384.
8   Gothard, Bill, *Institute in Basic Life Principles.*
9   Bunyan, John, *Pilgrim's Progress: First Part* (1678).
10   Ibid.
11   Jospehus, *The Works of Josephus, translated by William Whiston* (Lynn, MA: Hendrickson Publishers, 1984), p. 214.
12   Bowen, Barbara M., *Strange Scriptures that perplex the western mind* (Grand Rapids, Michigan: Wm. B. Eerdmans Publishing Company, 1944), p. 22.
13   Bunyan, *Pilgrim's Progress: First Part.*

Chapter 11

1   Erikson, Erik, *The Life Cycle Completed* (New York, NY: W.W. Norton & Co., 1982), p. 67.
2   Willmington, H.L., *Willmington's Guide to the Bible* (Wheaton, Illinois: Tyndale House, 1986), p. 244.

3   Ironside, H. A., *The Four Hundred Silent Years: From Malachi to Matthew* (Neptune, New Jersey: Loizeaux Brothers, 1914), p. 37.

4   Ibid., p. 40.

5   Ibid., p. 43.

6   Ibid., pp. 52-53.

7   Ibid., pp. 68-69.

8   Coleman, William L., *The Pharisees Guide to Total Holiness* (Minneapolis, MN: Bethany House Publishers, 1977). Yancey, Philip, *The Jesus I Never Knew* (New York, NY: Walker and Company, 1995). Mason, Steve, *Josephus and the New Testament* (Peabody, MA: Hendrickson Publishers, 1992). *Josephus: Thrones of Blood* (Uhrichsville, OH: Barbour Publishing, Inc., 1988).

9   *Josephus: Thrones of Blood.*

10   Bunyan, John, *Pilgrim's Progress: First Part* (1678).

11   Wiersbe, Warren, *The New Pilgrim's Progress* (Grand Rapids, MI: Discovery House, 1989), p. 144.

Chapter 12

1   Strong, James, *Dictionary of the Greek Testament* (James Strong, 1890), 3140, "charged."

2   Ibid., 3982, "persuade, have confidence."

3   Wiersbe, Warren, *The New Pilgrim's Progress* (Grand Rapids, MI: Discovery House, 1989), pp. 181, 182.

Made in the USA
Middletown, DE
09 June 2021